Richard Andrews is an archaeologist and underwater excavator with three decades of experience of the Middle East. He is co-author, with Paul Schellenberger, of the bestselling *The Tomb of God*.

Blood on the Mountain

A History of the Temple Mount
From the Ark of the Covenant
to the Third Millennium

RICHARD ANDREWS

PHŒNIX

A PHOENIX PAPERBACK

First published in Great Britain
by Weidenfeld & Nicolson in 1999

This paperback edition published in 2000
by Phoenix,
an imprint of Orion Books Ltd,
Orion House, 5 Upper St Martin's Lane,
London WC2H 9EA

A CIP catalogue record for this book
is available from the British Library.

ISBN 0 75381 054 9

Printed in Great Britain by
The Guernsey Press Co. Ltd, Guernsey, C.I.

Contents

Illustrations

Full-scale replica of the Ark of the Covenant
   (Author's design and model).
The Dome of the Rock viewed from north of the estimated
   position of Solomon's Holy of Holies.
The Temple Mount, with the south-eastern angle in the left
   foreground, viewed from the Mount of Olives.

Chronology

*c.*1800 BC	Arrival of Abraham and attempted sacrifice of Isaac.
*c.*1290 BC	Exodus from Egypt and construction of the Ark of the Covenant.
*c.*1000 BC	Founding of the City of David on the southern spur of Mount Moriah.
962–956 BC	Construction of First Temple under King Solomon and transfer of Ark from the City of David into the Holy of Holies in the Temple. Death of Hiram Abiff.
*c.*620 BC	King Josiah begs the Levites to bring the Ark out of hiding and place it back in the Holy of Holies (final reference to the Ark).
596 BC	Babylonians conquer Jerusalem.
586 BC	Babylonians destroy the Temple. Many Jews exiled to Babylon. Possible fate at Riblah of guardians of the whereabouts of the Ark. Jeremiah remains in Jerusalem.
*c.*538 BC	Return from exile.
520 BC	Foundation stone laid for the restoration of Solomon's Temple.

516 BC	Rededication of the Temple under Zerubbabel.
168 BC	Profanation of the Temple by Antiochus IV. Maccabaean Revolt breaks out.
63 BC	Profanation of the Sanctuary by Pompey.
19 BC	Herod the Great begins construction of Second Temple.
*c.*4 BC	Birth of Jesus.
c. AD 65	Josephus observes the Temple Mount.
AD 66	Outbreak of Jewish Revolt.
AD 70	Siege of Titus and destruction of the Temple; Josephus is eyewitness to the event.
AD 132–5	Bar Kokhba rebellion. Minting of 'Ark' coin. Return to Roman rule.
AD 362	Unsuccessful attempt by the Jews to rebuild the Temple.
AD 571	Birth of the prophet Muhammad.
AD 638	Moslem conquest of Jerusalem. The *sakhra* purified.
AD 688–91	Construction of the Dome of the Rock.
AD 1099	The Crusaders conquer Jerusalem.
AD 1115–42	The Dome of the Rock is converted into a Christian church, the 'Templum Domini', and an altar built over the *sakhra*.
1120	Formation of the Knights Templar. The Aqsa Mosque converted to Templar headquarters.
1187	Jerusalem falls to Saladin. The *haram* restored to a place of Moslem worship.
1260–1516	The architecture of the *haram* enhanced by the Mamluks.

1520–36	Walls of the *haram* strengthened by Suleiman the Magnificent. Ceramic tiling of the exterior of the Dome of the Rock.
1840–60	Revival of Christian biblical/archaeological interest in the Temple Mount.
1864–5	Ordnance Survey of the *haram* by Charles Wilson.
1867–70	Survey and excavation of the Temple Mount area by Charles Warren.
1909–11	Expeditions by Parker in search of the treasures of the Temple of Solomon.
1917	The Balfour Declaration promises a national Jewish homeland. The British army conquer Jerusalem. The *haram* remains a place of Moslem worship.
1948	The State of Israel declared. The War of Independence concludes with the Temple Mount in Arab hands.
1967	Jerusalem conquered by Israel during the Six-Day War. The Temple Mount falls under Israeli control. Moshe Dayan allows the *haram* to remain in Moslem hands.
1996	The red heifer is born, predictions of an imminent Messianic age.
1997	The Hasmonaean Tunnel is opened to the public; riots ensue.
1998	The Jewish ultra-Orthodox gain control over future archaeological excavation.

Foreword

The origins of this book go back to a brief encounter twenty-eight years ago. Coming from a Roman Catholic upbringing in England, I volunteered to work on a kibbutz in the Lower Galilee which gave me the chance to travel to Jerusalem, the city which had filled my imagination since reading letters of T.E. Lawrence written during the Arab Revolt of 1917. On a bus from Jericho I was persuaded by a young Jewish Orthodox couple to disembark before our final destination and walk the last few kilometres alone. They told me, with some passion, that I would remember the experience for the rest of my life. My first view of the Old City was thus of the Temple Mount seen from the south-east across the valley of the Kidron. My travelling companions, whose names I never knew, were right. At the age of seventeen I became a willing captive of Jerusalem's living history.

My first visit was to a united city. Only four years previously the Six-Day War of 1967 had brought Jerusalem under full Israeli control for the first time since AD 70. This gave Jewish people across the world unhindered access to the Wailing Wall, denied to them since the War of Independence in 1948.[1] Thus, to all Jews, the events of June 1967 symbolized a triumph of light over darkness, the triumph of the children of Israel over the Nazis, over the Arabs and over the soldiery of the British Mandate in whose ranks my grandfather had served from 1937 to 1938.

Unification of the city under the flag of Israel, however, has not brought peace. The years which separate my first visit to the city with the writing of this book have seen a changed atmosphere in Jerusalem. Following the Six-Day War General Moshe Dayan, as newly appointed Minister of Defence for Israel, decided to leave the Temple Mount under Moslem control, an act of benevolence which has continued to enrage many ardent Zionist and Orthodox Jews. At issue today are principles far more complex, and inherently more dangerous, than any reopening of a cross-border Arab–Israeli conflict; religious intolerance now threatens destruction of the Israeli nation from within. In addition, the advent of a new millennium is upon us adding impetus to the rebirth of religious fanaticism historically associated with such a momentous period in world history. The Temple Mount is the natural point of focus for this combined fanatical intent. The story of the Mount lies deeply embedded within the psyche and the religious ritual of the three great faiths of western history, Judaism, Islam and Christianity. Indeed, the Dome of the Rock stands guard over a slab of natural limestone, the *sakhra* – or summit of Mount Moriah – which can be justly described as the crucible of our modern-day monotheism. In religious terms the history of this place is linked to that of the majority of the western world, and its archaeology contains the stratified evidence of the successes and failures of inter-faith tolerance. Put simply, it is the living record of our relationship with one god. This story is ever changing, mutating as the power of religion increases or diminishes within society. With religious zeal on an upward spiral, and Jerusalem's fragile peace again threatened by religious intolerance, control of the Temple Mount remains the key issue.

In the past eight years there have been four (recorded) attempts by Jewish religious activists to blow up the Dome of the Rock. These extreme aims of a minority within the Jewish Zionist and religious Orthodox movements are supported by Messianic Christian groups from America who actively support a Jewish return to the Mount in order to re-establish the authority of the Old Testament. Such Christians wish to reach out and make contact with their historical past, once, that is, the debris from the Dome of the Rock has settled over the rooftops of surrounding Jerusalem and all traces of a Moslem presence on the Mount have been removed.[2] Since 1967 Israeli archaeologists, in an effort to replace conjectural history with scientific fact, have excavated an area to the south-west of the

Temple Mount. They have laboured valiantly under a barrage of threats and stones from their own religious Orthodox and amidst accusations of encroachment from the Waqf, the Moslem authority which guards the Temple Mount, or Haram al-Sharif – the Noble Enclosure, as it is known to the Arabs. Such intense emotion has given credence to the fear of many moderates that the Temple Mount is an historical time bomb and the millennium its fuse. For those living in such a place it is hard not to become caught up in the situation and many Israelis and Palestinians find the tensions intolerable. My own experience is that no one who becomes involved with the Temple Mount is exempt from the scrutiny or the opinion of others.

I have also been aware of the importance of historical writing which avoids the projecting of personal bias and the drawing of partisan conclusions. History written in this style may act as the only safeguard against distortion of the truth, the need for which has been amply demonstrated by comments made by revisionist 'historians' who have publicly denied the existence of the Jewish Holocaust of the Second World War. I have attempted within these pages to relate with objectivity and fairness the history of the Temple Mount as I have experienced and come to understand it. The Temple Mount still holds many secrets, perhaps not least the mystery surrounding the fate of the Ark of the Covenant which some people believe remains hidden within the network of subterranean vaults and secret passages which are known to riddle the foundations of the Temple Mount platform. The restrictions placed on archaeologists by both Moslem and Jewish religious authorities do little to alleviate speculation; rather they render legends surrounding Temple Mount history increasingly enigmatic as time passes.

Whilst living and working with both Arabs and Jews over the years and having experienced at first hand both war and peace in this divided nation, I have had the fortune to listen and observe, whilst at the same time storing away information in the hope of reliving the history of this most revered and disputed outcrop of rock, so aptly named in the Jewish liturgy 'the Navel of the World'.

I therefore stand deeply indebted to my unknown companions

who, many summers ago, set me down on the old Jericho road and thereby released me on the path towards this book.

Richard Andrews, May 1999

Introduction

The modern image of the Temple Mount of Jerusalem is unforgettable. Its most dominant feature, the Dome of the Rock, sits resplendent at the centre of an ancient man-made platform, the crowning glory of an archaeological jumble of battered limestone, the native stone of King David's city. The apparent peacefulness of this powerful and seductive scene is, however, an illusion. The Temple Mount is a place of human tragedy, with a turbulent history reaching back to the first millennium BC. Its story of cyclical upheaval, concentrated within such a reduced area, has no parallel in the annals of history.

The Temple Mount today covers an area of approximately 144,000 square metres, roughly one sixth of the area of the present Old City. Over the centuries its architecture has housed many treasures, but it has been faith rather than monetary wealth which has determined the development of the Temple Mount. The Jewish ancestors of the Israeli nation, under King David, were the first people to endow the Mount with religious significance. The location was chosen in circa 1000 BC as the final resting place of the Ark of the Covenant but after a lifetime of fighting David was considered too impure to create a sanctuary for the Ark so the task was passed to his son Solomon.

In 962 BC, four years after David's death, King Solomon's masons began their construction of a Temple to Yahweh, the God of the Hebrew nation. At its heart they built the chamber of the Holy of Holies, the *Kodesh Hakodeshim*, in which the Ark was placed. The Temple on the Mount thus became, one thousand years before the Christian era, the holy shrine of Israel and the most potent monotheistic symbol of its people. The death of Solomon in 926 BC led to a division of the Kingdom of Israel. Jerusalem and the Temple remained within the territory of the tribe of Judah which dominated the south of the kingdom, ruled by the line of David. The rest of Israel fell under the leadership of Jeroboam, the first king of the northern kingdom of Israel, and centres of worship to rival the Temple of Jerusalem were set up with golden calves in place of the Ark. The subsequent period of internecine struggle between the kingdom of Judah which encompassed Jerusalem and that of Israel to its north lasted from the tenth to the eighth centuries BC, a period which saw the rise of a force which even Kings and Princes could ill-afford to ignore: the power of written prophecy. The prophets of Judah played a crucial role in the consolidation of monotheistic belief, with the Temple Mount of Jerusalem its living epicentre. They also predicted that, should the people of Judah neglect their promise to serve faithfully Yahweh, destruction would befall the Holy City and the Jewish people would be dispersed into exile.

In 604 BC the Babylonian king, Nebuchadnezzar, began a campaign of conquest and in 597 BC, after a three-month siege, Jerusalem surrendered to his army. Nebuchadnezzar's men spared the Temple but stripped it of its treasures which were sent back to Babylon with ten thousand prisoners, including the Jewish King.

Nebuchadnezzar's magnanimity in saving the Temple was soon forgotten by the Jews who stayed in Jerusalem. Rebellion broke out in 587 BC and after a siege of eighteen months the Babylonian army breached the walls and re-entered the city. This time, they systematically destroyed the Temple. The building was set on fire and the Ark of the Covenant, containing the stone tablets given by God to Moses on Mount Sinai, disappeared. The destruction of the Temple was a disaster of unprecedented proportion to the Jewish people. Their covenant with Yahweh, which demanded his continuous worship from the location of Mount Moriah, had been broken and the physical link with his divine presence, the Ark of the Covenant, apparently looted by a strange people. However, despite this catastrophe in 538 BC Jewish captives and their descendants held in Babylon returned to rebuild their Temple and in 516 BC they completed a modest restoration of Solomon's original construction.

By the end of the first century BC the ancient Hebrew lands of Judah were under Roman military domination and Herod the Great was appointed governor of a province which included Jerusalem and its environs and was now appropriately named Judaea. Herod began a comprehensive restoration of the Temple Mount. His masons extended the walled boundaries of the earlier or Solomonic 'First' Temple precinct with massive blocks of squared and bordered limestone, the lower courses of which still form the base of the Temple Mount as we know it today. The Herodian 'Second' Temple, lavish and magnificent, stood not only as a monument to the abiding presence of Judaic monotheism within the sphere of Greek and Roman pantheism, but was the most extensive Temple complex of the Classical Age, covering over four times the area of the Acropolis in Athens.

In AD 66 the Jews rebelled against Roman occupation and full-scale war broke out. The story of the siege has been passed down to us by the historian Flavius Josephus in his work *The Jewish War*, which, completed in AD 75, provides us with an unrivalled window into this period of Temple Mount history. The struggle went on for four years culminating in victory for Rome. The Herodian Temple was completely destroyed by fire.

A new generation of Jewish resistance leaders provoked a further nationalist uprising and in AD 132 Simon Bar Kokhba attempted to overthrow and expel the forces of Imperial Rome from Judaean territory, but his army was crushed by the Roman military machine in AD 135. The ruins of the Temple Mount complex from the destruction of AD 70 were razed to the ground and the debris used as in-fill for the foundations of a new, Roman Jerusalem, *Aelia Capitolina*.

In the fourth century AD the adoption of Christianity as the official religion of the Roman Empire under Constantine sparked off a frenzy of creating holy locations within Jerusalem. Pilgrimage required established shrines so the Holy City and the Temple Mount were examined by the Byzantine Christian Church with this in mind. The sites of various events in Jesus' life, including his Passion and his burial, were identified as places of worship but for the duration of Byzantine Rule the area of the Temple Mount was largely shunned by official Christianity. However, the foundation of the Islamic faith under Muhammad in the early seventh century AD triggered the re-establishment of the Mount as a centre of monotheistic worship.

In AD 637 the Byzantines surrendered Jerusalem to the Moslem Caliph 'Umar. The new Arab masters of Jerusalem were profoundly shocked by conditions on the Temple Mount which the Byzantine authorities had converted into the city rubbish-tip. The Moslems, who revered many of the Prophets of Israel, transformed Herod's Temple platform by erecting buildings which permanently marked the site as a focal point of their monotheistic history. They also built the Dome of the Rock, which remains one of the world's architectural glories. The Dome was erected over the site where, by Islamic tradition, the Prophet Muhammad had ascended through the seven spheres of heavenly revelation, making the rock, known in Arabic as the *sakhra*, the third holiest shrine of Islam. The *sakhra* held further claims to greatness. Medieval Jewish scholars believed it was the site of the Holy of Holies, the resting place of the Ark of the Covenant, and Abraham, patriarch of Israel and Prophet of Islam, was eternally linked to the location through its identification as the summit of Mount Moriah – the mountain where Isaac had been offered up for sacrifice. Up until the end of the eleventh century the Temple Mount was untouched by political religious or military upheaval, but this tranquillity was cruelly shattered by the arrival of the armies of the First Crusade.

The legacy of Byzantine Jerusalem as Christendom's most Holy site of pilgrimage was rekindled by a papal speech exhorting Christians to conquer the Holy City. The First Crusade, launched in 1096, arrived at the walls of Jerusalem in 1099. On 15 July crusaders under the leadership of Godfrey de Bouillon breached the northern sector of the Arab defences and rampaged through the narrow streets of the city towards the Temple Mount, sparing neither women nor children, the old nor the infirm. The streets, as in AD 70, ran with human blood. The wanton slaughter shocked even the most hardened, but for the crusading army the fall of Jerusalem was a triumph of prophetic dimension. The rule of Christ had come to Jerusalem and, unlike Byzantium, the Kingdoms of Europe immediately recognized the unique spiritual and historical impor-tance of the Temple Mount. The Dome of the Rock was trans-formed into a Christian edifice and renamed the *Templum Domini* – the Temple of the Lord – and the *sakhra*, the exposure of rock under the Dome, was subjected to excavation and alteration by having foundations for an altar carved into its surface.

The founding members of The Order of the Poor Knights of the Temple of Solomon, or Knights Templar, were granted lodgings several hundred metres south of the *sakhra*, within the Mosque of Al Aqsa, which had become the Royal Palace for the Kings of the Latin Kingdom of Jerusalem following the Christian conquest. However, Christian involvement with the Holy site lasted for less than a century. In AD 1187 Jerusalem fell to Salah ed-Din, the legendary adversary of Richard Coeur de Lion of England and, with the exception of a brief period in the thirteenth century, the Temple Mount has prospered under Islamic rule.

With such a past it is hardly surprising that the imminence of the year AD 2000 is fuelling a steady increase in religious intolerance. But the seeds of today's conflict are as ancient as the Bible and to understand fully the crisis which faces the Mount we must look back to the monotheistic origins of Judaism, Christianity and Islam, to the time of the prophet Abraham who came to this location instructed by God to sacrifice his beloved son.

Mount Moriah

The hills of Jerusalem are cold in winter. Snow is not uncommon when the wind bears down from the mountains of Lebanon and the Syrian hinterland to the north. The summer months can produce an extreme and sultry heat in the city, but as Jerusalem lies at an altitude of over two thousand feet above sea level, the evenings can bring a blissful drop in temperature, providing a clear view of the surrounding skyline enhanced by the panorama of a star-studded night-time sky. Geographically, the city, lying at the heart of ancient Judaea, stands far inland from the western trading route of the Mediterranean seaboard and isolated from the ancient north–south highway of the Jordan rift valley to the east. But this isolation has never reduced the level of its strategic importance. A fortunate combination of natural assets has given the city an advantage over both these eastern and western byways. The ridge system of Mount Moriah, which supports the city, lends itself to defence, and fresh spring water, the essential prerequisite for survival, is in relative abundance.

The history of Jerusalem with its sieges and invasions has long been a magnet to inquiring minds. The steepness of its terrain makes its archaeology muddled and complex. Any serious modern investigators also have to negotiate the delicate obstacle of religious faith. However, in the second half of the last century a mission to map the city sparked off a major reappraisal of the history of the Temple Mount.

BENCH-MARKS AND THE BIBLE

On 3 October 1864 Captain Charles Wilson of the British Royal Engineers arrived in Jerusalem which was at this point under the control of the Ottomans who ruled from Constantinople. Wilson, together with his five-man team comprising Lance Corporals Francis Ferris and John McKeith, Sappers John Davison and Thomas Wishart, and Sergeant James McDonald, left England on 12 September 1864 from Southampton and after a journey of just over three weeks they entered the Holy City. Wilson was sent to Palestine to map the city and survey the water system in order to improve it for Christian pilgrims. The survey also provided the technical foundation for future archaeological expeditions set up by the Palestine Exploration Fund (PEF), a society, with Queen Victoria as its patron, dedicated to furthering our understanding of the ancient biblical sites of Israel. A hidden military agenda, not admitted at the time, was less philanthropic. The Suez Canal Project, designed to join the Mediterranean with the Red Sea, had begun in 1859 and was by the mid-1860s nearing completion. The opportunity to survey Jerusalem was, therefore, without doubt strategically attractive to the War Office as it would speed up the transport of troops and matériel to and from the Indian subcontinent and other British colonial possessions of the East.[1]

Wilson was sent out on secondment from the British army, his mission paid for by public donation and backed by the Church of England which wished to see sanitary conditions for Christian pilgrims to the Holy Land substantially upgraded. The idea of renovating the water supply of Jerusalem had originated with Miss (later Baroness) Burdett-Coutts whom the Prince of Wales and future King Edward VII described as 'after my mother the most remarkable woman in the Kingdom'.[2] Burdett-Coutts donated the sum of £500 to set the work in motion, every penny of which would be necessary if her objective was to be achieved. Wilson's task was daunting in its complexity. Sir Henry James, Director-General of the Ordnance Survey, had commanded him to execute a survey of ancient Jerusalem to the British standard. Because of religious sensibilities the hardest part of his mission was the detailed survey of the Haram al-Sharif, or Noble Enclosure – the Temple Mount. In the centre of the Temple Mount area stood the Dome of the Rock, and beneath its golden dome lay the surveyors' Holy Grail, the *sakhra* – the exposed area of bedrock traditionally accepted as part of Mount Moriah. This was the place where, according to the Bible and the Koran, Abraham had prepared the sacrifice of his son Isaac and the Prophet Muhammad had experienced divine revelation.

At twenty-nine, Wilson was already a veteran surveyor. He had previously worked for the Boundary Commission in North America for four years, experiencing one of the coldest winters there on record.[3] So, despite the haphazard procedure for selecting who should be sent to Jerusalem to carry out this mission, he was a sound choice:

> The conditions were that £500 was to cover all expenses, including the passage out and home of the surveyors, and the preparation of the fair plans. An Officer was to go, but he was to pay all his own expenses, and receive no extra pay whilst employed. The appointment was offered to several R.E. [Royal Engineer] officers; but the conditions were so hard, and the possibility of doing the work within the estimate so remote, that they all refused. I happened to be in the room of one of the Officers when he received the letter offering him the appointment; he said he would not go, and I then asked him, in writing his report, to say that I would go . . . I was generally considered to be going on a fool's errand: many believed I would come to grief in money matters: and even men who had had previous experience in Palestine and Jerusalem told me they did not believe the Turkish officials would allow me to survey the city.[4]

Not only did Wilson have a capacity for enduring the extremes of nature, he also possessed impressive powers of persuasion; soon he and his men gained the trust of the Turkish authorities and were granted unprecedented, and unlimited, access to the *sakhra*.

Local difficulties concerning the private ownership of property which abutted the *haram* and the city's unsanitary conditions were compounded by the labyrinthine processes of Ottoman bureaucracy, making Wilson's task predictably arduous. Undaunted, Wilson began his work by carving the mark of the British Survey on the walls of the city. This was achieved by cutting a permanent

bench-mark into the limestone blocks at the points at which he
wished to establish his permanent levels for mapping.

From *The Oxford English Dictionary*, second edition, volume II:

> bench-mark. A surveyor's mark cut in some durable material, as
> rock, wall, gate-pillar, face of a building etc., to indicate the starting,
> closing, or any suitable intermediate, point in a line of levels for the
> determination of altitudes over the face of a country. It consists of a
> series of wedge-shaped incisures, in the form of the 'broad-arrow'
> with a horizontal bar through its apex, thus ⊤. The horizontal bar is
> the essential part, the broad arrow being added (originally by the
> Ordnance Survey) as an identification. In taking a reading, an angle-
> iron 7 is held with its upper extremity inserted in the horizontal bar,
> so as to form a temporary bracket or *bench* for the support of the
> levelling-staff, which can thus be placed on absolutely the same base
> on any subsequent occasion. Hence the name.

Wilson and his team worked through the winter of 1864 and the
result was a masterpiece of surveying and technical drawing,
immediately recognized as such by his superiors.

> The survey…(which was only accomplished by the generosity of
> Captain Wilson, who gave his whole time and labour for nothing),
> has shewn how much may be done with tact, temper and opportu-
> nity, without arousing the opposition of the authorities or inhabit-
> ants. Recent letters of Sir H. James and others in the 'Times' have
> borne testimony to the remarkable fitness of Captain Wilson for such
> undertakings.[5]

For the first time, an accurate reproduction of the legendary rock of
Mount Moriah became available for study. All who have since been
involved in the archaeology of the Temple Mount have drawn on
the work conducted by Wilson, whose bench-marks still stand as a
level of excellence and precision amidst the architectural and
archaeological confusion of twentieth-century Jerusalem.[6] Despite
the adversities, Wilson completed his survey of Jerusalem and the
Temple Mount – the Haram al-Sharif – by the spring of 1865.

Two years after the completion of Wilson's work, the Palestine
Exploration Fund sent a fellow Royal Engineer officer, Lieutenant

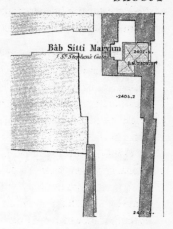

The Altitudes are given in feet above the level of the Mediterranean,

and those indicated thus { + B.M.2724-8 } refer to Marks made on Buildings, Walls &c.

100 Feet   50   0

Scale 1/500 or 10.56 Feet to One Statute Mile

FIGURE 1.1 Captain Wilson's bench-mark, 2409.3 of 1864, cut into the southern gate-pillar, Lion's Gate (a.k.a. Saint Stephen's Gate), north-eastern corner of the *haram* area, with extracts from the Ordnance Survey of 1864–5.

Charles Warren, to Jerusalem. Warren was of a different mould to his predecessor. If photographs can convey character, Wilson was by nature retiring and Warren quite the opposite. Later in his career, a decade after his posting to Jerusalem, Warren became famous as Commissioner of the Metropolitan Police involved in the investigation of the 'Jack the Ripper' murders of six London prostitutes.[7] When he was sent to Jerusalem Warren was a 27-year-old Lieutenant. He went to carry out further surveys of the *haram* area by excavation and, building on the ground-breaking work of Wilson, he threw himself into the task with dogged determination. By 1870, ill-health forced him back to England, but his achievement and contribution to the history of the Temple Mount remains, to this day, incalculable. Banned by the Ottoman authorities from excavating stratigraphically – by gradually exposing levels from the surface downwards – Warren sank vertical shafts into the ground

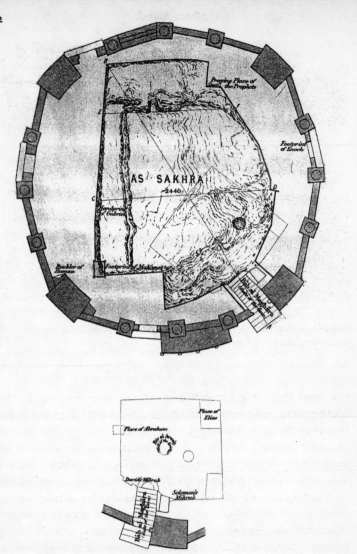

Scale $\frac{1}{200}$

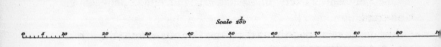

Engraved at the Ordnance Survey Office, Southampton, under the direction of Colonel Cameron, R.E. Colonel Sir Henry James, R.E., F.R.S. &c. Superintendent.

FIGURE 1.2 (a) Illustration of the *sakhra* from Captain Wilson's 1864–5
Ordnance Survey, Plate II. (b) A rare photograph of the *sakhra*, time exposure,
1930, taken from point B on Wilson's survey.

and from these dug tunnels quite literally into history. On the
south-eastern corner of the *haram* Warren found the base of the
Herodian Temple Mount platform, twenty-six metres below
ground level, and the 'Phoenician' inscriptions he recorded on
some of these blocks of stone have puzzled archaeologists and historians ever since. Lieutenant Warren and Sergeant Henry Birtles
explored the conduits and cisterns underneath the Temple Mount
area, confirming suspicions that the foundation of the *haram* was
an area of hidden tunnels, rooms and secret passages. Wilson and
Warren differed in their historical assessments but it is possible
that, perhaps unknowingly, both men came close to the greatest
archaeological discovery of all time: the long-lost Ark of the
Covenant.

The discoveries made by Wilson and Warren serve as the perfect
vehicle for a passage back through time. Charles Wilson's scientific
survey of Jerusalem's Temple Mount illustrates clearly both the

sanctity and the mystery surrounding its ancient past and the legendary episodes associated with it.

The 1864–5 Survey conducted by Wilson shows the plan, elevation and section of As Sakhra. This area of exposed rock under the Dome covers approximately 240 square feet and within its perimeter lies an impressive roll-call of kings and prophets. Wilson's plan view, drawn on the scale of 1:200, gives a list of the following features:

Praying Place of the Prophets
Footprint of Enoch
Footprint of Mahomet
The Handprint of Gabriel

Wilson then shows the detail of the rock which forms the roof of a cave, known in Arabic as the Maghara or the Mugharat al Arawah, the Cave of the Souls. Within this cave, circling around the Bi'r al-Arwah or Well of the Spirits – a mysterious and unexplored sealed hole in the centre of the floor – are places with names:

Place of Elias
Solomon's Mihrab (oratory)
David's Mihrab (oratory)
and finally, the Place of Abraham

For the Moslems, who constructed the Dome of the Rock over the *sakhra*, Abraham was revered as a prophet of God. Although a fellow Semite, Abraham was a Jew and not an Arab, and the path of this wandering Hebrew patriarch marks the beginning of the Temple Mount history, a story preserved in the Book of Genesis.

THE WANDERING PATRIARCH

The life of Abraham, father of Israel, mirrors the fate of the Jewish people who, for the greater part of their history, were forced to lead a nomadic existence. It is now generally recognized that the biblical stories of Abraham and the early Patriarchs were probably based on stories written down long after the events described. According to these legends Abraham was born somewhere in the Euphrates delta

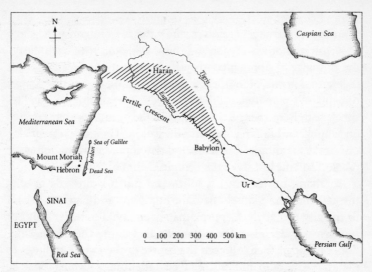

FIGURE 1.3 Map of the Near East, showing the Fertile Crescent, principal cities and the location of Mount Moriah.

between 1800 and 1700 BC. The Bible records that Abraham and his family left the ancient city of Ur[8] (whose people worshipped the moon) by the command of his God, to seek out, settle and populate a new land for the people of his clan. Post-biblical Jewish legend suggests that the singular nature of God's supreme being was revealed to Abraham at a young age.

> When he was three years old, Abraham came out of the cave. He reflected: Who created heaven and earth and myself? And all through the day he prayed to the Sun. But in the evening the Sun set in the West and the Moon rose in the East. When he saw the Moon surrounded by the stars, he said to himself: Here is the creator of heaven and earth and myself, and these stars are his ministers and servants. And all through the night he prayed to the Moon. In the morning, the Moon set in the West and the Sun rose in the East. He said: These two are powerless. They have one master, it is to him that I shall pray, before him that I shall prostrate myself.[9]

It is irrelevant to the history of the Temple Mount and the birth of

monotheism whether or not this tradition of revelation is authentic
or was compiled later to reinforce the status of Abraham as Patriarch
of Jewish monotheism. Since it is impossible to prove scientifically
the existence of Abraham and verify his role in the creation of the
oldest of known monotheistic faiths, argument on the subject
remains self-perpetuating. However, the overall story of his lifetime's search for the truth, resulting in the dramatic scene enacted
on Mount Moriah as recounted in the pages of Genesis, is essential to
our understanding of this historical development of monotheistic
religion and the history of the Temple Mount of Jerusalem.

Abraham, on leaving Ur, journeyed north-westwards passing
through the minor kingdoms of the Euphrates and Tigris delta land
to the city of Babylon, approximately eighty kilometres south of
modern-day Baghdad. From Babylon he went to the minor kingdom of Sippar, then followed the course of the river Euphrates to
the Mari Kingdom and its capital city, the ruins of which today lie
just within Syria's eastern border with Iraq. When Abraham, his
family and his followers reached Haran within the modern borders
of southern Turkey, they tried to settle. But his wanderings were not
over. According to Genesis, at the age of seventy-five Abraham and
his companions, by command of God, left the security of Haran to
travel south through Syria into the land of Canaan and the Judaean
hills before striking westwards across the northern Sinai desert and
entering the land of Egypt. Abraham's extraordinary path led him
over the Judaean hills, and the ridge system upon which Solomon
would build the first Temple to Yahweh, seven hundred years later.
Abraham did not forget the highlands of Canaan, which provided
both his last resting place and the scene of his greatest test. The Bible
tells us that Abraham's fellow tribespeople kept moving their flocks
of sheep and cattle until they reached the rich pastures of the Nile
delta which, not unlike those of the Euphrates, were well supplied
by annual floodwater.

Arriving in a foreign land, however, brought with it other problems than the search for mere subsistence. The beauty of Abraham's
wife, Sarah, did not go unnoticed by the Pharaoh, who, believing
her to be Abraham's sister, took her into his palace. This deception
was deliberate: Abraham was afraid that Sarah's beauty would cause

the Egyptians to dispose of him, should it be known that she was indeed his wife. Chapter XII, verse 17 of Genesis tells us that: 'the Lord plagued Pharaoh and his house with great plagues, because of Sarah, Abraham's wife'. The Egyptian Pharaoh, not surprisingly, requested that Abraham leave his territory, taking Sarah with him. Thus it was that Abraham and Sarah returned to Canaan in the company of their nephew Lot, their herds and their tents. Parting company from Lot, Abraham went northwards into the Judaean hills, again directed by God who, according to the Bible, left the Patriarch in no doubt about his continuing historic role in preparing the monotheistic framework of God's chosen people. Verses 14 to 18 of the thirteenth chapter of Genesis are an intensely moving summing-up of the immense responsibility laid on the shoulders of one man who, after a lifetime of incertitude and wandering in foreign lands, reaches the end of his trail:

> And the Lord said unto Abraham, after that Lot was separated from him,
> Lift up now thine eyes, and look from the place where thou art, northward, and southward, and eastward, and westward.
> For all the land which thou seest, to thee I will give it, and to thy seed forever.
> And I will make thy seed as the dust of the earth: so that if a man can number the dust of the earth, then shall thy seed also be numbered.
> Arise, and walk through the land, in the length of it, and in the breadth of it: for I will give it unto thee.
> Then Abraham removed his tent, and came upon the plain of Mamre, which is in Hebron, and built there an altar unto the Lord.

Abraham still had to make the hardest and yet possibly the shortest journey of his life. His destination: Mount Moriah, on the Jerusalem ridge system, just thirty kilometres north of Hebron.

MOUNT MORIAH

The southern route into Jerusalem follows the ridgeway of the

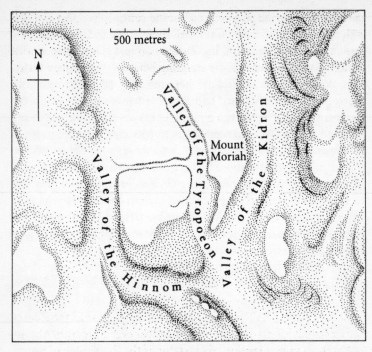

FIGURE 1.4 Geophysical map of Jerusalem, showing the valley of the Kidron, the valley of the Tyropoeon, the Hinnom valley and the location of Mount Moriah.

Judaean hill system upon which Hebron and Jerusalem constitute the principal southern and northern settlements. Owing to the gentle westward topographical decline, the rains of the winter filter unobtrusively into the subsoil. However, to the east of the ridgeway system in the direction of the river Jordan and the Dead Sea the scarp is far steeper and, because of the long periods of dryness, the water from Jerusalem runs fast, carving fresh channels into hardened wadis. This annual flood leaves a stratum of pebbles and rocks and frequently shards of terracotta, the fragments of broken pots, the visible evidence of countless households which have inhabited Jerusalem over the ages. Approaching Jerusalem from the south Abraham would have found on his right the valley of the Kidron, to his front, the valley of the Tyropoeon, and, curving in from his left, the valley of Hinnom which, running eastwards from his left to his right hand, links the southern end of the central Tyropoeon valley with the Kidron, thereby joining all three. This trident-like valley formation of the Hinnom, the Tyropoeon and the Kidron would have two north–south ridges standing between their valley forks. The Western Hill stands in between the Hinnom and the Tyropoeon and the eastern hill of Ophel between the Tyropoeon and the Kidron. The eastern hill of Ophel rises steeply and is today crowned by the Temple Mount, the area which covers the place known as the Mount of Moriah.

At the age of ninety-nine Abraham may well have considered that his contribution to monotheism was finally at an end, but the account of Genesis tells us that this was not the case. In the first seven verses of Chapter XVII, God, seemingly ever demanding, renews his covenant with Abraham and in so doing breaks the news of a future event which would eventually set Abraham back on the path of his wanderings towards the eastern ridge of Jerusalem and onto the high ground of the Temple Mount area. The events which preceded this journey by several years were crucial to its final outcome. In Chapter XVII, verse 5 of Genesis, God informs the elderly Patriarch that his name must be changed for evermore from Abram to Abraham in recognition of his status as the progenitor of future kings, and this was just the beginning of a new revelation. Chapter XVII continues with an explanation for an unmistakable and exclusive method of recognition, to set the people of Abraham apart from their fellow men – circumcision was to be instituted as the visible token of covenant between the Hebrews and Yahweh, the one God of all creation. In verse 15 the name of Abraham's wife is changed from Sarai to Sarah, and in verse 16 God reveals the fullness of his agenda: 'And I will bless her, and give thee a son also of her: yea, I will bless her and she shall be a mother of nations; kings of people shall be of her.' Abraham's reaction to the prospect of a renewal of fatherhood at age ninety-nine was perhaps not unpredictable for 'Then Abraham fell on his face, and laughed, and said in his heart, shall a child be born unto him that is a hundred years old? And shall Sarah, that is ninety years old, bear?'[10]

God's answer, however, remained affirmative, and in Abraham's one-hundredth year Sarah duly gave birth to Isaac. It was in the

company of his beloved son that Abraham began his journey northwards from Hebron, towards Jerusalem, and in the best tradition of
recorded human drama, the threat of a tragic ending hovered over
them. The account of Genesis continues the story, detailing God's
terrible instructions to Abraham: 'And he said, Take now thy son,
thine only son Isaac, whom thou lovest, and get thee into the land of
Moriah; and offer him there for a burnt-offering upon one of
the mountains which I will tell thee of.'[11] After a journey of three
days, Abraham, accompanied by two young men and his son, spot-
ted Mount Moriah on the horizon. Leaving the two men, father and
son progressed up the ridge, carrying the wood necessary for the
pyre. According to Genesis, Isaac, who up until this time was
unaware of his father's intent, conceded without opposition to
Abraham's wish. After building the sacrificial altar Abraham bound
the hands and feet of his son and laid him on the pyre, and with
knife in hand, prepared to complete God's order. At this moment
Yahweh, satisfied that his servant Abraham was obedient and faithful, stayed his hand, commanding him to do Isaac no harm. A ram,
caught in a nearby thicket by its horns, hitherto unnoticed was
swiftly brought as a substitute for sacrifice.

Because of the vast period of time which separates the life of
Abraham from the present day, it is not unreasonable to suppose
that the historical accuracy of Genesis may well be suspect and that
any real truth surrounding these events may have fallen victim to
the imagination of those who originated and reproduced the biblical account over the centuries. In an age where defenders of religious faith and scientific thinkers are rapidly parting company,
could the biblical account of Abraham's life be an entire fiction?
Whichever conclusion one wishes to draw, it remains undisputed
that the scene which unfolded on Mount Moriah, whether historically accurate or not, holds the seed of the three monotheistic religions of the West – of Judaism, Christianity and Islam, and the key
ingredient to their success – the promise of forgiveness – is shared
by all three. The concept of divine compassion, as demonstrated by
Yahweh to Abraham, still stands as the foundation stone of the
intense relationship between a singular all-powerful God and
humanity prepared to adhere to the concept of monotheism.

The identification of the *sakhra* as the sacred rock of Mount Moriah has ever since endowed the site with a powerful symbolic meaning and for the religious believer the story of Abraham elevated Mount Moriah to a position of paramount importance.[12] Consequently, by the middle of the second millennium BC, the eastern hill of Jerusalem became to the Hebrews the recognized junction between heaven and earth. Abraham was reputedly buried in Hebron and, whether legend or historical reality, what he began his descendants continued. Almost one thousand years later the most venerated holy temple of the ancient world – the Temple of Solomon – was erected on Mount Moriah and within its inner sanctum the united tribes of Israel placed the holiest of sacred relics, the Ark of the Covenant.

2

The Holy of Holies,
1290–963 BC

As the navel is set in the centre of the human body,
so is the land of Israel the navel of the world,
and Jerusalem in the centre of the land of Israel,
and the sanctuary in the centre of Jerusalem,
and the holy place in the centre of the sanctuary,
and the ark in the centre of the holy place,
and the foundation stone before the holy place,
because from it the world was founded.

Midrash Tanchuma, *Qedoshim*

The story of the Hebrew tribes from the time of Abraham circa 1800 BC to the founding of the First Temple under Solomon in 962 BC stands, when set apart from the overall history of Judaism, as an epic of survival. The most significant event during this period was the Exodus from Egypt which, although seemingly remote from the evolution of the Temple Mount, is critical to its history as it contains both the establishment of the Jewish Law and the birth of a legendary enigma which is to this day unsolved. The departure of the Hebrew tribes from Egypt has been placed in the early years of the reign of Rameses II, at circa 1290 BC,[1] over four hundred years after the death of Abraham, and although recent research points to the need for a major reappraisal of Egyptian and biblical parallel chronology, the thirteenth century BC is still the most widely accepted date.[2] The history of the Jewish Exodus is well known and has been a popular subject for Hollywood epics which have recounted Moses' struggle to weld his disparate following into a singly motivated community, the united people of Israel. Moses reinforced Abraham's message that Hebrews should worship one God and he went one crucial step further. By creating a written code, or Torah, he brought together the teachings that a united nation should follow. Enshrined in the Torah were the commandments, written on stone and relayed to God's chosen people through Moses. This written code of conduct also unified the tribes, and once they had accepted God's instructions and had entered into an agreement, or covenant, the engraved tablets of stone that were given to Moses by Yahweh on Mount Sinai – the Ten Commandments – were placed inside a specially constructed box, or Ark. The Ark – the visible evidence of a covenant with Yahweh – became the supreme symbol of Israel's power and in the twelfth century BC it began a long and eventful journey towards Jerusalem to its final resting place on the Temple Mount.

To a small nation within the ancient world of the second millennium BC subject to the encroachment of neighbouring empires, security was extremely important and largely depended on the strength of defensive walls. Transporting the Ark to a place of safety could thus only be achieved through political and military strength. In the two centuries that followed the Exodus, leading up to the construction of the First Temple under Solomon, the people of Israel provided the necessary location through conquest.

The Hebrew tribes, under Joshua, the appointed successor of Moses, invaded the land of Canaan, defeating first the Jebusites in the south and the Canaanites in the north.[3] It was the unification of these invading Hebrews with Jews who had stayed in Canaan which established the foundations of the Israelite nation, a people, the Bible tells us, chosen by God and favoured with the Law of Moses which provided the backbone of their social and religious order. Twelve tribes found a home in the land of Canaan governed by elders and ruled by judges who imposed the Mosaic Law. However, despite the successful adoption by nomads to a settled existence, there was a serious and permanent drawback. The land of Canaan was a poor choice for a young nation. The narrow coastal plain of Palestine, dominated by mountains to the north and east with the vast expanse of the Negev and Sinai deserts to the south, was a defensive military strategist's worst conceivable nightmare. Because of its elevated and central position, Jerusalem stood out as the only site which with its adequate walls could be defended. By the end of the second millennium Philistine encroachment from the south and from the Mediterranean coast to the west led to major confrontation which ended in an Israelite defeat. The Philistines displayed the torso of Israel's first anointed king, Saul, from the walls of Beth-Shan, a city on the west bank of the Jordan river, eighty kilometres north-north-east of Jerusalem,[4] and, to compound the horror of this ritualistic celebration of victory, they fastened his head to the wall of the neighbouring temple of Dagon.[5] Before he was captured, knowing he would be killed, Saul took his own life, an act of denial to the enemy that centuries later was repeated by Jewish rebels during the Roman occupation of Jerusalem and the Jewish War.

Several years before the anointment of Saul as King of Israel, the Ark was looted from the city of Shiloh during an incursion by the Philistines into Israelite territory, and installed as a trophy of war in the Temple of Dagon at Ashdod. But it proved to be a less welcome adornment than the head of an Israelite king. According to the Book of Samuel[6] a succession of ominous events, attributable to the Ark, caused a panic throughout the town, fuelled by the outbreak of an unexplained plague of tumours and the sudden death of Philistine citizens. After several months of unrest, the Philistine leaders convened and ordered the return of the Ark to Israelite territory. After the death of Saul the Israelite kingdom's fortunes decreased. Despite the supernatural powers attributed to the Ark of the Covenant, once the unifying force of the nation, it failed to keep Israel together. When unity seemed imperative, inter-tribal conflict broke out and only after seven years of infighting, when the tribal elders realized that in order to survive they would have to join together, did they congregate in Hebron. They elected David, leader of Judah and late armour-bearer to the dead King Saul, King of Israel. Although enjoying a senior position within the powerful tribe of Judah, David was chosen primarily for his military prowess which it was hoped would save the nation.

Jewish kingship was strikingly different from other pagan monarchies of the era. The anointed king was leader of the people, and power of divinity, attributed to Yahweh, was kept distinct from the temporal powers granted to the king. The power of the cult of Yahweh was reaffirmed as directly accessible to all Israelites, citizens and subjects. This remarkably democratic philosophy was only seriously challenged in later centuries by the Temple priesthood who imposed a religious hierarchy on the nation. The succession of David to the throne of Israel saw a new glorious dawn in the fortunes of the Jews and, like his legendary forefather Abraham, his path took him from Hebron to Jerusalem and up to the high ground of Mount Moriah.

Jerusalem had remained a Jebusite stronghold throughout the period of the Philistine invasion. It split the Jewish tribal lands of Judah to the south from those of Israel to the north. David's first step as military commander was to advance on the city in order to conquer it and convert the Jebusite salient into his capital and the base for his future operations. This he achieved in approximately 1000 BC.

Following his capture of the city of Jerusalem, David purchased an area of rock on Mount Moriah from the defeated Jebusite king, Araunah, who had been permitted to retain his ownership of land outside the city walls.[7] This piece of land is recorded in the Bible as being a threshing floor for wheat and it was on this site that David, forbidden by God to build a permanent home for the Ark of the Covenant, raised an altar to Yahweh. Scholars have since identified Araunah's threshing floor as the place chosen by Abraham for the sacrifice of Isaac.[8] For the historian and archaeologist the lack of archaeological evidence and documentation concerning the exact site poses enormous problems. A minimum of eight centuries separate Abraham from David and almost three millennia separate David from the end of the twentieth century AD. Added to the complexities of the Temple Mount area which covers the Mount Moriah location, scientific verification seems impossible. However, the case of David, Abraham and the threshing floor of Araunah demands less of an act of faith than other cases in the early history of the Temple Mount. David was in possession of the Ark, the most sacred object in the history of his people, and it seems likely that even if the threshing floor was not the exact spot of Abraham's sacrificial altar, David's identification of Araunah's property as the legendary high ground of Mount Moriah would have been close, if not correct.

David died an immensely successful warrior king. By the time of his death he had also expelled the Philistine invaders back to the Mediterranean coastal plain of Gaza, Ashkelon and Ashdod, and acquired a vast territory which stretched from the river Euphrates in northern Syria south to Aqaba at the head of the Red Sea. Israel, under his leadership, had become the most powerful nation within the Fertile Crescent. His son Solomon used the military and political stability his father had established as a foundation for the beautification of his kingdom. He enhanced his inheritance through the medium of architecture, a pursuit of excellence he could now afford, and thus almost one thousand years after Abraham had visited Mount Moriah with Isaac, the conditions for the safe housing of the Ark of the Covenant at the birthplace of Jewish monotheism were firmly in place.

THE HOLY ARK OF THE COVENANT

Arca, from the Roman, *arceo*, to enclose, preserve. A kind of box or strong chest used by the ancients as a receptacle for money, clothes, or any valuable effects.[9]

Aron, from the Hebrew, meaning a chest, translated as 'coffin' in Genesis 50:26.

When the Ark was returned to the Israelites by the Philistines, a new location, other than at Shiloh, was prepared. The Ark was taken to Kiriath Jearim, twenty kilometres west of Jerusalem, on the southwestern border of Saul's kingdom. It was placed by Levite priests in the house of a man called Abinadab and in this unpretentious setting the Ark of the Covenant remained until several generations later David had it transported to Jerusalem.

The Ark was built at the foot of Mount Sinai and details of its

FIGURE 2.1 Line graphic of the Ark of the Covenant, based on the Egyptian royal cubit of 21 inches, or 53.35 centimetres (seven palms, or 28 fingers). Dimensions: length: 133.375 centimetres, height and depth: 80.025 centimetres. Figure of cherubim based on sarcophagus of Ahiram, late Bronze Age King of Byblos, Beirut Museum (Author's design).

construction and outward appearance recorded in biblical texts allow us to picture it with some accuracy. The similarity with ritual containers found in Egyptian Pharaonic tombs is striking.[10] The Hebrew tribesmen who built its wooden carcass would have been trained in Egyptian methods of joinery, using panelled frames for the sides of the Ark, not unlike those on a chest found in the tomb of Tutankhamen. These panels were free to move along the inside grooves of the main frame so that when the panels shrunk no splits or cracks would have occurred. The Ark had two carrying poles – as did the chest found in Tutankhamen's tomb. Built of gum arabic or acacia wood, the Ark was two and a half cubits long, one and a half cubits wide and one and a half cubits high. Bezaleel, the craftsman whom Moses had charged with the overall task of completion, finished the casket in style: he plated the carcass inside and out with pure gold.[11] The lid, named the 'mercy seat', was also made out of solid gold as were the figures of two cherubim which stood at either end of the rectangular lid, facing each other with wings outstretched.

The length of a cubit is one of the great bones of contention within modern archaeology, as the approximation of eighteen inches generally ascribed to it cannot be verified with absolute certainty. To complicate things even further, various 'cubits' were employed at different times and places, as Mollet's *Dictionary of Art and Archaeology* for 1883 illustrates:

> **Cubit.** A measure of length among the Egyptians, Greeks and Romans. In Egypt there were two cubits; the *natural* cubit, or small cubit was equal to 18 inches (6 palms or 24 fingers); the *royal* cubit to 21 inches (7 palms or 28 fingers). Each of the subdivisions of the cubit was consecrated to a divinity. The Greek cubit was equal to about 18¼ inches; the Roman cubit to very nearly 17½ inches.

These discrepancies have plagued the efforts of researchers trying to work out the exact location and dimensions of the Temple of Solomon. To the less scrupulous, the varying length of the cubit is a godsend as it can be increased or decreased to suit particular theories, the advantages of which become immediately obvious when the cubit is applied and multiplied over distances on the Temple Mount. It also means that the past *location* of the Ark, which once stood in the Holy of Holies, can also be shifted, with obvious historical and archaeological consequences. The builders of the Ark were Egyptian trained and therefore probably employed the Egyptian cubit in its construction. Despite the fact that both the Ark of the Covenant and the Temple of Solomon disappeared within the course of the first millennium BC leaving little or no trace, the small dimensions of the Ark offer little room for error and mean that its probable size can be determined with some accuracy. The Ark was just over 1.33 metres in length, and almost exactly 80 centimetres in width and height.

Our popular contemporary image of the Ark derives from the Bible, which emphasizes the tremendous importance of the Ark to the Jewish people. It is hardly surprising, therefore, that, as the first Book of Chronicles, Chapter XV, verse 29 tells us, King David played music and danced during the transportation of the Ark from Kiriath Jearim to Jerusalem – the city he had captured and converted to the new capital of Israel. The Jebusite city of Jerusalem occupied the southern portion of Mount Moriah which today supports the Temple Mount. Comprehensive study of this site has only recently been completed by archaeologists of the Israel Antiquities

Authority. Excavation has produced evidence of successive defensive walls, making precise identification of the boundaries and extent of the later Davidic city extremely problematic. Archaeological assessments are compounded by the situation on-site. It is not difficult to imagine why excavation on a repeatedly reconstructed hillside city is a practical nightmare; past spoil, detritus and collapsed stonework complicate chronological identification of strata and add to the difficult job of maintaining stability in a sloping trench. Kathleen Kenyon, the renowned British archaeologist of the twentieth century who worked on the site of the City of David between 1961 and 1967, was convinced of its limitations: 'The Jerusalem of David is a key point in the history of Israel. Our excavations have revealed little of it. I am confident that we have delimited it. I believe that the archaeological evidence for anything more does not survive.'[12]

The prize of correct identification of the Davidic city has obvious allure, and archaeologists are continuing to investigate its strata. Essential material has been deliberately withheld between archaeologists – such as maps of past excavations – which could have provided information which, in turn, could have prevented unnecessary disturbance to a site of great importance.[13] But although the Davidic city was the first resting place of the Ark in Jerusalem, the limits of David's city walls have little bearing on the location of its final resting place. The threshing place of Araunah lying approximately seven hundred metres to the north up the Moriah ridge was the location chosen by David. Verses 3–11 of the First Book of Chronicles, Chapter XXVIII, tell us the instructions given by David to his son Solomon, for the construction of the Temple and the final positioning of the Ark:

> But God said unto me, Thou shalt not build a house in my name, because thou hast been a man of war, and hast shed blood ...
>
> And he said unto me, Solomon thy son, he shall build my house and my courts: for I have chosen him to be my son, and I will be his father ...
>
> Take heed now; for the Lord hath chosen thee to build an house for the sanctuary: be strong and do it ...

> Then David gave to Solomon his son the pattern of the porch, and
> the houses thereof, and of the upper chambers thereof, and of the
> inner parlours thereof, and of the place of the mercy-seat.

THE TEMPLE OF SOLOMON

The life of King Solomon represents the golden age of Israel. A large
part of Kings, Book 1, describes his reign and accomplishments.
However, during the last ten years objective criticism has been lev-
elled at the importance given to the Solomonic kingdom in the
Bible, which has generated heated debate.[14] But if the historical
influence of Solomon's reign within the Fertile Crescent of the Near
East is in doubt, what about the biblical description of the
Solomonic Temple?

According to the Old Testament the First Temple of Jerusalem was
planned and constructed to house the Ark of the Covenant and to this
end Solomon directed his energies and his resources. Building began
on the second day of the second month,[15] during the fourth year of
Solomon's reign. Faced with a severe lack of expertise and raw materials, Solomon approached King Hiram, ruler of the Phoenicians, the
greatest maritime trading nation of the ancient world. Tyre, the capital city of Phoenicia, lies on the Mediterranean coast of modern-day
Lebanon. King Hiram held great influence over the rich maritime
traffic of the eastern Mediterranean. Tyre was the gateway between the
rich land-based trading routes of the East and the diverse centres of
population scattered around the Mediterranean. The Phoenicians
were highly skilled craftsmen. Their ability as shipbuilders enabled
them to dominate the sea routes of the ancient world and their
shipbuilding skills overflowed into their architectural endeavours
wherever they had colonized. The slopes of Lebanon, which rise above
Tyre to the east, were well forested with the tallest and most versatile
tree indigenous to the Mediterranean, the Lebanon cedar. Jerusalem's
climate and soil were not conducive to the kind of timber suited to
building. So in order to carry out his task, Solomon required not only
the services of skilled craftsmen and masons, but also a considerable
amount of long and straight-grained tree-trunks to provide both

structural support and the furniture planned for the Temple. King Hiram had previously made favourable overtures of alliance to the Israelite kingdom,[16] and had supplied Solomon's father David with Lebanon cedar for his palace.[17] The Second Book of Chronicles tells us of the correspondence between Solomon and Hiram and the deal they struck. Solomon required a Master Mason, and in verse 7 of Chapter II he makes his request, asking the king of Tyre to send him 'a man, cunning to work in gold, and in silver, and in brass, and in iron, and in purple, and crimson, and blue, and that can skill to grave with the cunning men that are with me in Judah and in Jerusalem, whom David my father did provide'.

The stipulation by Solomon that Hiram's Master Mason should possess the skill of working in 'purple, crimson and blue' shows the extent of his forethought in completing his Temple. Solomon's vision was not only to build a sanctuary to Yahweh but to construct a royal palace with an elaborately furnished interior. The Phoenicians had long mastered the extraction of a purple dye from the body tissue of a Mediterranean marine snail, *Trunculariopsis (Murex) trunculus.* This dye was widely used in the Mediterranean for the production of royal purple and was a precious and prestigious commodity. Mention of this dye in Chronicles demonstrates that Solomon, before laying a single stone of the Temple, had fully visualized the complex as an entire entity. In exchange for timber, Solomon proposed an exchange of goods: 'And behold, I will give to thy servants, the hewers that cut timber, twenty thousand measures of beaten wheat, and twenty thousand measures of barley, and twenty thousand baths of wine and twenty thousand baths of oil.'[18] The Phoenicians of Tyre agreed to send a Master Mason, and in return for the grain, wine and oil proposed to float the timber southwards along the coast to Jaffa, reducing the overland journey to a minimum. By mutual agreement and cooperation, Hiram's craftsmen, complete with timber resources, engaged in the undertaking of Solomon's task.

MASONS OF THE KING

The secrets of the English and Scottish rites of Freemasonry are widely believed to derive from the building of Solomon's Temple. The association, which becomes immediately apparent to apprentices or lay investigators of the Freemasonic 'craft' or practice, is undeniable. The Masonic account of the building of the First Solomonic Temple is replete with intrigue, greed, murder and retribution. However, the key to understanding the intricacies of this human saga lies in the level or, in Masonic terms, the 'degree' of architectural expertise possessed by the artisans of Tyre and the scientific method and processes they employed. According to the Second Book of Chronicles, Solomon set all foreign inhabitants of Israel to work to achieve his aim – a total of 153,600 people.[19] The age and sex of these workers goes unmentioned in the Bible, although they may have numbered the 'cunning men' mentioned by Solomon as having been employed by his father David. It also seems unlikely that the Master Mason sent by Hiram would have arrived in Jerusalem unaccompanied, a fact highlighted by the discovery of 'Phoenician' lettering made during the excavations carried out by Lieutenant Warren in 1867–70.

Warren's shaft at the south-eastern corner of the *haram* took him to the base-layer of the Herodian Temple Mount foundations. A number of the beautifully dressed limestone blocks with typically flat panels projecting from a wide border, constituting the lower courses or levels, were found to bear two carved letters and several others painted in ochre. The presence of such marks, which were presumed to date from the *first* Solomonic Temple period of building, posed an immediate mystery. It is widely accepted that Herod employed Jewish, not Phoenician craftsmen, for his rebuilding and Warren was initially unsure if the earlier Solomonic platform had extended this far south on the Mount. Despite this, in his report to the PEF he concluded, because of the 'Phoenician style' of lettering, that the blocks were part of the First Temple construction. Further study of the inscriptions by Warren's contemporaries confirmed that the writing, although derived from the more ancient Phoenician, was in fact a sloppy version of Aramaean, a hybrid script much used by Jews in Herodian times.[20] Of greatest interest is the most prolific of the inscriptions, shown in Figure 2.2.

Found on a stone at the base of a wall (third stone from the right,

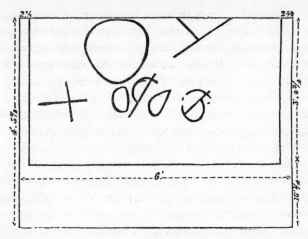

FIGURE 2.2 Reproduction of inscription found by Warren at the south-east angle of the *haram*.

'c', of Warren's second course 'f'), it told a story of Masonic cover-up. As it read *K'a k'ak'at*, literally, *carelessness of brand*,[21] it was evident that this stone, which has no border at its top but double the standard width at the bottom, had been condemned as imperfect and duly relegated to the lowest layer of the foundations where it would be covered over before inspection.

Warren, however, remained adamant that the base courses of the eastern wall were Solomonic, arguing that the western wall, which was known to be Herodian to its base layer, had its hidden, below-ground courses built from unfinished blocks. The blocks at the south-eastern corner were, by contrast, apart from their faulty borders, finished to a standard equal to those above ground. This convinced Warren of their Solomonic pedigree and if his deduction was correct, it meant that Aramaean script must have been in use since at least 960 BC. It would also credit him with identification of the first real evidence of King Solomon's Temple.[22] Warren had a secret ambition to uncover the Solomonic past of the Mount and went so far as to use gunpowder to clear a passage through the underground rubble barring his progress.[23] But Warren's personal motive did not entirely cloud his judgement. The ochre paint used for the writing ran upwards which was proof that the stones had been finished in the quarry. He deduced that the quality inspector had marked them with a brush, their top edge pointing down a slope, using too much paint which had trickled down before drying.

If the blocks found by Warren were Herodian and not Solomonic, conclusions concerning an earlier construction of the platform under Solomon can still be made. The building of the Solomonic Temple complex would have required a stable platform, and the blocks at the south-east angle indicate the massive size of hewn stone employed in its overall construction. The cutting and shaping of the stone would have demanded precise measurement given the dimensions involved. Under Solomon such blocks would have been similarly cut by saw, finished in the quarry to an exact template derived from a plan, then marked, transported up the Mount and placed in position.[24]

Payment made to labourers and artisans differed according to skill. It was given at various locations on the Temple site and, to ensure a just and fair reward, secret passwords and signs were distributed, according to an individual's degree, or level, of craft. This practice of payment by password, dating back almost three thousand years, is the origin of the passwords and signs which are employed within Freemasonry today, passwords which separate and define the *degrees* of Freemasonic brotherhood. The use of the word 'degree' is another indicator of the sophistication of the Phoenician craftsmen. The masonic skills of Solomon's artisans were exceptional for the era and contained a highly developed mathematical basis involving degrees or differences in level from a fixed point of survey. Mathematics, and in particular the application of geometry, is still upheld by Freemasons as a sacred science. Mount Moriah, as Warren so indisputedly proved in the last century, had a seriously undulating surface and the masons employed by Solomon must have succeeded in establishing accurate levels by using advanced methods of surveying. The Solomonic platform was nine centuries later integrated into the larger Herodian Temple complex and all traces of the Solomonic Temple and its surrounding buildings disappeared under the new Herodian, Second Temple. Although the Herodian expansion has left archaeologists and historians with little but the Old Testament account with which to attempt a reconstruction of Solomon's Temple, the biblical description is long and detailed; and it provides sufficient information with which to create a clear image of the First Temple on the Mount.

The Navel of the World,
962–955 BC

Although the Bible tells us nothing about the exact dimensions and method of construction of the First Temple platform, it is more informative about the Temple itself. The First Book of Kings confirms that when the foundations were laid Solomon's masons placed finished masonry *in situ*. The account makes it clear that this process of prefabrication was adopted not for technical reasons but rather to conform to religious requirements. Chapter VI, verse 7 tells us: 'the house [of the Lord], when it was in building, was built of stone made ready before it was brought thither: so that there was neither hammer, nor axe, nor any tool of iron, heard in the house while it was in building.' Such religious correctness indicates the degree to which the people of Israel venerated Yahweh. If such silence was indeed achieved, the scene atop the Mount must have been extraordinarily surreal, with thousands of workers moving amidst a quietly growing site. The Temple was finally completed in the month of Bul, the eighth month of the year, seven and a half years after the first foundation stone of the platform was set in place on Mount Moriah. There is no account of how long it took to construct the platform, or whether once a sufficient central area was completed, building work on the Temple proper was begun in parallel. However, the plan was for the Temple of King Solomon to be rectangular, and in the First Book of Kings its exact dimensions are given as sixty cubits long, twenty cubits in breadth and thirty in height.

Even if the biblical cubit is taken to be the largest of those described in Mollet's *Dictionary of Art and Archaeology* – the Egyptian royal of twenty-one inches – then the proposed Temple building was modest in size, standing at just under thirty-two and a half metres in length, a little over ten and a half metres in breadth and sixteen metres in height. There existed, however, a sound reason for the choice of such conservative dimensions. The construction of the Solomonic Temple followed the architectural design pattern of the era which required an open interior with a room free of internal columns, providing the requisite pure and uncluttered space for a planned antechamber giving onto the Holy of Holies, the chamber in which the Ark was placed. The breadth of the Temple would therefore have to be spanned by the only material capable of supporting unaided the weight of a roof – the straight baulks of precious Lebanon cedar, supplied by King Hiram of Tyre. The length and tensile qualities of a mature Lebanon cedar were the two factors which determined the maximum width separating the side walls of the Temple, a width which Solomon's masons had judged as being approximately eleven metres. Once they had raised the Temple walls to the required height, Solomon's masons placed the roof beams across the breadth of the building, leaving their ends free-standing on the top course of the stone side walls. This left the King ready to enter the next elaborate phase of his task which would demonstrate the versatility of Hiram's timber as a building material perfectly suited to the Temple Mount project.

The roof beams were overlaid from above with cedar boards and the internal face of these retaining stone walls was fully lined in a similar fashion, as confirmed in Chapter VI of 1 Kings. The words of verse 15 tell us how Solomon continued with the partitioning of the inside of his Temple: 'And he [Solomon] built the walls of the house within with boards of cedar, both the floor of the house, and the walls of the ceiling: and he covered them on the inside with wood, and covered the floor of the house with planks of fir.' With the walls lined, the Temple was ready for detailed work on its interior to begin. Cedar, with its close and straight grain, is ideal for carving large frieze decoration. Solomon's masons took advantage of this natural quality, creating 'knops' and 'open flowers'[1] out of the pliant wood of the walls and ceiling. Solomon gave instructions for all visible surfaces of the chamber to be overlaid with gold leaf.[2] Once all the finished woodwork was gilded, the interior of the

Temple to the Oracle or Holy of Holies, the internal chamber which would house the Ark of the Covenant, was decorated. If the biblical description can be believed, this small room, the most important and the most sacred location within the Kingdom of Israel which measured just twenty cubits square by twenty in height, received the fullest attentions of Solomon's most expert and able craftsmen. The result was a visually overwhelming design. The Bible describes the entrance to the Holy of Holies as measuring one fifth of the front wall, from both the side-posts and the lintel. We are told that the wall measured twenty cubits in breadth by twenty in height, which gives us both the breadth and height of the entrance. If the wall was twenty by twenty cubits the opening would have measured four cubits by four cubits, just over 2.1 metres. Leaving a possible twenty-five centimetre depth of frame on either side, the remaining width of each door would therefore have measured approximately eighty centimetres, and their height would have been 1.85 metres – the average height of a man.

Solomon used the native olive wood of Jerusalem for the construction of these doors, which had presumably been cut from trees growing in the Kidron valley next to Mount Moriah. This area was full of ancient olive groves, the oil of which was sent in vast quantities to King Hiram of Tyre in exchange for his precious Lebanon cedar. Dominated by the aptly named Mount of Olives, these terraced slopes still contain, despite the ravages of history, ancient trees of sufficient girth and height to complete a contemporary reconstruction of the doors described in the First Book of Kings. Undaunted by the natural hardness of olive wood, Solomon's workers carved the doors with 'cherubims and palm-trees and open flowers'[3] and, in the style of the rest of the Temple, they were then overlaid, inside and out, with pure gold.

Progressing through the gilded olive wood doorway, into the Holy of Holies, his craftsmen embarked on the decoration of this innermost sacred chamber. The cedar of the walls and ceiling were carved to match the entrance doors and the whole of the interior, floor, ceiling and walls, was coated in gold. Within this chamber Solomon placed his first pieces of furniture – a pair of cherubim, carved, like the doors, from olive wood and both gilded. They were positioned side by side and stood ten cubits in height, with inner wing-tips joined and outer wing-tips touching opposite walls.

Some archaeologists have argued that the profusion of gold in the Temple and the Holy of Holies was unnecessarily ostentatious.[4] But the presence of gold in the Temple is historically significant in itself for what it tells us about the politics of the time. Although the absence of hard archaeological evidence means we have to rely on biblical description, the detailed description in the First Book of Kings is immensely vivid, giving quantities as well as measurements, and this information concerning the use of gold, combined with details of its provenance, helps us to complete the large picture of the Solomonic Temple period. Solomon's security as the ruler of Israel enabled him to conclude an initial building deal with King Hiram of Tyre. Without the valuable national commodities of oil, wheat and wine, there would have been no cedar and, thereby, possibly, no Temple construction. To the King of Israel, gold ore, necessary for the final embellishment of the Temple, was, like cedar, nowhere to be found in the Israelite territory. Notwithstanding this disadvantage, the lands Solomon had inherited from his father David offered rich possibilities. Solomon's domain was the central trading link in the Near Eastern arena. His territory straddled the ancient trade routes of the Transjordan, which ran from the Arabian peninsula northwards, up the Jordan rift valley, into modern-day Syria, thereby linking the gold-rich Arabian and Indian markets with the heart of the ancient Mediterranean world. For the rulers of the Arabian peninsula and beyond, the freedom to move goods along this route was crucial to their national economic expansion. Solomon was, therefore, courted by his neighbours north and south, as an ally.

Early in his reign Solomon married the daughter of the reigning Egyptian Pharoah. This was a move of political astuteness on the part of Egypt – if not one of pleasure on the part of Solomon who, so the Bible tells us, later confirmed through the construction of a personal palace[5] his Egyptian wife's pre-eminence in a growing harem of 'many strange women, women of the Moabites, Ammonites, Edomites, Zidonians, and Hittites'.[6] This dynastic link with Egypt laid the foundations for further diplomacy aimed at keeping the trade routes of the Transjordan open. Use of gold in the Temple, ostentatious or otherwise, was an unmistakable symbol of kingly power signalling to outsiders the status of the cult of Yahweh in the eyes of the Israelite nation. This quantity of gold seems relatively small when compared to the vast quantity of foreign tribute that was offered to Solomon once the Temple and its surrounding royal precinct was completed – a period of immense riches encapsulated by the visit to Jerusalem of the legendary and mysterious Queen of Sheba. In the meantime, the Holy of Holies awaited only the installation of the Ark of the Covenant.

THE WIDOW'S SON

To complete the furnishing of the Temple and the elaborate buildings planned to its south, the King required people highly skilled in metalwork and, in particular, the casting of bronze, or brass. Solomon turned once again to the Phoenician Kingdom of Tyre: 'King Solomon sent, and fetched Hiram out of Tyre, he was a widow's son of the tribe of Naphtali, and his father was a man of Tyre, a worker in brass: and he was filled with wisdom and understanding and cunning to all works in brass. And he came to king Solomon, and wrought all his work.'[7] Hiram the 'worker in brass' was given a task of truly regal proportions by Solomon. However, the quality of work he was commanded to execute must have paled into insignificance when he learnt the immense size of the castings required for the Temple. Hiram was asked to construct two massive bronze pillars, a large vessel called the Great Sea for holding purified water and a number of other furnishings and tools including ten bronze lavers or large cleansing basins. Ancient bronze was usually an alloy of copper and tin with an added element of arsenic. The arsenic would render the final bronze more or less brittle depending on whether the final product was a decorative item or a working tool. Whilst it is generally accepted that Hiram was casting bronze, the modern Bible, based on the translation ordered by King James I of England, calls it brass, an alloy of copper and zinc. Although brass weathers in a similar way to bronze – both are resistant to water corrosion – brass is less pliant, more brittle and therefore less suitable for casting large objects. The brittleness of brass, however, holds an important clue to the content of Hiram's bronze.

It seems probable that Hiram of Tyre was master of a further, more complicated alloy, a triple phase bronze which consists of copper, zinc and tin. This alloy, when fused in certain proportions by cannon makers of the sixteenth, seventeenth and eighteenth centuries, was known as gunmetal but often described as ordnance *brass*. Hiram's own, ancient, triple phase bronze, of copper tin and *arsenic*, would have entered the Authorized Version of the King James Bible compiled in the sixteenth century as brass, because of its similarity to gunmetal.

Hiram, a master architect and metallurgist, was revered by all who worked under him and his skills became legendary. Two thousand years after his alchemic achievements, the mystery surrounding Hiram was further embellished by the clandestine activities of a medieval military order: the Knights Templar. Formed as a monastic military order after the Christian capture of Jerusalem in AD 1099, the Templars, who initially took the name the Poor Knights of the Temple of *Solomon*, revived the Solomonic glory of Hiram's achievements with the result that Hiram of Tyre was installed from the 12th century onwards within the highest echelons of western Freemasonry under the name, Hiram Abiff.[8] Hiram's work has thus become shrouded in mystery, a fact which has complicated any historical assessment of his life. But, apart from legend, if Hiram held secrets important enough to be prized by King Solomon and resurrected by Christians later, is there any recorded evidence which might indicate the true level of his skill? The answer lies in the First Book of Kings. According to this account, the list of furniture and working utensils requested by King Solomon was far from modest. Hiram's triple phase castings were the finest bronze products of the Solomonic era.

THE TEMPLE TREASURE

Solomon was determined that Hiram's initial castings would be the most ambitious. Hiram had to create two pillars, Jachin and Boaz, which would stand side by side flanking the main entrance of the Temple on the Mount. Boaz was to be on the left; Jachin to the right. The size of these pillars was a constant visual and physical reminder to all who entered the Temple of King Solomon's ambitious plans for the Mount and the cult of Yahweh.[9] Jachin and Boaz might be described as part of the fixed architecture of the Temple, and therefore not *per se* a component of the Temple treasure of gold, silver and bronze utensils. But in monetary terms their value was high as they were castings of a size never before attempted by workers in the Kingdom of Israel. Their planned dimensions presented Hiram with a task which bordered on the impossible.[10] We are told by the chronicler of Kings that the shaft of each pillar measured eighteen cubits – approximately 9.6 metres in height. Kings gives their cubit circumference as twelve which, when calculated on the Egyptian royal measurement, gives a diameter of just over 1.9 metres, an ambitious casting even for modern times, particularly given the nature of the material being used. At the time of Solomon, standard bronze was valued at approximately one fourth of the value of gold;[11] the monetary value of such bronzes was therefore not

FIGURE 3.1 View of the Temple showing the main, east-facing entrance with Jachin and Boaz *in situ*, from Stade.

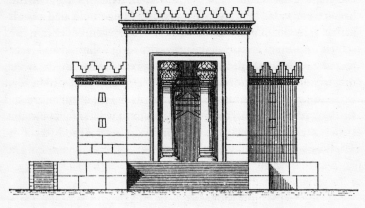

insignificant. Just how and where Hiram created Jachin and Boaz is uncertain. However, verse 46, Chapter VII of the First Book of Kings describes the creation of the *tools* used in the Temple: 'In the plain of Jordan did the king cast them, in the clay ground between Succoth and Zarthan.'[12]

The 'clay ground' between the ancient locations of Succoth and Zarthan lies approximately forty kilometres north-east of Jerusalem, in the valley of the Jordan, and the words of verse 23 suggest that this Jordan clay formed the moulds into which bronze mixed by Hiram was poured. Perhaps Hiram cast Jachin and Boaz at the same place as the tools, since the moulds for these pillars would have required an enormous amount of clay. Although the location of Hiram's largest casting remains uncertain, how he did it is easier to grasp. Both the Bible and the work of the Jewish historian, Flavius Josephus, give virtually identical accounts. On the casting of Jachin and Boaz Josephus says: 'this Hiram made two [hollow] pillars, whose outsides were of brass; and the thickness of the brass was four fingers' breadth.'[13] Josephus was obviously well versed in the Old Testament for this specific information came not from the most commonly used source of the Books of Kings or Chronicles which hold the bulk of biblical information on the Solomonic Temple, but from the account of the Prophet Jeremiah, Chapter LII, verse 21: 'And concerning the pillars...the thickness thereof was four fingers: it was hollow.' If Jeremiah's description and the account of Josephus in *Antiquities* are true, Jachin and Boaz were cast hollow either in single lengths around a clay or limestone core, or constructed from sections. The words of Jeremiah have a significant place in the historical jigsaw of both the Temple Mount and the fate of the Ark of the Covenant as Jeremiah not only prophesied but also witnessed the destruction of the First Temple of Solomon under the Babylonians in 586 BC. It remains a tantalizing prospect that Jeremiah might have measured the broken columns, or the gap they left after they were looted, with his own fingers.

Josephus was writing more than ten centuries after the construction of the First Temple and almost seven after Jeremiah. By the time of Josephus, all physical evidence of the First Temple would have been relegated to memory but his description of the Solomonic period often contains information which cannot be found in the Bible. We can only therefore assume that Josephus had tapped into an oral tradition or, more importantly, writings which have been lost. In *Antiquities*, Josephus provides a clue to the provenance and location of long-forgotten secrets of the Temple of Solomon. In Book VIII, Chapter II, he describes the initial agreement between Solomon and King Hiram of Tyre which involved the exchange of goods in return for the invaluable Lebanon cedar and the expert services of Hiram, the Tyrian Master Mason. This deal was confirmed in writing as both the First Book of Kings and the Second Book of Chronicles record. Josephus' eighth verse begins: 'The copies of these epistles remain to this day, and are preserved not only in our books, but among the Tyrians also; insomuch that if any one would know the certainty about them, he may desire of the keepers of the public records of Tyre to shew him there, and he will find what is set down to agree with what we have said. I have said so much out of a desire that my readers know that we speak nothing but the truth.' This clearly indicates that Josephus had had access to records from Tyrian archives – or copies of them: archives which may have held further information concerning the mysterious workings of Hiram. Josephus' words in verse 8 reveal his preoccupation with 'the truth' and an awareness that distortion of the written record was as threatening to *true* history in his own time as in ours. This underlines the central problem we have today in understanding the history of the Temple Mount, and in particular the history and archaeology of the First, Solomonic Temple. Our contemporary written sources are far more limited even than those which were once available to Josephus so it is only archaeology that can enhance our knowledge of the First Temple with any great accuracy. For those who sought out greater mystery, the hollow nature of Jachin and Boaz was significant. Freemasons believe that these pillars contained, inside their hollow section, writings which described the lost secrets of the 'widow's son', Hiram Abiff.

Hiram's next task was to cast the Great Sea. This huge receptacle, over five metres wide,[14] was supported by twelve bronze oxen. Placed in groups of three, the oxen faced outwards from the centre towards the four cardinal points of the compass, shouldering the weight of the

FIGURE 3.2 Illustration of the Great Sea, from Stade.

bronze basin which Kings records as being 'an hand-breadth' in thickness. Kings leaves us in no doubt that the basin, a thumb wider than Jachin and Boaz, was a single casting.

The Great Sea was, according to Josephus, designed to be used as a purification bath for the hands and feet of all priests who entered the Temple and were entitled to conduct sacrifice. The rim of the bath stood at ten cubits, or approximately 5.3 metres, from the ground. At this height the purifying water must have been decanted to wash the feet. By following a similar process to wash the hands the waters in the bath would have remained clean and pure. But personal bodily purification was only one part of the ritual. Sacrificial offerings to God required careful preparation, and the Jewish Temple priesthood, proficient in butchery, were provided by Hiram Abiff with ten intricately designed and lavishly constructed bronze basins to assist them in their bloody purpose.

Four cubits in diameter, set upon intricate four-wheeled bases, and modelled, according to the biblical account, on the contemporary chariot wheel, these basins, or lavers, were used to cleanse the entrails and feet of animals before they were sacrificially burnt on the bronze altar. After being washed the animals were incinerated on the bronze altar in order to produce the sacrificial burnt offering for Yahweh – a continuation, more elaborately produced, of the legendary burnt offering presented to God by Abraham on

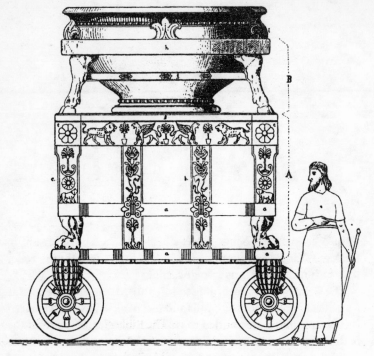

FIGURE 3.3 Illustration of bronze laver, from Stade.

the same location one thousand years previously.[15] The lavers were designed for use around the main entrance to the Temple.

Once the bronze pillars Jachin and Boaz were installed on either side of the main Temple entrance, Hiram capped them with two capitals of five cubits. This brought their height from eighteen to twenty-three cubits, just over twelve metres. These highly decorated capitals were then covered by beaten chainwork in the shape of palm trees, and as a final embellishment two hundred bronze pomegranates were set in place circling the top of each pillar.

With the major bronzes completed Solomon instructed his workers to place the Great Sea in the south-eastern corner of the Temple courtyard and the ten lavers either side of the external side walls of the Temple, five to the north and five to the south.[16] The account in the First Book of Kings then describes the casting of the

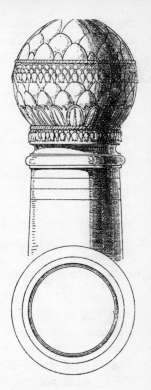

FIGURE 3.4 Illustration of bronze capitals to Jachin and Boaz, from Stade.

smallest bronzes, the 'pots, shovels and basons' required by the priests within the Temple for tending the sacrifices.[17]

Only the Temple priesthood and the tribe of the Levites were allowed access to the Inner Courtyard. This placed the Ark of the Covenant, the Temple and the Inner Courtyard out of bounds to the common men and all women of Israel, which restricted any experience of the fully equipped and working Temple to a few privileged chosen men. For the small number of workers and masons who laboured with Hiram of Tyre and the scribes whose job it was to keep a record of the works, the production of the treasure must have presented a task of vast complexity in proportion to the overall construction of the Temple. For the majority of the Jewish nation, the reported quantity and magnificence of the treasure would have raised the status of their cult to new heights. However, the veil of Masonic knowledge surrounding the works, coupled with a denial of access to the innermost places of the Temple, had a lasting effect. An air of secrecy had entered the Temple Mount and this atmosphere is fully reflected in the Old Testament. It is generally believed that the two Books of Kings were compiled in the seventh century BC, several centuries after the Solomonic era. By this time the exact quantity of Solomon's treasure was forgotten, with the author or authors admitting, in near apologetic tone, that 'Solomon left all the vessels unweighed, because they were exceeding many: neither was the weight of the brass found out.'[18] This tone of coyness present in the First Book of Kings was not, however, repeated by Josephus in his own description of the bronze or brass vessels. His pride in his Jewish heritage is apparent in his description of this particular part of the treasure which he claims looked 'in splendour and beauty as gold'. Josephus completes his narrative of the First Temple treasure by listing the almost unbelievable amount of gold and silver utensils:

> The king also dedicated a great number of tables, but one that was large and made of gold, upon which they set the loaves of God; and he made ten thousand more which resembled them, but were done after another manner, upon which lay the vials and the cups; those of gold were twenty thousand, those of silver were forty thousand. He also made ten thousand candlesticks, according to the command of Moses…The king also made pouring vessels, in number eighty thousand, and a hundred thousand golden vials, and twice as many silver vials: of golden dishes, in order therein to offer kneaded flour at the altar, there were eighty thousand, and twice as many of silver. Of large basins also…sixty thousand of gold and twice as many of silver. Of measures…there were twenty thousand of gold, and twice as many of silver.[19]

Outside the Holy of Holies, a smaller golden altar was positioned with on one side a single large gold table to hold holy loaves and on the other a single candlestick – one of the ten thousand listed in *Antiquities*. This inventory concludes by telling us how many golden censers were used by the priests. Twenty thousand were used to carry incense across the Inner Courtyard to the large bronze altar and another fifty thousand were made specifically for ceremonies around the golden altar. These censers were important tools in the ritual of the Temple. They were designed to carry incense which once ignited was taken from the bronze altar and carried through the Temple entrance flanked by Jachin and Boaz towards the Holy of Holies. Once inside, the priests, purified by the waters of the Great Sea, stood directly in front of the doors to the inner sanctum containing the Ark of the Covenant, swinging the golden censers filled with incense to purify the burnt offering as it was placed on the golden altar.

With Hiram's work on the Temple utensils complete, King Solomon sent out word to his people and their tribal elders to gather in Jerusalem. The invitation to participate in and witness the permanent installation of the most holy relic of Judaism within the Holy of Holies on the Temple Mount linked the soul of Judaic faith with the city of Jerusalem for ever and constituted a turning point in the history of Israel. Thus, some thirty generations after Moses had come down from Mount Sinai with the words of God carved in stone, preparations were set in motion for the Ark of the Covenant, together with its divine cargo, to make its final recorded journey from the lower, adjoining City of David up to the Temple of Solomon on Mount Moriah.

THE MULTITUDE, THE LEVITES AND THE PRIESTS

From the time King David first moved the Ark to Jerusalem, it stayed within the safety of the walls of the city he had built on the tongue of high ground which stretched away southwards from the Temple Mount. According to the First Book of Kings these walls were built of three layers of hewn stone, capped by a course of cedar beams.[20] In *Antiquities* Josephus describes the wall as exactly three cubits in height and in Section 9 of Chapter III he elaborates further, stating that the wall was designed for 'the exclusion of the multitude from coming into the Temple, and shewing that it was a place that was free and open only for the priests'.[21] Three cubits, whether Egyptian royal or Egyptian natural would have given a wall of approximately five feet or 1.6 metres. This, whilst denying the 'multitude' personal access, would at least have allowed them to view the sacrificial activities of the priests.

The ultimate responsibility for the fulfilment of sacrifice before the Ark lay with the priests of Israel. According to Josephus, 612 years separate the Exodus and the completion of the First Temple and during this period he calculated that thirteen High Priests had served at the head of the cult of Yahweh.[22] In the new Temple of Solomon, the High Priest and the priests of Israel retained their hereditary rights and by establishing a permanent altar in the Holy of Holies, Solomon granted these priests almost unassailable religious power within the heart of his kingdom. It seems evident, however, from the biblical account that only a small group of people knew the specific process by which the Temple was built. The handling of the sacred relic remained the privilege of the members of one tribe – the Levites. When an attempt was made to allow non-Levites to become involved it ended in disaster with the non-Levite Uzza, who reached out to steady the Ark, dropping dead as soon as he touched it.[23] The effect of this on the Israelites was profound, and whether this event actually happened or not, this Levitic privilege was never again contested.

The installation of the Ark on the Mount called for a high degree of ceremony in which the Hebrew nation excelled. In addition to duties of transport the Levites, since the early years of King David's reign, were responsible for providing religious music, both choral and instrumental. Music lay at the very heart of the cult of Yahweh and, with the Ark now in a permanent setting, the Levites were instructed by Solomon to prepare a special musical service to accompany the priestly sacrifices that would take place on the Mount.[24]

> The sacredotal [sic] garments which belonged to the high priest, with the long robes, and the oracle, and the precious stones, were a thousand; but the crown upon which Moses wrote [the name of God] was only one, and hath remained to this very day. He also made ten thousand sacredotal [sic] garments of fine linen, with *purple girdles* [author's italics], for every priest; and two hundred thousand

trumpets, according to the command of Moses; and also two hundred thousand garments of fine linen, for the singers that were Levites; and he made musical instruments, and such as were invented for the singing of hymns, called *Nablae* and *Cinyrae,* [psalteries and harps] which were made of electrum, forty thousand.[25]

The dye used for the 'girdles' was extracted from the marine snail *Truncalariopsis (Murex) trunculus.* This process was perfected by the Phoenicians, hence the relevance of Solomon's initial demand, made seven years previously to King Hiram of Tyre, for a master craftsman 'cunning', not just in the craft of building and metal-work, but also in the manufacture of purple. Hiram Abiff's abilities would also have served the King well in the production of *Nablae* and *Cinyrae.* Electrum, like bronze, was an ancient and highly prized alloy and although it was simpler to manufacture than bronze, it surpassed bronze in value. The electrum of the psalteries and harps contained a high content of gold – 75 per cent – and the remaining percentage was made up of 22 per cent silver and 3 per cent copper.[26] If Josephus' calculations are correct these forty thousand instruments of electrum would have added considerably to the value of the Temple's treasure.

The Levite tribe was also assigned the duty of maintaining the sanctity of the Temple and safeguarding the Ark. They were made doorkeepers to the Temple as verses 17–19 of Chapter XXVI of the First Book of Chronicles relate: 'Eastward were six Levites, north-ward four a day, and toward Assupim two and two. At Parbar west-ward, four at the causeway, and two at Parbar, these are the divisions of the porters.' This gave them a unique position of power. As doorkeepers, they were privy to the secret passages, hidden chambers and hiding places within the Mount, a knowledge which had far-reaching consequences in the future.

OF STAVES, THE ARK AND THE BIBLE

It took a total of seven months for all the tribal leaders and people of Israel to receive the King's summons. The assembly in Jerusalem must have been an extraordinary moment for the populace. Most people would have travelled from Israelite territory lying outside and beyond Jerusalem and for them the occasion would have been their chance to glimpse Solomon's construction on Mount Moriah, now transformed from barren rock into a magnificent platform crowned by a Temple.

On the day ordained by the King, sometime in the summer or early autumn of 954 BC,[27] the Ark of the Covenant was lifted up by Levite bearers to begin its journey from the Davidic city up to the Temple Mount. The weight of the golden reliquary, which contained the stone tablets, made the ascent from the City of David to the Mount extremely arduous. Today the view northwards from the ruins of David's city to the Mount of Moriah is dominated by the towering south-eastern corner of the *haram* or Temple Mount enclosure. This is the highest corner of the existing Mount and it still holds the Aramaean Masonic inscriptions of 'carelessness of brand' or imperfection discovered on its lower courses by Lieutenant Warren in 1867. The huge *haram* masonry to the north, rebuilt on Herod's Second Temple foundations, dwarfs the modern viewer into insignificance. The Dome of the Rock covering the *sakhra* cannot be seen, giving the whole of the Mount an air of mystery and seclusion.

By contrast, the 'multitude' of 955 BC would have had a clear view of the Temple complex. Josephus tells us that the platform area of Solomon's Temple was half that of Herod's.[28] The lower walls would have given a less foreboding vista but no less impressive with the freshly cut limestone of the new Temple and the glistening bronze of Jachin and Boaz rising up from the centre of the Mount in the high distance, beckoning the people forward. The procession of the Ark, led by King Solomon, was accompanied by sacrifices and oblations and the burning of an immense amount of incense[29] which 'filled the onlookers and participants, even at a distance' with such celebratory energy that 'they did not grow weary, either of singing hymns, or of dancing, until they came to the temple'.[30] At the gates of the Inner Courtyard, or at the main Temple entrance itself, the multitude were held back, excluded from direct access to the ceremony. The priests and Levites lifted the Ark up the front steps of the Temple and, passing between Jachin and Boaz, continued a further distance of approximately eighteen metres up to the entrance of the Holy of Holies. The sacred relic was carried inside and laid to rest under the protective wings of the golden cherubim. The Ark of the Covenant had reached its final known resting place.

The Temple Mount, a man-made platform built on an easily quarried bedrock of limestone, is an ideal site for constructing places of concealment. During their respective researches in Jerusalem three thousand years after the Solomonic era, Captain Wilson and Lieutenant Warren demonstrated that not only could such locations exist, but that they could remain undetected for centuries. They came to realize the importance of the secrets entombed within the substrata of the Temple Mount, and in his official report to the Palestine Exploration Fund (PEF) in 1867 Wilson described the existence of a passage under the Temple Mount which he could investigate no further as it had been sealed off. Charles Warren, who followed in Wilson's footsteps, wrote the words 'secret passage' on many of his maps. Soon after his arrival in Jerusalem, the Turkish governor of Jerusalem, Izzet Pasha, nicknamed Warren, who had quickly established a reputation as being obsessive about his digging work, 'the Mole'.[31]

In the Sanctuary (on the Temple Mount) live, for the protection of the place, certain African or Nubian men...their fanaticism knows no bounds; but I found means to be friendly with these people. They once ate a very large pet lizard of mine which I wanted to send home to the Zoological Gardens in London, and I took advantage of the occurrence to make friends with them, so that instead of coming and throwing stones at me when I entered the Temple area by myself, they would stand up and deferentially salaam. However, I never attempted to test their good feeling too far, and on this occasion they were given a hint that they might obtain a smell of grilled lizard if they went in a certain direction. This was enough for them; they are greedily fond of the large lizard, which happens to be my namesake, Warren, and were thus out of our way.

The blows of our hammers resounded in the vaults, and soon our Moslem friends got into the greatest fright lest all would be discovered: however, we were in for it; if we were to be set upon and eaten up instead of the lizard, we might as well complete our work first. Accordingly, whenever we were implored to stop, we made more noise until our friends lay in a corner tearing their beards and plucking at their garments in the greatest state of agonised terror.[32]

It is clear from this and other reports that the Turkish authorities were often completely unaware of how extensive the 'Mole's' penetration of the sacred *haram* or Temple Mount area was. As a result, they were equally ignorant of the enormous significance of Warren's discoveries. In his official report of 1871 Warren states: 'That in places there may be objects of the greatest interest hidden, I think there can be no doubt.'[33] Warren uncovered 'objects' not necessarily of great value but of immense archaeological importance, which he described in detail in his reports to the PEF. He did not find the Ark nor has he left any description of what he thought the Ark may have looked like. What, then, does the Bible tell us about the most important relic of Yahwism?

The first 'clue' concerning the Ark might seem irrelevant. In effect, it is nothing more than the discrepancy between a single word in a parallel text found in the First Book of Kings and in the Second Book of Chronicles, concerning the use of a pair of long poles or staves. For their journey up the Mount the Levites used staves to facilitate the lifting and carriage of the Ark. The Bible, describing its construction in the desert some five hundred years earlier, confirms the original function of the staves: 'And two golden rings shalt thou make to it under the crown of it, by the two corners thereof, upon the two sides of it shalt thou make it; and they shall be for places for the staves to bear it withal.'[34] The staves can thus be assumed to have run through rings set into the sides of the Ark which, most probably for reasons of stability, were positioned along its length. The First Book of Kings then gives a description of the moment in which the Ark was lowered onto the floor of the Holy of Holies by the Levites: 'And they drew out the staves, that the ends of the staves were seen out in the holy place before the oracle, and they were not seen without: and there <u>they</u> are unto this day.'[35] (Author's underlining.) The Second Book of Chronicles, which post-dates Kings, contains one word which is crucially different:

'And they drew out the staves of the ark, that the ends of the staves were seen from the ark before the oracle, but they were not seen without. And there <u>it</u> is unto this day.'[36] (Author's underlining.)

It is widely accepted by biblical scholars that the two Books of Chronicles were compiled after the sacking of Solomon's Temple by the Babylonians in 586 BC.[37] It seems, therefore, that the verse in the First Book of Kings has been changed in the Second Book of Chronicles to record the fact that the Ark was still hidden inside the Temple Mount following the Babylonian destruction when it 'disappeared' from the Holy of Holies.[38] If the author of Chronicles was recording 'secret' information what were his sources? Was he in contact with the descendants of the Temple doorkeepers, the Levites, or was he himself a Levite who wished to pass on a message concerning the Ark for the benefit of posterity? When compared to the text of the earlier First Book of Kings, the Chronicler's text is distinctly pro-Levite.[39] Furthermore, his emphasis on the importance of one particular musical guild – the Levite guild of Asaph – indicates that he was indeed a member of the Levite community.[40] If this was the case his birthright would have allowed him access not only to the secret places on the Mount but also to the secret location of the Ark of the Covenant.[41]

When dealing with the evidence of the staves, we are relying on written testimony and, as in the case of the recorded legend of Abraham preserved in the Book of Exodus, we may never know the truth which lies behind such words. The problem of historical veracity is a subject which has been recently taken up by the historian Felipe Fernandez-Armesto who emphasizes the pitfall of the many 'historians' who claim to be 'priests of the cult of truth'.[42] The Chronicler *may* have been working from a historically faulty oral tradition; his sources *may* have been suspect; transcribers and translators *may* have altered the words and the meaning of his original text. But perhaps the Chronicler can be seen as a forerunner of a select group of people concerned with the 'true' preservation of Solomonic secrets, a preservation which was continued by the Knights Templar and European Freemasonry. A sense of mystery is also projected by Josephus. With the Ark laid to rest inside the Holy of Holies, he gives the following description of events as they unfolded within the Temple: 'Now, as soon as the priests had put all things in order about the Ark, and were gone out, there came down a thick cloud, and stood there...This cloud so darkened the place that one priest could not discern another; but it afforded to the minds of all a visible image and glorious appearance of God's having descended into this temple.'[43]

4

God's Covenant,
953–597 BC

Whether or not the 'thick cloud' signalled the presence of God or merely the quantity of incense, Solomon was quick to exploit the atmosphere. Having remained seated for the ceremony,[1] he rose up and, turning towards the Ark, addressed Yahweh as if he were present in the Temple.[2] Solomon's choice of words, as recorded by Josephus, formed the blueprint for prayer which was copied by future religious groups emanating from the Middle East and, in particular, from Jerusalem:

> I beseech thee, for the time to come, to afford us whatsoever thou, O God, hast power to bestow...that our kingdom shall continue...and successively receive it to ten thousand generations...I humbly beseech thee that thou wilt let some portion of thy Spirit to come down and inhabit this temple, that thou mayest appear to be with us on earth...But if this people be found to have sinned...have mercy upon them, and deliver them from their afflictions.[3]

According to the Second Book of Chronicles, Solomon's prayer, in which the structure of the Lord's Prayer can be detected, was accompanied by a rush of fire 'which came down from heaven, and consumed the burnt offering and the sacrifices', a fitting conclusion to the ceremony.

There is no report of this godly intervention in the parallel narrative in the Book of Kings which only mentions the cloud descending on the Ark of the Covenant once it was installed in the Holy of Holies. This could be because the Chronicler was a Levite who wished to perpetuate the mystical aura surrounding the Ark, and promote the role of his fellow Levites – involved in its preservation at the heart of Temple sacrifice – as essential.

THE 'HOLOCAUST'

Holocaust. Whole burnt-offering; wholesale sacrifice or
destruction.

[Greek *holos* whole, *kaio* burn] *The Oxford Dictionary*

Today, when standing on the eastern ridge opposite the eastern wall
of the Temple Mount, every detail of the illuminated walls of the
haram can be seen with perfect clarity. Three thousand years ago the
campfires of the tribes of Israel would have covered the Kidron
valley below, the path of the ancient watercourse which stood as a
natural north–south divide between the Mount of Olives and the
Temple Mount. The majesty of the view and the experience of
the installation of the Ark of the Covenant had a lasting impact on
the collective memory of the Israelite people. The Second Books of
Kings and Chronicles both describe the inaugural ceremony in
much the same vein, telling a story of an extensive and extremely
bloody sacrifice. Twenty-two thousand oxen and one hundred and
twenty thousand sheep were slaughtered in the Temple precincts as
an offering of peace to the God of Israel. This immense sacrificial
offering or holocaust overwhelmed the normal working capacity of
the Temple. The bronze altar proved inadequate so Solomon
demanded that the entire area of the Inner Court be used as a place
for the preparation of burnt sacrifice.[4]

The extent of the sacrifice is conveyed by Josephus who said that
'the temple did first of all taste of the victims'.[5] The holocaust of
animals lasted for several weeks, until, with the blessing of their
king, the tribespeople and their leaders, with the exception of those
resident in Jerusalem, left Mount Moriah and the new Temple. The
dispersal of Solomon's people back to the towns and villages of
Israel was the religious high-point of his reign. The instructions
given by his father David with regard to the Ark had been fulfilled
and his actions endorsed by the tribes of Israel. However, with this
success came a threat – the transgression of divine will. Israel was
about to enter a time of prophecy and dreams about the fate of the
future generations and the prospect for the cult of Yahweh, for the
kingdom of Israel and the Temple seemed to be fated.

KING SOLOMON'S DREAM

> Now mine eyes shall be open, and my ears attent unto the prayer that
> is made in this place.[6]

With the Ark of the Covenant installed, building work was resumed
on the Temple Mount in order to fulfil King David's wish to establish Mount Moriah as the centre of religious and political administration within his kingdom. However, the Bible records that prior
to this his son Solomon received a divine warning. Both the First
Book of Kings and the Second Book of Chronicles describe the
appearance of Yahweh to King Solomon in a dream. Yahweh
warned Solomon that unless the message in the dream was heeded
the nation of Israel would suffer dire consequences. Solomon was
ordered by Yahweh to walk before his God in the manner of his
father David, with 'integrity of heart and uprightness', whilst maintaining the statutes and judgements laid down in the law given to
Moses – in particular the commandment not to worship other
gods.[7] Adherence to this would be rewarded by a guarantee that the
kings of Israel would reign unhindered over their domain for ever.
If these commands were disobeyed not only would royal sovereignty come to an end but also the existence of the Temple as the
centre of the Yahwist cult, as the prophetic words of verse 8,
Chapter IX of the First Book of Kings implies: ' And at this house,
which is high, every one that passeth by it shall be astonished, and
shall hiss: and they shall say, Why has the Lord done thus unto this
land, and to this house?' Verses 3–9 of Chapter XI in the First Book
of Kings tell us that Solomon, after ruling for forty years, broke the
commandment of Yahweh not to worship foreign gods:

> And he [Solomon] had seven hundred wives, princesses, and three
> hundred concubines: and his wives turned away his heart.
>
> For it came to pass, when Solomon was old, that his wives turned
> away his heart after other gods: and his heart was not perfect with the
> Lord his God, as was the heart of David his father.
>
> For Solomon went after Ashtoreth the goddess of the Zidonians,
> and after Milcom the abomination of the Ammonites.
>
> And Solomon did evil in the sight of the Lord, and went not fully
> after the Lord, as did David his father.

Then did Solomon build an high place for Chemosh, the abomination of Moab, in the hill that is before Jerusalem; and for Molech, the abomination of the children of Ammon.

And likewise did he for all his strange wives, which burnt incense, and sacrificed unto their gods.

And the Lord was angry with Solomon, because his heart was turned from the Lord God of Israel, which had appeared unto him twice.

If we are ready to believe that such harsh accusations in the Bible of Solomon's later life are accurate, we must give equal credence to Solomon's initial dedication to Yahweh – reflected by the glory of the Temple, and, according to the First Book of Kings, he spent further energy and vast resources on the construction of additional buildings to complement the architectural achievement of the Temple on the Mount.

Once they had finished the main Temple, Solomon's masons began work on the surrounding precinct to provide living quarters and an efficient working environment for the priesthood, and accommodation for the King and his Egyptian wife. A series of buildings were erected to the south of the Temple precinct (x) which took thirteen years to complete. These comprised: the House of Pharoah's daughter, adjoining Solomon's palace – both enclosed within a walled precinct (y); a Throne Room adjoining the Hall of Columns; and the House of the Forest of Lebanon which was the last building to be constructed. Situated furthest from the Temple, it completed the plan envisaged by Solomon and his father David. A final outer precinct wall (z) was then built to surround the Temple, Royal Palace and both Inner and Outer Courtyards.

THE 'TRUE' LOCATION OF KING SOLOMON'S TEMPLE

The debate surrounding the exact location of Solomon's Temple remains intense, particularly in Jerusalem. As tensions rise in the Old City, positions and opinions are becoming more entrenched. Orthodox Jews believe unremittingly in the Old Testament account

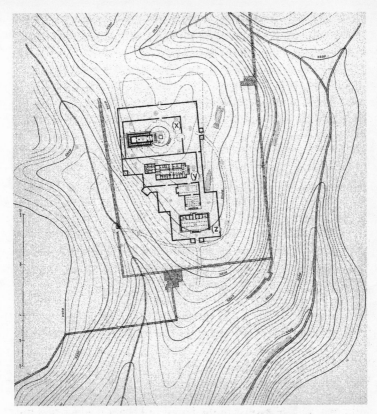

FIGURE 4.1 Plan of Jerusalem, circa 950 BC, showing details of Solomon's Temple, and the adjoining royal buildings, superimposed on the plan of the present-day *haram* precinct, after Stade.

of the Solomonic Temple Mount. Consequently, they now wish to reclaim it as their own on the basis that their ancestors were the first people to identify Mount Moriah as a holy place. Their beliefs are strongly supported by additional Jewish traditional literature, such as the *Mishnah*, a compilation of ancient Jewish texts first edited in the third century AD. Arab Palestinians, on the other hand, resident on the Mount since the seventh century AD, question the legitimacy of the Jewish Orthodox claim. As Moslems, they share in the reverence of Abraham as a great prophet and they perceive the *sakhra* as

an historically Islamic site. When pressed on the validity of the
Jewish heritage they raise the question: does any archaeological
evidence exist of the Solomonic Temple on the Mount?

Archaeologists and historians suspect that Herod the Great
rebuilt the Temple from the foundations upwards but left little or
nothing Solomonic in place. In so doing, Herod unwittingly created
an insoluble puzzle. Since the end of the last century, scholars,
historians, explorers, archaeologists and military engineers have
argued over the exact position of Solomon's Temple. If the position
of the Temple were determined, the last known resting place of the
Ark could be accurately assessed. Warren, ever meticulous, made a
list of the various opinions of his contemporaries concerning the
Temple's location. In 1871 no fewer than fifteen academics shared a
total of five different theories about the position of the Temple.[8] A
plan drawn up by a German professor, Bernhard Stade, in 1887,
firmly places the large bronze sacrificial altar which stood outside
the Temple entrance on the site of the *sakhra*, the holy rock of
Mount Moriah. This would have placed the location of the Ark
within the Holy of Holies at exactly thirty metres west of the
present-day western entrance to the Dome of the Rock. Warren, on
the other hand, on the conclusion of his survey and excavation in
1871, estimated the original location of the Ark at approximately
fifty metres south-west of the *sakhra*. Using as evidence the underground passages which may have serviced the Temple and his
knowledge of the bedrock of Mount Moriah gained from tunnelling around the present-day *haram*, Warren's method of practical investigation remains the only available scientific approach to
the biggest mystery facing all serious researchers of Temple Mount
history.[9]

The majority of modern scholarly opinion disagrees with both
Stade and Warren and identifies the *sakhra* as being not the site of
the altar but the actual *centre* of the Holy of Holies itself and, therefore, the exact resting place of the Ark. This assumption is based on
the logic that the Holy of Holies would have been constructed on
the highest geographical point on the Temple Mount. Claude
Reignier Conder, who as a fellow Royal Engineer officer and military surveyor followed in the footsteps of Wilson and Warren, was

an early advocate of this particular line of thinking. In 1909, after studying the architecture of the Temple Mount, he published his own findings. Conder had already contested Warren's identification of the painted 'Phoenician' characters found on the southeastern corner of the Mount. He identified them as 'Aramaean' and therefore 'definitely Herodian', failing to take into consideration the possibility that 'Aramaean' script might have been in use well before the time of Herod and possibly since the time of Solomon.[10] Conder, in his book *The City of Jerusalem*, justified his theory about the position of the Holy of Holies thus:

> The *Sakhra* itself is the controlling feature, because it rises at its crest 8 feet above the average level of the surrounding rock terrace. If the Holy House [Holy of Holies] was built over the *Sakhra*, then the levels of the descending courts naturally agree with those of the rock site. But if the Temple itself is placed to the south or to the west of the *Sakhra*, it is no longer on the top of the mountain; and any student who draws a section, in accordance with the ascertained levels of the rock, will find that he has, in these cases, to suppose foundations of at least 30 feet necessary to support the heavy walls of the building.

Conder cited Josephus as further justification of his theory since Josephus had claimed that the Temple was on 'the top of the mountain'. But to apply such a generalization and identify it with the *sakhra* was highly tenuous. Solomon's Temple had been constructed almost three thousand years before Conder first set foot in Jerusalem. Likewise, Josephus' account of the First Temple dated from the first century AD and was largely drawn from biblical sources. In the intervening period, it was not unlikely that the presence of man could have changed the overall topography of the Temple Mount. The Romans had carried out a massive levelling of the Mount following the destruction of the Second Herodian Temple in AD 70, and Warren would have been acutely aware of the effect human disturbance could have on remnants of its predecessor, the Temple of Solomon. One of Warren's primary objectives was to establish the bedrock levels supporting the complex jigsaw of Temple Mount archaeology, the result of which gave him the key to the historical evolution of Mount Moriah.

In December 1997 the Palestine Exploration Fund yielded the original hand sketch from Charles Warren's bedrock survey of Mount Moriah. Measuring 32 by 42 centimetres, this important document of stiff paper, outlined in pencil and finished in black ink, showed the position of the 'sacred rock', or *sakhra*, in relation to the surrounding bedrock topography of the Mount. Over lines of contour, built up on a pencilled grid, Warren outlined the present day *haram* area, marking 'The Temple' and 'Solomon's Palace'. Never published, despite being dotted with editorial corrections requesting a reduction by half to 1:5000, it demonstrates conclusively that Warren believed that the only reasonable position for the Temple and thereby the Holy of Holies was south of the *sakhra*, an opinion he later reiterated in his official report to the PEF and in his own book *Underground Jerusalem*.

According to Warren's meticulous survey there is no doubt that the highest natural point on the platform in the nineteenth century AD was the *sakhra*, situated under the protection of the Dome of the Rock. The traditional identification of the *sakhra* as the threshing floor purchased by King David tied in with this since threshing floors were traditionally placed as high as possible so that the wind could help sort the wheat from the chaff. Conder's assumption that this summit marked the site of Solomon's Temple still remains, however, wide open to criticism.

The Solomonic era was not handicapped by any lack of building method or imagination. At the time that Solomon succeeded to the throne of Israel, the Great Pyramid at Giza had been standing for over fifteen hundred years. It is therefore impossible to rule out the fact that human intervention might at some stage have given a new man-made summit to Mount Moriah. The thirty feet, or approximately ten metres, of foundation necessary to support Warren's hypothesis would have been well within the capabilities of Hiram Abiff and his fellow masons. Was Warren, not Conder, therefore correct? Could Solomon have constructed his Temple in a different place, to the south as Warren suggested? Solomon's Temple complex was built as a series of gradually descending courtyards, which would have required substantial raised foundations to produce a horizontal surface at each stage. Could Solomon's completion of the Temple with its foundation platform and Inner and Outer Courtyards have raised the 'top' of the Mount above the present day *sakhra*? Had Herod the Great rebuilt from the same level?

Warren, after spending three years above and below the surface of the Temple Mount, suspected that this was what Herod had done, and by 1871, having completed his tour of duty in Jerusalem, Warren felt he had the proof. By combining the results of his archaeological research with the bedrock levels of Mount Moriah he was able to explain the architectural evolution of the Temple Mount to the PEF. The hand sketch of the Mount discovered in the archives of the PEF threw up another controversial fact. Conder had exaggerated the difference in height between the *sakhra* and the area to the immediate south: Warren's sketch showed the true discrepancy to be twenty, not thirty, feet. The difference of opinion between Warren and Conder illustrates the continuing difficulties in the search for the truth behind the history and archaeology of Jerusalem. Conder, who published his work in 1909 – thirty-three years after Warren, had either not understood Warren's findings, or, worse still, had chosen to ignore them. Warren too, had had to face the dangers arising from political and religious fervour, in addition to which for over three years, from 1867 to 1870, he had been constantly exposed to the dangers of excavation. But his method of deep mining had given the 'Mole' of Jerusalem a major advantage over other investigators and his achievement has never been surpassed. Indeed, out of all researchers, past or present, Warren alone was in a position to discover the real truth behind the complex mysteries of the history and archaeology of the Temple Mount.

THE SOUTH-EAST ANGLE AND THE 'STRAIGHT JOINT'

From the moment of his arrival in Jerusalem Warren was convinced that the walls of the Temple Mount platform, and the subterranean passages and cisterns which once served the area, held the key to unlocking the whole mystery of the location of Solomon's Temple. He knew that if the extent of the Solomonic platform could be

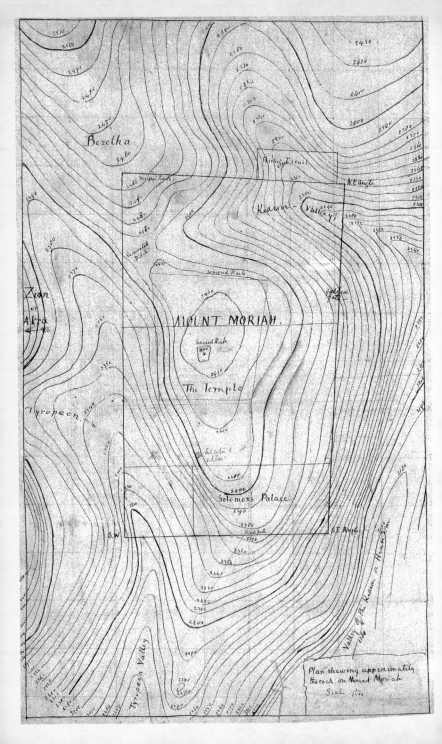

Plan shewing approximately
the rock on Mount Moriah
Scale

determined, the position of the Temple itself would fall into place. The philanthropic pretext assigned to Wilson's mission of survey in 1864–5 – to provide up-to-date intelligence for the War Office and information which would enable the water supply to the Old City to be improved – was completely overshadowed by the archaeological zeal of his successor. On Warren's final return to England in 1870, he admitted his sojourn in Jerusalem had been for the 'purpose of examining those walls'.[11] Through his intensive subterranean efforts, Warren reached the base of the existing walls, a feat unrivalled to this day. In 1871 the Dean of Westminster was invited by the committee of the Palestine Exploration Fund to write an introduction to *The Recovery of Jerusalem*, a narrative which contained an edited account by Warren of his three years spent in the Holy City. Warren was suitably modest about the dangers he and his men had had to face, but the words of the Dean give an intimate glimpse of what exactly these were:

> The whole series of their progress was a succession of 'lucky escapes'. Huge stones were day after day ready to fall, on their heads. One of the explorers was so severely injured that he could 'barely crawl out into the open air'. Another extricated himself with difficulty, torn and bleeding; while another was actually buried under the ruins. Sometimes they were almost suffocated by the stifling heat; at other times they were plunged for hours up to their necks in the freezing waters of some subterranean torrent; sometimes blocked up by a falling mass, without light or escape.[12]

Conder had never taken such personal risks to arrive at his conclusions although if he was wrong about the original position of Solomon's Temple he was almost certainly correct about the age of the base stones at the south-eastern angle of the present-day *haram* which are, in all probability, Herodian. But if this is the case, where had the Solomonic wall once stood? Perhaps it had never occupied the line of the present eastern wall of the *haram* but had run, either inside, or even outside, the present-day *haram* area. Warren,

FIGURE 4.2 Hand sketch of the topography of Mount Moriah, with the position of Solomon's Temple and palace superimposed on an outline of the present *haram* area, shown in reduced scale, from Warren's survey. (Courtesy of the PEF.)

however, did more than simply dig in one area of the south-east angle. He uncovered evidence linking it to the City of David, indicating a continuity of the north–south line of the eastern wall of the Temple platform since the time of King Solomon.

The ancient City of David which occupied the ridge to the immediate south of the *haram* would have been fortified. Warren reasoned therefore that the City of David must have been connected to the southern wall of the Solomonic Temple Mount platform by an extension of these fortified walls. In a letter to the Palestine Exploration Fund dated 2 October 1868 Warren described his attempt to locate the remnants of just such a Solomonic extension. His report, complete with a diagram, was characteristically conclusive. He announced the cutting of eight exploratory shafts which proved the existence of ancient towers linked by a wall joining the south-eastern corner of the present-day *haram* to the eastern side of the City of David.

Warren had in fact discovered the remains of a Byzantine wall of the Christian era with earlier, unidentified deposits beneath it, but he had neither the time nor the funds to explore further. It took the excavations of Kathleen Kenyon between 1961 and 1967 to confirm the importance of Warren's discovery. In 1974 Kenyon concluded:

> Any Solomonic extension [of the Davidic city wall] must have taken place only on the crest of the ridge....Interesting supporting evidence was derived from [a site] 105 metres south west of the present south eastern corner of the Temple platform. Here we located Warren's Byzantine wall, with spectacular evidence of his perilous trench beneath it by which he followed its line. Beneath...was a wall on bedrock...the date of these earliest walls...is, on the field estimate of the pottery eighth century BC or earlier...The combined evidence...therefore indicates that on the east side Solomon joined the town to which he succeeded to the platform of his new temple by a wall on the eastern crest of the eastern ridge.[13]

If Solomon had joined the City of David to the south-eastern corner of the Temple Mount, Warren could be forgiven for thinking that the painted letters he had found on the eastern wall of the *haram* were ancient enough to be Solomonic. But, as Kenyon indicated,

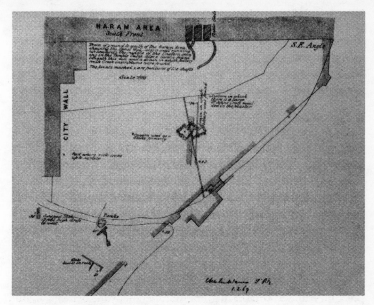

FIGURE 4.3 Warren's plan of the wall linking the south-eastern corner of the *haram* with the City of David. (Courtesy of the PEF.)

only the rescue and subsequent analysis of archaeological artefacts from underneath the base level of the south-eastern corner could provide any certainties about its date.

The problem of the eastern wall of the *haram* was not, however, just a question of the base course being Solomonic or Herodian. Approximately a dozen paces northwards from the south-eastern angle an abrupt change in style is visible in the exposed masonry. This and the fact that there appears to be no deliberate attempt to interlock the two styles has led archaeologists and historians to label this junction as the 'Straight Joint'. This is the only such point in the *haram* enclosure; nowhere else does a break appear.

In the spring of 1870, Warren resumed his work at the south-eastern corner of the *haram*. Using the same shaft from which he had uncovered the painted letters close to the south-eastern corner, he drove a gallery towards the platform wall which he struck at a point 9.75 metres north of the angle. The instability of the earth and the danger that it could cave in meant that he could only uncover a height of three courses of stone whilst he continued extending a horizontal gallery northwards. However, at 32.9 metres north of the south-eastern corner he observed a continuous horizontal break in the wall and a change of style in the masonry which seemed to match, at least on the surface, that of the visible 'Straight Joint'. From this Warren concluded that the Straight Joint was continuous from the exposed portion above ground to the foundation of the existing Temple Mount platform. A century later Kenyon concluded that this was definite evidence of the southern limit of the Solomonic platform. She argued that the stones to the north of the joint, which displayed the unfinished central panel, dated from the time of the restoration of the First Temple in the fifth century BC. Kenyon quoted evidence of similar, datable ancient structures across the Middle East at Eshmoun and Byblos[14] which belonged to the Persian period of between the sixth and early fourth centuries BC. However, in the eyes of many of her archaeological successors this supposition remains inconclusive.

On 11 December 1997 an archaeological symposium was held at the Bar Elan University in Jerusalem. Much of the day's discussion was taken up with the problems still surrounding the archaeology of the Temple Mount, not least the enigma of the Straight Joint in the eastern wall of the *haram* platform. The Bible describes how the Jews who returned from exile in Babylon in 538 BC had begun to repair the damage done to the Temple Mount by King Nebuchadnezzar's army forty-eight years earlier. The attempt was so moderate that those who remembered the glory of Solomon's original Temple apparently wept at the sight of the restoration.[15] Kenyon presumed that the Straight Joint showed the delimitation of the southern limit of the Solomonic platform rebuilt by the exiles but she had no solid archaeological evidence from the base of the wall to support her theory. By the 1990s some commentators on the Straight Joint departed even further from a possible post-exilic alteration,[16] suggesting that the embossed masonry to the north of the joint was of a much later Greek style. This would place it firmly in the second century BC, adding greater confusion to an already complex problem. There was thus no concrete evidence to add to the Solomonic debate. Without permission to excavate inside the *haram* area, or even to explore the external base courses briefly uncovered by Warren in the nineteenth century, nothing extra could be added. However, new evidence concerning the method of wall construction employed by the stone-masons of the Second Herodian Temple came to light in the mid-1990s which would help clarify at least part of the archaeological and historical enigma of the walls of the Temple Mount.

In the spring of 1997 the Israelis reopened one section of an ancient tunnel which ran alongside the present *haram* platform in the vicinity of the Western Wall, roughly opposite the eastern wall Straight Joint. Control of the tunnel was in the hands of the Jewish Ministry of Religious Affairs and the opening was seen by Moslems as a violation of the sacred status of the *haram* area. Rioting followed and many people were killed. One positive factor emerged from the situation. In what is perhaps the single instance where the politics of religion have assisted, albeit indirectly, in the archaeological investigation of the Mount – and in particular of the masonic precision of the stonework forming the base layers of the *haram* platform – archaeologists were able to investigate the platform interior. They found that an incredible degree of accuracy was achieved on the external face of the masonry so that it is difficult to insert the blade of a pocket knife between the joints. This is even more remarkable given that the blocks of stone used weighed tens if not hundreds of tons. So how did the masons manage to finish the wall in this fashion?

The blocks of stone which made up the wall of the platform were not square, but trapezoidal.[17] Their sides were adjoined to each other at an angle either greater or lesser than ninety degrees in relation to their external face. The reason for this becomes clear when considering the immense weight of the blocks. By positioning the longest and heaviest blocks and leaving lesser gaps in between, a smaller and more manoeuvrable block could have been introduced into the gap and then coaxed forward.

This meant that the heaviest of the stone blocks need only be placed and not fitted. The smaller and lighter blocks could be introduced into gaps between them from the inside of the wall, achieving the narrowest of joints. Once in place, the protruding face of the smaller stone block could be chiselled back to match the completed faces of its flanking partners to finish the course. In his letter to the PEF dated 22 January 1869 Warren described the painted and carved 'Phoenician' or 'Aramaean' letters on the base courses close to the south-eastern angle of the *haram*. He also made some revealing comments on methods of stone jointing:

> On the sixth course there are red paint-marks on nearly every stone; on the first none, on the second the O Y Q, which is supposed to be some numeral; on three to nine are single paint characters at the left-hand top corner; on the tenth there are a great number of flourishes in red paint, and on the eleventh occurs something curious: the face projects about ⅛th of an inch too much, and has been worked down over about half its surface, on the *raised part* is a + cut in the stone, two straight lines perpendicular to each other; on the *worked face* [author's italics] is a painted + much larger, and with a bend down at the right end of the horizontal stroke. Many of the other stones in this course have characters on them.

Warren does not draw any particular conclusions from this but in the light of the new observations of jointing made by archaeologists from within the Hasmonaean tunnel in 1997, his description has fresh relevance. The existence of an 'unfinished' stone at the south-eastern angle indicates that an attempt had probably been made to finish it *in situ*, projecting from the face of the wall. Had the same trapezoidal method of construction found at the western wall therefore been employed at the south-eastern section? The evidence of the single unfinished block on the eastern wall suggests strongly that this might well be the case. As the western wall blocks are known to be Herodian, this is evidence that the construction of the base of the south-eastern angle dates not to King Solomon but to the Herodian Second Temple as Conder had stated in 1909. Furthermore, a Herodian block excavated in 1997 below the western wall has two crosses – identical to the one found by Warren on the block at the south-eastern angle – cut into its unfinished surface.[18] Without reopening Warren's shafts and galleries, a solution to the extent of the Solomonic platform and the true age of the south-eastern angle may never be found. However, further study of the carved and painted letters uncovered by Warren may still cast some light on this ancient mystery. The incised marks on the raised unfinished part of the eleventh stone, in the form of '+' and two straight perpendicular lines, were probably the personal marks of the stonemason charged with the task of finishing the front of the block. In the platform wall itself the one 'unfinished' block Warren had uncovered had its finished section similarly marked with a painted letter, as had so many other completed blocks already within the course. A possible process emerges of inspectors paint-marking any pre-finished stone in the quarry and then marking the remainder as they were finished *in situ* – on the wall itself. But do these inspection marks tell us anything further?

Freemasonic tradition indicates the use of 'passwords and signs' employed by the masons involved in the building of the Solomonic Temple. Whereas passwords were essential to confirm the masonic degree of each craftsman and thus his eligibility for payment, the password on its own would not give any indication of the amount of work finished by each mason at the end of every day. Given the size of the workforce engaged on the Mount, a register of progress claimed daily by the workers employed on site would have been kept. Each block completed on the Temple Mount, satisfactorily or otherwise, was inspected, marked accordingly and a record kept of its position. The painted letters uncovered by Warren are the only existing archaeological proof of the control exercised by either a masonic foreman or a member of the royal treasury – or possibly both – over the progress and cost of work on the Temple Mount.

If the marks on stone were connected to masonic payment, they might have been part of a secret language, a Masonic script, dating back to the time of Hiram Abiff. 'Aramaean', like Hebrew, had distinct roots within ancient Phoenician[19] – the language spoken by Hiram Abiff – which had formed the backbone of many offshoots within the Middle East from the eleventh century BC onwards. It is possible that the carved marks and painted letters found by Warren, although Herodian, would have been the same as those used by Solomon's inspectors and perhaps even by Hiram himself. The daily wage of the Solomonic workforce, like that employed by Herod, was considerable, and the overall expenditure daunting to the ruler of a country such as Israel whose natural resources were limited.

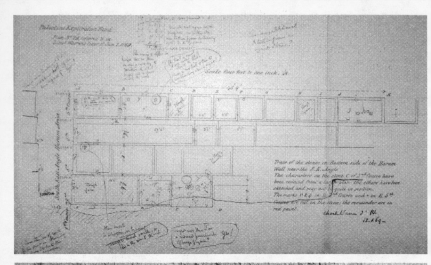

FIGURE 4.4 (a) Copy of the original drawing by Warren of the base courses of the eastern wall forming the south-eastern corner of the *haram*, complete with his editorial comments. The 'unfinished' stone lies furthest to the right in the top course shown.

(b) Detail of 'crosses' on the unfinished Herodian stone from the western wall.

According to the Bible, the fame of Solomon's achievement soon spread throughout the Near East, bringing wealth into the kingdom by way of tribute which alleviated any financial problems incurred during the architectural development on the Mount. But construction of a fixed abode for the Ark created new challenges for the people of Israel.

THE MOUNTAIN OF THE LORD

Great is the Lord, and greatly to be praised in the city of our God, in the mountain of his holiness.[20]

The Solomonic precinct wall surrounding the Temple complex and the platform on which it stood separated the religious administration from the rest of Jerusalem. Today it is impossible to deduce from the evidence we have inherited whether David or Solomon realized the inherent dangers which lay within the vision of a safe haven for the Ark of the Covenant. However, if Solomon's dream had indeed been a reality, and not a later biblical invention, the experience would at the very least have given the King an indication of the possible trouble which lay ahead. In 942 BC Solomon handed over control of Isreal's monotheistic ceremonial religion – the true source of power within the nation – to the priests and Levites. By doing so Solomon believed he was providing a centre of faith supported by an exact ritual around which the Jews of his kingdom could build an enduring religious structure. To a certain degree he was right: stability for the cult was a prerequisite to good kingly management. But, perhaps unknowingly, he had sown the seeds of destruction. Solomon had installed a religious class system over a people nomadic by nature, tribal and fiercely independent. Concentrating the cult of Yahweh at the Temple Mount centralized national power and wealth in Jerusalem which was seen as the only place within the nation where legitimate sacrifice could be offered up to Yahweh. Envy and resentment caused inevitable internal division. Solomon was destined to fulfil the omen within his own dream by failing to stay faithful in his sole worship of Yahweh. His worship of 'foreign gods', common to the region of Israel since before the time of David, questioned his interpretation of Mosaic Law and fuelled the arguments of those who opposed his rule. This opposition grew in strength as Solomon's reign progressed, seriously weakening the defences of the state. Jerusalem and its treasure became under threat from the enemies of Israel, as Solomon's dream readily forewarned.

The Old Testament Books of Kings and Chronicles are our only major source of information concerning the remainder of Solomon's reign. Completion of the royal, religious and administrative buildings situated to the south of the Temple drew heavily on his finances. A great quantity of precious material was required by his craftsmen if the standard achieved in the Temple was to be upheld throughout the Temple Mount complex. The military successes of David had guaranteed Solomon both a national source of wealth from the new Kingdom of Israel and payment in tribute from neighbours, which enabled him to finance construction of the Mount Moriah platform and the building of the Temple. Solomon's links with Egypt were an important component of this national wealth and security. Good relations with the ruling Pharoah secured his southern borders and allowed commerce to proliferate. To this end Solomon built a fleet of ships on the shores of the Red Sea at a location close to modern-day Eilat, receiving, so the Bible tells us, further assistance from his oldest ally: 'And Hiram [King of Tyre] sent in the navy his servants, shipmen that had the knowledge of the sea, with the servants of Solomon. And they came to Ophir, and fetched from thence gold, four hundred and twenty talents, and brought it to King Solomon.'[21] Gold, ivory and other precious materials which could not be found within Israel's borders were brought to Israel and were used to embellish the royal complex, details of which were spreading throughout the Levant. And with fame came a visit from the Queen of Sheba.

Sheba, who hailed reputedly from southern Arabia,[22] arrived in Jerusalem in order to experience for herself the Solomonic Temple Mount and to question in person the king who was so associated with 'the name of the Lord [Yahweh]' and so 'prove him with hard questions'.[23] Sheba's hard questioning, however, was sweetened by the richest of gifts: 'She came to Jerusalem with a very great train, with camels that bare spices, and very much gold, and precious stones.'[24] The First Book of Kings also tells us that the gift of gold amounted to one hundred and twenty talents, approximately six kilograms.[25] Sheba's monetary contribution to King Solomon's treasury was thus not insignificant, although the Bible hints of a possible secondary motive behind her visit to Jerusalem: 'and when she came to Solomon, she communed with him of all that was in her heart'.[26] The romantic encounter between Solomon and Sheba entered into the folklore of Jerusalem. It is impossible to deduce exactly how many days, weeks or even months Sheba remained as his guest, but it was sufficiently long for Solomon to give 'unto the queen of Sheba all her desire, whatsoever she asked, beside that which Solomon gave her of his royal bounty'.[27]

Once the Temple Mount complex was finished Solomon moved the living quarters of his Egyptian wife from the lower City of David to his royal precinct which, as Warren suggested, probably stood on the platform somewhere to the south-east of the Temple. Exactly what effect the visit of Sheba had on the royal marriage will for ever remain a mystery, but their legendary meeting had a magical effect on Solomon's standard of wealth. According to the First Book of Kings, as soon as Sheba returned to her native land Solomon began to receive a fabulous influx of precious commodities from the Arabian peninsular, presumably from the trading route of the Red Sea via the Gulf of Eilat, which was controlled by his navy and manned by the expert seamen from Hiram's Kingdom of Tyre: 'Now the weight of gold that came to Solomon in one year was six hundred threescore, and six talents of gold, beside that he had of the merchant-men, and of the traffic of the spice-merchants, and of all the kings of Arabia, and of the governors of the country.'[28] The Royal Palace on the Temple Mount became a showcase for Solomon's wealth. The First Book of Kings continues, describing the objects of treasure composed by the craftsmen of Jerusalem:

> And king Solomon made two hundred targets of beaten gold: six hundred shekels [approximately ten kilograms] of gold went to one target.
>
> And he made three hundred shields of beaten gold; three pound of

gold went to one shield: and the king put them in the house of the forest of Lebanon.

Moreover the king made a great throne of ivory, and overlaid it with the best gold.[29]

In 1996 fragments of carved ivory were found at the south-western angle of the *haram* by archaeologists of the Israel Antiquities Authority. Believed to be fragments from the furniture of the Second, Herodian Temple, and thus not Solomonic, they were, however, an important find which demonstrated the probable validity of this particular verse from Kings. If Solomon's ivory and gold throne was a reality and not a biblical exaggeration, perhaps the rest of the golden treasure as described in the First Book of Kings had also actually existed. Verse 23 of Chapter X claims that Solomon 'exceeded all the kings of the earth for riches and for wisdom'. His drinking vessels, and all the vessels within the House of the Forest of Lebanon, so the Book tells us, were made of solid gold.[30] However, this treasure could not have been assembled under the guidance of the man most credited with the actual Temple and its furniture of bronze masterpieces. According to Freemasonic tradition, Hiram Abiff, the Tyrian Master Mason, had already died of unnatural causes, and King Solomon was under suspicion.

THE DEATH OF HIRAM ABIFF

To this day the death of Hiram Abiff, Master Mason of the Temple, remains mysterious. The western, or European, Freemasonic theory about Hiram can be traced back to the early fifteenth century AD.[31] The 'passwords' and 'signs' which still differentiate the varying 'degrees' of Freemasonic rank lay at the heart of Hiram's reported demise. Hiram, having worked with such diligence, applying all his skills to the Temple and its bronze furnishings, was not only intimately familiar with the Temple but was probably permitted unlimited access to the interior. According to Freemasonic legend, not long after the building had been completed Hiram was approached by three masonic apprentices inside the Temple. They had chosen their moment well as the Temple was deserted except for Hiram. The apprentices demanded that he tell them the secret passwords and signs so that they could claim payment greater than their expertise warranted. Hiram refused to divulge these secrets and was dealt a blow to the head. Attempting to escape, he was caught and killed at the eastern entrance to the Temple, the doorway flanked by Jachin and Boaz. Hiram's body was then taken out of the Temple through the precincts and buried on a surrounding hillside.

Although legendary, this tale possesses a great deal of self-supporting logic. The apprentices were obviously anticipating a further period of sustained work, during which they intended to make more money than was their due. The killing must therefore have taken place before completion of the second phase of building work on the Mount – that of the construction and furnishing of the royal complex – as the legend recounted. For Hiram to have been pursued and successfully brought down within the Temple indicates that the doors to the exterior may well have been closed or even locked which suggests the incident took place at a time when it was unfrequented by the priests and Levites – during the small hours of the night when sacrifice was not being offered. But even if this was the case the Levites were supposed to guard the Temple day and night. Had the apprentices therefore obtained the co-operation of the Levites and, with their detailed knowledge of the Temple, used a secret passage to remove Hiram's body? It is highly unlikely that three men carrying a corpse, even in the dead of night, could have gone unnoticed. Hiram, as Master Mason of the Temple, would, like the Levites, have known of the existence of any secret routes in and out of the Temple and surrounding area. With the knowledge that hidden passages still exist inside the Temple Mount, the scenario supporting the legend is certainly feasible, but is there any historical basis for such a story? The Bible is unspecific about Hiram's death[32] but the Freemasonic story claims that Hiram was killed as a result of a failed attempt at extortion. Could this explanation mask a more sinister plot?

In 1922 Sir James Frazer, a Fellow of Trinity College, Cambridge, published a work which has become a landmark study of ancient ritual practices. *The Golden Bough* contains a section on building rituals still in use up to the early twentieth century:

> In modern Greece, when the foundation of a new building is being laid it is the custom to kill a cock, a ram, or a lamb, and to let its blood flow on the foundation stone, under which the animal is afterwards buried. The object of the sacrifice is to give strength and stability to the building. But sometimes, instead of killing an animal, the builder entices a man to the foundation stone, secretly measures his body, or a part of it, or his shadow, and buries the measure under the foundation stone; or he lays the foundation stone upon the man's shadow. It is believed the man will die within the year... Not long ago there were still shadow-traders whose business it was to provide architects with the shadows necessary for securing their walls... Thus the custom is a substitute for the old practice of immuring a living person within the walls, or crushing him under the foundations of a new building, in order to give strength and durability to the structure, or more definitely in order that the angry ghost may haunt the place and guard it against the intrusion of enemies.[33]

Frazer's description demonstrates the survival of an ancient practice well known within the Mediterranean sphere – the use of human sacrifice to dedicate the foundation or completion of buildings, in particular those with a religious purpose. If the Freemasonic tradition concerning the Temple involved the unnatural death of its architect could King Solomon be implicated? The Bible describes how Solomon had late in life 'built an high place' in 'the hill that is before Jerusalem' for the worship of 'Chemosh' and of 'Molech'. Worship of Molech was commonly known to have involved human sacrifice. Was the description of the 'high place' on the 'hill before Jerusalem', like the Freemasonic story, a smokescreen, a substitute description for the Temple Mount composed to preserve the monotheistic reputation of the cult of Yahweh on the Temple location?

To extract the central 'truth' from the surrounding web of Freemasonic legend and recorded biblical history would be an impossible task. However, there are certain parallels which are too striking to be ignored. The Bible blames women for leading Solomon's heart astray from Yahweh in the latter part of his life. But it is not unrealistic to assume that King Solomon was engaged in the worship of foreign gods on the Temple Mount earlier than the Bible admits. According to Freemasonic legend,[34] the body of Hiram Abiff was found by fellow masons in a place identical to the biblical description of Solomon's 'high place' of human sacrifice on a hillside before Jerusalem. On retrieval, Hiram's fellow Master Masons are said to have 'reburied' the body somewhere on the Temple Mount. Allowing for the fact that the ritual sacrifice described by Sir James Frazer has a provenance dating to the time of Solomon, it is possible that Hiram was sacrificed and 'immured in a wall' of the Mount, so that his ghost might protect the Ark of the Covenant from future predation by the enemies of Israel.

THE TEMPLE INHERITANCE

The story of Hiram Abiff has joined the legend of Abraham and Isaac, tainting the location of the Temple with suspicions of human sacrifice. But the Temple was built for the purpose of sacrificing animals in the name of Yahweh and with inauguration complete, this process became the focal point of daily ritual. Strict observance of the laws of Yahweh did not result in sustained national harmony. The unity of Israel came under increasing pressure as Solomon's reign went on. The Kingdom of Israel which lay to the north of Jerusalem was unfairly taxed by Solomon. Many of his subjects felt Solomon had exploited the manpower and resources of the northern Kingdom of Israel to build the Temple Mount complex, which created jealousies within the Hebrew nation and threatened internal dissension. In the final years of his life Solomon put Jeroboam, the son of his servant Nebat, in charge of the northern Kingdom of Israel. Solomon had been initially impressed by the 'industry' of Jeroboam, 'a mighty man of valour',[35] but Jeroboam was to turn on his former master. Solomon's dream of Yahweh's punishment, should he transgress the commandment not to worship foreign gods, would soon become reality.

The Bible tells us that one day Jeroboam met Ahijah, a Hebrew prophet from Shiloh, the town where the Ark had once lain. Ahijah foretold the division of the united Kingdom of Israel and how he, Jeroboam, would be responsible for the upkeep of Yahweh's commandments. Solomon would be deprived of all royal control, except over the city of Jerusalem and the tribe of his father David, because Solomon and his wives had 'worshipped Ashtoreth the goddess of the Zidonians, Chemosh the god of the Moabites, and Milcom the god of the children of Ammon'. This prophetic explanation in the Bible supports the fact that the true cause of rebellion was a power-struggle between Jeroboam and King Solomon fuelled by an old grievance: Solomon's exploitation of northern resources for the building of the Temple. The Bible continues: 'Solomon sought therefore to kill Jeroboam and Jeroboam arose, and fled into Egypt, unto Shishak, king of Egypt, and was in Egypt until the death of Solomon'.[36]

After the death of King Solomon in 926 BC the fortunes of his people went into decline. Despite Solomon's achievement of securing political and economic stability for Israel, for Israel's neighbours the riches of the Temple represented potential revenue, in the form of plunder. Within a century the Egyptian descendants of Solomon's wife invaded and demanded tribute from the king in Jerusalem, which included a portion of the wealth of the Temple.

ISRAEL AND JUDAH

On the death of King Solomon his son Rehoboam succeeded to the throne and became king of both Israel and Judah. Judah's heavy demands on Israel in terms of manpower and money increased even further under Rehoboam. He had little respect for the councils of his elders and steadfastly refused to accommodate the wish of his fellow Hebrews to establish a fairer and more equal system of labour and taxation. So Jeroboam, who escaped the wrath of Solomon by fleeing from Judah to Egypt, returned to Israel and was made king, which separated Israel from Judah and Jerusalem. Rehoboam's Kingdom of Judah was now effectively surrounded by potentially hostile neighbours and it was not long before the first attack on Jerusalem and the Temple Mount was planned.

In the second year of Rehoboam's reign, 925 BC, Judah was invaded by Shishak, Pharoah of Egypt.[37] Shishak crossed into Rehoboam's territory approximately thirty kilometres to the north-west of Jerusalem, leading a massive army of foot soldiers, twelve hundred chariots and sixty thousand horsemen.[38] It has been argued by many biblical scholars that Shishak's primary aim was the subjugation of Israel and that Judah and Jerusalem were not on his itinerary. But his military juggernaut proceeded relentlessly south and east, laying waste the Judaean cities of Aijalon, Gibeon and Kiriath Jearim which stood at the entrance to the foothills of Jerusalem. According to the Bible, the invasion by Shishak was the direct result of Israelite infidelity to Yahweh. Both Israel and Judah stood accused.

> And Judah did evil in the sight of the Lord, and they provoked him to jealousy with the sins which they had committed, above all that their forefathers had done:
>
> For they built them high places, and images and groves, on every high hill and under every green tree.
>
> And there were also sodomites in the land; and they did according to all the abominations of the nations which the Lord cast out before the children of Israel.[39]

In order to prevent the desecration of the Temple and the plundering of the city, Rehoboam gave Shishak 'the treasures of the house of the Lord', the 'treasures of the King's House' and the 'shields of gold which Solomon had made'.[40] As a result, the Temple survived and Rehoboam's humility in front of his God was rewarded: 'They have humbled themselves, therefore I will not destroy them, but I will grant them some deliverance; and my wrath shall not be poured out upon Jerusalem by the hand of Shishak'.[41] The critical point is how much of the Solomonic treasure was handed over to the Egyptian Pharoah and whether this included the greatest prize of all, the Ark of the Covenant. The Bible does not mention the Ark as being part of the tribute paid to Shishak. Other biblical references refer to the presence of the Ark on the Temple Mount in the seventh and sixth centuries BC which suggests the Ark was not included within this payment.

After Solomon's death the Temple continued to serve as the main repository for tribute and taxes. Since the time of the Exodus under Moses every Jew was obliged to make an annual contribution to the cult of the nation which meant the finances of the Mount were continually replenished. However, the Bible tells us that Rehoboam replaced with bronze the golden Solomonic shields from the King's House, an indication that the cost of keeping at bay the army of Shishak had temporarily drained the coffers of the Temple. The accumulation of golden objects in the Temple served a twofold purpose – firstly as a rudimentary banking system and secondly to supply an immediate and acceptable international currency should the payment of tribute or ransom be demanded, thus affording a degree of protection to the Ark of the Covenant.

The Temple treasure was repeatedly plundered over the course of the next four centuries. The period which preceded the arrival of Nebuchadnezzar, King of the Babylonians, in 596 BC would see a gradual decline in the cohesion of the Hebrew nation. The conflict begun by Rehoboam and Jeroboam between the Kingdoms of Judah and Israel continued, interrupted only by the graver threat to both kingdoms posed by foreign invaders. The Temple Mount and its treasure remained permanently at the centre of local and foreign policy. Rehoboam's grandson Asa who reigned between 913 and 873 BC stripped the Temple complex of gold and silver in order to bribe the Syrians of Damascus away from their allegiance to Israel. One major attempt at reconciliation, however, was made. During the reign of Asa's successor, Jehosophat, the Kingdoms of Israel and Judah were linked by marriage when Jehosophat's son Jehoram married Princess 'Athaliah of Israel. The resulting brief lull in internecine strife allowed these two kingdoms to pursue a united struggle against Syria, whose armies presented a continuous threat to both Israel and Judah.

The domestic scene on the Temple Mount, however, remained unstable. Her husband Jehoram succeeded his father to the throne but in 842 BC after only eight years of rule Jehoram died of an incurable disease. His son Ahaziah took the throne but within a year, he died on the field of battle. His mother 'Athaliah became the first woman to rule over Judah, Jerusalem and the Temple Mount.

Although a princess of Israel, 'Athaliah's ancestors were Phoenician and did not practice monotheism. From the beginning of her marriage to Jehoram she reintroduced the worship of 'strange' gods, the major threat to the cult of Yahweh.

'STRANGE GODS' AND YAHWEH

The Bible tells us that since the death of Solomon the successive Kings of Judah oscillated by varying degree between faithful observance of Yahweh and sacrifice to 'strange' or 'foreign' deities. However, the language of the Bible masks the true severity of the struggle which was taking place within Hebrew society. Amongst the united tribes of the Hebrew nation there existed a trend towards non-monotheistic worship which, despite the constant efforts of the supporters of the Yahwistic cult, was deeply rooted within the national culture. The Bible portrays this situation by describing a people faithful to Yahweh repeatedly beset by religious crisis. It tells us that this problem always surfaced when the leader of the nation had strayed away from the strict laws of observance derived from the Covenant or Ten Commandments, enshrined on stone within the Ark of the Covenant. The historical reality, however, is somewhat different. There was certainly nothing 'strange' and very little that could be classed as truly 'foreign' about the deities such as Ashtoreth and Molech who so tempted Solomon and successive kings and queens of Israel and Judah.

One other form of worship was endemic within Israel. Since the time of the Exodus and the wanderings of the Hebrew tribes in the desert, the worship of a god in a graven image in the form of a calf or bull was at the centre of the 'problem'. This adherence to the bull cult has received extensive scholarly recognition in the twentieth century and has been amply backed up by archaeological excavation. Research has focused on events which occurred during the Exodus immediately prior to the construction of the Ark of the Covenant under the supervision of Moses. Historians have proposed that Aaron, Moses' brother, was the progenitor and first 'priest' of the bull or Ba'alist cult.[42] The bull cult intermingled with the fertility god of Adad and Ba'alism became a generic term for fertility cult worship.[43] With this in mind the scene in the Book of Exodus which describes the reaction of Moses on coming down from Mount Sinai with the words of Yahweh carved in stone has great significance for the history of the Temple Mount during the three centuries following the completion of Solomon's Temple. Moses' anger at the transgression of his fellow tribespeople signalled the beginning of a long conflict between the Aaronite priesthood of Ba'al and the tribe of Levi, the backbone of the cult of Yahweh, servants to its priesthood, and protectors of the Ark of the Covenant.

While Moses was on Mount Sinai, Aaron had supervised the restless Hebrew tribes in the construction of a golden calf. Moses, when he arrived back at the Hebrew camp with the words of Yahweh carved in stone, set about the destruction of this golden idol. The events which followed show how seriously the threat of Aaronite Ba'alism was taken by the adherents of monotheism:

> Then Moses stood in the gate of the camp, and said, Who is on the Lord's side; let him come unto me. And all the sons of Levi gathered themselves together unto him.
>
> And he said unto them, Thus saith the Lord God of Israel, put every man his sword by his side, and go in and out from gate to gate throughout the camp, and slay every man his brother, and every man his companion, and every man his neighbour.
>
> And the children of Levi did according to the word of Moses: and there fell of the people that day about three thousand men.[44]

During this period of the Exodus the golden calf was destroyed and the Aaronites massacred by the Levites, leaving the Yahwists in a position of temporary supremacy. In the years that saw the settlement of Palestine, the establishment of Jerusalem as the capital city of the United Israel and the building of the Temple under King Solomon, Hebrew worshippers of Ba'al remained faithful to the image of their bull god conceived in the deserts of the Sinai. The conflicting religious interests of the Aaronites and Levites became deeply entrenched within the national psyche casting a pattern of crisis within the Hebrew nation. The unification of the Hebrew tribes under King David only highlighted the difference between the religious factions. A religious division had been drawn between Jerusalem and the rest of the country.

The Aaronites have been historically associated and archaeologically identified as predominant within the northern Kingdom of Israel, and despite fulfilling his father's wish to create a sanctuary to Yahweh, we are told in the Bible that Solomon succumbed to the temptation of other gods by building 'altars in high places' to 'strange' gods.[45] However, evidence of a more solid kind once existed on the Temple Mount itself in the form of the bronzes cast under the direction of Hiram Abiff. As we have seen, the Great Sea comprised no fewer than twelve oxen supporting the basin which more orthodox Yahwists felt contravened God's commandments against the creation of graven images. The use of this particular animal for such an important piece of Temple furniture cannot have been arbitrary. In the second millennium BC the ox shared the identical form of lettering, in this case the cuneiform *remu*, with the word for a bull.[46] Thus the twelve oxen could be correctly described as twelve bulls – symbols of the Ba'alist cult. As if this were not enough, in more than one instance the Bible uses the word Ba'al to describe more than the one specific cult. This generalization for the naming of foreign deities was the result of the influences of trade and of migration which caused the central tenets of the bull-cult to spread into the region of Judah and Israel and to take on different guises depending on the cultic influences already established in the region. Thus, from the root of the 'Ba'alist' or fertility cult, stemmed many different branches, all of which posed a threat to monotheism.

Fertility lay at the centre of this polytheism. The Phoenician goddess of Ashtoreth, in whose name Solomon had set up an altar 'on high' on the hills of Jerusalem, was one example of a Ba'alistic form of fertility-rite worship practised under another named deity. It is likely that the religious influence of Solomon's many wives was fertility-based and was similar to the native Phoenician religion of Hiram Abiff.

But what alternative evidence can be found to support the contention of the Yahwist Levites that the fertility cult of Ba'al was a direct threat to the principles laid down under Mosaic Law? The cult of Yahweh, with its Ark of the Covenant safely installed on the

Temple Mount of Jerusalem as its epicentre, represented an alto-
gether different religious concept to that of the cult of Ba'al and its
many variations. The followers of Yahweh were worshippers of an
abstract ideal: the word of God was the law of their society. The cult
of fertility represented by Ba'alism was by comparison liberal and it
was this liberalism that posed the greatest threat to the cult of
Yahweh. One of the main aims of any fertility cult was to ask the
gods to bless the agricultural endeavours of the community, but
there is also abundant historical evidence that the use of the human
body in the form of prostitution was central to its beliefs. The
Yahwist religion was the forerunner of the strict moral code of marriage and sexual behaviour which was later adopted by Christianity
and Islam. The control of women, who within the Ba'alist cults held
centre stage, was an obvious necessity to the exclusively male priesthood of the Yahwist tendency. Thus the accession of 'Athaliah, a
princess of Phoenician descent and worshipper of Ba'al, to the
throne of Judah in 841 BC was alarming in the extreme to the priests
and Levites on the Temple Mount.

The consequences of 'Athaliah's actions following the death of
her husband and her son were far-reaching. Whether overcome by
grief compounded by the isolated position in which she now found
herself or motivated by political ambition, 'Athaliah embarked on a
killing spree aimed at eliminating the hereditary Davidic line of
Judah. Her plan of murder was successful in all but one case. A
grandson, Joash, was 'stolen from among the king's sons that were
slain'[47] and rescued alive. The six-year-old Joash only survived the
murderous attentions of his grandmother thanks to the intervention of Jehoiada', a Temple priest, who hid him within the holy
complex. Joash became the nucleus of revolt and the Temple
Mount became, not for the last time, a site of human bloodshed.
According to the Bible it took five years before the priest Jehoiada',
who was organizing the insurrection, was ready to confront
'Athaliah. During this time he gathered the support of the tribal
elders around Jerusalem – a show of strength on the Temple Mount
would be necessary if the revolt was to be successful. Joash was
hidden for seven years and although this was an extremely long time
there may have been a simple explanation for the leaders of the

uprising not acting sooner. Joash would, by then, have passed through the perilous stages of infancy and early childhood and the existence of an heir who was approaching manhood would have given heart to those who were secretly plotting 'Athaliah's overthrow. Joash's more mature age would also help attract the support of the non-committed; after all, the price of failure to the followers of Yahweh was great and they knew that the re-establishment of the Davidic bloodline rested entirely on the survival and accession of Joash to the throne of Judah, once he had reached maturity.

With our knowledge of the Solomonic Temple Mount the scene of 'Athaliah's demise given in the Bible can be well visualized. Chronicles informs us that the Levites played an instrumental role in the revolt which took place on the sabbath, a day of increased activity on the Mount. The Levites, the doorkeepers to the Temple complex, were reinforced by brethren from outside Jerusalem.[48] A further group of Levites was moved into the Temple to form a bodyguard to the young Joash: 'And the Levites shall compass the king round about, every man with his weapons in hand; and whosoever else cometh into the house, he shall be put to death; but be ye with the king when he cometh in and when he goeth out.'[49] It would have been an open declaration of rebellion for any visitor to the Temple Mount to enter the complex carrying arms, so to preserve the secrecy of impending revolt Jehoiada' was forced to use the instruments of war which were already in the Temple precincts including a number of weapons dating from the time of King David. These 'spears, bucklers and shields'[50] were taken from their sacred resting place and distributed to the captains at the head of the revolutionary cohorts.

With preparations on the Mount as complete as possible, Joash was brought out of his hiding place and presented to the people in order to confirm the existence of a Davidic heir. He was then taken back into the interior of the Temple of Solomon where the crown of Judah was placed on his head. The noise of the resulting tumult reached 'Athaliah who hurried from the Royal Palace to the Temple. Surrounded by her enemies and with no one willing to come to her aid, she was dragged out of the Temple precinct and butchered in the proximity of the horse-gate of the Royal Palace.[51]

People then proceeded to tear down the images which 'Athaliah had erected in honour of Ba'al.

Joash succeeded to the throne of Judah in 836 BC, bringing new hope to the followers of Yahweh. The Temple of Solomon was by this time over one hundred years old and badly in need of repair. Joash instructed the priests to finance the work from the income of the Temple which was paid to the treasury in precious metal bearing the King's stamp. The stamp attested to the purity and weight of the pieces, bars or ingots submitted. Religious offerings to the Temple fell generally into three categories: the 'value' requested from an individual for the implementation of a sacrifice made by a priest; 'free' offerings or donations without request; and 'sin' and 'guilt' moneys which were accepted as sufficient repentance for the discharge of individual shortcomings.[52] Joash allowed the priests to retain the sin and guilt moneys, but the first two categories of payment had to be used to fund the repairs. His faith in this process, however, was ill founded and after a lapse of twenty-four years during which time no repairs had begun, a new system was established. A box was placed to the right of the Temple entrance in which all offerings had to be dropped. The King's scribe then had to distribute correctly the revenue. This relatively minor adjustment, recorded in the Bible, indicates the influence of the monarchy over the daily affairs of the Temple and emphasizes the growing importance of the Temple as a repository of the wealth of the nation. The temptation for the monarch to plunder the Temple treasury during times of national emergency would have left the priests and Levites in no doubt of the precarious situation existing for the Ark of the Covenant which, quite apart from its spiritual value, contained a considerable amount of gold in its construction. This fact, together with the threat to the monotheistic faith of Yahweh posed by Ba'alism from within Jewish ranks, caused the Levites to reconsider the security surrounding the Ark and to find a place of hidden sanctuary known only to themselves. It is likely that well before the Babylonian invasion in 596 BC the Levites of the Temple Mount had already prepared a secret repository for the Ark of the Covenant somewhere beneath the Temple complex. The Levites' caution was prudent. In the two and a half centuries leading up to this event the

Temple Mount continued to be a place of increasing importance for the cult of Yahweh, but religious growth was matched step for step by dire warnings uttered by the prophets of the nation such as Isaiah and Jeremiah.

THE GATHERING STORM

The fate of 'Athaliah underlined a constant dilemma facing the nation of Israel. Within such a confined location as the Temple Mount, a conflict of interest between the secular kingship and the religious priesthood was unavoidable and, as successive monarchs lurched from crisis to crisis, so the impact and importance of the prophets in the life of the nation increased. From the earliest days of kingship under Saul, circa 1020 BC, up to the Babylonian invasion in 596 BC, the expansion of this prophetic movement – which proclaimed destruction for Israel if Yahweh was not obeyed – followed the development of the priestly hierarchy on the Mount. The ancient words for the term 'prophet' provide us with a perfect reflection of this evolution.

Historically, the earliest word for 'prophet' in Hebrew is *ro'eh*, or 'seer', which derives from the root *ra'ah* meaning 'to see'. This word was later replaced by the word *nabi'*, which derived from *nabu* in the ancient Babylonian tongue of Akkadian, 'to call out or to speak'.[53] Thus it was that the original function of the 'prophet' was as a mouthpiece for God. In the case of the early prophets, such as Samuel and Nathan, the Bible shows that this was their wholly and only perceived function. The 'speaking out' was often accompanied by uncontrolled bodily action in the form of religious ecstasy and, although there is no evidence that this took on the more orgiastic forms of celebration found in Ba'alistic religious ceremony, the behaviour of the early prophets of Yahweh did little to establish a reputation for purity of mind. The Bible on several occasions refers directly to their complete madness.[54]

The construction of the Temple under Solomon had resulted in the emergence of 'prophetic' groups, which functioned as a professional body, 'prophesying' in a united voice.[55] Despite their independent function the prophets of Israel initially went the same way as the priesthood of the Temple, with money determining their existence. But during the eighth century BC, the prototypic voice of prophecy, fashioned in the old mould of the 'seer', re-emerged on the Temple Mount. Amos, born the son of a prophet, broke away from the accepted trend. Uninspired by a future of divination for payment, Amos began a movement which challenged the prophetic order on the Temple Mount, initiating what became a sustained deluge of warning on the people of Judah and Israel should the Law of Moses be transgressed and the cult of Yahweh be in any way diminished.

In the year 740 BC Isaiah took up the challenge laid down by Amos and began his own work of individual prophecy in Jerusalem. It is believed that Isaiah was born into the royal family of Judah and was a serving priest in the Temple at the moment of the 'vision' which led him to become a prophet. Isaiah saw Yahweh sitting on the Ark of the Covenant surrounded by seraphims in smoke-filled air. Isaiah's recorded words – the epitome of the voice in the wilderness – had a profound effect on the attempt to restore fundamental monotheism to Jerusalem. His prophecy laid the foundations of popular belief in a Messiah who would deliver the people of Israel from a Temple priesthood which depended on blood sacrifice, a form of worship which ardent Yahwists recognized as still prevalent amongst Jews still sympathetic to Ba'alistic methods of worship:

> To what purpose is the multitude of sacrifices unto me? saith the Lord: I am full of the burnt offerings of rams, and the fat of fed beasts; and I delight not in the blood of bullocks, or of lambs, or of he-goats...
>
> And when ye spread forth your hands, I will hide my eyes from you; yea, when ye make many prayers, I will not hear: your hands are full of blood...
>
> Learn to do well; seek judgment, relieve the oppressed; judge the fatherless; plead for the widow.[56]

Isaiah lived and wrote under the kingship of four Jerusalem monarchs: Uzziah, Jotham, Ahaz and Hezekiah, from circa 760 to 698 BC. His prophecies reflected the challenges faced by the nation, giving instructions on how to maintain the correct path of monotheistic Yahwism and warning of the dire consequences of any deviation. Because of Jerusalem's geographical location, danger from an external source was always close at hand and in 734 BC a military campaign of merciless brutality for ever altered the precarious relationship which had existed between the Israelite monarchies of Israel and Judah for over two centuries. The Assyrian army, led by Tiglath-Pileser III, a former soldier made king, swept up from the Fertile Crescent and invaded Palestine via north-eastern Syria, posing a threat to the very continuation of the Kingdom of Israel. An annual per capita levy of fifty shekels – the modern equivalent of approximately 350 grams of silver – kept the Assyrian army at bay.

But this was not a situation which the economy of the Kingdom of Israel could endure. Resistance to the Assyrians grew and Syria and Israel – old enemies – formed an alliance to combat the Assyrian army. King Ahaz, ruler of Judah, refused to join the fight against Assyria with the result that Israel and Syria marched south on Jerusalem. Ahaz sent a message to the Assyrians detailing his imminent plight, and backing his appeal for help with a substantial donation from the Royal Palace and the treasury of the Temple.[57] The Bible indicates that Ahaz's worship of foreign gods, the hated Ba'alim, caused the situation he found himself in: he had made 'his son to pass through the fire, according to the abomination of the heathen, whom the Lord cast out from before the children of Israel'.[58] The Second Book of Chronicles suggests that more than one of his children suffered a premature end: 'and [Ahaz] made also molten images [bronzes] for Ba'alim. Moreover, he burnt incense in the valley of the son of Hinnom, and burnt his children in the fire, after the abominations of the heathen, whom the Lord has cast out before the children of Israel'.[59] The sacrifice of his own children betrayed a level of desperation which he obviously felt lay beyond the powers of Yahweh to resolve. However, any successful attempt to save Jerusalem and the Temple from the wrath of the Assyrians ultimately depended on the size of tribute rather than the degree of human sacrifice, and with monetary donation came a temporary reprieve for the nation of Judah.

With his army's southern flank and the mountains of Jerusalem secure, Tiglath-Pileser attacked Israel and Syria, relieving the threat to the city of Jerusalem. At the conclusion of his campaign, Samaria alone escaped destruction, a small Hebrew enclave in the tide of Assyrian invasion. This remnant of the Kingdom of Israel recommenced the transfer of tribute to Assyria in a last-ditch effort for survival. The future of Judah rested on the horns of a similar dilemma of payment or conquest. Despite the magnificence of the initial treasure paid by Ahaz, the spectre of annual tribute to keep the Assyrian army away from the gates of Jerusalem drew closer each day. To the dismay of Isaiah and the Yahwistic faithful, Ahaz attempted to appease Tiglath-Pileser by introducing an Assyrian religious influence into Jerusalem. He gave orders for a newly constructed altar of Assyrian pattern to be placed within the Temple. According to the Second Book of Kings, this altar became a general place of sacrifice.[60] The parallel text of the Second Book of Chronicles is more explicit: Ba'alism had returned to Jerusalem and Ahaz 'shut up the doors of the house of the Lord',[61] with disastrous results. The King's transgression was 'the ruin of him, and of all Israel'.[62] This lament in Chronicles was clearly made by a Levite who, with the benefit of hindsight, wished to reinforce the perils awaiting all who strayed from the path of Yahweh.

But leaving human destiny aside, the outlook for the Temple was little better. Short of money and with the treasury depleted, Ahaz turned his eye to the furnishings within the Temple Courtyard. Bronze, which weight for weight was worth approximately one third of the value of silver, was plentiful. Hiram Abiff's ten bronze lavers were stripped of their wheeled carriages and the twelve oxen supporting the Great Sea were similarly destroyed. The massive bronze basin was dumped, according to the Bible, 'on a pavement of stones'.[63] Some biblical scholars have interpreted the destruction by King Ahaz of the decorated wheeled carriages and the twelve oxen as an act of belated repentance – an attempt to remove idolatrous images from the Mount to appease Yahweh. There is no mention of such a motive in the Bible but whatever Ahaz's intentions, his measures succeeded. The Assyrians were kept on the outside of Jerusalem; Judah, the Temple and the scions of the royal family of David whom Ahaz had not 'passed through the fire', survived. Samaria, however, the last stronghold of the Kingdom of Israel, was not so fortunate.

In 722–721 BC, the Assyrians finally overran Samaria, and the Kingdom of Israel ceased to exist. Twenty-seven thousand, two hundred and ninety[64] Hebrew inhabitants of the enclave were marched eastwards into captivity, finally putting an end to any hope of a return to the glorious days of the United Davidic Kingdom. Jerusalem, capital of Judah, remained alone, surrounded by her enemies. Although two different dates for the death of Ahaz are given in the Second Book of Kings,[65] it is believed that the King lived to see the destruction of Samaria and died the following year in 720 BC. The reign of Ahaz was a crucial episode in the struggle between, on the one hand, the Yahwistic priesthood of the Temple who sacrificed before an Ark containing the word of God, and on the other a monarchy and populace who at different times, and to greater or lesser degree, reverted to Ba'al and engaged in the horror of human sacrifice. The biblical description of the sacrifice by Ahaz of his own children records the continued existence of this Ba'alistic form of worship. The passage of the next 124 years, leading up to the Babylonian invasion, resulted in a final escalation in sacrifice providing a decisive outcome to the struggle between Yahweh and Ba'al.

By the eighth century BC the plains of Palestine, to the north and west of Jerusalem, had long been established as an historic battleground. The Assyrians were successful invaders in the region, but their role as conquerors was far from over. In 705 BC Jerusalem once again became the focus of their military endeavours. Hezekiah, King of Judah, led a coalition to throw off Assyrian domination, a move as politically unsound as it was strategically unwise. The coalition partners in Babylon and Phoenicia fell one by one to the Assyrian forces, led by Sennacherib, and in an attempt to save Jerusalem from an inevitable act of retribution Hezekiah reverted to eleventh-hour diplomacy. The Second Book of Kings tells us that 'Hezekiah gave him [Sennacherib] all the silver that was found in the house of the Lord, and in the treasures of the king's house. At that time did Hezekiah cut off the gold from the doors of the temple of the Lord, and from the pillars which Hezekiah king of Judah had overlaid, and gave it to the king of Assyria'.[66] Hezekiah's act of appeasement failed, however, to persuade the Assyrian command of his sincerity and Jerusalem and the Temple Mount came under siege.[67]

Sennacherib's army possessed both the manpower and the engineering expertise to break down the walls of the city and destroy the capital of Judah but, not long into the siege, Jerusalem was delivered by, so the Bible tells us, 'the angel of the Lord' who 'went out, and smote in the camp of the Assyrians an hundred and four score and five thousand: and when they arose early in the morning, they were all dead corpses'.[68] The overnight demise of the Assyrian army is still commonly attributed to a virulent plague in their camp. It is more likely that the real cause of infection was disease caused by poor sanitation. The Assyrian force, camped on the hillsides around the city, was in excess of a quarter of a million men, and water collection for so many soldiers was a complicated task. A major source of water known as Hezekiah's Tunnel had also been denied to them. Through a feat of engineering Hezekiah had diverted the waters of the Gihon Spring on the eastern side of the City of David, back inside the city walls. The nineteenth-century mission of Wilson to improve the supply of drinking water indicates that this was still a problem. Fresh water would have been a prime consideration to maintain the health of such a large number of men encamped outside the city, and a possible explanation is that choleric dysentery, the scourge of all Middle Eastern armies from ancient times to the twentieth century, took a sudden hold on Sennacherib's forces.

Hezekiah had already paid tribute to the Assyrians and at some point during the siege Sennacherib received news of the revolt of his vassal Bel-Ibni in Babylon. A combination of sickness and bad tidings probably saved the City of David. For the prophet Isaiah the outcome was a triumph. Jerusalem had been saved through the intervention of Yahweh. Towards the end of his reign, Hezekiah fell ill and, having received presents from Babylon after his recovery, he invited Babylonian representatives to Jerusalem. The Babylonians were emerging as serious contenders to the Assyrians for military domination of the region and Hezekiah, aware of their potential, was only too willing to ingratiate himself to them by showing their envoys the treasures of his palace and the Temple Mount. Isaiah was horrified:

Then came the prophet Isaiah unto king Hezekiah, and said unto him, What said these men? and from whence came they unto thee? And Hezekiah said, They are come from a far country, even from Babylon.

And he said, What have they seen in your house? And Hezekiah answered, All the things that are in mine house have they seen: there is nothing among my treasures that I have not showed them.

And Isaiah said unto Hezekiah, Hear the word of the Lord.

Behold the days come, that all that is in thine house, and that which thy fathers have laid up in store unto this day, shall be carried into Babylon: nothing shall be left saith the Lord.[69]

After the death of Hezekiah, Yahwists such as Isaiah would have even greater cause for alarm because of the behaviour of Hezekiah's son, Manasseh.

HINNOM, THE VALLEY OF HELL

Before his death Hezekiah, spurred on by Isaiah, attempted to rid the Temple Mount and the 'high places' or idolatrous hillside shrines around Jerusalem, of all vestiges of Ba'alism. Manasseh, imitating his father's appreciation of Babylon and paying no heed to diplomacy, introduced the rite of the solar cult and calendar of Babylon onto the Temple Mount[70] and, as if wishing to compound this injury to the Temple priesthood of Yahweh, he encouraged a return to all forms of Ba'alistic religious ritual. His zeal for a return to the polytheistic ways of Israel was unlimited and Manasseh set a new standard of religious degeneracy in Jerusalem.

According to the Second Book of Kings, Manasseh filled the Temple and its courts with altars of the Ba'alim – the various foreign deities so feared by the followers of Yahweh. But his actions went beyond the reinstatement of fertility rites such as those of Ashtoreth in the place sacred to monotheism. The Second Book of Chronicles tells us: 'he caused his children to pass through the fire in the valley of the son of Hinnom: also he observed times, and used enchantments, and used witchcraft, and dealt with a familiar spirit, and with wizards'.[71]

The Hinnom runs in from the west below the Temple, completing the left-hand branch of the three-pronged fork which constitutes Jerusalem's principle valley network. For reasons of topographical convenience, augmented by the impossibility of performing human sacrifice and witchcraft on a Temple Mount controlled by the priesthood of Yahweh, Manasseh and his followers found a location for their ritual in this valley: the son of Hinnom. Natural erosion has endowed the Hinnom with narrow ravines in which were built fire pits, the Hebrew *topheth*, a name which derives from the word for a 'thing abhorred'.[72] The *topheth* were designed to receive the sacrifice of a complete human body. The use of such offerings had long been anathema to the Yahwists as the story of God's substitution of a ram for Isaac, son of Abraham, illustrates. The Yahwists had, however, made one concession to Ba'alism in the past, although this had no direct link with human sacrifice. Moses, returning from the heights of Mount Sinai with the Ten Commandments, destroyed the golden calf built under the guidance of his brother Aaron and ordered the construction of the Ark, but crowned it with two figures that Yahwists considered idolatrous. The Ark, so the Bible tells us, was crowned by two 'cherubim'. The derivation of the word cherubim is revealing. The *Jewish Encyclopaedia* says: 'The origin of the cherub myth predates history ... in Babylonia there is the winged sphinx having a king's head, a lion's body, and an eagle's wings ... Following Lenormant's suggestions, Friedrich Delitzsch connected the Hebrew with the Assyrian "kirubu" = "shedu", the name of the winged bull.' The application of the cherubim to the Ark was therefore an act of compromise by Moses to the worshippers of the Bull or Ba'al cult. Solomon too had placed figures of oxen, or bulls, under the Great Sea which stood outside the Temple. But Manasseh was not interested in any reciprocal compromise; he was determined to reinstate 'foreign gods'. He took the fight into the heart of the city, shedding the blood of the Yahwists, the 'innocents', 'till he had filled Jerusalem from one end to another [with their blood]'.[73]

The human sacrifices performed on the *topheth* in the valley of the son of Hinnom were, according to the Bible, intended as an offering to Molech, or Molek. Scholars have suggested that Molech, in some references, was not a separate deity, but simply Melech, or Melek, 'The King'.[74] The Hinnom valley of Jerusalem where human sacrifice was practised and encouraged by its kings became known as the place of abomination or hell. The 'hell' of the valley of Hinnom and the 'heaven' of the Temple Mount served as the model for the later Christian concept of a greater Kingdom of God. Was the truth of Hinnom therefore even more disturbing for the adherents of Yahweh than the Bible has led us to believe? Had kings of Judah, in times of danger to the city, allowed human sacrifice to be made in their name in order to receive the strength of divine power? Self-deification, as the lives of Alexander the Great and several Roman emperors have proved, was not uncommon amongst the leaders of the ancient world.

Manasseh died in 640 BC. Later a prophet condemned the position of his tomb as being too close to the sacred precincts of the Temple which suggests that Manasseh had either claimed or had been elevated to God-like status during his lifetime.[75] His surviving son and heir Amon ruled for only two years and was murdered by the people of Jerusalem for continuing the idolatrous practices established by his father.[76] They made Manasseh's eight-year-old grandson Josiah king, hoping that such a youthful ruler could be educated to cleanse the Temple Mount of foreign gods.

JEREMIAH, PROPHET OF DOOM

The priests said not, where is the Lord? and they that handle the law knew me not: the pastors also transgressed against me, and the prophets prophesied by Ba'al, and walked after things that do not profit.[77]

The reign of Josiah is known for the reforms which were undertaken in the presence of Judah's gloomiest prophet, Jeremiah. If Isaiah's prophetic outlook was at times made miserable by the prospect of the degeneration of the Yahwistic cult, the recorded utterances of Jeremiah made the words of his predecessor look positively optimistic.

King Josiah reigned for thirty-one years. At some time between 621 and 620 BC, in the eighteenth year of his rule, an ancient book containing the Mosaic Law was discovered during the course of restoration work which he had ordered to be conducted on the Temple. The book contained not only the Law but further information which, when brought to the King's notice, alarmed him. According to the words contained within the hidden document, the protection afforded by Yahweh to the people of Israel was not guaranteed unless the Mosaic Law was fully observed on the Temple Mount. The King, spurred into action by these words, saw an opportunity to rid his monarchy once and for all of the stain of Ba'alism and instigated a series of reforms. 'All the men of Judah and all the inhabitants of Jerusalem'[78] were summoned to the Temple for a reading of the book. Josiah then reaffirmed, by the use of correct sacrifice at the Temple, the covenant made with Yahweh. The Temple and its courtyards, and even the valley of the son of Hinnom, were cleared of all traces of Ba'alistic cult worship 'so that no man might make his son or his daughter pass through the fire to Molech'.[79] Extending his reforms to the countryside of Judah, Josiah then attempted to purge his kingdom of all traces of alternative religions, killing priests of alternative cults and burning their bones on their own altars.[80]

Unlike his predecessor Isaiah, Jeremiah was not a native son of Jerusalem. He was born between 650 BC and 645 BC in 'Anathoth, four miles east of Mount Moriah. For this legendary prophet, however, four miles might well have been four hundred. Jeremiah was a wanderer, more at home with the freedom of open spaces such as the Judaean wilderness than the tumult of Jerusalem's busy streets and Temple Mount. Throughout his life he longed for a return to the rural existence into which he had been born and raised, but in the thirteenth year of Josiah's reign, in about 625 BC, Jeremiah received the calling of Yahweh. In a city used to prophets in the streets and on the Temple Mount his lone figure and his message must have seemed familiar to the people of Jerusalem. The warnings uttered by Jeremiah of imminent destruction for the people of Judah went unheeded.

The balance of power in the region of Palestine was about to change. The reaffirmation by the Jewish people of their covenant with Yahweh and the false sense of security it created led Josiah to an unfortunate military decision. In 609 BC he challenged an Egyptian army led by Pharoah Necho II. The two armies met at Meggido, the legendary site of Armageddon, north of Jerusalem, which lay in the central area of the fertile Palestine plains which so favoured large forces of battle. During the early stages of the battle Josiah was hit by an Egyptian arrow and mortally wounded. He returned to Jerusalem with the survivors of his defeated army where he died.[81] The Pharoah, now influential in the politics of Jerusalem, elevated Josiah's son Jehoiakim over Jehoahaz, the son and first heir initially chosen by the native Jerusalem hierarchy.

In 605 BC the forces of Egypt and Assyria were defeated by the Babylonian army. Jerusalem fell under the vassalage of Babylon, and for several years Jehoiakim paid tribute to keep the Babylonians at bay. However, the situation did not endure for long. Jehoiakim, the Bible tells us, 'did that which was evil in the sight of the Lord his God,'[82] a sure sign that the curse of Manasseh had not departed from the line of David. Jehoiakim rebelled against the distant power of Babylon, throwing his lot and the fate of his city in with the fortunes of an Egyptian alliance. The time of destruction, prophesied by Jeremiah, was fast approaching. The King of Babylon, whose name would become forever linked with the Solomonic Temple, gathered his forces against Judah: Nebuchadnezzar marched on Jerusalem.

From Destruction to Jesus,
596–4 BC

THE FIRST BABYLONIAN CONQUEST

In the weeks it took Nebuchadnezzar to mobilize an army, Jehoiakim died. The crown passed to his son, Jehoiachin, who at eighteen years of age faced the gravest external peril ever to beset the Kingdom of Judah and the Temple Mount cult of Yahweh. The Bible mentions briefly the young king's reign, informing us that Jehoiachin followed the familiar path of his ancestors doing 'that which was evil in the sight of the Lord'[1] – suggesting that the *topheth* in the valley of the Hinnom had been put back into service. However, for once the gods of the high places and the Hinnom smiled on the young sons of the line of David – the potential victims of the king. Jehoiachin's reintegration of human sacrifice was short lived when the appearance of Nebuchadnezzar's army at the gates of the city placed the Hinnom out of bounds. The arrival of the Babylonians concentrated the mind of the young king on military matters and the survival of his kingdom. After a siege of only three months, during which time Nebuchadnezzar joined his army below the walls of the city, Jehoiachin capitulated. The Bible tells us that the King of Judah in the company of his mother Nehushta, their servants and officers, and the surviving princes of the line of David left the protection of the Temple Mount and surrendered themselves to Nebuchadnezzar.[2]

For the first time since the completion of the Temple under Solomon, three and a half centuries previously, the Temple Mount was set to suffer the indignity of forced entry into its precincts by a foreign invader. Nebuchadnezzar, however, was not intent on destroying the Solomonic complex. With an army to pay and a large region to administer he had other more immediate aims. The Temple Mount was the treasury of Judah and to the victor the spoils. What silver had been refused in tribute, Nebuchadnezzar would take as conqueror. The buildings of the Temple Mount were thus targeted for treasure: 'And he [Nebuchadnezzar] carried out thence all the treasures of the house of the Lord, and the treasures of the king's house, and cut into pieces all the vessels of gold which Solomon king of Israel had made in the temple of the Lord, as the Lord had said.'[3] The reign of Jehoiachin lasted only three months and ten days.[4] By surrendering, the King of Judah had saved Nebuchadnezzar the losses inherent in a long siege and in turn protection for the royal family as they left the city was guaranteed by Nebuchadnezzar. This royal entourage, led by Jehoiachin, was sent on the long road to the south-east and exile in the Euphrates delta, the heart of Babylon.

Nebuchadnezzar's next move, the removal of craftsmen, reflects a high degree of military astuteness. His personal experience of besieging the Holy City of Yahweh had obviously impressed him. Despite the application of overwhelming force, militarily Jerusalem had proved a difficult conquest. If Jehoiachin had not opened his gates to the Babylonian commanders, the time taken to reduce the city may have run into years, rather than months. Nebuchadnezzar therefore made a prudent decision. The masonic descendants of Hiram Abiff, the men skilled and cunning in the art of metalwork, represented an essential human resource to any future rearmament of Jerusalem. The Second Book of Kings gives the number of masons as one thousand.[5] Their removal from the city was therefore an utmost necessity for Nebuchadnezzar, especially if he was to rule the city from afar. Overriding promises he had made to Jehoiachin,[6] the Babylonian king ordered the 'craftsmen and smiths' of Jerusalem to join a captive train of 'all that were...apt for war,'[7] in preparation for deportation into deepest Babylon. Thus the craftsmen and warriors of Jerusalem were sent to accompany their king, Jehoiachin, in exile.

Nebuchadnezzar's next action, however, was by necessity political and in contrast to his military thinking it displayed a distinct lack of sound strategy. Although the older members of the nobility of Judah had been sent into exile, a younger nucleus stayed behind in Jerusalem. Nebuchadnezzar appointed a younger brother of Jehoiachin, Mattanaiah, to the throne, changing his name to Zedekiah in the process. An inexperienced king of apparent weak character was thus left to rule over a youthful court – an invitation to disaster, which did not take long to materialize. With an empire to administer the Babylonian king could not remain indefinitely in Jerusalem so he departed, leaving Zedekiah to rule in his place. Seduced by a semblance of autonomy the newly established monarchy quickly found itself at odds with those of more experienced years and, not surprisingly, the prophet Jeremiah who was living through events he had himself predicted soon made his own judgement of the new situation, influenced by visionary experience.

Not long after the departure of the captives, Jeremiah noticed several baskets of figs which had been left outside the gates of the Temple. In his own words, the prophet thought them to fall into two categories: 'very good figs' of a quality as if first picked, and 'very naughty figs' which because they were so bad could not be eaten.[8] But then, in a vision, Jeremiah received a different interpretation from Yahweh. According to the God of Moses, the good figs represented those exiles who were faithful and would one day return to Jerusalem and re-establish correct Temple worship.[9] The bad figs – or deviants from the true cult – were so evil that Yahweh would 'deliver them to be removed into all the kingdoms of the earth for their hurt, and to be a reproach and a proverb, a taunt and a curse, in all places wither I shall drive them. And I will send the sword, the famine, and the pestilence, among them, till they be consumed from off the land that I gave unto them and their fathers.'[10] The warning which Jeremiah passed on shocked the population of Jerusalem. Jeremiah's many enemies, when they heard this news, began to feel increasingly intolerant of the prophet. But the hostility shown to Jeremiah was only one symptom of an emerging crisis. The majority of the young nobility favoured a renewed alliance with Egypt, whilst those with more experience – Jeremiah amongst them – warned against the folly of raising the ire of Nebuchadnezzar. The outcome of this internal struggle was to decide the fate of the Jewish nation.

FALSE PROPHETS AND YAHWEH

Jeremiah was not the first prophet of Judah to be disliked by his contemporaries. At the beginning of Jeremiah's prophetic career King Jehoiakim sent a posse of men into Egypt in pursuit of the prophet Urijah who had sought sanctuary there. Brought back to Jerusalem, Urijah was put to death by Jehoiakim who had the body of the prophet 'cast into the graves of the common people'.[11] Jeremiah would now face a similar threat of death.

Verse 1, Chapter 28 of the Book of Jeremiah tells us that during the early part of Zedekiah's reign Jeremiah had a confrontation with a fellow prophet, Hananiah, which took place in the Temple in the presence of the priests 'and in the presence of... all the people'. The location and the attendance of so many people suggests a growing national awareness of the threat facing the cult of Yahweh. Hananiah opened the debate prophesying imminent redemption for the exiled people. Yahweh, he promised, would within 'two years' bring back the looted vessels of the Temple and reinstate Jehoiachin, the exiled King of Judah.[12] Jeremiah's reaction was damning. He told the assembly before him to open their ears to the truth of the situation. Considering the words of Hananiah as an incitement towards rebellion against Babylon, Jeremiah warned of the dangers of such false prophecy and outlined his own definition of 'true' prophecy: 'The prophet which prophesieth of peace, when the word of the prophet shall come to pass, then shall the prophet be known, that the Lord hath truly sent him.'[13] With emotions running high Hananiah tore off Jeremiah's 'yoke' or collar piece[14] and, breaking it in two, announced that in such a fashion would Yahweh break the neck hold of Babylon within the time he had predicted.[15] As the period of two years elapsed, however, and the prophecy of Hananiah did not come to pass, the warnings from Jeremiah – which had continued unabated – took on an even more relevant urgency to those who were willing to listen. The power on the Mount – the court of King Zedekiah – pursued the Egyptian alliance, ignoring the constant warnings of Jerusalem's most dedicated prophet.

The exact extent of armed help promised by Egypt to Judah in support of the raising of a rebellion against Babylon remains unclear. But it is evident from the Bible that the Jerusalem leaders of Judah felt their forces had been sufficiently strengthened by the accession of the Pharoah Apries to the Egyptian throne in 588 BC, and were able to reject the conditions of vassalage imposed by Nebuchadnezzar. Judah, together with Ammon – a region which lay some seventy kilometres to the north-east of Jerusalem – revolted against Babylon. Nebuchadnezzar mobilized his forces and, for the second time in a decade, marched towards the region. Judah and Ammon, however, were not his only problem. The military situation in northern Syria also required his presence and the Babylonian king established his field headquarters at Riblah on the Orontes.[16] From there he dispatched the necessary forces south-westwards towards Jerusalem to invest the city. Thus it was that in the first months of 587 BC the army of Babylon surrounded the walled City of David and the Temple Mount.

As a result of the past endeavours of King Hezekiah, the city remained well supplied with water and, unlike his older brother Jehoiachin a decade previously, Zedekiah showed little inclination to surrender to the Babylonians. The pro-Babylonians within Jerusalem, with Jeremiah their most vocal advocate, pressed Zedekiah for an immediate capitulation but to little or no avail. The Egyptians, aware of the divisions still present within the walls of Jerusalem, nevertheless crossed the border and moved north into Babylonian-dominated territory, causing the Babylonians to march southwards to engage them which meant breaking the siege of Jerusalem. Little is known of the resulting encounter except that the Egyptians were defeated.[17]

Having thwarted this rescue attempt, Nebuchadnezzar's forces retraced their steps to the scene of their main intent: the capture of Jerusalem. During the lull in Babylonian operations against the city, relations between Jeremiah and his opponents deteriorated even further. As a prophet, Jeremiah was zealous to perfection but to the pro-Egyptian faction his incessant reminders of their deviance from the true path of Yahweh finally resulted in a decision to curtail his activities. Jeremiah was no easy target, however. He had already been arrested and imprisoned by the hereditary royal princes and, although incarcerated in the house of the scribe, Jonathan, he still had access to the ear of the King. Zedekiah was reluctant to ignore the words of a prophet so proven and summoned Jeremiah to a meeting in the Royal Palace on the Mount. But the message of the prophet was unchanged and Zedekiah felt obliged to continue his arrest, stipulating that 'until all the bread in the city is spent' the prophet of Yahweh should be fed a piece daily.[18] Jeremiah heard rumours that his enemies were scheming his ultimate downfall and during their encounter he begged Zedekiah to change his place of imprisonment to a more secure location, a plea to which the King conceded. After the meeting Zedekiah's orders were obeyed but the princes who first arrested Jeremiah had deadlier plans for the famous prophet. Entering the courts of the city prison, they recaptured him and lowered him into a cistern by the use of ropes. The cistern was empty of water but deep in mud, and he was left for dead.[19]

THE DESTRUCTION OF SOLOMON'S TEMPLE

To enforce the isolation of the besieged city the Babylonian commanders constructed a series of walls around it. At strategic locations in the City of David and on the Temple Mount complex[20] they placed towers from which to launch arrows and other missiles. After eighteen months of fighting Nebuchadnezzar's army stood on the brink of success, helped as Jeremiah had predicted[21] by famine and pestilence. On the ninth day of the Jewish month of Av, the second day of August, 586 BC,[22] the Babylonian army breached the weakened defences of Jerusalem from the north, geophysically and militarily her weakest point. With the knowledge that they were fighting for their lives, the defenders put up a desperate resistance and it took until midnight for the Babylonians to gain overall control of the city.[23] The Babylonian commanders, Nergal Sharezer, Samgar Nebo, Rabsaris, Sarsechim and Rabmag, entered the Temple of Solomon, their path lit by brazier or torch, determined to take total revenge. In the eyes of the priests and Levites who survived the siege, the pestilence and the fighting, the predictions of Jeremiah were coming true and the worst was still to come.

The presence of Babylonian commanders on a victory tour inside the Temple finally ended the state of prolonged procrastination which had so hampered the decision-making capacity of Zedekiah throughout his reign, prompting him to flee. He left the city through 'a gate between two walls which is by the king's garden',[24] accompanied by his 'wives and his children, and his captains and his friends',[25] who made their 'way toward the plain'.[26] Judging from the account in the Bible the 'king's garden' butted up against the southern perimeter of the Royal Palace, which itself lay in the south-eastern sector of the Temple Mount enclosure. It is therefore likely that 'the gate between two walls' stood at the junction between the present-day south-eastern angle and the adjoining ancient walls of the Davidic city, the remains of which were discovered by Warren in 1868. The route taken by the last Davidic King of Judah was probably that of today's 'old' Jericho road which leaves the valley of the Kidron and, in a direct line with the south-eastern corner of the *haram*, runs over the Mount of Olives towards the open spaces of the Judaean wilderness. The events which followed Zedekiah's escape from the city give some support to this theory as Zedekiah and his party were immediately pursued and captured in Jericho.

The King of Babylon decided to stay at Riblah throughout the eighteen-month siege, and Zedekiah and the royal entourage were taken northwards to his headquarters. Here, Nebuchadnezzar confronted his rebellious vassal and invoked the sentence of traitors. Zedekiah was made to watch as his sons and friends were butchered in front of him. Zedekiah's captains, who also witnessed the slaughter, next saw sentence passed on their king: Zedekiah's eyes were put out. Nebuchadnezzar then dispatched the captain of his own guard, Nebuzaradan, to Jerusalem who arrived there on 'the seventh day of the fifth month',[27] four weeks after the Babylonian commanders had taken the city and the Temple Mount. He carried with him strict orders from Nebuchadnezzar to destroy the city and the Temple Mount – once it was stripped of all treasure. So Nebuzaradan 'burnt down the house of the Lord, and the king's house, and all the houses of Jerusalem, and every great man's house burnt he with fire'.[28] Before the Temple complex had been fired, however, the complete looting of all treasures had, in accordance with Nebuchadnezzar's instructions, been ruthlessly carried out. Jachin and Boaz were broken up and the Great Sea, which since the time of Ahaz had been without its base of twelve oxen, was shattered into pieces. The destruction of Hiram Abiff's masterpieces was probably not a simple act of vandalism. The bronze Temple furniture was a ready source of material from which a new generation of workers could manufacture weapons. Hiram's broken bronzes were, therefore, added to a train of booty bound for Babylon which included 'the pots, and the shovels, and the snuffers, and the spoons, and all the vessels of brass...And the fire-pans, and the bowls, and such things as were of gold...and of silver.'[29] The Second Book of Kings relates how Nebuzaradan left only 'the poor of the land to be vine dressers and husbandmen',[30] exiling the merchant classes, the artisans, the civil and royal servants and any surviving warriors to Babylon where they would join their fellow Jews who had gone there a decade before. Thus, through the efficient organization of Nebuzaradan, King Nebuchadnezzar concluded a second attempt to prevent Jerusalem from becoming a future threat to his sovereignty and this time Nebuzaradan ensured that the political choice of his king would be as sound as the hard-won Babylonian victory.

Gedaliah, the son of a nobleman, was chosen to govern the city of Jerusalem and the Jews left behind in the Kingdom of Judah. According to the Bible, he was a man of peace[31] and, most importantly for Nebuchadnezzar, pro-Babylonian.[32] Gedaliah's attitude of compromise with Babylon followed the advice of the prophet Jeremiah who until Gedaliah's appointment continued to languish at the bottom of the cistern into which he had been lowered.

The mud in which Jeremiah stood reached up to his neck. Undaunted, the prophet offered his words of warning to such captors or passers-by who might have been inclined to listen[33] and if it seems likely that his utterances may have been largely ignored we are told by the Bible that he did not go unnoticed. An Ethiopian named Ebed-melech, a eunuch of Zedekiah's palace, took pity on him. He approached the King and informed him of Jeremiah's situation, saying that if left unaided the prophet would soon die. Zedekiah commanded Ebed-melech to gather together thirty men to rescue him.[34] Ebed-melech and his rescue party hastened to the cistern with old clothing and rags taken from a room under the palace treasury. Casting a makeshift rope into the depths of the cistern, Ebed-melech instructed Jeremiah to pass it under his arms. He was then hauled out. It probably did not require thirty men to raise the prophet out of the mud, so unless this was an exaggeration it can be reasonably deduced that this number had served to guarantee a successful rescue without interruption from Jeremiah's enemies.

Brought once again before his king who felt it safer for Jeremiah's own good not to release him, Jeremiah was re-incarcerated and spent the remainder of the siege within the courtyard of the prison.[35] After the fall of Jerusalem Jeremiah was finally released by the Babylonians who gave him into Gedaliah's care.[36] In the days that followed, however, he was innocently caught up in a mass arrest and placed in chains ready for deportation. When Nebuzaradan heard that the prophet was bound for Babylon he intervened and suggested that 'If it seem good unto thee to come with me unto Babylon, come, and I will look well unto thee: but if it seem ill unto thee to come with me unto Babylon, forbear: behold, all the land is before thee: whither it seemeth good and convenient for thee to go, thither go.'[37] The fame of Jeremiah's tenacity had obviously spread and Nebuzaradan's diplomatic intervention had the effect he desired: Jeremiah opted to remain in Judah.

THE ARK AND THE FATE OF THE DOORKEEPERS

The authenticity of the Bible's account of the destruction of Jerusalem, like the description of Solomon's Temple, has often been questioned. However, in 1933 the Assyriologist E.F. Weidner confirmed the biblical description of the Babylonic conquest with his study of tablets and pottery shards which had been excavated by the German Oriental Society from the site of Nebuchadnezzar's capital city of Babylon in 1899. On a large number of shards and tablets the daily administrative inventory for the city was recorded. This list included names and one in particular caught Weidner's eye. It was 'Ja'-u-kinu', [Jehoiachin] 'King of Judah'. The inventory dated from 592 BC, five years, according to the biblical testament, after Jehoiachin had surrendered to Nebuchadnezzar and gone into exile in Babylon. In 1955 similar research on Babylonian tablets held by the British Museum produced further startling evidence in support of the biblical account. D.J. Wiseman, a scholar of cuneiform, came across the following:

> In the seventh year of the month Chislev, the king assembled his army and advanced on Hatti-land [Syria]. He encamped over against the city of the Judeans and conquered it on the second day of Adar. He took the king [Jehoiachin] prisoner, and appointed in his stead a king [Zedekiah] after his own heart. He exacted heavy tribute and had it brought to Babylon.[38]

Such historical confirmation of the factual truth of the Bible is of great significance when taking into consideration the history of the Ark of the Covenant during the final years of Judah and the period of the Babylonian destruction. The Ark of the Covenant is not mentioned in the inventory found at Babylon or in the biblical account of the looting of the Temple. Many observers have deduced that this may have been an oversight and that the Ark was either destroyed or taken to Babylon, but this is highly unlikely. Despite the fact that the Ark was of little value compared to the rest of the treasure in the Temple, as a trophy of war it was a worthy prize. Its capture, or its complete loss, would surely have been recorded. Had the Levites, therefore, successfully created a secret location somewhere within the Mount, a hiding place known only to themselves, and once perhaps to the long-dead Hiram Abiff? Evidence that they had done so lies within the Second Book of Chronicles. During the Passover of 620 BC, a generation before the arrival of the Babylonians at the gates of Jerusalem, King Josiah addressed the Levites: 'And [Josiah] said unto the Levites that taught all Israel, which were holy unto the Lord, put the holy ark in the house which Solomon the son of David king of Israel did build: it shall not be a burden upon your shoulders [any more]; serve now the Lord your God and the people of Israel.'[39] According to the Bible, the Levites had removed the Ark from the Holy of Holies and placed it in a location unknown to the monarchy, afraid that it might be included in the periodic tribute paid to belligerent nations or spiritually contaminated because of worship to 'foreign gods' on the Mount. There is no mention in the Bible of the Levites obeying Josiah; with the religious record of the kings and queens of Judah, they had little reason to do so and during the course of the next thirty years when the political situation deteriorated towards war they would have protected the Ark and its hidden location with vigilance.

The looting of the Temple and its destruction by fire which followed the second Babylonian Conquest of 586 BC would have revealed any hiding place which existed above ground level on the Mount. But the Temple Mount offers the ideal place of concealment for the Ark *underground*. If it was hidden underground it could have remained in its hiding place, protected from the ravages of war and preserved for posterity. In this context, verses 24 to 25, Chapter LII of the Book of Jeremiah, have gone unnoticed. They tell us that before finally departing from Jerusalem to Babylon with his chained prisoners, Neburazadan received additional, urgent orders from Nebuchadnezzar to find 'Seraiah the chief priest, and Zephaniah the second priest, and the three keepers of the door' and to bring them to Riblah. Once one accepts the possibility that a select group of individuals – the Levites – knew of a secret place where the Ark had been hidden, the words of the verses have a crucial bearing on the mystery. Seraiah alone, as chief priest, had official access to the Ark of the Covenant and Zephaniah would have substituted for Seraiah in case of Zephaniah's incapacity to fulfil his duties. The three doorkeepers were senior Levites who protected the Temple and they would, therefore, have known the Ark's location. The reigning king of Judah, Zedekiah, had been dealt with and his heirs and successors executed. In addition, the Temple had been destroyed and all possible articles of value looted. So by sending for the chief priest, the second priest and the 'three doorkeepers' of the Temple, Nebuchadnezzar may only have wanted one thing which his trusted captain Nebuzaradan, had not yet discovered: the whereabouts of the Ark.

Without accurate maps, which probably did not exist, the exact location of an entrance into the underground of the Temple Mount would have been difficult for the captives to convey. The Temple

Mount was also strewn with the debris of destruction. It is therefore likely that Nebuchadnezzar wished to obtain the compliance of one or more of the group to return to Jerusalem and reveal – in person – their secret knowledge. Nebuchadnezzar either had no success with his proposal or, quite simply, grew so impatient that he executed the entire group and some other eminent Jews that Nebuzaradan had brought to Nebuchadnezzar including seven of Zedekiah's close friends, his scribe, and a eunuch who had been the King's military chief of staff.[40] It is possible that the secret of the exact location of the Ark of the Covenant died at Riblah on the Orontes in northern Syria in 586 BC.

THE DESOLATE MOUNTAIN

How doth the city sit solitary, that was so full of people…

Jerusalem hath grievously sinned, therefore she is removed…

Because of the mountain of Zion which is desolate; the foxes walk upon it.[41]

With the Temple in ruins and the city of Jerusalem destroyed, the Jewish people had suffered a seemingly irreversible blow. Their king was a blinded prisoner, the senior members of the Temple dead and the majority of Hebrew craftsmen and men of warrior age sent into exile. Jerusalem and the Temple Mount lay desolate. Jeremiah's Lamentations, which are believed to be his personal observations of the city in the immediate aftermath of destruction, were written in five chapters and they convey the horror of a once thriving city, looted and abandoned.[42] The 'poor of the land' who had been left behind inhabited a city of ghosts with wild animals roaming the Temple Mount, once the religious and political heart of the Jewish nation.

But the predicament in which Jeremiah and the remnants of the Jewish population of Judah found themselves was probably not as dire as has been portrayed. The number of those sent into exile, as given in the Bible, are few:

First Babylonian conquest (597 BC)	3,023 persons
Fall and destruction of Jerusalem (586 BC)	832 persons
Five years after the destruction	745 persons
Total	4,600 persons

These conservative figures from the Book of Jeremiah[43] suggest that the Babylonians took only key personnel into exile, leaving behind the bulk of Jerusalem's population which can be estimated at five to six times that number. The exile was not to be indefinite. Within several generations – in 538 BC – there would be a return. Josephus tells us that 'all Judaea and Jerusalem' was deserted.[44] But in view of Jeremiah's figures this was probably an exaggeration. To the adherents of Yahweh the calamity which had befallen the nation confirmed the power of the God of Moses. After all, Mosaic Law stipulated that what God had given he could equally take away. The warnings of Isaiah and Jeremiah had proved accurate. To the survivors of the Babylonian conquest the facts were undeniable: Yahweh had punished his people for their sins; Nebuchadnezzar had burnt the Temple and the Ark had vanished. But Mount Moriah, the legendary location of Abraham's attempted sacrifice of Isaac, could not be obliterated by any human hand and on this place the ruins of Solomon's Temple, the man-made limestone blocks of the Temple Mount, still stood, a fact which would have sustained the hopes of the Jerusalem faithful. In all probability the desolate Mount still contained the Ark of the Covenant within the Temple foundations.

There existed sound practical reasons why the destruction of the Solomonic structure may not have been as complete as Babylon would have wished. Without the technology of explosives the act of demolition was often as laborious as the process of construction. Fire would quickly consume timber and furnishings but limestone – the principle building material used in Solomon's Temple – would react by merely splitting along natural lines of weakness or with surface flaking, when heated to a high degree. Although the cedar beams and wooden furnishings of the Temple and palace would have produced a conflagration, parts of the limestone walls and all of the foundations would have survived. Any remaining walls would then have been toppled by hand, forming a heap of material over the original foundations. If the Levites had hidden the Ark underground, the entrance would probably have been covered over by this mass of stone.

The period of the Babylonian exile can be estimated as having lasted for forty-eight years, although the precise dating is much disputed by biblical scholars.[45] During this period the Jews left behind in Jerusalem continued to make a token sacrifice to Yahweh on the Mount. There is a reference in the Book of Jeremiah to pilgrims from the outlying area of Shechem, Shiloh and Samaria who came to Jerusalem to participate in the Yahwist sacrifice.[46] The Second Book of Chronicles also informs us that the city was faithful to Yahweh, and kept the sabbath.[47]

Gedaliah set up his political centre not at Jerusalem but at Mizpah, about eight kilometres to the north-west of the city. This was perhaps because the city was in such ruins, but it could also have been because some members of the population wanted to shun the Temple Mount site and the cult of Yahweh. The conflict between the faithful of Yahweh and the followers of the Ba'al was by no means over and Ba'alist fears amongst the Yahwists still persisted. However, the Jews who continued to follow the Law of Moses were not left without prophetic assistance. Jeremiah remained behind in Judah to continue the fight for monotheism and the Jews sent to exile in Babylon were soon to receive the services of another prophet from within their midst.

EZEKIEL'S VISION

The prophet Ezekiel was exiled in the first group of prisoners sent to Babylon following the initial conquest in 596 BC. At the age of thirty he received a vision from Yahweh. In Ezekiel's vision four cherubim were the heavenly escort of Yahweh. The God of Moses appeared to Ezekiel in the form of an enthroned man composed not of flesh but of the brightest fire.[48] During the course of this encounter, the 'spirit of fire' – the word of God – entered Ezekiel and began a discourse with him,[49] making the exiled priest the mouthpiece of God, the prophet of Yahweh for the Jewish exiles in Babylon. Not surprisingly

the prophecy of Ezekiel was viewed by the Jewish exiles as an affir-
mation of the supreme nature of Yahweh. The cherubim which he
encountered in his vision match those on the Ark of the Covenant
which sat on either side of the 'mercy seat' or lid of solid gold.
Ezekiel's prophecy went further, describing a vision of a new
Jerusalem with, at its centre, the ideal Temple. Giving the measurements in cubits, the Book of Ezekiel gives details of both the interior
and the exterior of a new house of God.

By the time the second group of exiles reached Babylon in 586 BC
Ezekiel was already well established in his prophetic role. The fate of
the exiles was mixed. Some were put to forced labour[50] but the
majority were allowed by Nebuchadnezzar to settle in family clans
and pursue the living of their choice. Whilst this can be seen today
as a sensible and humane course of action on behalf of a conqueror,
it poses an historical enigma. This policy stood in stark contrast to
the treatment meted out to the senior priests and Levites interro-
gated at Riblah, suggesting that Nebuchadnezzar believed the
Temple hierarchy alone was in possession of information concerning the whereabouts of the Ark of the Covenant.

Back in Jerusalem, however, the political scenario had changed
little, despite the disaster which had befallen the city. Divisions
amongst the remaining population still existed and in 582 BC
Gedaliah was murdered by Ishmael, a descendant of the line of
David. Backed by pro-Egyptian officers, he wished to win back
control of Judah from the Babylonians. The population of Judah,
memories of the consequences of rebelling against Babylon fresh
in their minds, refused to back Ishmael who was left with no alternative but to flee into the mountains of neighbouring Ammon.
The Babylonians responded by installing another governor in
Gedaliah's place. Jeremiah informs us that a further 745 persons
were deported to Babylon from Jerusalem in 581 BC, probably as a
result of investigations into the murder of Gedaliah.[51] Jerusalem
and the remnants of Judah, further depleted in essential manpower
and reduced to a far-flung vassal of Babylon, became prey to incur-
sions from stronger neighbours. This desolate situation lasted for
almost fifty years until the supremacy of Babylon itself was
challenged by the Persian Empire.

THE RETURN OF THE EXILES

In 539 BC, forty-seven years after the fall of Jerusalem to the Babylonians, King Cyrus II, King of Persia, defeated the Babylonians at Opis. Opis lay one hundred kilometres north-east of Babylon, between the Euphrates and Tigris, the great river network which formed the backbone of the Fertile Crescent. With their new territory the Persians engulfed the ancient Babylonian kingdom. The rise of Cyrus had been hailed by the prophets in exile as heralding the dawn of a new age for Judaism. According to the Jewish prophets, Cyrus would champion the cause of the cult of Yahweh, giving back their religion to the subjects of his territories, and the Jews in exile believed that should he defeat Babylon their return to Jerusalem would be guaranteed. They were not disappointed.

> Thus saith the Lord to his anointed, to Cyrus, whose right hand I have holden, to subdue nations before him; and I will loose the loins of kings, to open before him the two-leaved gates; and the gates shall not be shut:
>
> I will go before thee... And I will give thee the treasures of darkness, and hidden riches of secret places...
>
> I form the light, and create darkness; I make peace, and create evil.
>
> I the Lord do all these things.[52]

It is tempting to conclude from the words 'I will go before thee... and I will give thee... hidden riches of secret places' that on their return the exiles, as Cyrus' subjects, would be shown the hiding place of the Ark of the Covenant. The inference from the phrase 'I form the light, and create darkness', however, is clearer. By the end of the Babylonian exile a major change had occurred. The Jews in Babylon who were faithful to Yahweh no longer saw their God as simply supreme above all others. He was now viewed as active in a 'dualist' role of 'light' and 'darkness'.

This concept of dualism had its origins in the teachings not of a Jewish prophet but of an Iranian who lived in neighbouring Persia during the period of the Jewish exile in Babylon from 618 BC to 541 BC. Zarathustra, or to give him the Greek form of his name, Zoroaster, began his prophetic ministry at the age of thirty and, although not himself of Hebrew origin, the influence of his teaching radically changed the religious ideology of the Jewish exiles. A monotheist like the Yahwists, Zoroaster taught that God's creation was based on a concept of two spirits, Ohrmazd, the Spirit of Good, and Ahriman, the Spirit of Evil. These spirits, or common principles emanated from a single source: Ahura Mazda, the Supreme God of Light. Zarathustra proposed that all individual human beings had a right to a freedom of moral choice during their lifetime on earth, a choice between order and chaos, good and evil, light and darkness. This was Yahwism with popular appeal, offering as it did direct participation with the work of God without the necessity for priestly intervention. Deprived of their centre of worship in Jerusalem, it is not surprising that the exiles incorporated the Zarathustran principles into their religion. The acceptance of such dualism by the Jews in Babylon threatened in a new way Mosaic Judaism which the exiles imported back into the heart of Judah. The evolution of Zarathustran philosophy challenged the Temple priesthood as it would make priests, the traditional intermediary between God and man, redundant. Zarathustra also advocated a life beyond death for all men, declaring that resurrection would be preceded by the coming of the Saoshyant, or Saviour at the end of time when the forces of evil would finally be overcome by the forces of good.[53] Zarathustra died a few years before the defeat of the Babylonians by Cyrus and promise of Jewish return to Jerusalem, but the seed of his revolutionary religious ideas had been laid sufficiently deep within Jewish ideology.

In Babylon Zarathustrianism took root and flourished, gradually producing within Yahwism profound divisions and a common expectancy of a Messianic age. However, the possibility of rebuilding the Temple was paramount in the hopes of the faithful and both the Bible and Josephus furnish us with substantial detail of the events surrounding the return of the exiled people of Judah. In 538 BC, immediately following the defeat of the Babylonians at Opis, Cyrus released the Jews from captivity. Although there were less than five thousand exiles from Jerusalem[54] the number of exiles from Judah as a whole was considerably greater. The Jewish people, whilst in captivity, had been allowed to prosper, and we are told that a total of 42,462 people took the road back towards their ancestral homeland.[55]

In anticipation of their arrival Cyrus issued a decree to the governors of neighbouring Syria which, according to Josephus, ran as follows:

> King Cyrus to Sisinnes and Sathrabuzanes, sendeth greeting.
>
> I have given leave to as many of the Jews that dwell in my country as please to return to their own country, and to rebuild their city, and to build the temple of God at Jerusalem, on the same place where it was before. I have also sent my treasurer, Mithridates, and Zorobabel, the governor of the Jews, that they may lay the foundations of the temple, and may build it sixty cubits high, and of the same latitude, making three edifices of polished stones, and one of the wood of the country, and the same order extends to the altar whereon they offer sacrifices to God.[56]

Forty-eight years had elapsed since the destruction of the Temple of Solomon. Men and women who had witnessed the event returned to the Temple Mount to begin the task of rebuilding from the foundations up, as prophesied by Ezekiel and the Book of Isaiah. Initial funding was not a problem. Cyrus generously restored much of the looted treasure back into Jewish hands, and directed taxes from the surrounding area of ancient Judah towards the repair of the Temple.[57] The Temple alone received 'fifty chargers of gold and five hundred of silver; forty Thericlean cups of gold, and five hundred of silver; fifty basons of gold, and five hundred of silver; thirty vessels for pouring [the drink offerings], and three hundred of silver; thirty vials of gold, and two thousand four hundred of silver; with a thousand other large vessels'.[58]

The foundation of the new Temple was planned for 536 BC but the rebuilding was impeded by disagreements between the exiles and the inhabitants of Samaria who feared that any architectural reconstruction in Jerusalem might rekindle a desire for independence, inviting retaliatory warfare back to the region.[59] It was not until 521 BC, eight years after the death of Cyrus and following the death of his successor Cambyses, that the stalemate was broken by the new Persian monarch Darius I. As a reward for loyalty to the Babylonian throne Darius appointed Zerubbabel, a descendant of the royal line of David, as governor of Jerusalem. Plans to rebuild the Temple received a new impetus spurred on by the alleged 'rediscovery' of a copy of Cyrus' original edict in the Persian royal treasury.[60] It appears, however, from further biblical evidence, such as that found in the Book of the prophet Haggai which has been dated to 520 BC, that a different story exists concerning the initial intentions of the exiled Jews. The Book of Haggai is relatively short – only thirty-eight verses – but revealing. Cyrus' suggestion that the Jews should return to their homeland was not received by the Jews in Babylon with unanimous enthusiasm, and the return to Jerusalem was undertaken by only a relatively small number of exiles with the majority preferring to stay. Whilst there is no reason not to believe that a successful attempt was made to reinstate sacrificial offering on the Temple Mount, it is more than likely that the first 'return' was made in insufficient number to effect a rebuilding.

Despite the intervention of Darius, by 520 BC work had still not begun. Jerusalem had suffered a drought which, according to Haggai, had come about because construction of private property in Jerusalem had proceeded apace and the faithful were ignoring their obligation to Yahweh.[61] Haggai's description exposes the reality of the situation in which the exiles found themselves. The offer of an immediate return in 538 BC would only have been taken up by those free from obligations of family and business. In addition, after their emotional arrival and faced by the opposition from the people of Samaria, the initial optimism of the exiles would soon have waned. Since they were small in number, and possibly without a remit from Cyrus, the task of reconstructing the Temple complex would have rapidly appeared impossible to them. Indeed it would have been far easier and simpler to reconstruct their private houses and wait for help.

Haggai tells us that the laying of the foundation stone of reconstruction took place not in 536 BC but on the twenty-fourth day of the sixth month of 520 BC.[62] We are told in the Bible that 'many of the priests and Levites, and chiefs of the fathers, who were ancient men, that had seen the first house, when the foundations were laid before their eyes, wept with a loud voice; and many shouted for joy.'[63]

The task ahead was immense and complicated by the fact that

rather than constructing a new complex, they decided to restore an old and severely damaged site. Also, there was no Hiram Abiff and, although the Bible says that cedar was fetched from Tyre,[64] there was a lack of skilled labour. The realization that the reconstruction would never match the old Temple quickly dawned on the population, whom Haggai attempted to console:

> In the seventh month, in the one and twentieth day of the month, came the word of the Lord by the prophet Haggai, saying,
>
> Speak now to Zerubbabel, the son of Shealtiel, governor of Judah, and to Joshua the son of Josedech, the high priest, and to the residue of the people, saying,
>
> Who is left among you that saw this house in her first glory? And how do ye see it now? Is it not in your eyes in comparison of it as nothing?
>
> Yet now be strong...for I am with you...
>
> According to the word that I covenanted with you when ye came out of Egypt, so my Spirit remaineth among you; fear ye not.[65]

Darius, the new monarch of Babylon, supported the work of the Yahwists. Darius ordered a search of the royal archive to find the original decree in favour of rebuilding issued under Cyrus. When it was found he studied it and drew up one of his own. The contents of his decree were fundamentally similar to that of Cyrus' with the exception of one verse in which Darius declares that the penalty for hindering the Yahwists in their work on the Temple would be severe: 'Also...whosoever shall alter this word, let timber be pulled down from his house, and, being set up, let him be hanged thereon; and let his house be made a dung hill for this.'[66]

Crucifixion, killed by being nailed to the beams of one's own house, much used by the Persians as a form of capital punishment, had made its official religious debut in Jerusalem. Whether or not this extreme penalty was ever invoked at the time is not mentioned in the Bible. What is certain is that after this alarming decree work on the Mount continued unhindered. It took four and a half years to complete the restoration and in March of 516 BC the Temple was finished. It looked much simpler than Solomon's original structure as Zerubbabel's masons lacked the raw materials to embellish the interior. The bronze altar which had once stood outside the main

Temple entrance was probably made of undressed limestone, twenty cubits, or 10.6 metres, square and ten cubits, or 5.3 metres, high.[67] Jachin and Boaz and the Great Sea were not replaced and the Holy of Holies which had once housed the Ark was empty.[68]

HIGH PRIESTS AND SCAPEGOATS

The destruction of the Temple and the Babylonian exile left deep scars in the psyche of the Jerusalem population. The fulfilment of prophetic warning could not be denied and this prophetic 'truth' gave heart to the Yahwists in their fight for monotheism. The city remained without a king which endowed the Temple priesthood with greater power. Persia was concerned primarily with the stability of the region and as long as taxes were paid and military requirements met, Darius looked favourably on the re-building of the Temple Mount in the name of Yahweh.

The Jews in Jerusalem, therefore, faced a religious challenge and the priesthood had a radical proposal. Five centuries earlier Solomon had created a shrine to Yahweh on the Temple Mount, an island of monotheism in a sea of Ba'alistic worship. To the advocates of the new Jerusalem, in the fifth century BC, there no longer existed any challenge for godly supremacy. There was only one God, Yahweh, and as his chosen people, the Israelites could benefit from the observance of his law. The way was open for Yahweh's people to establish a Jewish theocratic state within the realm of the Persian Empire, fully able, through the daily guidance of the codes of Mosaic Law, to fulfil their covenant with God. For the priesthood this was an ambitious gamble: the more the concept of self-improvement was taken to heart, the more the functional importance of the priest, and in consequence the Temple, would diminish. But the priesthood had an insurance policy. At the heart of Yahwism lay the ritual of sacrifice and far from becoming diminished, sacrificial offerings at the Temple increased. Moreover, the immediate decades following the rebuilding of the Temple saw an upsurge in the compilation and updating of existing religious texts and the institution of new festivals which placed the priesthood at the pinnacle of national existence. A new ritual for the Day of Atonement, or Yom Kippur, was created.

The Day of Atonement was originally a day of individual repentance, celebrated by fasting, observing periods of rest required under the laws governing the sabbath and making sin offerings fit for feast days in the religious calendar.[69] Under the High Priesthood it was given a new significance and became a communal Day of Atonement, or Yom Kippur, in memory of the destruction of King Solomon's Temple in 586 BC. In this new ritual a bullock was sacrificed in the name of the High Priest and the priesthood, and the burnt offering of a ram was placed on the altar before the Holy of Holies in the name of the people. Two live goats were then chosen. Lots were cast and one goat was killed and prepared as a further sacrificial offering to Yahweh. The High Priest placed both his hands on the head of the remaining animal, transferring into it all the sins of the people. After this part of the ceremony was over, the goat was taken away from the Temple Mount, out of Jerusalem and released into the wilderness. To prevent the faithful from breaking the laws of the sabbath which prohibited the faithful from travelling more than a certain distance in one day a series of manned booths were set up along the route to the wilderness. When the scapegoat reached each station, scarves were waved to signal its progress to the Temple priesthood. Once the goat was at its final destination,[70] the priest in charge of the goat divided a thread of crimson. A description of this is given in the *Yoma*, a tractate specifically intended for the Day of Atonement found within the *Mishnah*:[71] 'What did he [the priest] do?...half of it he tied to the rock, and half he tied between its horns, and he pushed it backwards; and it went rolling down, and it was dashed to pieces before it reached half-way down the hill.'[72] If the thread of crimson which was tied to the rock turned white on the death of the goat, the person leading the goat would be assured that the sacrifice had worked in the way Isaiah prophesied: 'Though your sins be scarlet, they shall be as white as snow.'[73]

The role of the 'scapegoat' is common to ancient societies. Still randomly practised until fairly recent times within tribes in Africa, America and the Indian subcontinent, human scapegoating in 'civilized' societies of Mediterranean classical antiquity was already well established by the sixth century BC. In Massilia, a colony of ancient Greece, a volunteer of the lower classes would be maintained at public expense 'on choice and pure food' for a whole year. When the year was up, the 'scapegoat' would be paraded through the streets dressed in sacred garments before being taken outside the city walls. Here he was either released into the wilds, like the scapegoat of Jerusalem, or stoned to death.[74] The city of Athens which, like Jerusalem, was built around a sacred Temple mountain, ritually killed a man and a woman every year in May during the festival of Thargelia in order to exorcize the nation of the burden of their sins and misfortune and, by thus appeasing the gods, avert the threat of famine and pestilence for the coming year.[75] The Jerusalem ritual of scapegoating, performed by the monotheist Yahwists, had strong links with polytheistic culture and despite the re-establishment of Mosaic Law, the reality of Ba'alism – the worship of strange gods and the threat of unlawful sacrifice – had not fully departed the city of Jerusalem and the Yahwists still felt threatened. The God of Israel speaks through his prophet Isaiah:

> I said, Behold me, behold me, unto a nation which was not called by my name.
>
> I have spread out my hands all the day to a rebellious people...
>
> A people that provoketh me to anger continually to my face; that sacrificeth in gardens, and burneth incense upon altars of brick;
>
> Which remain among the graves, and lodge in the monuments; which eat swine's flesh, and broth of abominable things in their vessels...
>
> Behold it is written before me; I will not keep silence, but will recompense, even recompense into their bosom,
>
> Your iniquities, and the iniquities of your fathers together, saith the Lord, which have burned incense upon the mountains, and blasphemed me upon the hills: therefore will I measure their former work into their bosom...
>
> But ye are they that forsake the Lord, that forget my holy mountain...
>
> Therefore will I number you to the sword, and ye shall all bow down to the slaughter.[76]

While Jewish monotheism continued to struggle against the legacy of inbred ancient pantheistic ritual, in-fighting still existed within the cult of Yahweh. The priesthood endeavoured to establish their rule over the state but many people worried about not having a king and believed that a new king, a 'Messiah', or 'anointed one' from the line of David would soon emerge. But the prospect of accommodating a Davidic king into the carefully established framework of the new Jerusalem represented only half of the challenge facing the priesthood. The Davidic kings of the past had signally failed to protect the integrity of the Mosaic Law, the priesthood and the Temple, and the religious hierarchy were unwilling to back the reinstatement of a monarchy. There were also practical problems to contend with which affected everyone's security. Despite repairs to the Temple under Zerubbabel, the walls of the city and the Temple Mount complex were largely unrepaired, which meant that Jerusalem was defenceless. But some seventy years after the restoration of the Temple, in the middle of the fifth century BC, one man took specific action to remedy the situation.

NEHEMIAH AND THE WALLS OF JERUSALEM

Nehemiah was born into a Jewish family who came from Jerusalem and after being exiled stayed abroad in Babylon. In the year 445 BC he was employed at the court of Artaxerxes I, the King of Persia,[77] as a eunuch. This allowed him access to the royal harem. He was also appointed cup bearer to the Persian monarch which gave him direct access to King Artaxerxes. Reports of the conditions in Jerusalem reached the court, and Nehemiah found it hard to conceal his feelings of grief and concern for his ancestral home. Artaxerxes, recognizing the demoralized state of his servant, quizzed Nehemiah on the cause of his unhappiness upon which Nehemiah begged leave to undertake a mission of restoration, a request to which the King gladly obliged. Thus, in the year 444 BC, accompanied by a detachment of king's horse, Nehemiah returned to Jerusalem and, entering through the broken gates, he rode straight into difficulty.

Artaxerxes had armed Nehemiah with a letter giving him full licence to raise the necessary men and materials to restore the city walls, but by the third day of his arrival Nehemiah's plans met with considerable resistance. Not wishing to draw attention to himself he surveyed the outside of Jerusalem at night, mounted on horseback and alone,[78] at a time when his detractors would hopefully be asleep. 'And I went out by night, by the gate of the valley, even before the dragon-well,[79] and to the dung-port, and viewed the walls of Jerusalem, which were broken down, and the gates thereof were consumed by fire.'[80]

Although it is difficult to match all the places mentioned by Nehemiah to modern-day archaeological sites, it is probable that Nehemiah exited to the south-west and passed around the walls of the Davidic city in an anti-clockwise motion. The 'king's pool' is the present-day Pool of Siloam, constructed under King Hezekiah in the eighth century BC.[81] The Siloam lies on the southern tip of the eastern ridge of the City of David, and from here Nehemiah found his way barred by rubble. Faced with the prospect of picking his way over it or turning back with his reconnaissance incomplete, Nehemiah abandoned the idea of following a path along the base of the city wall and went down the slope into the Kidron valley or the *brook*,[82] the name by which it was then known and by which it was still referred to even up to the nineteenth century.[83] Here his going would have been easier and his view of the walls under moonlight clearer. By this route, Nehemiah would have progressed north, parallel to the eastern side of the City of David, heading towards the south-eastern corner of the Temple Mount. From the junction of the Hinnom and the Kidron, Nehemiah would have had a view of the entire eastern wall of the City of David, including its junction with the walls of the Temple Mount platform.

The task on which Nehemiah had set his heart was daunting and when he discussed the plan with the inhabitants of Jerusalem he stirred up deep-rooted fears. In the years since the Jews returned from exile the priesthood had gradually established themselves at the religious helm of Jerusalem and the arrival of Nehemiah was perceived by many Jews as menacing to the status quo. The rebuilding of the city walls could be construed by Jerusalem's neighbours as an attempted refortification and a threat to the established peace of the region which would put Jerusalem at risk.

In addition to this concern, the people of Samaria, and their fellow Jews who had remained in Judah, posed a threat to the lawful re-establishment of Yahwism in Jerusalem. This was because many of them had married non-Jewish settlers, amongst whom it was feared Ba'alism was still very much alive. The historical precedents of the Samaritans in particular were a constant source of worry. As Jews, they had access to the Temple Mount and the possibility of another 'Samaritan' from the old Kingdom of Israel – such as 'Athaliah – gaining control of the Temple was too dreadful for the members of the new Babylonian-influenced orthodoxy to contemplate. In this charged atmosphere, Nehemiah began work on the restoration. It took just fifty-two days for him to complete his task.[84] Each gate and section was repaired by a specific group including priests and Levites of the Temple as well as merchants and goldsmiths of the city.[85] Within the ranks of those who laboured, the atmosphere was tense. They expected to be attacked and each worker had 'his sword girded by his side'.[86] Nehemiah describes the non-stop nature of the restoration: 'So we laboured in the work...from the rising of the morning till the stars appeared ...neither I, nor my brethren, nor my servants, nor the men of the guard which followed me, none of us put off our clothes, saving that everyone put them off for washing.'[87]

With the walls secure, the city and its Temple was defendable for the first time since the destruction of 586 BC and the second half of Nehemiah's plan – the tightening of religious orthodoxy – ready to put into effect. At this stage, Nehemiah compiled a census, listing the Jews who had returned from Babylon with Zerubbabel, and their descendants.[88] For those whose families had stayed in Judah throughout the period of the exile and intermarried, exclusion from the list was eventually put to a sinister use.

After a brief visit to the court of the Persian king in 432 BC, Nehemiah returned to Jerusalem armed with new civil powers. The commitment he had applied to the rebuilding of Jerusalem's walls met with the approval of his Persian masters and his efforts were now directed towards providing political support for the religious orthodoxy so favoured by the Babylonian Jewry. In his absence, the struggle between the Yahwists and those Jews more disposed to ancient Ba'alistic ritual had resurfaced. Following a ceremony to celebrate the completion of the city walls, the Law of Moses had been openly read to the people congregated on the Temple Mount, during the course of which reference was made to the thorny issue of intermarriage. The potential for damaging the visionary purity of Judaism was made clear. The Ammonite and the Moabite 'should not come into the congregation of God forever' because 'they met not the children of Israel with bread and water, but hired Ba'alam against them'.[89]

To try to lessen the tension Nehemiah decided to strengthen the power of the Temple priesthood. Under ancient Law every Jew was obliged to render unto the priests and Levites a tithe – a tenth of annual agricultural produce – to assist in the maintenance of the Temple.[90] Nehemiah demanded that this practice, which had fallen into disuse, be restored.[91] He also carefully noted the movement of agricultural produce and other merchandise into the city on the sabbath, such as wine, grapes and figs from the surrounding countryside, and fish sold by merchants from Tyre.[92] He forbade such practices which were prohibited by the laws of the sabbath. He also admonished any Jew who had intermarried and he went out into the streets of Jerusalem to confront, and in some cases physically assault, any fellow Jew he thought culpable of such an offence. The legacy of Solomon's wives had not been forgotten, as this description of Nehemiah's angry progress, confirms:

> And I contended with them, and cursed them, and smote certain of them, and plucked off their hair, and made them swear by God, saying, Ye shall not give your daughters unto their sons, nor take their daughters unto your sons, or for yourselves.
>
> Did not Solomon king of Israel sin by these things? Yet among many nations there was no king like him, who was beloved of his God, and God made him king over all Israel: nevertheless, even him did outlandish women cause to sin.[93]

At this point Nehemiah, his duty done, disappears from the Bible. His final words, however, were reserved for the Levites and the priests of the Temple. He claims to have 'cleansed them from all strangers' and appointed 'everyone to his business'[94] on the Temple

Mount. Within less than two generations the city went through another religious upheaval.

In approximately 397 BC[95] the city of Jerusalem received the visit of a Jew who had been born in Babylonian exile and was keen to continue the work undertaken by Nehemiah to restore the city walls and to reinstate the religious and moral purity of Jerusalem. Ezra was a priest and a 'scribe of the Law of the God of heaven',[96] and his outlook was simple. The Temple Mount, the heart of the new religious state, had to be cleansed of the scourge of all Ba'alistic influences. Unlike Nehemiah who had travelled with a small military escort, Ezra arrived in Jerusalem with a group of fellow Jews from the area of Babylon who, despite their civilian status, provided him with moral if not military support for his mission. Ezra came bearing precious gifts. Before he left Babylon Artaxerxes II, King of Persia, gave Ezra 'all the silver and gold' that could be found in Babylon which was to be presented to the Temple on the Mount – a gift from Persia to the God of Israel.[97]

The situation in Jerusalem was worse than Ezra had imagined.[98] Distraught at the apparent lack of religious discipline amongst his resident fellow Jews, he set about improving the situation. Artaxerxes had invested him with considerable power to appoint magistrates and judges in order to enforce the Law of Moses. Ezra could impose the penalties of death, banishment, confiscation of goods or imprisonment should anyone stand in his way.[99] He announced that all Jews of the exile should attend a meeting at the Temple Mount. They were given three days to comply and if they failed to do so their land would be confiscated and they could even face expulsion from the religious congregation.

It was raining on the day Ezra addressed the people of the city who stood without cover in the Temple Courtyard. Ezra demanded that they confess to the 'Lord God' of their fathers and separate themselves immediately 'from the people of the land, [Samaritans and Jews of Judah who had intermarried with them] and from the strange wives'.[100] The congregation complained and played for time telling Ezra that they could not possibly stay any longer on the Mount in such bad weather. They also felt that the segregation he was proposing could not be achieved in such a short space of time since there were many people who had 'transgressed in this thing' – or intermarried.[101] With the combination of inclement weather and logistics making an immediate settlement impractical, a compromise was struck and ten days later[102] a process of registration was begun. Ezra sat at the head of his chosen group of inquisitors and, aided by the census taken thirty-five years previously by Nehemiah, received formal submissions of guilt from all 'transgressors'[103] who promised to banish their 'strange' wives from Jerusalem.

The work of Ezra altered the course of history on the Temple Mount. The concept of a theocratic state based around the Temple in Jerusalem was, after a period of instability lasting for well over a century and a half, finally implemented. People's lives now revolved far more around religion and the sacrificial rituals dedicated to Yahweh. With Yahweh the only form of recognized religious truth, the Goyim, or Gentile neighbours already forbidden to marry the Jews of Jerusalem, were – because of the rigidly observed laws of purity – excluded from the Temple Mount. However, with the successful establishment of monotheistic worship came a new danger. The Temple sacrifices generated an immense annual wealth for the priesthood which created constant rivalry for power, centred on the Mount. Whilst the Persians dominated the region of Judah the situation in Jerusalem remained relatively stable, but a new force was in the ascendant centred around the military genius of one man, which would bring Jewish religious factions into conflict with each other.

HELLENISM VERSUS ONE GOD

In the autumn of 333 BC Alexander of Macedon defeated Darius III, King of Persia, at the battle of Issus. Although Issus lay more than five hundred kilometres north of Jerusalem,[104] the outcome of the battle brought profound changes to Jerusalem and the Temple Mount. Unlike Persia with its principles of Zarathustran monotheism, Greek society had evolved around an elaborate tradition of pagan ritual. Following Alexander's success in battle, the region of ancient Judah fell under Greek dominance, and Jerusalem and the

Temple faced a fresh challenge to the hard-won supremacy of the Yahwistic monotheistic priestly tradition. The control that the Temple priesthood had over everyday life contrasted strongly with the fabric of Greek society. Hellenism advocated civil control of state policy and, although religious rites played a major role within society, Greek politics were designed to operate free of interference from religion. To those Jews who resented the power of the Jerusalem priesthood, Hellenism seemed an attractive alternative. To the priesthood, however, and to the more orthodox members of Jewish society who upheld the Mosaic Law, the new influence was perceived as a potential menace.

The death of Alexander the Great in 323 BC sparked an immediate rivalry between his generals for the succession to his empire. This power struggle rapidly deteriorated into a full-scale conflict between the Greek-controlled regions of Asia and Mesopotamia, which encompassed ancient Babylon and Egypt. History was repeating itself. Jerusalem, lying to the immediate south of the fertile plains – and battleground – of the ancient Kingdom of Israel, stood perilously close to the passage of invasion and counter-invasion between Egypt and Syria. But despite such regional instability, its overall influence on the daily life of Jerusalem and its Temple Mount was minor. Pilgrimage to the Mount continued and the ritual of sacrifice at the Temple was unaffected.

After twenty years the Egyptian monarchic dynasty founded under Ptolemy I gained a more lasting supremacy over the region and brought a relative calm to the Holy City. The Ptolemaic Kingdom of Egypt was noted for its religious tolerance and the High Priests of the Temple Mount of Jerusalem were left to their own devices.[105] But Hellenistic ways were keenly felt, leading to deep divisions within the established religious state. The internal Jewish political situation was already complicated with the High Priesthood anxious to maintain their influence over their own people.

At some point during the early Ptolemaic rule the Samaritans separated from the Jerusalem community and founded their own religious sanctuary at Mount Gerizim, fifty kilometres north of Jerusalem in Samaria, the territorial heart of the ancient Kingdom of Israel. This act of schism, whether freely chosen by a Samaritan community which found itself constantly on the fringes of the new religious order or actively enforced by an increasingly intransigent Orthodox community wedded to the legacy of Ezra's separationist policy,[106] broke the final ties which had existed between the people of Israel and Judah since unification of the Israelite monarchies under King David seven hundred years previously.

The Bible had been a useful tool to the advocates of separatism. It is generally recognized by biblical scholars that the Books of Chronicles and the final version of the Books of Ezra and Nehemiah were completed during this period of Ptolemaic rule.[107] Their content must have provided formidable support to the theocracy of the Temple priesthood, and the bias of these writings in favour of the Jerusalem hierarchy when combined with the departure of the Samaritans concluded the policy of religious exclusivity which Ezra had first openly advocated in 397 BC.

Despite the religious success of Orthodox Judaism, Jerusalem and Judah were still vulnerable to the political and military ambitions of their neighbours. Between the years 219 to 200 BC the Greeks of the Mesopotamian region, led by Antiochus III of the Seleucid dynasty, attacked Palestine from the east. Antiochus' challenge to the Ptolemaic dynasty was initially seen by the more conservative elements of Jewish society in Jerusalem as an opportunity to stem the influences of Hellenism and was therefore regarded as favourable to the city, although the trust placed by the Jews in the Seleucid alliance was proved ill founded. After almost twenty years of conflict between Ptolemaic Egypt and the Seleucid forces during which Jerusalem was repeatedly attacked, the city in the spring of 199 BC fell under Seleucid control.[108]

Antiochus III was magnanimous in his victory and Josephus records that he issued several edicts to strengthen the Jewish Orthodox position.[109] Backed by their new ruler but still facing some fierce internal dissension despite the absence of the Samaritans, the Temple priesthood continued in their efforts to hamper the seductive influences of Hellenism. Greek domination of the Middle East gave rise to a Jewish diaspora throughout the Mediterranean, and although the accession of Ptolemy I resulted in a forced deportation of Jews from Judah, voluntary Jewish migration and colonization continued into the Seleucid era with Alexandria becoming a centre of commerce and learning. These Jewish communities even when living away from Jerusalem remained loyal to the concept of the Holy City as the heart of their faith, but those who stayed in Jerusalem still seemed tempted by Greek influence. Marooned in what they perceived as a widening ocean of religious impurity, the High Priesthood gradually but firmly tightened the laws governing the Temple Mount. Strictures on the recognized purity of sacrificial animals were increased and a higher degree of ritual ablution became compulsory for all Jewish males who wished to enter the Inner Court of the Temple. The Inner Court became forbidden territory for any 'impure' Jews, every Gentile and all women, regardless of their religious background and standing. The all-male priesthood of Jerusalem successfully separated the ritualistic centre of their religion from contact with the female sex. Such a separationist move figured high on the Orthodox Jewish agenda, especially when faced by the reality of female involvement in Greek religious ritual. The prospect of Hellenic priestesses in the city of Jerusalem would have resurrected haunting memories of Ba'alism.

The tightening of religious law led to a further development which had unforeseen ramifications in twentieth-century Jewish history. It was during the second century BC that the Asidaeoi or Hasidim, a religious party dedicated to the rigorous upholding of the Mosaic Law, was established. The Hebrew noun from which the word Hasidim derives signifies both love towards God and fidelity towards the Covenant of Law, once enshrined in the lost Ark.[110] The Hasidim – the 'Pious' or 'Devout' ones – continued the work started by Ezra several generations previously and, in the physical absence of the Ark of the Covenant, the word of Yahweh, newly embellished by Books of the Old Testament such as the Chronicles, Ezra and Nehemiah, became more important within this exclusive grouping. The endeavours of the Hasidim strengthened the power of the High Priesthood, but did little to mend the existing division between those people in Jerusalem who wished for a more liberal society, based on Hellenistic ideals, and those who, like the Hasidim, wished for a totally theocratic society.

Since the rebuilding of the Temple under Nehemiah, the priesthood of the Temple, in the absence of a king, represented the power
within the city hierarchy and these priestly families proved not to be
immune to the forces of change. Monotheistic Judaism was facing a
deepening crisis, partly because of the influences of Greek religion
and politics, but mainly because it was struggling to define and hang
onto its own identity. Mosaic Law was on collision course with
Hellenism. Sanctity stood against liberalism, and the contrast could
not be greater. Whilst Hellenism continued to expand its horizons,
promoting a varied and growing path of free choice to the individual, Orthodox Jews were so strict that even the word Yahweh could
only be pronounced once a year by the High Priest on Yom
Kippur.[111] The contrast in lifestyle between the Hasidim and the
Hellenizers was great and in the confines of the Holy City the situation was precarious. It would take little to turn internal division into
a major crisis and it was not long before just such an occurrence
took place.

Antiochus III, anxious to underline his support of the Temple,
granted money to the Jews of Jerusalem in aid of Temple sacrifice
and withheld the imposition of tax on cedar wood imported from
the Lebanon, used in repairs.[112] However, the motives of the
Seleucid king may not have been as reverent to the Jewish faith as
Josephus suggests. Control of the region required a standing army.
Soldiers generally demanded payment in hard currency and the
cost of this was enough to deplete the finances of any kingdom. As
long as Mosaic sacrifice was performed at the Temple Mount, the
coffers of the Temple were regularly replenished and it was hard
cash, or rather the Seleucid need of it to finance their army, which
ultimately sparked an explosion of violence and bloodshed.

In the spring of 187 BC, Antiochus III was killed in battle. His son,
Seleuchus IV, subsequently ruled the Seleucid Empire for twelve
years, during which time he sent his chief minister Heliodorus to
investigate claims that moneys unrelated to sacrificial payment
were being hoarded in the Temple. The Second Book of Maccabees
recounts that Heliodorus, when he attempted to enter and seize the
due tribute, was confronted by a 'great apparition' which put an
immediate end to his sacrilege, although it is more likely that the

contrivance of an ambush, giving Heliodorus a fright, was to blame.[113] When asked by Seleuchus who should be sent to accomplish the task of retrieving the money, Heliodorus advised the dispatch of 'any conspirator against the state' as the King would receive him back well scourged. There was, Heliodorus concluded, the 'power of God' on the Temple Mount.[114] These events dissuaded Seleuchus from plundering Temple wealth and the treasury remained inviolate. However, there was little honour amongst thieves. In 175 BC Heliodorus murdered his king and Seleuchus' brother, Antiochus IV, succeeded to the throne.

By all accounts Antiochus was impulsive and lavishly generous. An ardent champion of Hellenism, his mode of living left him constantly short of money. Various Hellenizing factions in Jerusalem saw their chance to bribe their way into the office of the High Priesthood by offering Antiochus greater tribute than was his normal due from the Temple. By this method Onias, the hereditary High Priest, was removed from office and, much to the dismay of the Hasidim, Jeshua, a Jew who had assumed the Greek name of Jason, seized control. Jerusalem was finally exposed to the reality of the Hellenic world. Under Jason's direction a gymnasium was built in the city and youthful elements of the Jewish secular population adopted Greek fashion and manners. Even young members of the Temple priesthood were lured to the game of the discus which took place in the Tyropoeon or Kidron valleys.[115] The opinion of the pious, amongst them many from the lower, underprivileged classes, reached new levels of disgust, but worse was still to come. Competition for the High Priesthood degenerated into a bidding war for Seleucid favour, backed by internal armed conflict. In 170 BC false reports reached Palestine that Antiochus IV had died campaigning against Egypt. Jason had temporarily lost Seleucid backing – and thereby the power of the High Priesthood – to Menelaus, a fellow priest who through bribery engineered the removal of Jason so that he could take his place. Jason had taken refuge across the Jordan river. When news of Antiochus' death reached him Jason seized the opportunity to regain his position as High Priest and successfully attacked Jerusalem with a thousand armed men, killing many fellow Jews who were loyal adherents of Seleucid power. He reclaimed control of the Mount by force of arms, but his troubles were far from over. The intelligence surrounding the fate of Antiochus was correct. When he heard of the struggle for control of the Temple, Antiochus, forced away from Egypt by the Romans, decided to cut short his campaign and, anxious to make it known that rumours of his death were greatly exaggerated, headed for Jerusalem. Determined to reinforce his supremacy by military means, his actions following his arrival in the city opened a new phase of bloodshed on the Mount and fulfilled a prophecy in the Old Testament Book of Daniel.

THE HORN OF THE BEAST

And as I was considering, behold, an he-goat came from the west, on the face of the whole earth, and touched not the ground: and the goat had a notable horn between the eyes.

... the he-goat waxed very great: and when he was strong, the great horn was broken: and for it came up four notable ones, toward the four winds of heaven.

And out of one of them came forth a little horn which waxed exceedingly great...

Yea, he magnified himself even to the prince of the host, and by him the daily sacrifice was taken away, and the place of his sanctuary was cast down.[116]

The Book of Daniel is generally believed to have been written between 168 and 165 BC[117] and describes, in the manner of a seer, the rise of Alexander the Great, and the consequences of the arrival of the 'little horn', Antiochus IV, in Jerusalem.

On his accession, Antiochus IV, true to character, adorned himself with the additional title of Epiphanes, or God-Manifest. His detractors, quick to discern his arrogance, nicknamed him instead Antiochus Epimanes, 'The Maniac'. After the recapture of Jerusalem, Antiochus unleashed his troops on the city and for three days Jewish blood filled the streets and the Temple Mount. Antiochus entered the Temple precincts, pulled down the dedicated offerings of other kings and plundered the Temple and treasury. He left Jerusalem taking with him the golden altar and candlestick of the Temple[118] and ordered that sin-offering sacrifices, held on a daily basis at the Temple, should cease for a period of three and a half years.[119]

In 168 BC Antiochus sent his chief collector of tribute, Apollonius, to Jerusalem. At first feigning friendship, Apollonius soon showed his true intentions and copied the bloody actions of his master Antiochus which had taken place only two years previously. On this occasion, however, the killing and the looting were merely the prelude to a final solution to what the Seleucid dynasty saw as a distinctly Jewish problem: the supremacy of Yahwist monotheism. Antiochus instigated a regime of religious persecution which lacked any vestige of godly concession and seemed to be fuelled by vindictive madness.

Circumcision of newborn males was forbidden, as was observance of the sabbath. Pious Jews were forced to eat pork and the sacrifice of unclean animals as idols was ordered. The purity of the Temple and the Law surrounding the Yahwistic tradition was disastrously compromised. According to Josephus, the Seleucid soldiery may not have been alone in their task of imposed Hellenization. The 'impious and wicked part of the multitude'[120] caused the citizens 'many and sore calamities', leading to a suspicion that elements of 'Hellenized' Jewry may have assisted the troops of Antiochus in their work.[121] But even if this had been the case the collusion of a number of Jews in the destruction of their fellow men was an insignificant factor given the totality of Greek persecution:

> but the best men, and those of the noblest souls, did not regard him…on which account they every day underwent great miseries and bitter torments; for they were whipped with rods, and their bodies were torn to pieces, and were crucified while they were still alive and breathed: they also strangled those women and their sons whom they had circumcised, as the king had appointed, hanging their sons about their necks as they were upon the crosses. And if there were any sacred book of the law found, it was destroyed; and those with whom they were found, miserably perished also.[122]

Anti-semitism had made its debut at the Temple Mount, the supreme sanctuary of Mosaic Law. To crown the opening of this new episode in the history of the Temple, on the fifteenth day of Kislev – December 168 BC – the altar of the burnt offering in the Inner Courtyard of the Temple was replaced by one to Olympian Zeus. Ten days later, sacrifices were begun.

The efforts of Antiochus to expunge Judaic monotheism from the Mount appeared to have been entirely successful. The response of the pious was not, however, passive. Under Jason and Menelaus, the hereditary continuity of the High Priesthood had been broken and their usurpation had established a barrier to future Jewish reunity concerning the Temple. The High Priesthood had signally failed to protect the sanctuary of Yahweh so Jews, loyal to the Yahwistic tradition, took matters into their own hands and rebelled against their Seleucid masters.

JUDAS MACCABAEUS

By the second century BC the Romans were gradually increasing their influence in the Near East and Antiochus had to bow to their demands of withdrawal from Egypt. Beset by internal intrigue and coming under constant pressure from Rome, the region of Palestine entered a period of intense political and military turmoil. The nationalist religious uprising of the Jews which followed the actions of Antiochus took place in the midst of this transition from Greek to Roman dominance. The rebel leader was Judas Maccabaeus. His surname, meaning either 'The Hammerer' or 'The Exterminator', represented an appropriate metaphor for his abilities as a general. Fighting had begun when Judas' father, Mattathias, an elderly priest of the Hashmon family, received orders to consummate a heathen sacrifice in the village of Modein, thirty kilometres north-west of Jerusalem. Mattathias, infused with religious fervour, chose not to submit to Antiochus' demands and taking up his sword he struck out and killed the King's emissary. This act, fuelled by one man's pious outrage, provoked a national uprising. Mattathias charged his five sons with leading the revolt and Judas was given the role of military leader. The revolt from its inception was successful. Judaea became a stage for open warfare between Greeks and Jews. The initial encounter between the Seleucids and the Maccabaean forces ended in victory for Judas and the death of the Seleucid leader, Apollonius. Judas thenceforth carried Apollionius' sword in all his military engagements. In 164 BC Judas, taking advantage of a temporary withdrawal of Greek forces, entered Jerusalem and occupied the Temple complex. Although the Greek forces still retained control of the Akra fortress which stood to the north-east of the Temple Mount, rededication of the Temple in the name of Yahweh was joyfully completed.

Judas' achievement was immense. Jewish religious freedom had been restored and the revolt was a triumph for the pious who had actively assisted in the revolt. The Hasidim also interpreted the reclamation of the Temple site as of prophetic significance. Since the rebuilding of the Temple by Zerubbabel and its reconstitution under Nehemiah and Ezra, the Messiah had been long anticipated, and a new concept of the Redeemer of the Nation was becoming popular.[123] The Messiah would arise from amongst the common people: 'Rejoice greatly, O daughter of Zion; shout, O daughter of Jerusalem; behold, thy King cometh unto thee; he is just, and having salvation; lowly, and riding upon an ass'.[124] This extract from the Book of Zechariah indicates that by 164 BC the religious expectations of the Jerusalem community were ideally suited for the coming of Jesus of Nazareth.

But Jesus' role in Jerusalem would be played out on a very different Temple Mount to that rededicated by Judas Maccabaeus and his faithful followers. By the time of Jesus' birth, the man who had the greatest architectural influence on the history of the Temple Mount had just died. Herod, known to history as the Great, had rebuilt the Temple and in so doing had erased all trace of Solomon's original construction.

THE COMING OF THE ROMANS

The history of the Temple Mount up to the time of Herod is fraught with intricacies brought about by the decline of the Greek Empire, the rise of the power of Rome, and incessant outbreaks of in-fighting which had continued amongst Jewish factions. In April 160 BC Judas Maccabaeus died in battle at the head of a valiant band of eight hundred soldiers after the bulk of his army had deserted in the face of a superior Seleucid force. Judas' brothers had to continue the guerrilla resistance and maintain the nationalist cause. The Hellenistic party in Jerusalem temporarily regained control, and Alkimus, their newly incumbent High Priest in a move to modern-ize ritual, attempted to tear down the dividing wall between the Inner and Outer Courtyards of the Temple. But before he could complete the task he died, a fact which pious Jews interpreted as a sign from God. However, the sacrifice shown by Judas in defence of Jewish independence was not totally in vain. The Greeks, faced with their own internal problems, preferred stability over conflict and Jerusalem began a period during which the High Priesthood once again became a bargaining counter in a game of higher politics. In 142 BC Judas' brother, Simon, was confirmed as High Priest and granted rule over the region. Israel was reunited as a nation under a Hasmonaean kingship and in the cause of religious orthodoxy. The Hasmonaeans extended their dominion over the ancient territories of Judah and Israel and by 76 BC the Hasmonaean Kingdom encom-passed much of the area of Israel once governed by David and Solomon.

But the cost of unity had been high, and human barbarity and bloodshed continued under the Hasmonaeans. In 134 BC John Hyrcanus succeeded to the office of High Priest left vacant by the death of his father Simon who was murdered by his own son-in-law, a champion of Hellenism. During the course of his reign Hyrcanus forcibly extended religious orthodoxy into the country surrounding Jerusalem. In 108 BC he destroyed the Samaritan Temple at Mount Gerizim and laid siege to the city of Samaria. In 107 BC he razed it to the ground, putting an unhappy end to Samaritan religious independence. Hyrcanus' actions were not, however, universally popular amongst the Jews of Jerusalem. Resentment towards the Hasmonaean royal priesthood manifested itself through protest. Civil revolts in the Holy City led to bloody suppression and under John Hyrcanus' son Alexander Janaeus,

Hasmonaean abuse of power grew steadily worse. The attitude towards the Hasmonaeans as saviours of Judaism was changing and Alexander, by reason of his liberal personal behaviour, had become to the pious an object of ridicule and revulsion.

Pelted with lemons during the ceremony of the Feast of Tabernacles – which were normally used for ritual purposes only – Alexander responded by killing approximately six thousand of his fellow Jews. He then erected a wooden palisade around the perimeter of the Inner Courtyard to prevent any further attempt by the Hasidim to demonstrate against him during ceremonies conducted at the Temple.[125] The worst fears of the faithful were now confirmed. The Hasmonaeans, far from being liberators, were imitating the religious trends of the Seleucid Greeks, a fact which had already prompted several members of the Hasmonaean dynasty to make a complete break with tradition. Many Orthodox Jews believed that the Temple was, despite the apparent Jewish 'unity', still polluted as the Hasmonaean High Priesthood, because of the changes to ritual they had introduced, was not legitimate. So, during the early years of the Hasmonaean period they set up a rival Temple at Leontopolis in Egypt under the direction of Onias, the legitimate heir to the High Priesthood.[126] This drastic step indicated the width of the divide which existed between the Jewish factions of Jerusalem concerning the use of the Temple Mount site. For the faithful, correct maintenance of the Temple site was becoming an uphill struggle and the increase in factionalization was hardening attitudes.

Josephus mentions the existence of another pious sect dating from this period whose written legacy provides the modern historian with a clear image of the depth to which theocracy permeated Jerusalem society. The members of this sect were known as the Essenes, from the Greek Essenoi, a name which possibly derives from the Aramaic 'Pious Ones', although this is disputed.[127] The Essenes were a monastic community intent on the written preservation of the Law of Moses and the attainment of salvation through spiritual enlightenment. They maintained a communal presence in Jerusalem until 140 BC[128] when many of them departed along the old Jericho road to establish the Qumran community. This was a monastic settlement at the base of the arid escarpment which formed the junction of the wilderness of Judaea and the north-western shoreline of the Dead Sea. The first cave containing part of the written material now known collectively as the Dead Sea Scrolls was discovered in 1947, since which a total of 813 documents have been officially retrieved from eleven caves. The attraction to scholars of written material dating to the historical period immediately preceding the birth of Christ has led to competition and secrecy surrounding their dating and interpretation. It is rumoured that many other locations have been plundered and that scrolls found there now reside in private collections. Despite claims that they may be a part of the library of the Herodian Temple destroyed by the Romans in AD 70, the scroll material is generally attributed to the Essenes of Qumran, and recent studies of their contents continue to demonstrate how deeply the tenets of Persian Zarathustrianism, brought back to Jerusalem by the Jews who had returned from the Babylonian exile, influenced the thinking of Jewish orthodoxy. The Essenes lived under the direction of a community rule. The simplicity of their life and their dedication towards preserving the written word of God means that they can be correctly recognized as the historical prototype for Christian monasticism. Conditions were harsh. Fresh water at Qumran was scarce and had to be carefully conserved. The intense heat of the summer – regularly above 40 degrees centigrade – made daily life a question of basic survival. In stark contrast Jerusalem, barely thirty kilometres to the west, offered a much more comfortable standard of living.

Roman rule initiated the most splendid architectural era in the Temple's history, but it was short lived, ending in a destruction of the Temple Mount area which overshadowed even the terrible events of the Babylonian invasion of 586 BC. By 65 BC the Seleucid Empire was in terminal decline and the Romans, who had successfully invaded their Syrian territory, set their sights southward on Jerusalem. The expansionist policies of Rome coincided with problems within the Hasmonaean dynasty of Jerusalem. Alexander Janaeus died in 76 BC and the death of his wife and chosen successor Salome in 67 BC left the kingship and High Priesthood in the hands of her two sons Hyrcanus II and Aristobulus II. A bloody conflict broke out between the two who both appealed for outside help in support of their respective claims to the throne. Whoever held Mount Moriah would have an immediate advantage in any power struggle. During the early Hasmonaean period the city of Jerusalem had undergone considerable expansion to the west of the Moriah ridge, the area which held the Temple and the City of David. The walled area of the Temple complex represented an attractive bastion to any commander. It could be easily defended, it was the symbolic heart of the nation and it possessed in its many underground cisterns that most essential of siege commodities: water. Aristobulus seized his opportunity and destroyed the bridge connecting the Mount with the city to the west. Hyrcanus, unable to dislodge his brother by his own means, begged Antipater, governor of Idumea, the desert region to the east of Jerusalem, and then Pompey, whose Roman legions lay to the north, to assist him. Pompey obliged, and marched on the city. After three months of siege, in 63 BC, Pompey's legionnaires broke into the Temple complex from the northern side, its most vulnerable point. The Temple Mount became a scene of mass human slaughter.

When the battle ended and the carnage had ceased, Pompey walked through the scene of his victory and entered the Temple. His action was a diplomatic disaster. Despite the apparent perversity of Jew killing Jew on the Temple Mount, the Temple and the Holy of Holies was in the mind of all Jews sacrosanct. Pompey, an impure Gentile, had entered the sacred reserve of the High Priesthood, the repository of the Ark of the Covenant, on a victory promenade. If Pompey hoped to find the Ark he was disappointed. Josephus, listing the treasures of the Temple viewed by Pompey, makes no mention of it being in the Holy of Holies.[129] The relationship between the Jews of Judaea and the Romans had, because of Pompey's insensitivity, received a severe setback and the future looked grim. Time was running out for the Jews of Israel and the scene of Jew fighting Roman on the Temple Mount was soon to be repeated.

Thanks to Pompey's intervention Hyrcanus was victorious over his brother and gained control of the office of High Priesthood. The Jewish people, despite the presence of new Roman masters, were left to pursue the worship of Yahweh on the Mount. But the

Romans, like the Greeks before them, required a constant supply of hard revenue to maintain their forces in the field and, although Pompey had reportedly left the treasury of the Temple intact, the lure of easy riches proved too much for Crassus, a fellow general. In 54 BC, Crassus, on his way eastwards to wage war against the Parthians of Mesopotamia, changed the course of his march southwards towards Jerusalem.

Josephus tells us that Crassus was helping himself to the coin in the Temple treasury when he was momentarily diverted by a priest named Eleazar. Anxious to avert the catastrophe of a total plunder, Eleazar offered Crassus a deal fixed by oath. If Crassus left the coin intact, Eleazar would show him the location of a gold ingot hidden within a hollowed-out wooden beam of the Temple. Crassus readily agreed, took the ingot and, unfearful of breaking his oath, took the coin as well.[130] Crassus left Jerusalem with sufficient money to continue his campaign without the worry of having insufficient funds with which to pay his legions.

Prosperous local economies were the key to providing wealth and manpower for the empire. Consequently the Romans, like the Greeks before them, desired stability over plunder and Crassus' action was in this respect untypical. However, the expansion of Republican Rome was founded on the success of her generals and a power struggle for control of the empire inevitably developed amongst them. In 49 BC civil war broke out between Pompey and Julius Ceasar. Antipater, father of Herod the Great, represented the most powerful Jewish force in the region. His influence was matched by his political astuteness and in 48 BC, following Pompey's defeat at Pharsalus, Julius Caesar rewarded his support. Hyrcanus II was reconfirmed as High Priest and Antipater promoted to Prefect of all Judaea. Antipater's sons were appointed as tetrarchs of the region, Herod receiving Galilee and Phasael Jerusalem. However, peace did not endure.

In 40 BC, the Romans suffered a military setback. The Parthians invaded Palestine, captured Jerusalem and installed the Hasmonaean heir, Antigonus, to the High Priesthood. Phasael committed suicide by dashing his own head against a stone and Hyrcanus – the deposed High Priest – was brought, captive and bound, before Antigonus. Ritual Law prevented the officiation of the High Priesthood by any person with a physical blemish and, anxious to ensure that his role of usurper would never be reversed, Antigonus devised a solution. When Hyrcanus fell to his knees in front of him Antigonus chewed off Hyrcanus' ears.[131] Herod escaped to Rome and in 40 BC the senate appointed him King of Judaea. Temporarily a king without a kingdom he soon returned to Palestine and, after having conquered Galilee with the help of Mark Antony, he laid siege to Jerusalem in 37 BC.

Herod's forces were considerable. Backed by Mark Antony, who had appointed the Roman general Sosius to assist in the task, Herod's army of Romans and 'own countrymen'[132] amounted to eleven legions of foot soldiers, six thousand cavalrymen and an indeterminate number of auxiliaries who had been recruited from Syria. Herod was aided by the Jewish calendar. Thirty-seven BC was a Sabbatic Year, which by Law prohibited the normal agricultural activity around Jerusalem.[133] By early summer, despite fierce resistance, the city lay weakened and close to famine, leaving the poorly defended walls vulnerable to a final assault. Twenty chosen men from Herod's army scaled the city wall, followed by Sosius' Roman centurions. Josephus tells us that it took a further fifty-five days of fighting before the defending Jews, who had fought a gradual retreat through the streets of the upper city and the Temple precincts, were defeated.[134] The stubbornness of the Jewish defenders was remarkable and the heat of the summer did nothing to lessen the anger felt by the attacking troops at the resistance they encountered. No mercy was given, and along with male defenders, Jewish women and children, the old and the infirm were indiscriminately butchered in the narrow streets of the city. Once again, the courtyards of the Temple ran with Jewish blood. Herod's army was on the rampage.

But Herod, intent on preserving his religious inheritance, attempted to limit the disaster. By offering hard cash to each victorious soldier, he subdued their desire to loot, and saved the Temple from desecration. This left him one final problem which required a quick resolution. Antigonus, the defeated High Priest, had survived the siege and the ensuing slaughter. He was of royal

Hasmonaean descent and as long as he remained alive he represented a serious threat to Herod's sovereignty. Offering Mark
Antony 'a great deal of money',[135] Herod sealed Antigonus' fate: the
last of the royal Hasmonaean High Priesthood met his end under
the blade of a Roman axe.

KING HEROD AND THE SECOND TEMPLE

History portrays Herod as a despot and megalomaniac who murdered at whim. Herod in his attainment of Judaean kingship was
indeed ruthless. He cleared his path to power with murder, and
once he saw this strategy was successful, he continued to apply it in
order to safeguard his rule even against members of his own family.
But when the archaeological record of his reign is fully considered it
is undeniable that this assessment of his character is incomplete.
Josephus professed shock at Herod's behaviour, but such tactics of
self-preservation in ancient times, as Josephus well knew, were not
unusual. The city that Herod conquered had no established prece-
dence for neighbourly tolerance but it had a glorious past.
Jerusalem was a place well suited to Herod's style of rule.

Although Herod married ten times and was clearly attracted to
women, his admiration and respect was reserved for his father
Antipater and his brother Phasael, both of whom had died prema-
turely at the hands of their enemies. Herod's desire to succeed
where they had failed fuelled his ambition and the guaranteeing of
personal safety often required radical decisions. With age Herod's
cruelty worsened. The onset of illness during the final months of life
prompted him to issue an order for the execution of leading members of the Jewish community. The men, held captive in the
Hippodrome in Jerusalem, were to be shot down with arrows at the
moment of his own death. The lamentation for their loss would,
Herod reasoned, ensure the correct degree of mourning for his own
passing.[136] He was also responsible, allegedly, for ordering the
deaths of many babies.[137] Despite the contrivances of what was by
this stage of life a sick and tortured mind, Herod was in many
respects a man of remarkable vision. He was a strong and

charismatic ruler in a part of the world notorious for rebellion and by the time of his accession to the throne of Judaea the city of Jerusalem, including the Temple Mount, had suffered human brutality unparalleled in the ancient world. But his life has endowed Jerusalem's Temple Mount with a rich heritage and the massive blocks which still support the *haram* are testimony to the immensity of his achievement made possible to a great degree by his political skill.

Herod's first decade of rule was unaffected by internal Roman affairs. But Mark Antony's defeat by Octavian at the battle of Actium in 31 BC left Herod in a difficult and dangerous position. Astute and often ruthless, Herod was held in high esteem by his Roman masters. As the romantic saga of Mark Antony and Cleopatra ran its course, resulting in Mark Antony's suicide, Herod had to make appropriate changes to maintain his position of favour with Rome. He hastened to Rhodes to appeal personally to Octavian who was now emperor. Impressed by Herod's frank style and reassured by his reputation for strong rule, Octavian reconfirmed Herod as King of Judaea. Following the death of Cleopatra in 30 BC, Octavian, now elevated to the title of Augustus, ceded all territories once governed by Cleopatra to Herod's dominion. Jerusalem entered a phase of stability rarely enjoyed by its citizens. The Holy City began to prosper, not least because of the immense building work Herod planned for the Temple Mount.

Josephus describes Herod's prime motive for rebuilding the Temple as the desire to construct a perfect house of God which would stand as an 'everlasting memorial' to himself.[138] But whilst Herod's ego may have guided his actions against those he perceived as enemies, his reverence for and recognition of the Temple Mount site as the physical and spiritual heart of the Jewish nation was the driving force behind his architectural ambition. It remains quite possible that his plans to reconstruct the house of Yahweh represented a genuine attempt not to erect a monument to his own memory but to create a lasting sanctuary of God which through its architecture would break the historic pendulum of violence on the Mount and rid the place once and for all of the spectre of tragedy. His design for a new Temple was of a complexity which, if reconstructed today, would still remain astonishing. He began his work on the Temple Mount thinking on a grand scale and he pushed his materials, his architects and his craftsmen to the very limit of their physical capabilities. In 19 BC with his workforce of ten thousand he began his programme of work.

To attempt a major rebuilding of the Temple, Herod had to begin at the foundations of the existing Mount area. The Solomonic platform had been restored under Zerubbabel in the sixth century BC and this older structure needed to be enlarged in order to accommodate Herod's plan. Herod's Temple would obliterate any surviving architectural evidence of the First Temple but he was scrupulous in his observance of religious law and would have placed the Holy of Holies of his construction over the original site chosen by Solomon. For the Jewish faithful, this location was vital as the site of the Solomonic Holy of Holies had contained the Ark of the Covenant.

Since the Roman period, however, the position of both the First and Second Temples has been uncertain. In AD 70 the Second, Herodian Temple was destroyed and the entire site covered over with rubble. The lower levels of Herod's platform walls are all that can now be seen of his Temple Mount. However, before laying the first block of stone Herod broke the news of his plans by addressing the population of Jerusalem directly and in so doing he left a clue to the solution of the lost location of the Holy of Holies.

A SOLUTION TO THE ENIGMA OF THE STRAIGHT JOINT

Herod's speech began with a reminder to his people of the inadequacies of the initial rebuilding carried out under Zerubbabel. Herod gave an intriguing detail about the size of Zerubbabel's 'rebuilt' Temple: 'Our fathers, indeed, when they were returned from Babylon, [re]built this temple to God Almighty, *yet does it want* sixty cubits of its largeness and altitude; *for so much did that first temple* which Solomon built *exceed this [Zerubbabel's] temple*' (author's italics).[139] This statement appears to refer only to the Temple. However, when the number of cubits mentioned are taken into account a question arises: was Herod referring to the Temple or to the Temple Mount complex as a whole? The number of cubits quoted by Herod holds the answer.

It would have been impossible for the returning exiles when rebuilding under Zerubbabel to reduce the original Solomonic dimensions of the *Temple* by sixty cubits as the original Temple of Solomon, excluding the twenty-cubit porch or entrance, was only sixty cubits in length and twenty in breadth. In addition, the Solomonic Temple, according to the First Book of Kings, had never reached sixty but was only ever thirty cubits in height.[140] It is possible, therefore, that Herod *was* referring in his speech not to the size of Zerubbabel's 'repaired' *Temple* but to the overall external size of the Temple Mount *complex*. When viewed from this perspective, the mathematics throw up a surprise about the Straight Joint.

Warren stated that the cubit of the Herodian era was approximately twenty-one inches,[141] the same 'Egyptian royal' unit of measurement – 53.35 centimetres – which would have been used in the construction of the Ark of the Covenant and Solomon's Temple. Herod's 'sixty cubits of largeness' would thus be 32.01 metres in length. The distance from the south-eastern corner of the existing *haram* platform, northwards to the Straight Joint, is exactly 32.72 metres. This leaves a discrepancy of just *seventy-one centimetres* between Herod's declared extension and the existing distance from the Straight Joint to the corner of the south-eastern angle. Warren also observed that the Straight Joint had continued to the bedrock, suggesting that the Joint had functioned at some stage in history, as the south-eastern corner of the Temple platform.[142] With such a close measurement, a possible new chronological sequence of the development of the Temple Mount platform emerges.

Although unproven by archaeological excavation, this sequence of architectural evolution provides a logical answer to the enigma of the Straight Joint – that it represented the south-eastern angle of the platform when the walls of Jerusalem were rebuilt at the time of Nehemiah. But if so, why has it escaped the notice of so many observers in the past?

Most commentators have concluded that since the construction of the first platform under Solomon the length of the eastern wall

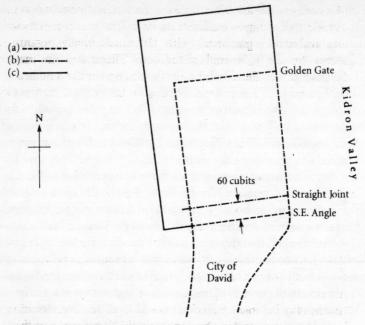

FIGURE 5.1 (a) Construction of the walls of the City of David and the Temple Mount platform under Solomon and his successors to the limit of the present (and Herodian) south eastern corner.
(b) Rebuilding under Zerubbabel and the reduction of the platform size by sixty cubits, under Nehemiah: construction of the Straight Joint.
(c) Construction of the Second Temple Complex under Herod, and re-extension of the platform back to the original Solomonic position by replacing the 'wanting' sixty cubits.

would have always been increased southwards with Herod the Great adding a final extension. But this new interpretation of Herod's speech suggests the opposite – that at some time after the Jews returned from exile, under Nehemiah's direction, the south-eastern limit of the Temple Mount complex was *reduced* from its Solomonic dimension by sixty cubits which Herod several centuries later restored. Herod's speech therefore supplies an answer to the mystery of the Straight Joint – an answer which is further supported when looking at the Straight Joint as might a mason.

Without explosives, the only way to destroy effectively a walled platform would have been to throw the stones downwards on the outside. Following the exilic return, reconstruction of the city walls was undertaken piecemeal, with Nehemiah finally organizing, sector by sector, overall restoration. There was no massive Solomonic workforce to draw on. To reconstruct the southern end of the complex to its original length would have required the complete removal of all fallen stones and the recutting of hundreds, if not thousands, of new blocks, a costly exercise in manpower and money, both of which were wanting. It would have been far simpler, therefore, to reduce the platform from the south by, say, sixty cubits. This would eliminate part of the area of the Royal Palace but since there was no King of Judah there could be no objection. Herod faced no such problem. He had manpower, materials, ambition and money, and the continuation of his speech in which he mentions the sixty-cubit enlargement confirms his determination to revive the days of Solomonic glory: 'I will do my endeavour to correct that imperfection which hath arisen from the necessity of our affairs and the slavery we have been under formerly, and to make a thankful return after the most pious manner to God, for what blessings I have received from him, by giving me this kingdom, and that by rendering his temple as complete as I am able.'[143] If these sixty cubits were replaced under Herod, then the question of the dating of the carved and painted letters found by Warren on their lower courses would also be attributable to the Herodian period. The courses of stone containing the painted and carved letters were accurately drawn by Warren and are unmistakably of Herodian style, a fact which confirms that the existing construction of the south-eastern corner – the sixty-cubit extension from the Straight Joint to the south-eastern corner – definitely took place during the building of the Second Temple.

Another crucial deduction can be made from the sixty-cubit restoration undertaken by Herod southwards from the Straight Joint. If the Herodian south-eastern angle was extended – albeit with a discrepancy of seventy-one centimetres – to match that of the original Solomonic angle, we have for the first time a fixed point on the map of Mount Moriah for the extent of the Temple Mount complex at the time of King Solomon. We can then go one step further. From this position at the south-eastern corner of the Solomonic platform, we can calculate the site of the Holy of Holies, the precise location where, almost three thousand years ago, King Solomon had placed the Ark of the Covenant. In this we are assisted by both Josephus and Warren.

THE RELATIONSHIP BETWEEN THE SOLOMONIC AND HERODIAN TEMPLES AND THE POSITION OF CISTERN V

Josephus tells us that Herod eventually doubled the area of the Temple Mount complex, encompassing 'a piece of land about it [the Temple] with a wall, which land was twice as large as that before enclosed'.[144] Assuming that the enlargement included the sixty cubits southwards from the Straight Joint, what can we deduce from this information when it is applied to the archaeological map of today? When viewed from above ground it is evident that the walls of the *haram* or Temple Mount were constructed on the remains of Herod's Temple Mount enclosure, a fact which was first archaeologically endorsed by Warren. But Warren's knowledge of the underground drainage and water storage systems of the *haram* area led him to suggest a more southerly location for the Solomonic Temple than was acceptable amongst scholars of his time. This view was strongly contested by Lieutenant Conder, who believed that the location of the Holy of Holies was either on or level with the *sakhra* which lay under the Dome of the Rock. Warren's surveys and drawings are staggeringly accurate and detailed. To achieve this precision Warren studied closely every cistern and passage he could find and one in particular attracted his attention. Warren's Royal Engineer predecessor, Charles Wilson, numbered it as Cistern V and had made an accurate survey of its interior.

Of cruciform shape, the main axis of Cistern V pointed south-eastwards, following the natural decline of the Temple Mount bedrock. From this Warren made a logical deduction. This 'cistern', he claimed, represented the original course of drainage for the blood and offal of the First Temple – which meant that the bronze altar of Solomon's Inner Courtyard would have been at the north-eastern extremity of Cistern V. This led Warren to decide that Solomon's Temple stood approximately forty metres to the *south* of the *sakhra*. With these co-ordinates of the Temple and the south-east angle pinpointed on the map, a logical plan of the Solomonic complex emerges.

Archaeological evidence such as that found by Warren and the biblical testimony of Nehemiah suggest that the Davidic city was at some stage joined to the Temple Mount complex. From this we can work out the position of the east- and west-facing walls of the Davidic city as they ran northwards to join the south-eastern and south-western angles of the Solomonic Temple complex. By extending northwards from these junctions we can deduce the line of the eastern and western Solomonic Temple complex wall. This leaves only the position of a northern wall linking these eastern and western walls, to complete the picture.

The Golden Gate lies in the northern sector of the eastern wall of the *haram*. The external image of the present-day gate looks forbidding. The twin doorway has been walled up and a Moslem cemetery placed across the hillside of the Kidron to prevent the entry of a Jewish Messiah.[145] According to at least one Jewish rabbi, Leibel Reznick, the Golden Gate stands on the probable location of a Solomonic entrance to the Mount.[146] Warren's survey sketch of the rock contours of Mount Moriah shows a scarped line of rock running roughly east–west across the Mount, just north of the level of the Golden Gate. If this was indeed the case, could the location of the Golden Gate mark the north-eastern entrance to the Solomonic Temple complex? If we use Warren's original contour sketch of Mount Moriah, which contains his outline of the Herodian Temple complex, we can attempt to draw in the walls of the Solomonic complex. Starting clockwise from the sixty-cubit south-eastern corner of Herod's plan – and possibly that of Solomon's – we can progress westwards to a junction with the northern end of the Davidic city western wall. If we follow this line north, once the scarped rock is reached, we turn eastwards. By running to the south of the scarp – which would in any case have provided a natural line of demarcation – we then join the eastern wall just north of the Golden Gate, completing an enclosed area: the Solomonic Temple Mount complex.

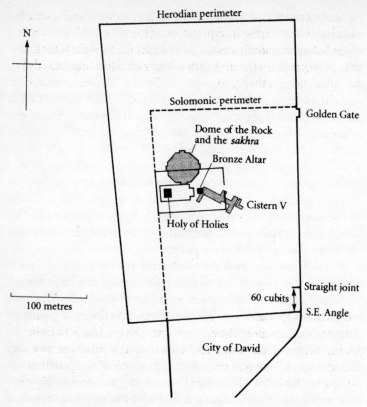

FIGURE 5.2 Position of the Holy of Holies (based on Warren's Cistern V position of the bronze altar) drawn on plan of Solomon's Temple complex perimeter superimposed on the Herodian (Based on a clockwise continuation from the 'sixty-cubit' position of the south-eastern angle, to the junction with the Davidic city western wall, northwards to the line of the natural scarp, and eastwards to a junction with the *haram* wall, just north of the Golden Gate.)

When measurements of the area of the Solomonic complex are calculated by using Charles Wilson's 1:2500 Ordnance Survey map of 1864–5 and compared with the known Herodian area, the result is revelatory. The Solomonic area measures 73,700 square metres – only slightly more than half the 142,500 square metres of Herod's construction.[147] These figures confirm Josephus' assessment that the area of the Mount was doubled under Herod. These measurements also confirm the interpretation of the sixty-cubit restoration of the Solomonic south-east angle and date the Straight Joint to the time of Nehemiah – the mid-fifth century BC. Most importantly for the Jewish faithful they lend weight to Charles Warren's conclusion that the Holy of Holies was situated south of the *sakhra* which allows the establishment of a fixed location for the site of the Holy of Holies.

THE HOUSE OF GOD

Herod was most anxious to restore the Holy of Holies and the Temple to its former glory. He declared to the people that when the old Temple was pulled down a new one would soon be erected in its place. Josephus describes how Herod's trained band of priests took a mere eighteen months to finish the building of the new Temple.[148]

Herod was extremely wary of not upsetting the religious hierarchy in Jerusalem so he would have followed regulations dating from the time of the exilic return. The tractate *Middot* in the Jewish *Mishnah*, compiled and edited in the third century AD, includes a description of the religious practices and regulations set up under Ezra for the rebuilding of the Solomonic Temple destroyed by the Babylonians. Ezra decided that the use of iron on the building blocks of the main altar of the Inner Courtyard would render the stone impure. Iron was used in the manufacture of weapons of war and was prohibited for use on the Inner Temple area on the grounds that it shortened rather than prolonged man's God-given life. It was probable that the same law applied to the rebuilding of the Temple under Herod and in particular to the construction of the main sacrificial altar in front of the Temple entrance. However, any comparison between the restoration attempted under Ezra and the planned new proposal of Herod ended there. If returning exiles had wept with emotion at the sight of Ezra's mediocre restoration of the Solomonic Temple, the Herodian Temple, as described by Josephus, would have completely overwhelmed them.

Herod maintained the basic layout of the Solomonic Temple, with the Holy of Holies separated from the main part of the interior. The height of the Temple was increased to a total of one hundred cubits. Jachin and Boaz were not reconstructed. Instead Herod's craftsmen placed an imitation vine made entirely of gold, the branches of which, laden with fruit, hung down over the entrance 'from a great height'.[149] The doors of the Temple under the vine were 'adorned with embroidered veils, with their flowers of purple and pillars interwoven'.[150] In the Inner Courtyard the original Solomonic bronze altar was replaced with one of stone and was isolated from the Outer Courtyard by a high wall. The sanctity of both the Inner and Outer Courtyards was visually reinforced by signs written in Greek and Latin. Posted at regular intervals, they warned of the dire consequences of intrusion by any ritually impure person from the area of the colonnades into the Courtyards. The penalty for such an act was death.[151] Around the perimeter of the Outer Courtyard, along each side of the platform, Herod's masons constructed a series of cloisters, with those on the southern wall greater in depth and in height than the rest and supported by columns of the Corinthian order.[152] The southern section which departed from the south-east corner of Herod's new platform was named the Royal Portico, further evidence perhaps that the original Solomonic platform containing Solomon's Royal Palace had indeed extended beyond the Straight Joint to this position at the south-eastern angle. Josephus also tells us that Herod had the trophies and spoils taken from 'barbarous nations' fixed to the cloisters, including those which he himself had taken, giving us an indication that although the coin of the treasury had been regularly ransacked over the centuries, some carefully hidden treasure had survived. The greatest relic of the Temple – the Ark – was still missing, and the Holy of Holies, now also known as the House of Atonement,[153] was symbolically empty. The entrance to the Holy of Holies had under Solomon been closed by a pair of highly carved gilt olive wood doors. The entrance to the Holy of Holies in the new Herodian Temple was, according to Josephus' account in *Wars of the Jews*, covered by a 'Babylonian curtain'. The composition and the colours of the curtain reflected the elements of earth, fire and water, the whole 'being an image of the universe'.[154] Other furnishings of the Temple were also faithfully restored including the golden altar and the symbolic candlestick, which had seven branches. All the furnishings of the Temple, from the golden vine and the colourful veils to the golden furniture inside the building itself, reflected cosmic imagery inherited from the Zarathustrans. The Zarathustran concept of the cosmic forces of light and dark, good and evil were fully reflected in the holiest location of Judaism, demonstrating the influences on Jewish monotheism of the Persian religion.

Despite the exilic return of the sixth century BC many Jewish families had remained in Mesopotamia. During the period of Greek domination others had left Judaea to form Jewish communities in the prosperous cities and towns around the Mediterranean. However, Jerusalem was still the epicentre of the Jewish faith and to these families the city stood as the only place of pilgrimage. One such pilgrim, who left us his impressions of the Holy City, was Philo of Alexandria.

The son of a wealthy family, Philo, like many of his Jewish kin who lived outside the confines of Judaea, was influenced by Hellenism and in particular by the philosophy of Plato which advocated the application of geometric concepts to explain the communion between man and creation. Philo saw at the Temple Mount much to reinforce this philosophy, which led him to conclude that the structure of the Temple opened a pathway to the cosmos, enabling communion with God. This kind of belief had deep implications. To the priesthood and the people of Herodian Jerusalem, Herod's 'new' Temple symbolized a 'new' beginning. The despair of the Babylonian destruction was to a great extent alleviated by the magnificence of Herod's construction. Although devoid of the physical link with Yahweh – the relic of the Ark – the Temple of Jerusalem had come of age. It had become an Ark of the Covenant in its own right; to enter and sacrifice at Herod's Temple was to commune directly with God. The Mount had become the Navel of the World, the gateway to the heavenly cosmos.

Herod went to great lengths to restore the glory of Solomon's Temple. Did he follow the concept of creating the perfect building for God, a concept perhaps initiated by Solomon and realized by

Hiram Abiff? Was this – the masonic blueprint for a perfect Temple – the information for which the apprentices had killed Hiram? It is improbable that the apprentices attacked their master in such a deadly fashion simply to acquire promotion and a mere increment in pay. The blueprint for a building of such balanced dimensions was of far greater importance to the apprentices than extra wages as it would have rendered them power as skilled masons. An understanding of mathematics was essential for the transmission of architectural knowledge. Mathematical formulae were, therefore, at the centre of the Hiramic murder. This would explain the legend which for centuries has also surrounded the Solomonic symbol. The 'Seal of Solomon' – the present-day Star of David – is a hexagram from which most mathematical constructions, useful to architects and masons, can be derived.[155]

This concept of a geometric pathway to God, originally set in place on the Temple Mount of Jerusalem, was resurrected in the Middle Ages and became the backbone of European Freemasonry, implemented through the Order of the Knights Templar in the eleventh century AD. The Knights Templar are reputed to have conducted archaeological excavations on the Mount, apparently in search of treasure. There is no record of them finding gold or silver, but like Warren they would have encountered the massive stones of Herod's construction, and this would certainly have made them aware of the level of architectural skill involved in the building of both Herod's and Solomon's Temple. Some of Herod's blocks are so large that even in the twentieth century the method by which they were set in place is still debated.

THE ARCHITECTURAL LEGACY OF THE SECOND, HERODIAN TEMPLE

Josephus in his descriptions of Herod's achievement gives the individual dimensions of the stone blocks used in the building of the 'Temple' as twenty-five cubits long by eight cubits high. He estimates their 'breadth' at 'about' twelve cubits deep.[156] These measurements translate to approximately 13.3 by 4.2 by 6.4 metres.

But, as in the case of Herod's 'sixty cubits', it would seem unlikely that Josephus was referring to the construction of the actual *Temple*. To begin with, it would have been impossible to include any details such as windows and doors in a building one hundred cubits in length which was made out of blocks of twenty-five cubits. It therefore seems probable that he was referring not to the Temple but to the walled platform. Possible confirmation of this surfaced in the 1990s as a result of excavations which had begun in Israel in the immediate aftermath of the Six-Day War.

In June 1967, after the Six-Day War which had resulted in the defeat of Egyptian, Jordanian and Syrian forces, Jerusalem fell under Jewish control for the first time since the destruction of the Second Temple in AD 70. The Religious Orthodox groupings in the city were still a minority and had little political power. They objected to the exposure of ancestral Jewish grave sites but, despite their protestations, there was an overwhelming national desire to reveal archaeologically the biblical past of Israel. A programme of archaeological excavation was set up by the authorities and excavations began close to the western wall at Robinson's Arch, the name given to the remains of the main entrance onto the Mount which dated from the Herodian era. The base levels of Herod's original Temple Mount wall were still intact and the large, easily identifiable blocks of stone continued northwards to the area known in Warren's time as the Wailing Place of the Jews, which today is called the Wailing or Western Wall. As the name suggests, this location was, since the destruction of the Second Temple by Titus in AD 70, a focal point for Jewish prayer and lamentation. The Herodian stonework had become a symbol to the Jewish faithful for the past glory of the Temple of Yahweh.

By the late 1980s Israel's Ministry of Religious Affairs undertook the task of exposing the rest of Herod's western wall which was known to run from the wailing area to the north-western corner of his complex. Digging underground along the outside of the *haram* and directly below Moslem houses of the Old City, archaeologists traced the course of the surviving Herodian masonry. By 1997 they were ready to open up this extraordinary underground site, 'the Western Wall Tunnels'. For reasons of safety and practicality, it was necessary to find an exit from the extended tunnel site. Access was achieved from the north by reopening an ancient aqueduct dating to the Hasmonaean period of rule, which had preceded that of Herod. This channel took them to the northernmost limit of the Herodian western wall and passed within several metres of the present-day precinct of the *haram*. It was the opening of this exit route – the 'Hasmonaean Tunnel' – which sparked the riots of spring 1997. Moslems took to the streets of Jerusalem, objecting to what they perceived as a violation of the status of the *haram* containing the Dome of the Rock and the *sakhra* – the third most Holy Shrine of Islam and an area which, following the Six-Day War, had been left in Moslem hands. Thirty-two Arabs and Israelis were killed in the rioting which followed the inauguration of the site to the public. The question of access to the Western Wall via the 'Hasmonaean Tunnel' has since become a critical issue in the deteriorating relationship between the Moslem and Israeli authorities in Jerusalem. However, deep underground at a point seventy metres north of the Wailing Wall area, the public had their first view of an extraordinary block of stone.

The blocks Warren had recorded in the eastern wall were big, but this one exceeded them all. The western wall block measured 13.7 metres in length and 3.5 metres in height, dimensions which were almost too close to Josephus' account for coincidence. He stated in *Antiquities* that individual stone blocks of 13.3 metres in length and 4.2 metres in height had been used to build the 'Temple'. But if this size of block – perhaps this very stone – had prompted Josephus to make his claim about its length, what of its breadth? Josephus was unsure of the breadth of the blocks he was quoting. He was only an eyewitness to the completed Temple Mount complex and therefore had no simple means of ascertaining this fact, other than perhaps asking a surviving mason who had worked on the Mount at the time of its construction. He estimated that his 13-metre-long blocks of stone had a breadth of 'about' twelve cubits or 6.4 metres.

In AD 1997, Israeli archaeologists faced a similar problem. They couldn't dig openly under the Mount for fear of creating a full-scale Moslem uprising and they certainly couldn't ask a Herodian mason. They therefore brought in the latest technology to find the answer. Using ground-penetrating radar, experts from Haifa University worked out that the 13.3 metre block was between 4.2 and 4.9 metres wide.[157] The weight of this single block of stone has since been calculated at 570 metric tons – more than the weight of three Boeing 747 'Jumbo' Jets.[158] The closeness of the measurements of the block discovered inside the Western Wall Tunnels to Josephus' description suggests that Josephus had possibly measured this stone in person. We know from his own testimony that he was a great scrutinizer. When describing the columns which helped to form the southern cloisters on the Mount, Josephus recorded that it required the efforts of three men with arms extended and hands joined to encompass fully each of its pillars.[159]

It is evident from such comments that Herod's Temple was a source of great pride to Josephus. Despite his adoption of Roman citizenship, Jewish blood ran in his veins, carrying constant memories of the glory of his nation. One particular passage in *Wars of the Jews* suggests that at some time before the destruction of AD 70, he had watched the sun rise from a position on the Temple Mount platform: 'Now the outward face of the temple in its front [facing east] wanted nothing that was likely to surprise either men's minds or their eyes: for it was covered all over with plates of gold of great weight, and, at the first rising of the sun, reflected back a very fiery splendour, and made those who forced themselves to look upon it to turn their eyes away, just as they would have done at the sun's own rays.'[160] Josephus must also have discussed the impression the Temple had made on travellers and pilgrims bound for Jerusalem who, on reaching the hill crests around the city, saw for the first time the work of Herod: 'But this Temple appeared to strangers, when they were at a distance, like a mountain covered with snow; for, as to those parts of it that were not gilt, they were exceeding white.'[161]

The description of parts of the Temple being 'exceeding white' is problematic. The only major extant evidence of Herod's Temple is the massive foundations built from blocks of limestone. The blocks have weathered and stained over the centuries giving their surface a patinated colour varying from off-white to light brown. These colours change dramatically as the sun's rays pass over the stones which still form the base of the *haram* enclosure, reflecting a kaleidoscope of golden light back to the eye of the modern-day observer. But Josephus describes the Temple as looking 'like a mountain covered with snow'. Josephus had been raised in Jerusalem. Born into a family of Hasmonaean descent he was educated at a rabbinical school in the city between AD 49 and 55. Some weathering of Herod's Temple Mount would have taken place by this time so was Josephus referring to a particular part of the Mount, such as for example the cloisters and the façade of the Temple itself?

Archaeological excavation at the base of the southern *haram* wall during the 1990s showed that some blocks had been damaged by fire. The heat had cracked the surface of the stone and some pieces which had fallen to the ground revealed the original, internal, unpatinated colour of the limestone. The natural colour was white, but not an intense white. Had the walls of the platform, therefore, ever been smoothly finished to reflect the light and enhance the natural colour of the stone? Closer inspection showed that Herod's masons had finished the external face of each block of stone placed on the Mount with a dentate chisel. The cutting end of such a chisel would have been beaten out from a length of metal to form a wide, flat head. A series of notches would have then been cut into the leading edge to form a row of teeth – hence the chisel's name. Judging from the small indentations left on the face of the stone, these dentate chisels had twelve teeth. The external face of the walls of the sacred enclosure was not deemed sacrosanct, and thus it is probable that the dentate chisels were made not of bronze, but more durable and efficient iron, an economic necessity when the scale of work on the platform is taken into consideration. When looked at closely, the surviving Herodian blocks of the *haram* wall show the sweeping curves of a cutting action, indicated by separate lines as Herod's masons made their final pass over the face of each block. The overall result produced a surface similar to that of an orange: lightly pitted, it refracted rather than reflected the light of the sun. Such indentations were perfect receptacles for dust, and although the walls of the platform were made of white limestone, it is unlikely that with this finish they would have been 'exceeding so' for long. So had the stone of the

Temple and its cloisters been finished any differently to make it more resistant to the weather and, possibly, the same time, whiter?

In the summer of 1997, work began at the south-east angle of the *haram* to 'tidy up' the area and bulldozers moved in to create flower beds and walkways. A last view of the site turned up a fragment of carved lintel in limestone bearing all the characteristics of the Second Herodian Temple period.[162] Carved from identical fossil-bearing or oolitic limestone utilized in the construction of the Herodian platform wall, its surface was white. The surface of the stone had been finished with a chisel which had a single flat point of exactly two centimetres' width. The result left a patina without indentations, smooth as it if had been polished. When placed in the summer sunshine, it reflected back to the eye an intense white. The fragment had been found directly below the site where the colonnade of the Herodian Temple had once stood, which had a front, according to Josephus, 'all of polished stone, insomuch that its fineness, to such as had not seen it, was incredible, and to such as had seen it, was greatly amazing'[163] – proving once more the accuracy of Josephus' description of the Second Temple.

Herod never saw the Mount in all its finished glory. By 27 AD when the Temple Mount project was finally completed, forty-seven years after work began, Herod the Great had been dead for thirty-one years. His death in 4 BC was shrouded in controversy, violence and mystery. In his final years, Herod suffered from a life-threatening disease.[164] Conflict with his sons and other members of his immediate family had taken their toll on him and his life-long attempt to be recognized as legitimately Jewish by the Jews of Jerusalem had come to nought. In the eyes of the Orthodox Jewry Herod, despite the scale and magnanimity of his work on the Temple Mount, represented all that was wrong with the Roman Empire. Roman influence on traditional Judaism was seen as little better than the Greek influence it had replaced and in many cases elements of both had combined to present a formidable threat to Mosaic tradition. True to his principles of religious observation, Herod's statue did not adorn the Temple of its Courtyards, nor was his portrait displayed on coins of the era. There is no surviving confirmed likeness of Herod.[165] His loyalty to Rome, however, finally caused him to infuriate the Jews of Jerusalem and provoke amongst them a rebellion. Herod, ever anxious to display his loyalty to those who had given him power, had placed a golden eagle, the symbol of Imperial Rome, over the main gate to the Temple.

When it became apparent that Herod was ailing, the young blood of the nation sprang into action. In the middle of the day, in full view, they abseiled down the front of the building and using axes cut the eagle down.[166] Herod's Temple guard apprehended about forty of the perpetrators and brought them before Herod. In their defence the young men claimed that the eagle contravened the Law against the use of graven images. They professed to have no fear of the consequences of their actions; they preferred death over life because 'after life they should enjoy greater happiness.'[167] This zealous concept of self-sacrifice was fully endorsed by Herod. Appealing to the population of Jerusalem, he accused the young men of sacrilege and condemned them, together with their rabbis, Judas and Matthias, to death by burning. Josephus writes that after this episode Herod's illness took a sudden turn for the worse. The King had 'a gentle fever upon him, and an intolerable itching over all the surface of his body, and continual pains in his colon, and dropsical tumours about his feet, and an inflammation of the abdomen' and 'a putrefaction of his privy member'.[168]

Death was certainly on Herod's mind. Having already murdered two of his sons, Alexander and Aristobulus, and their mother Mariamme, Herod turned his attention to Antipater the surviving son of ruling age and, convinced that Antipater was a threat, had him killed. Five days later Herod succumbed to his illness. One modern diagnosis states that Herod died from gangrenous complications brought on by arteriosclerosis. Josephus, who, despite admiring the Herodian Temple, obviously disliked Herod, was more explicit. Herod, Josephus informs us, died slowly and in great pain; with his entrails ulcerated, his breath foul and his putrefacient penis producing worms.[169]

Meanwhile, ten kilometres to the south of Jerusalem and the Temple Mount, a Messiah had been born.

From Jesus to Destruction,

3 BC–AD 70

The final resting place of the most influential man in the architectural history of the Temple Mount of Jerusalem continues to be a mystery. Josephus records a funeral procession to Herod's mausoleum at Herodion, twenty kilometres south of Jerusalem,[1] but the excavation and study of the site have revealed nothing to substantiate this claim. Herodion is a desolate ruin, little frequented by visitors – unlike the town of Bethlehem, ten kilometres to its north, where people flock to see the place where Mary, wife of Joseph, a carpenter, gave birth to Jesus of Nazareth.

JESUS: FROM THE GREEK, 'GOD IS SALVATION'

The millennial anniversary of Christ's birth has placed the traditional calendar method of historical dating under scrutiny. The 'star in the east' mentioned in the Gospels[2] is widely accepted as being the conjunction of Jupiter and Saturn in the constellation of Pisces, which was visible in the skies of the Middle East during the month of December in 7 BC.[3] If this dating is accepted, then at the time of Herod's death, Jesus was three years old. The timing of Jesus' birth could not have been more propitious. Jerusalem, despite having enjoyed relative stability under Herod, was a place of deep religious and social division and a hotbed of Messianic expectation. The new Temple was the focal point of these divisions, a fact which would become apparent in the way it influenced the life, and the death, of Jesus.

The death of Herod ushered in a new wave of bloodshed and

violence on the Temple Mount. Herod left two contradictory wills. His three surviving sons, Antipas, Philip and Archelaus, were forced to travel to Rome to ask the Emperor Augustus which of them should succeed to the throne of Judaea. But before they could leave for Rome, a national uprising broke out. The common people of Jerusalem and Judaea were still enraged at the execution of the young men who had cut the golden eagle from the Temple, and their rabbis, Judas and Matthias, subsequently became martyrs to the cause of Orthodox Jewry. The imminence of Passover brought many Jews into Jerusalem from the surrounding countryside and, as numbers increased, rioting broke out. A group of protesters, described by Josephus as 'the seditious', took control of the Temple and the area of the Inner Courtyard.[4] Archelaus' response was to send a regiment of a thousand men under a captain to restore order. The soldiers, attacked by stones, retreated from the scene, leaving Archelaus with a simple choice: to give up his plans for Rome, and thence the crown, or to evict the protesters by the sword. He chose the latter, and the Temple Mount became once again the scene of mass slaughter.

Archelaus sent his foot soldiers into the Temple complex and surrounded the Mount with cavalry. As the survivors of the slaughter in the complex fled, the cavalry pursued and cut them down. An estimated three thousand perished in the onslaught.[5] Archelaus' decision to set Jew upon Jew quelled the immediate insurrection, but did little to solve what was rapidly becoming a national cause of discontent. The occupying Romans and all those who profited from their rule were fast becoming an object of intense hatred. After Archelaus finally sailed for Rome, Varus, the Syrian legate, reinforced the Roman army in Jerusalem. Varus soon departed the city, leaving behind an extra legion of foot soldiers.

The Temple treasury survived these events intact but, as so many times before, this situation was only temporary. Sabinus, the Syrian procurator, found the lure of easy cash too much to resist. With Herod's heirs away in Rome and Varus in Syria, Sabinus marched to Jerusalem, entered the Temple and searched it for coin. It was Pentecost, the fiftieth day after Passover, and with the attention of the nation already focused on the Temple Mount, Jerusalem erupted into violence at his outrageous actions. Sabinus was besieged on the Temple Mount and surrounded by enraged Jews. He appealed to Varus for help, but Varus procrastinated. To gain an advantage over the Roman legionnaires a number of Jews climbed onto the roofs of the cloisters which ran around the perimeter of the Mount. They loosed arrows and javelins on the Roman troops below, 'destroying', according to Josephus, 'a great many of them'.[6] This advantage however, was not maintained. The Romans set fire to the cloisters and some Jewish fighters, realizing the hopelessness of their own situation, threw themselves into the flames or committed suicide by falling on their swords. Those who descended found the legionnaires waiting for them and were either killed or captured. Having lost control of the Temple perimeter, the Jewish forces immediately decided to recapture the complex, not through frontal assault but by tunnelling under the Herodian walls,[7] a process which would take weeks if not months. Sabinus once again sought Varus' assistance. With the situation in the whole of Judaea rapidly deteriorating, and confronted by the possibility of escalating violence on a massive scale, Varus finally took action. Varus' legions marched on Jerusalem and overcame the rebels. Retribution was swift and bloody; Josephus tells us that two thousand Jews were put to death by crucifixion.[8]

Archelaus and his brothers returned to Jerusalem from Rome without the kingship. The Romans had decided that, given the unrest in the province since their father's death, administration of the region should be divided amongst them. Antipas and Philip were appointed to govern the Galilee and Peraea, and Archelaus was given Judaea. His arrival coincided with some difficult decisions concerning the future of the Holy City. A strong High Priest had become an essential prerequisite if stability was to be preserved and any choice of priest he made would come under attack from opposing factions. Archelaus possessed the ruthlessness of his father but he soon proved incapable of maintaining the confidence either of the Romans or his own people and in AD 6 he was finally deposed. The region, now under Roman prefectship, entered a period of uneasy truce, with the ruling classes of Jerusalem longing for stability, and the common populace, who had borne the brunt of

Archelaus' inept and brutal policies, aggrieved and revengeful. Ensconced on the Temple Mount the religious hierarchy were represented by both sides of this divided society.

The most numerous participants were the Pharisees. Their name derived from the Greek for 'separated ones',[9] and Pharisaic doctrine can be seen as a continuation of the orthodox traditions of the Hasidim or Pious Ones, who first came to prominence during the Hasmonaean dynasty. Pharisaean numbers were drawn from the middle classes of Jerusalem society and they believed themselves to be the upholders of religious righteousness for the good of the common people. But ultimate control on the Mount lay with the Sadducees, named after Zadok, High Priest of King Solomon. The Sadducees had strong political leanings and influential connections, and by supporting the Roman dominance of the Judaean region they reaped the reward of power. By the time of Jesus' birth, they dominated the Sanhedrin, the supreme religious Council of Jerusalem. In AD 6, when Jesus – if he had been born in 7 BC – was in his thirteenth year, the Sanhedrin appointed the Sadducee Annas High Priest of the Temple. After he was deposed nine years later by Valerius Gratus the Roman procurator of Judaea, Annas' son-in-law, Joseph Caiaphas, succeeded him in the High Priesthood. It was under Caiaphas' tenure that the 'Messianic' rumours about Jesus of Nazareth came to the attention of the Sanhedrin.

The Gospels suggest that Jesus' father Joseph settled in Nazareth in order to fulfil the words of the ancient prophets[10] which foretold of a future Nazarene Messiah.[11] Whatever the truth of this statement, Jesus spent most of his childhood in Nazareth, a thriving agricultural town and a place which would have offered constant work to his father. It is probable that Jesus' first visit to the Temple of Jerusalem occurred at the time of his circumcision, when he was brought to the Temple Mount by his parents 'to do for him after the custom of the Law'.[12] His early childhood was one of strict traditional observance to the Law of Moses and as a young man he demonstrated an advanced, if not precocious, degree of religious awareness. When he reached the age of twelve Mary and Joseph took him to Jerusalem to attend the Feast of Passover. When they left the city at the end of the feast, they assumed he was with the other pilgrims. But at the end of the day's march Jesus was nowhere to be seen. After retracing their steps they found their son in the Temple, 'sitting in the midst of the rabbis [teachers], both hearing them, and asking them questions'.[13]

The expectation of a Messianic Coming was rife amongst the population of Judaea. From Josephus alone, we are told that during the national uprising against Sabinus in the immediate aftermath of Herod's death, no fewer than three 'Messiahs' had emerged on the scene. They represented a cross-section of Judaean country society. Judas was the son of a bandit leader, Simon a Herodian slave, and Athronges a shepherd.[14] But their bids for the title of true Messiah were unsuccessful and popular demand went unfulfilled. By the time Jesus began his ministry in Galilee John the Baptist, amongst others, had raised the hopes of the poor and middle classes of Judaea to fever pitch.

The image of the life and work of Jesus reported in the New Testament Gospels is powerful. Jesus is portrayed as a unique phenomenon within Judaea, standing in solitary opposition to the powerful Sanhedrin. But this could not have been strictly accurate. The fact that the Sadducaean-dominated Sandhedrin collaborated with the Romans left them much despised and, as the case of the golden eagle had so amply demonstrated, there were many young men willing to die for the Jewish religion. Jesus did, however, stand out from his contemporaries. His encounter with the rabbis in the Temple is indicative of his own deep interest in the intricacies of Mosaic Law and, if at the age of twelve he had conversed on an equal level with teachers of his day, by the time he was thirty his own reputation as a rabbi was considerable. In addition, his approach to daily living, and the application of religion to it, was revolutionary. Although Jesus conformed to the basic tenets of his ancestral Judaic faith, he advocated the existence of a compassionate God, an attitude which gained him much support from the common people of Galilee and Judaea who felt that Yahweh had been hijacked by the priesthood of Jerusalem.

Jesus spent most of his life in the countryside of Galilee and Judaea and his way of life has strong historical parallels with the Essenes or 'Pious Ones', the group which originated in Jerusalem but broke away from the established Temple worship during the time of the Hasmonaean High Priesthood. It has been suggested that Jesus' parents were affiliated to this sect and that they followed the basic tenets of Mosaic Law, raising their son in the same tradition.[15] When Jesus began his ministry around AD 28, the Essenes at Qumran still had several causes for dissatisfaction. They believed that since the hereditary line of David had ceased under the Hasmonaeans, the Temple sacrifice would continue to remain invalid until a High Priest of the Davidic line was reinstated. They also considered the lunar calendar which had been adopted by the Hasmonaean priesthood as inaccurate, so that their sacrifices were being made on the wrong days, thereby rendering them impure regardless of the lineage of any High Priest.

The passionate conviction of the Essenes in the righteousness of their cause might never have come to light had it not been for the discovery in 1947 of the first jars containing the 'Dead Sea Scrolls'. Muhammad adh-Dhib – Muhammad the Wolf – a Bedouin boy of the Ta'amireh tribe, was walking along the rocky escarpment of the Dead Sea one thousand metres to the north of Wadi Qumran tending his herd of goats. Bored, he started throwing stones against a nearby rock. The Qumran cliff side, composed of fractured limestone, is a place of numerous fissures and caves of all sizes. One of Muhammad's missiles ricocheted from the face of the rock he was aiming at and flew into a narrow opening, producing as it fell the sound of broken pottery.[16] His curiosity aroused, Muhammad adh-Dhib cleared the entrance and entered the cave. Inside he found approximately forty earthenware jars, many of which contained complete or fragmented scrolls written on goatskin parchment. The importance of adh-Dhib's discovery was soon overshadowed by the ineptitude of the scholars and archaeologists who set about investigating the area for further scroll deposits. Teams of Bedouin were hired to search the surrounding cliff face while archaeologists collated the results at the bottom. Numbers allocated to caves became muddled, leading to a highly confused and inaccurate survey. Fragments of jars which contained scroll material were left behind in the caves in the hurry to empty them of their precious contents.[17] But the scrolls themselves fared no better on reaching the 'laboratory'.

The scandal of the initial conservation and study of the scrolls has become infamous. Many fragments were stuck together with Sellotape and there was uproar when it was discovered that the first international team set up in Jerusalem to examine the scrolls had not one single Jewish member – they were all Christians. Almost without exception, the content of the scrolls and their translation was jealously guarded by the scholars studying them. The value to collectors of the Qumran deposit meant that several scrolls were sold on the black market and it was only after the Six-Day War of 1967 that the Israelis managed, through the efforts of their Antiquity authority and several of their leading military generals, to bring together most of the material found at Qumran under a professional team of conservators. It is alleged that in the late 1950s, Moshe Dayan had even planned a military operation to invade the Rockefeller Museum via the underground sewage system of Jerusalem and take the scrolls into Israeli custody.[18]

But was it just amateurism that caused the first research team to drag their feet or were they reluctant to reveal the written contents of the material? In hindsight, now that the contents are known, the original all-Christian international team had little to be pleased about. The majority of scrolls were of minor significance to Christians as they had been compiled many years before Jesus was born. However, some of the fragments dating to the beginning of the first century BC[19] described a coming 'Messianic age':

> The Heavens and the earth will obey His Messiah . . . He will not turn aside from the Commandments of the Holy Ones. Take strength in His service, you who seek the Lord. Shall you not find the Lord in this, all you who wait patiently in your hearts? For the Lord will visit the Pious Ones [Hasidim] and the Righteous will He call by name. Over the Meek will his spirit hover, and the faithful will he restore by his power. He shall glorify the Pious Ones on the throne of the eternal kingdom. He shall release the captives, make the blind see, raise up the downtrodden . . . He will heal the sick, resurrect the dead, and to the Meek announce glad tidings.[20]

This scroll fragment could be describing the life of Jesus as reported in the Gospels of the New Testament and, were it the last scroll to be written, could easily be classified as an extraordinarily accurate prophecy. But there were some scrolls from the Qumran site which were written after the death of Jesus and they give no mention of the arrival of a Messiah, nor is there any recognition of a prophet or teacher of Jesus' name. The members of the community who lived at Qumran up until AD 68 – over thirty-five years after Jesus' death – were still awaiting the Messianic Coming. For Christians who believe the Gospel stories of Jesus' work and miracles amongst the people of Judaea, his apparent lack of impact on the Qumran community was hard to explain since the 'Holy Ones' of Qumran, the natural successors to the Hasidim of Hasmonaean times, were precisely the people with whom the aims of Jesus should have coincided. There may, however, be an explanation for the omission of Jesus within the scroll material.

During Jesus' brief life the Jerusalem Temple Mount complex was architecturally integrated with the rest of the city. Shops continued to be built around the periphery of the platform to service the needs of pilgrims who wished to pay for sacrifices on the Mount and attend the annual celebrations of the Jewish faith. With such a magnificent Temple to the name of Yahweh, the spectre of Ba'alism had receded. But the ruling priesthood was acutely sensitive to this old threat and to any other form of challenge to their authority. By AD 30 their sensitivity became almost a paranoia concerning purity and correctness on the Temple Mount and it was against this unyielding attitude that the words of Jesus collided. To the ruling elite of the Temple, Jesus' teachings proposed a personal development of religious life through the word of God *outside* the confines of the Temple precinct. Such a message was threatening to the correct maintenance of Yahwism and undermined the power of the Temple priesthood. The Essenes who, like the Jerusalem priesthood, were an elitist religious grouping, would have found Jesus' doctrine equally disturbing. Jesus' liberal philosophy threatened the rigid social structure which maintained their status as a community. It would thus have been impossible for any member of the Essene sect to recognize Jesus as the Messiah; neither would any Essene be encouraged to preserve his words and deeds on parchments and conserve them for posterity.

Jesus may well have been a radical breakaway Essene with his own agenda, and if he wanted to restore the covenant with Yahweh on a popular level he was not alone. Judging by his popularity, he shared the wish of many of his generation to break the stranglehold of the Sanhedrin on the Temple, and he seemed the perfect candidate for the role of Davidic Messiah who would restore the days of independent glory of Israel.[21] The contempt felt by the common people was not limited to the priesthood and the ruling Sadducees of the Sanhedrin. The Pharisees, who upheld the Law, were seduced by the riches pouring into the Temple from the remittance of sacrifices and had fallen well short of their role as defenders of the faith. There was considerable wealth on offer. The treasury received an annual tax of half a shekel from every adult Jewish male – roughly the equivalent of two Roman silver pennies or denarii. All Jews, including those in most distant lands, were required to submit this sum to support the maintenance of the Jerusalem Temple. The priesthood and the Levites of the Temple also profited from contributions towards sacrificial offerings and took a tithe from all the agricultural produce given to the Temple. The priests alone could eat the flesh of the sin and guilt offerings and could share with their families and servants certain portions of any other sacrifice.[22] They enjoyed a standard of living far above the average for the citizens of Judaea, including the Pharisees.

Jesus viewed this emphasis on creating wealth with a sceptical eye. When approached by Pharisees who wished to ensnare him into a denunciation of Roman rule by asking if it was lawful to give tribute to Caesar, Jesus asked to see a 'tribute penny'. Looking at the inscription on the silver denarius, he made the famous reply: 'Render unto Caesar the things that are Caesar's and unto God the things that are God's.'[23] Comments such as these suggest that Jesus judged the activities within the new Herodian Temple as based on values that he considered unscrupulous and immoral. He felt the Pharisees were equally to blame for the degenerate state of affairs:

> all their works they do for to be seen of men...they enlarge the borders of their garments,
>
> And love the uppermost rooms at feasts, and the chief seats in the synagogues,

And greetings in the markets, and to be called of men, Rabbi,
Rabbi.

Woe unto you, scribes and Pharisees, hypocrites! For ye shut up
the kingdom of heaven against men.

. . .

Ye fools and blind! For whether is greater, the gold, or the temple
that sanctifieth the gold?[24]

If the religious inheritance of the Temple of Jerusalem had provided
Jesus with a standard of sanctity for his own revolutionary view of
the Jewish faith such insulting words to the Pharisees[25] ultimately
sealed his fate. Although the date of Jesus' crucifixion is uncertain it
is probable that he entered Jerusalem in the days leading up to the
Passover of AD 30. Once inside, he proceeded to the Temple Mount,
the scene of his childhood rabbinical discussions, in a mood for
confrontation. Surrounded by a crowd which proclaimed him the
Davidic Messiah he strode into the Courts where he overturned the
tables of the money changers and the seats of the dove merchants,
shouting that they had transformed the Temple of Yahweh into 'a
den of thieves'.[26] Such behaviour did not go unnoticed, and the
New Testament tells us that the Sanhedrin lost no time in plotting
an abrupt end to Jesus' interference in their business.

Judas Iscariot was responsible for Jesus' betrayal, according to the
New Testament. This view, however, is challenged by the fact that
Judas was Jesus' most beloved disciple. The possibility that Judas
became the community 'scapegoat' for the death of his master is one
that cannot therefore be discounted.[27] The historical accuracy of
Jesus' betrayal is difficult to assess, with the 'truth' of the New
Testament – like that of the Old – the determining factor. But,
whether Judas' testimony was a matter of fact or fiction, Jesus' end
was certain. He was arrested on charges of blasphemy and when
asked by Caiaphas if he was the Son of God, Jesus remained non-
committal,[28] which infuriated his interrogator and led other members of the Sanhedrin to spit in his face and slap him. The Sanhedrin
decided he should die. By law the Sanhedrin could not execute their
fellow Jews. The governorship of Judaea was now in the hands of
Pontius Pilate, and the chief priests and scribes of the Sanhedrin
turned to Pilate anxious that he put Jesus to death as an agitator,

Charles Wilson, Royal Engineers, in his mid-twenties, *c.* 1860.

A large fragment of carved limestone from the Temple Mount in the Second Temple period.

Burnt shop outline from the destruction of AD 70 at the southern *haram* wall.

(i)

Three coins of the Roman period:
(i) 'Tribute' denarius;
(ii) Titus denarius;
opposite (iii) sestersius of Titus Vespasian, 'Judaea Capta' (obverse and reverse).

(ii)

(iii)

View of Robinson's Arch from the south showing the collapsed stones from the destruction of AD 70.

Charles Warren, in his early forties, *c.* 1880.

Montagu Brownlow Parker photographed at Taormina, Sicily in 1912 following his unsuccessful attempt to return to Jerusalem.

Above Detail of 'Masonic' gravestone from Temple, Scotland showing compasses and set square.

Left 'Templar' figure from Kilmory, Scotland.

The Straight Joint, 32.72 metres north of the south-eastern angle of the *haram.*

Detail of actual joint in the Western Wall, showing six-centimetre nail for scale.

Kaiser Wilhelm II leaving the Qubbet as-Sakhra in the company of his wife and entourage, autumn 1898.

Rejected stone

Photograph of the south-east angle showing the 'rejected stone'.

Detail of the triangle.

Full-scale replica of the Ark of the Covenant, constructed by the author.

The Dome of the Rock viewed from north of the estimated position of Solomon's Holy of Holies.

The Temple Mount, with the south-east angle in the left foreground, viewed from the Mount of Olives.

ridding Jerusalem and the Temple Mount of his influence. At the Feast of Passover, as was the established custom between Romans and Jews, Pilate was obliged to release one Jewish prisoner. Finding no fault with Jesus, Pilate proposed to set him free. But the chief priests demanded that Pilate release Barabbas – who was awaiting the execution of sentence for sedition and murder – and crucify Jesus instead. Unable to appease them in any other way Pilate bowed to the demands of the chief priests and the scribes and gave his men orders to carry out the task. In the brief space of one day – from the time that the sun rising over the Mount of Olives would have illuminated the 'exceeding white' face of the Temple, to the moment that the last rays of its light would have flooded the massive stones of the western wall – Jesus of Nazareth underwent both trial and execution.

Jesus was crucified at Golgotha, or the Place of the Skull. Its location, like almost every other question surrounding the history and archaeology of Jerusalem, is debatable. *The Historical Atlas of Jerusalem* compiled by Dan Bahat, the experienced Israeli archaeologist, places Golgotha inside the present-day walls of the Old City of Jerusalem, just to the north of the present Church of the Holy Sepulchre.[29] If this was the case, and if Jesus had been crucified facing eastwards, his last view before losing consciousness would have been cruelly dominated by Herod's Temple rising above the walls of the Temple Mount complex, the place which, he prophesied with extraordinary accuracy, would not have 'one stone upon another, that shall not be thrown down'.[30]

Crucifixion was a particularly brutal form of execution which could leave victims alive for many hours if not days. By AD 30 thousands had suffered in this fashion. The length of time that Jesus spent on the cross was brief by comparison with other sufferers, which has led to doubts surrounding the historical accuracy of the Gospel accounts of his 'death' and whether or not his crucifixion killed him. We know from Josephus that it was possible to be crucified and live.

Forty years after the execution of Jesus, following the destruction of the Temple in AD 70, Josephus obtained permission from Titus, the Roman commander, to rescue three former comrades. As the leg bones of a crucified man would support the body in a sufficiently upright position to allow the lungs to function, death by crucifixion was slow. Taken down from the cross, two of Josephus' friends succumbed to their injuries but one survived.[31] When a crucifixion site became overcrowded or, as in the case of Jesus, the imminence of the sabbath required the removal of the crucified from the cross, the leg bones of the victims would be broken. Jesus, unable to support the weight of his own body, would then have suffocated.

We are told in the New Testament, however, that Jesus' leg bones remained intact.[32] This was because the soldiers charged with dispatching the two thieves crucified alongside him thought Jesus had already expired. Pilate had apparently marvelled at the fact he was dead and asked the centurion in charge of the execution if this was indeed the case. When told that it was, he released Jesus' body into the care of Joseph of Arimathaea, a wealthy member of the Sanhedrin who had secretly become one of Jesus' followers.[33]

So did Jesus, like Josephus' comrade, survive his ordeal? In recent years, the author Barbara Thiering has speculated that Jesus may well have entered a state of unconsciousness, possibly induced by the effect of the liquid offered to him in a sponge on the point of a lance, which may have sedated him. At the time of the crucifixion Joseph of Arimathaea was in the process of finishing his own tomb. The Gospels tell us that Jesus was taken to this sepulchre together with a large quantity – over thirty kilograms – of aloes and myrrh. Here Jesus could have been resuscitated by the ministrations of his friends and followers before being taken to a place of safety. He would have been physically able after several days to begin a series of final encounters with his followers before leaving Judaea where, being officially 'dead', he could no longer live. He could then have begun a new life in a country where he was not known and could not be easily recognized.[34] The Gospel version attributes the reappearance of Jesus after crucifixion as proof of the resurrected Christ. But in the absence of archaeological and historical evidence, the suggestion that Jesus was revived and not embalmed by the aloes and myrrh brought to the unfinished sepulchre by Joseph of Arimathaea is one that cannot be wholly discounted for the simple reason that the alleged resurrection of Jesus' body neither proves nor disproves the ultimate fate of his physical remains.

With Jesus apparently dead, the Sanhedrin could resume their running of the Temple without interference. But they had not considered the determination of the disciples Jesus had left behind.

PAUL OF TARSUS

After Jesus' body was handed over to Joseph, it mysteriously vanished. In the minds of his contemporaries the exact whereabouts of his body may not have mattered as much as the significance of his words and his example. Jesus' work in Jerusalem was continued by his closest followers led by his brother James. The adherents of 'Christianity' were exclusively Jewish; Gentiles were considered impure as they were uncircumcised. This changed when Paul, the son of a Pharisee from Tarsus, entered the Christian scene, causing an upheaval which transformed the small Judeo-Christian Church of Jerusalem into the official religion of the Roman Empire. His first contact with the Christians of the Holy City was, however, in the role of persecutor.

Paul began his religious life following in the steps of his father. He studied for the rabbinate and at the age of thirteen entered the synagogue in his home city of Tarsus, which was situated close to the north-eastern coast of the Mediterranean in what is modern-day Syria. In AD 28, at the age of eighteen, he travelled to Jerusalem to study theology under Rabbi Gamaliel, a member of the Sanhedrin who was much respected for his wisdom. There is no indication that Paul ever met Jesus but shortly after the crucifixion he came into conflict with Jesus' followers. In AD 36 the Sanhedrin ordered the persecution of members of the Christian Church. Stephen, an ardent disciple of Christ, was stoned to death on the charge that he was using the Jewish scriptures to support the Messianic status of Jesus. Paul was an active participant in Stephen's death and having demonstrated his willingness to attack the Christians he was sent to Syria to eradicate Christianity wherever he might find it. Struck by a blinding light while approaching the gates of Damascus Paul fell from his horse. In the three days that it took him to recover his sight Paul was visited by Ananias, a Christian disciple. Ananias converted him to Christianity and declared that from that moment Paul would become a powerful witness to the way of life advocated by Jesus.

Paul now directed his fanaticism towards rather than against the spread of Christianity. His energy was boundless and with his theological training he soon devised an invincible formula for the promotion of his newly acquired faith. His methods, however, caused deep upset both to Jews who had remained loyal to their religion and to Christian converts. Everywhere Paul went he provoked anger from Orthodox Jews who were enraged at his attack on their faith. He had to be lowered in a basket over the city walls of Damascus at night to escape arrest by the ruling king, Aretas, and even in Jerusalem, where he returned to spend time with his fellows of the Christian community, Paul was an unwelcome guest. Grossly unhappy with the convert in their midst, the elders of the Christian Church persuaded him to leave Judaea and a small group accompanied him to Caesarea, the closest port on the Mediterranean coast to Jerusalem, where they put Paul on a ship back to Tarsus. Paul was not seen in Jerusalem for fourteen years but when he finally came back, he engineered the most important decision in the history of the new Church.

Despite his rejection from Judaea Paul continued his efforts to spread the message of Jesus in his own individual style. His direct and dynamic approach won him increasing support throughout the Hellenized Jewry of the Mediterranean and, if Jesus' message was revolutionary, Paul's interpretation of it was a stroke of genius. Unconstrained by his Jewish inheritance, Paul promoted a doctrine of salvation for Gentile and Jew in the name of a resurrected Messiah, Jesus, son of God. He arrived in Jerusalem to challenge the authority of the Judeo-Christian Church, demanding that James relax the rule regarding circumcision and allow uncircumcised Gentiles access to Christianity. James consented but only on the condition that the law be upheld governing sacrifice of animals, fornication and idolatry. Despite the work of Jesus, the fear of Ba'alism still existed amongst the converted Jews of Jerusalem, although Paul did not feel this threat. He left Jerusalem triumphant and returned to Antioch. Christianity could now offer the message of redemption throughout an empire renowned for efficient communication. The prospect for the Jerusalem Church, however, was bleak.

Christians were facing increasing hostility from the Sanhedrin and when Paul, having travelled to such major cities as Athens and Corinth to spread the word of Christ, returned on a visit to the Temple Mount in AD 58 James advised him to follow the traditional Jewish ritual of self-purification and sacrifice in order to avoid confrontation. Within a week of his arrival, however, Paul was accused of introducing Greek Gentiles onto the Mount. A riot ensued and only the intervention of the Roman guard saved Paul from death at the hands of the mob. Brought before the members of the Sanhedrin, Paul attempted unsuccessfully to influence proceedings against him by reminding the Council of his Pharisaic upbringing. Paul was locked up in the Fortress Antonia, the Roman governor's military headquarters, which stood at the north-western edge of the Temple Mount complex. There were threats on his life from angry Jews and the Roman authorities transferred him to Caesarea where he was kept under arrest for two years. The Sanhedrin made constant efforts to have Paul returned for trial in Jerusalem but he escaped their clutches by claiming Roman citizenship. This permitted him to be tried by the Emperor and in the autumn of AD 60 he was put aboard ship for Rome where he was executed in AD 67. During the persecution of the Christians under Nero, Paul's particular doctrine of Jesus as resurrected son of God became firmly rooted throughout the Roman Empire.

The Judeo-Christian Church in Jerusalem meanwhile had suffered an irreversible blow. In AD 62 James the brother of Jesus and leader of the Church had been apprehended by the populace and thrown over the wall of the Temple Mount at its highest point, the south-east angle, by order of the Sanhedrin. This, they thought, would put an effective end to the Judeo-Christian Church of Jerusalem. After the death of their leader the Judeo-Christian community left the city, dispersing into Jordan and Egypt. The death of James and his disciples, and the crucifixion of Jesus, at the hands of fellow Jews, provided Gentile Christians with an excuse to scapegoat the entire Jewish race, which had the most terrible consequences for the future. The most sacred relic of the Jewish religion was also subjected to a new Christian interpretation. The body of Jesus came to symbolize to the early Christian Church a replacement for the lost Ark of the Covenant.[35] Meanwhile in Jerusalem the events which had such bearing on the development of the Christian Church went unnoticed. Archaeological excavation has revealed a thriving economy during post-Herodian times with the Temple Mount fully serviced by an infrastructure wholly dedicated to sacrificial offerings. In the years following the crucifixion of Jesus, however, the city slid inexorably towards war.

THE DESCENT INTO WAR

The liberal Roman attitude to religion did not mix easily with that of the monotheistic Jews. Pilate, from his earliest days in Judaea, encountered this problem in particular where the Temple Mount was concerned. True to the style of Roman conquerors and eager to ingratiate himself with the Emperor, Pilate soon after his appointment in AD 26 sent images of his Caesar in the form of standards to the city of Jerusalem.

The soldiers charged with carrying the standards arrived at night and the Jews of the city awoke the following morning to the sight of graven images in their midst. Although the standards were not carried inside the Temple complex, their proximity to the Mount was enough to cause a national outcry. Zealous Jews hastened to Caesarea where Pilate was residing and begged for the immediate removal of the offensive objects. Pilate at first refused and his petitioners responded by lying down in protest. Josephus informs us that after five days of the first recorded lie-down protest in history, Pilate resorted to a ruse. He invited the protesters to parley and had them surrounded by three ranks of soldiers. Roman swords were drawn and Pilate declared that the Jews should allow the standards to remain in Jerusalem or they would be killed. The protesters responded by falling back down on the ground and, crying out that they were 'sooner ready to be slain, than that their Law should be transgressed',[36] they exposed their necks to Pilate's troops. Faced with such an impasse, Pilate relented and ordered the removal of

Caesar's standards from the Holy City. But the acute sensitivity surrounding the sanctity of the Mount and the zealotry it inspired prompted Pilate, who had learnt his lesson once, to devise a more covert means of suppressing mass demonstration. He was soon given a chance to put his method into practice.

During the early days of his governorship Pilate was determined to improve the water supply of the city and ordered the construction of aqueducts. This was a noble and necessary cause. The Temple in the first century AD was a place of mass pilgrimage and great animal slaughter, the combination of which must have led to an extreme lack of sanitation. Once again, however, Pilate's actions caused uproar. He demanded that money dedicated to the *Korban* – the sacrifice made at the altar in front of the Temple – should be used to finance the building of the aqueducts. When he arrived in Jerusalem he was warned of impending trouble, so Pilate mixed his troops, who were dressed as civilians, with the crowd attending his regular tribunal. At the first public complaint, Pilate gave a signal to his soldiers who laid into the protesters with the staves they had been carrying as part of the disguise.[37] Many Jews were beaten to death and, in the ensuing crush to escape the scene, more were suffocated.

Pilate left Judaea in AD 36, and, according to one Christian legend, ended his days as an exile in Gaul.[38] His rule as governor had been fraught with difficulty, and the Temple Mount was the source of most of his problems. When the Emperor Tiberius died in AD 37 – whose reign since AD 14 had spanned the ministry and crucifixion of Jesus – the portents for peace received yet another blow.

Gaius Caligula, Tiberius's grandson, succeeded him to the throne and, despite enjoying a reign of only three years and eight months, Caligula managed to widen the already unbridgeable rift between Rome and the Jews of Judaea. To the Jews the supremacy of Yahweh pre-empted any mortal claim to a godlike status. But in Rome, by the time of Caligula's accession, the trend of self-deification was well established. As Emperor-god, Caligula perceived the Temple of Jerusalem as a worthy site for his image. He gave orders that his statue should be erected in various locations within the Temple complex.[39] The Jews challenged this planned desecration by appealing to Petronius, the Roman legate of Syria who had the unenviable task of carrying out Caligula's orders. The Jews who met Petronius were forthright in their assessment of the inherent dangers of the situation. They reminded Petronius that they offered sacrifice in the Temple 'twice daily for Caesar and the Roman people'[40] and if Petronius persisted in carrying out Caligula's orders he would precipitate a holocaust of the entire Jewish nation who were ready 'to expose themselves, together with their children and wives, to be slain'.[41] The situation, which dragged on for several months, threatening all the time to escalate, was only relieved by the death of Caligula in AD 41, following which Judaea and Jerusalem re-entered a temporary phase of calm.

Claudius, the Emperor-elect of Rome, returned hereditary lands to Herod's grandson Agrippa I, making him ruler of Judaea and thereby restoring some status to the Jewish people. The situation, however, did not endure. He died in Caesarea in AD 44 and, as his successor Agrippa II was not yet of adult age, the Judaean region passed back into the hands of a Roman procurator. Rome thus maintained a tight grip on the affairs of Jerusalem but religious and political tensions still simmered under the surface. Cumanus held the procuratorship from AD 48 to 52 and it was under his rule that an incident occurred which emphasized the vast gulf between the Roman and the Jewish attitude towards religion and which, in the opinion of Josephus, signalled the true beginning of the hostilities destined to devastate Judaea.

During Passover the people of Judaea thronged to the Temple and the Roman authorities, anticipating skirmishes which habitually marred such festivals, positioned a cohort of 450 legionnaires[42] in the cloisters around the Temple Courts. Whilst the religious ceremony was in progress a legionnaire, unimpressed by the service and bored, decided to make his feelings known. He lifted his tunic and, turning his back on the pious assembly, he bent over and farted in their direction. The mature members of the congregation clamoured for the Procurator Cumanus to punish the soldier and 'the rasher part of the youth' started to throw stones at the legionnaires. Cumanus, afraid that his cohort might be unable to handle the deteriorating situation, rushed reinforcements into the Temple precincts. In the fighting and the stampede that followed, ten thousand Jews were crushed or trampled to death.[43] The whole nation was thrown into mourning at this event but calm at least in the Temple area was quickly restored and daily sacrifice resumed.

In AD 59 Agrippa II was installed in the Hasmonaean Palace of Jerusalem as King of Judaea and for a brief time Jerusalem society fell under the ancient Jewish hierarchy of a king and a High Priest. Work around the Temple Mount was finally completed, including paving and sophisticated drainage with raised kerbs and drain covers cut from solid limestone that would have pleased Pilate.[44] In spite of these practical improvements to the Temple Mount area, control of the national political situation was rapidly slipping away from the grasp of the Sanhedrin. Since the days of Herod the Judaean countryside sheltered organized bands of robbers and groups opposed to the rule of Jerusalem. This area became a battleground between various lawless bands and the Roman army who were trying to impose law and order. In the midst of this turmoil the Messianic expectations of the common people were ripe for exploitation and any imperious act by Rome served as perfect propaganda for the more zealous elements of Jewish society. Moderate Jews, who favoured a peaceful co-existence with Rome, found any moral ground for their argument repeatedly taken from under them. A generation after the crucifixion of Jesus of Nazareth, one ultra-Orthodox militant group – the Zealots – achieved supremacy over the moderates and, through active promotion of their nationalistic ideals and by their refusal to compromise with the superior forces of Rome, they dragged the entire nation into war.

In AD 66, under the rule of the procurator Florus, insurrection aimed at forcing Jewish independence from Rome began to break out across Judaea. Josephus describes a 'multitude' of robbers within the Judaean countryside, so great they were 'not to be enumerated'.[45] To compound the disorder Jerusalem was rife with false prophets who 'deceived and deluded the people under pretence of divine inspiration'.[46] Pre-eminent amongst these were the Sicarii[47] named after the curved daggers employed in the assassination of their victims. The Sicarii were fanatically motivated and selective about whom they killed. Jonathan, the High Priest of the Temple, was their first victim, suggesting that they disapproved violently of the political allegiance between the priesthood and the Romans. Their favourite method of operation was to mingle with the crowds and, having stabbed their victim, to conceal their weapon and participate in the indignation of the crowd over the ghastly crime perpetrated within their midst.[48] With extremists at work within society creating fear and distrust it required only one minor confrontation to provoke a war between Romans and Jews and just such an incident took place on the Temple Mount.

The procurator Florus had not resisted the lure of easy money and, like so many before him, had plundered the Temple treasury. The violent protests which followed led to the deaths of 3600 people in one day. Jewish members of the Equestrian Order amongst the arrested were scourged and crucified in direct contravention of Roman law.[49] With peace on a knife edge, King Agrippa II appealed to his people to maintain relations with Rome. He addressed them from a gallery leading onto the Temple Mount and warned of the dangers of going to war with an empire which had defeated remote places such as the British Isles and people such as the Germans who were 'strong and tall' and had 'minds greater than their bodies, and a soul that despises death'.[50] Agrippa's words created a brief lull in the escalating atmosphere of hostility. But the divisions within Jerusalem society ran too deep for peace to succeed. Eleazar, the son of Ananias who had succeeded Jonathan as the High Priest and governor of the Temple, persuaded those who officiated at sacrifice to refuse gifts or sacrifices from any non-Jew. The Jerusalem Temple rejected the established sacrifice made on behalf of Caesar and by so doing symbolically broke all relationships with Rome. The rashness of this decision was not unanimously approved by the Jews of the city.

THE JEWISH WAR AND THE SIEGE OF JERUSALEM

The Jewish War, as the rebellion came to be known, was as much a civil war as a conflict with the Roman Empire. It took four years and the intervention of her ablest generals for Rome to quench finally the flames of revolt which had begun at the altar of the Temple in AD 66. Following the decision to stop all sacrifices made on behalf of Caesar, a dispute broke out between Jews who wanted a reconciliation with Rome and fanatical Zealots who were eager to fight for independence. The Zealots murdered Ananias the High Priest of the Temple and his brother Hezekiah, and the Roman soldiers within Jerusalem found themselves as the despised peace keepers between warring factions. Besieged and with no choice but to parley, the Romans agreed to surrender and lay down their arms if allowed to leave Jerusalem. Once the arms had been relinquished, Eleazar and his Zealot followers broke their oath and massacred the Roman contingent. In an attempt to extinguish this nucleus of rebellion, the Roman general Cestius Gallus marched on Jerusalem at the head of the Twelfth Legion. The Jewish forces defeated him, killing 5300 Roman infantrymen and a contingent of 380 cavalry.[51] The outcome convinced the Romans that they had a determined and fanatical enemy on their hands. The ruling emperor Nero, who had succeeded Claudius in AD 54, appointed Vespasian, a general of proven ability, to the supreme command of Palestine forces with orders to crush the Jewish revolt. Titus, Vespasian's elder son, was appointed his second in command. It took two years for Vespasian to reconquer the greater part of Judaean territory. The Jewish forces fought with great ability and in several instances the Romans were obliged to lay siege to cities and towns in their effort to reclaim control of the province. However, by AD 69 Vespasian's troops were in a position to march on Jerusalem, the stronghold of Jewish resistance.

That same year Nero, abandoned by his supporters, was put to death on his own request by a member of his court. There then followed a struggle for the throne between the generals of the Roman army. Vitellius, who commanded the legions in Germany, outmanoeuvred his rivals but his reign as emperor only lasted for eleven months. Condemned by the populus of Rome for his extravagant and licentious behaviour, he was murdered and his body thrown into the river Tiber. Vespasian, temporarily stationed in Alexandria, was proclaimed emperor by his troops, a decision later approved by the senate and the people. Wishing to depart for Rome once the winter weather had subsided, Vespasian ordered Titus to leave Egypt, march north into Judaea and conclude the war with the Jews by conquering Jerusalem. Titus left, taking with him Josephus Flavius, the Jewish historian.

At the outbreak of war in AD 66 Josephus had been appointed Jewish commander of Galilee. In AD 67 he was captured by the Romans but was released two years later when his prophecy that Vespasian would one day attain the throne became true. Josephus, rewarded with his freedom and protected by Vespasian's patronage, thus accompanied Titus as his official interpreter and biographer of his campaign.

Titus arrived outside Jerusalem at the head of a redoubtable army. He was accompanied by three battle-hardened legions of hand-picked men and by contingents from his royal allies – auxiliaries from Syria, and had all the equipment necessary for a prolonged siege. His first act was to make a reconnaissance of the city walls, during which he nearly lost his life. When he approached the city he could see no enemy movement. Titus left his troops and went on with a small escort. Close to the walls, he was ambushed. Separated from his main contingent he and his handful of companions had to force their way through the Jewish attackers. He succeeded in extracting himself unharmed but two of his comrades were killed and many suffered wounds. Josephus tells us that this encounter gave the Jews 'ill-grounded hope' that fortune was on their side.[52] But Titus was determined to conquer the city at all costs.

The Roman siege of Jerusalem began in the spring of AD 70. The city was crammed with pilgrims who had arrived to celebrate Passover, so many Jews found themselves trapped far from their homes and without the means to subsist for more than a few days. To the residents of the city the presence of such visitors posed a logistical problem. The infrastructure of Jerusalem was not designed to sustain such large numbers of people over a lengthy period so what had begun as a festival rapidly became a frenzied mass of trapped and frightened people. To add to this, the political situation within Jerusalem was verging on the anarchic. Josephus describes how three 'treacherous factions' were waging a guerrilla war against each other. Eleazar and his Zealot supporters on the Temple Mount were still engaged in bitter fighting with citizens of the Upper City who had chosen Simon, son of Gioras, as their leader. A further, third faction was formed when the behaviour of one of Eleazar's supporters, John of Gischala, caused a split in their own alliance. John controlled the periphery of the Temple for Eleazar and as a result of his dispute with John, Eleazar and his Zealots were obliged to retreat to the Inner Courts of the Temple. John was thus left sandwiched between Eleazar and Simon. The result of this rivalry was that by the time of Titus' arrival, much of the work in weakening the city in preparation for assault had been done for him. The multi-partisan conflict within Jerusalem had degenerated into mindless destruction. During the course of house-to-house fighting huge quantities of the city's store of corn and vital supplies went up in flames, severely escalating the famine which so seriously weakened the population prior to the conquest of Jerusalem five months later. Josephus records how all the buildings around the Temple were burnt to the ground, transforming the area between the Mount and the rest of the city to its west into a desolate no man's land.[53] With the blood of strangers and priests, pilgrims and citizens creating 'lakes in the Holy Courts',[54] we are told by Josephus that people of the city wished for the success of the Romans even though they were the enemy. The Temple Mount once again became a killing field, with Jew pitted against Jew.

Titus' reconnaissance of the city walls convinced him of the need to carry out a methodical siege which would involve the achievement of several objectives. With the arrival of the Tenth Legion, which had been recalled from Mesopotamia, his men began to fortify their positions. Whilst the Tenth Legion set up their encampment on the Mount of Olives directly opposite the eastern wall of the present-day *haram*, the Twelfth Legion dug in on Mount Scopus to the north-east of the Temple Mount across the valley of the Kidron, with the Fifteenth Legion behind them. Watching the Roman soldiers fortifying their positions brought the battling factions in Jerusalem to their senses. Fearful of the potential danger, they decided to put an end to their internal fighting and to unite. Choosing the early morning to launch their attack they left the safety of their walls and attacked the Romans who, without arms readily to hand and deprived of the defensive effectiveness of their traditional phalanx, suffered heavy losses. This Jewish success encouraged more Zealots to join the battle which continued well into the afternoon. The day ended when Titus rallied his men and succeeded in forcing the Jews back across the Kidron. With a stalemate established, the Jewish factions soon rekindled their enmity for one another.

On the day of Passover, Eleazar's Zealots made the fatal mistake of partially opening the gates of the Inner Courtyard to worshippers. John's men, dressed as pilgrims, with weapons concealed in the folds of their garments, entered the Inner Temple area and once in threw off their disguises and began to slaughter the followers of Eleazar. Most of Eleazar's Zealots survived, saving themselves by hiding in the Temple vaults, but hundreds of innocent pilgrims were killed. John's men were left in possession of the entire Temple Mount complex. Titus meanwhile, with the fortifications of his encampment now complete, was about to make his first attack. In mid-May, leaving the Tenth Legion on the Mount of Olives, he moved the Twelfth down from Mount Scopus to within four hundred and fifty metres of the north-eastern corner of the city wall in order to approach Jerusalem via its weakest geophysical point. It was also, as Titus had observed, the weakest link in her military fortifications. Before the Romans arrived the northern defences were strengthened by the hurried completion of an extensive wall described by Josephus as the 'Third' wall, as it was the outermost of the three walls which protected the city. This fortification contained the urban extension of the Upper City, which had previously been enclosed by a much shorter 'Second' wall. Titus brought up his siege engines and it was now just a matter of time before the city fell.

By the fifteenth day of the siege, at the beginning of June, Titus' troops captured the 'Third' wall and five days later they breached the Second. The determination of the Jews was, however, undiminished and sacrifice was still being performed at the Temple. The Romans realized that they faced a bloody struggle with the Zealots in order to capture the city, a prospect which Titus did not relish. Josephus' ability to speak Hebrew led Titus to ask Josephus to make

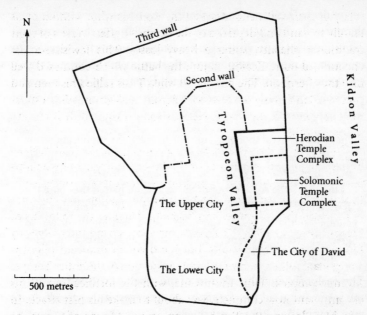

N

Third wall

Second wall

Tyropoeon Valley

Kidron Valley

┤ Herodian
Temple
Complex

┤ Solomonic
Temple
Complex

The Upper City

┤ The City of David

The Lower City

500 metres

FIGURE 6.1 Map of Jerusalem at the time of the Roman siege of AD 70 showing the 'Second' and 'Third' city walls in relation to the 'First Wall' of the Temple Mount and the Davidic city.

an appeal on his behalf to the Jews inside the besieged city. Josephus chose an area close to the walls so that he could shelter from the arrows of his fellow Jews, and launched into a lengthy speech. The core of his argument was that if his former comrades did not relinquish possession of the city to the Roman forces, the Temple would be in great danger. Josephus' address attracted abuse and ridicule, the Jews assuring him that the Romans would never succeed in capturing the city. But Jerusalem was beginning to feel the effects of famine and his words did not fall entirely on deaf ears. Some people left the city, surrendering to the Roman soldiers on the surrounding hillsides, having first swallowed any gold or silver coin in their possession. Titus released most of these deserters into the countryside and they departed for a new life, carrying their meagre wealth undetected inside them.[55]

The refusal by the majority of the Jerusalem population to

surrender to the Romans exasperated Titus. Many Jews kept leaving the city walls at night to scavenge for food. Some were captured and Titus, despite his previous clemency towards deserters, decided to make an example of the plight of the starving in the hope of weakening the resolve of the Jews still defending the city. Josephus, who probably witnessed the proceedings, left a gruesome account of what happened:

> they [the captives] thought it too late to make any supplications for mercy: so they were first whipped, and then tormented with all sorts of tortures before they died, and were then crucified before the walls of the city...the soldiers out of the wrath and hatred they bore the Jews, nailed those they caught, one after one way, and another after another, to the crosses, by way of jest; when their multitude was so great, that room was wanting for the crosses, and crosses wanting for the bodies.[56]

The Zealots invited the relatives of those being crucified to witness the scene and used the occasion to warn against the dreadful fate which awaited all Roman prisoners.

THE DESTRUCTION OF HEROD'S TEMPLE

Titus now faced a dilemma. Despite his wish to end the siege, his commanders advised him that the strength of the Jewish forces was sufficient to repel a full-scale Roman assault. The weakening of the Jewish garrison through starvation was the only solution which could help alter the balance in favour of an eventual Roman attack. But Titus was well aware that it was virtually impossible to prevent food from entering the city as provisions would probably find their way along the secret passages and sewers which entered the Mount.[57] So he made a decision to build a wall around Jerusalem which would prevent people from leaving the city to forage in the neighbouring countryside. His action had the desired effect. Jerusalem, already low on food, quickly fell into severe famine. The dead lay in the streets and when money from the public treasury to finance burials ran out, the corpses were thrown over the city walls to rot on the open ground below.[58] Houses of the dead were pillaged and anarchy took hold of the city.

The severity of the situation brought out the worst in Simon who still controlled the Upper City. He put to death eminent figures from the priestly families on the grounds that they were planning to defect to the Romans. Josephus' parents, descendants of the priesthood, escaped death but were imprisoned as a national danger because of their son's collaboration with the Roman enemy. Josephus, during one of his trips around the city, was struck on the head by a stone and knocked unconscious. Although he was rescued by Roman soldiers, the word soon passed around Jerusalem that he was dead. Those Jews who hated Josephus for helping Titus rejoiced. His mother on hearing the news, lamented that she would not even be able to bury her son whom she had expected all her life to bury her.[59]

Despite the dangers of being captured and tortured by the Romans, attempts to defect from the siege continued unabated with Jewish deserters trying to slip through the Roman defences at night. The Romans found out that people leaving Jerusalem were swallowing their coins. Many deserters were captured and cut open to have their stomachs and intestines searched for gold. Titus felt this would lead to disorder amongst his troops so he attempted, unsuccessfully, to stop it.[60] By July, Titus judged the city sufficiently weakened to recommence his assault and took the northern part of the Upper City.

With this area of the city in his hands, Titus decided that if he managed to seize the Temple Mount the rest of Jerusalem would fall. So, once inside the Third and Second walls of the city, the Roman forces concentrated their efforts against the northern perimeter of the Temple Mount complex. But Herod had done his work well. The complex gave the defenders a great deal of advantage. They had height and shelter on their side, in addition to which the Romans, in their efforts to force a breach of the wall, found themselves constrained to fight man-to-man on a narrow front, all of which hampered any progress.[61] It took a week for the Romans to bring down Herod's wall and build a point of easy access for the legions to reinforce their position. Having finally established a bridgehead on the northern end of the Temple platform, Titus again requested Josephus to persuade John – who since defeating Eleazar now controlled the Mount – to surrender and save the sanctuary of the Jewish nation. John and his men took no heed of Josephus' supplication and the final battle for the Temple began in earnest.

On the seventh day of the month of Av, approximately the thirty-first day of July AD 70, with the Zealots still defending the Temple from behind the Inner Courtyard wall, Titus' men brought battering rams across the Outer Courts in an attempt to penetrate their position. Jewish resistance was so fierce and the Roman losses so great that Titus ordered his troops to set fire to the gates of the Inner Court. The next morning Titus took stock of the situation and prepared his legions for an attack against the Inner Court wall for the following day. At eight o'clock in the morning on the ninth day of Av, the Jewish defenders of the Temple made a final desperate sortie from the East Gate but were thrown back. Titus retired from the battle but a few hours later was called out from his tent where he was resting: the Temple precincts were on fire. According to Josephus, the Roman soldiers, under orders from Titus to stop the spread of fire towards the sanctuary, were prevented from doing so by further sorties of Jews into the Outer Courts. One of the Roman legionnaires, disregarding Titus' instructions, decided that it was better to destroy rather than preserve the Temple and climbed on the back of a fellow soldier to launch a blazing piece of wood from the cloisters through a chamber window on the northern side of the Temple building.

The fire was at first confined to the chambers surrounding the Temple which were used as a repository for precious goods but before long it spread to the interior. The heat and intensity of the flames threw the Zealots into total confusion. The Roman legions, seizing their chance, poured through the gates of the Inner Court and fought like men possessed, slaughtering Zealots and priests alike, regardless of age or rank. Around the altar a pile of corpses grew higher and higher whilst down the sanctuary steps 'poured a river of blood, and the bodies of those killed at the top, slithered to the bottom'.[62] In the mayhem, Titus entered the Temple and saw for the first time what a magnificent building it was. Tragically his endeavours to save it had been in vain. As his soldiers rampaged across the Temple Courtyards in an orgy of bloodshed and looting, Herod's Temple exploded into flame. The hanging curtains, the holy oils, and the furniture, fed the Lebanon cedar of the roof. Josephus, an eyewitness, described the final moments of the Second Temple of Jerusalem:

> The Temple Hill, enveloped in flames from top to bottom, appeared to be boiling up from its very roots; yet the sea of flame was nothing to the ocean of blood, or the companies of killers to the armies of killed: nowhere could the ground be seen between the corpses, and the soldiers climbed over the heaps of bodies as they chased the fugitives.[63]

From Rome to Saladin,
AD 71–1187

It took Titus another month to capture the Upper City. By September he achieved his objective of conquering Jerusalem. For Jews worldwide the calamity was total. The Babylonian destruction of the Temple had left some stones standing, but this time the devastation was so severe that there was little prospect of rebuilding it. For those who paid attention to prophecies and looked for God's hand in the catastrophe the date that the Roman soldiers broke into the Second Temple complex was significant since it was the anniversary of Nebuchadnezzar's destruction of 586 BC.

Josephus claims that when the fire had subsided on the Mount a surviving priest by the name of Jesus 'son of Thebuthus' struck a deal with Titus. In return for his life Jesus would enter the ruins and deliver to Titus 'certain of the precious things that had been reposited'. He emerged with two candlesticks ' like to those that [once] lay in the holy house, with tables and cisterns and vials, all made of solid gold, and very heavy'.[1] Jesus also produced veils and garments embedded with precious stones which formed part of the Temple worship. Encouraged by the existence of these hidden valuables, Titus persuaded the treasurer of the Temple Phineas to make a careful search which resulted in a great many other objects being discovered.[2] Titus transported this booty to Rome where it was carried in procession through the streets. Josephus makes no mention of the Ark of the Covenant being amongst the trophies on display.[3] However, the treasure that was found was so valuable that it financed new building work in Rome such as the construction of the Coliseum and a triumphal arch with a bas-relief of Titus' soldiers carrying the looted Temple furnishings from the Temple.

Jewish presence on Mount Moriah came to an abrupt end and the Romans were in no mood to make concessions. It took Roman legions another two years to capture the remaining pockets of Zealot resistance and when the fortress of Masada – which had once been Herod's summer palace – fell in AD 72 the war was finally over. The Jewish War cost the Romans many casualties and they imposed harsh conditions on the defeated Jews. King Agrippa II, who tried in vain to avert the outbreak of war, was given conditional rule over Galilee but only on the understanding that upon his death the Jewish monarchy would cease to exist. Josephus' brother and fifty friends were released unharmed and Titus gave Josephus a number of unidentified 'holy books' from the Temple, confirming that, as well as drawing on the Tyrian archives he mentions as a source, Josephus wrote his histories referring to works that may well be unavailable to us today.[4]

Jerusalem lay desolate and in the months that followed, the ruins of the Temple Mount platform were systematically demolished to clear the area. Josephus was given leave by Titus to enter the Temple complex and search for friends and acquaintances amongst the prisoners held there. In this way Josephus managed to have freed a further 190 fellow Jews.[5] The immediate prospects for the remainder were grim. The Temple Courtyard of the Women was turned into a prison and Titus gave Fronto, one of his commanders who had participated in the battle for the Temple, power of life or death over the captives. Surviving Zealots and partisans were killed, the 'tallest and most beautiful' young men Fronto reserved for Titus' triumph in Rome and the 'rest of the multitude' above seventeen years of age were chained up and dispatched to the mines of Egypt. Of the Zealot commanders, John was condemned to perpetual imprisonment and Simon, once he had been paraded through the streets of Rome, was put to death.[6] Josephus tells us that the walls of the city which John and Simon battled over were entirely demolished by the Romans. The south-western corner of the Mount has now revealed evidence that this included all the walls of the Temple and its cloisters. In 1867 Warren, through use of his shafts and galleries, reached blocks of fallen Herodian masonry close to the external wall of the *haram*. As the result of recent excavation these blocks of stone, many of which still bear the signs of the fire of the second day of August AD 70, can be seen lying in a massive heap on top of the pavement which was so scrupulously finished under Agrippa II. In several places the weight of the stone has caused the collapse of the huge paving stones, themselves almost twenty-five centimetres thick, into the drainage tunnels below. In all probability these blocks did not fall from the platform as a direct result of fire. It is much more likely that they were pushed, and the excavations at Robinson's Arch conducted in the 1990s have revealed that Roman soldiers probably used their Jewish captives to do the work because of the considerable quantity of human bones of a certain type uncovered from amongst the blocks of stone. The majority of bones found were from arms and fingers indicating that, as the enormous blocks were moved, they took human extremities with them – cut off in the process of toppling them over the edge. Thus it appears that the Jews who survived siege, famine, battle, execution or transportation, were put to work on the final destruction of their Temple and that many were crippled as a result.

When Titus departed in triumph for Rome the Tenth Legion was left to guard the ruins of the Holy City. The Tenth had been summoned from the Euphrates delta of ancient Babylon to fight in Jerusalem, so their military postings during the first century AD were in the two places most influential to Jewish history. The ruination of Jerusalem was so complete that living conditions during the first winter after the destruction must have been squalid. Those who died in battle or because of the famine lay rotting in the ruins of the city and, as the famous 'Judaea Capta' coins of the era minted by Vespasian show, the once proud Jewish nation was now under the sword of Rome. The Mount, home of the largest and most glorious Temple of the known world, had now become quite literally the graveyard of Jewish independence. After the fall of Jerusalem, Titus' troops hunted down and killed any survivor bearing arms. Many sought refuge in the sewers but the Romans ferreted them out and few escaped alive. The Tenth Legion built permanent quarters at a location in the Upper City which, judging by the archaeological remnants of the terracotta tiles they produced bearing their legionary stamp, stood within the south-western corner of the present-day Old City, four hundred metres to the south-west of the Temple Mount.[7] Jerusalem, which had been the scene of battle for so many years, was now a place of peace, but with such a reduced population that there was little demand for shelter and many of the damaged houses were knocked down. As the years passed the winter rains carried the debris and ash from the Temple Mount down into the Tyropoeon valley filling in the cavities between the fallen stones and cementing the evidence of destruction for posterity.[8]

As the years following Jerusalem's destruction passed, a small number of Jews continued to live there eking out an existence, but the bulk of the population in Jerusalem was made up of Roman soldiers and immigrant Gentiles. The city needed to be rebuilt from the ground up and exactly sixty years after the events of AD 70 the city was visited by one of Rome's most prolific builders, the Emperor Hadrian, who saw the devastation as an opportunity to glorify his own name.

AELIA CAPITOLINA, THE BAR KOKHBA REVOLT AND A FINAL IMAGE OF THE ARK?

In AD 130 Publius Aelius Hadrianus, Emperor of Rome, arrived in Judaea. Although some scholars believe that he visited Jerusalem there is no firm evidence that he actually went into the city.[9] Hadrian was firmly wedded to the belief that monumental construction was the key to the long-term preservation of his empire, and Jerusalem, with its ravaged houses and ruined Temple, was the perfect candidate for his imperial policy. He proposed that a new city be constructed on the rubble of the old, bearing his name, *Aelia*, and *Capitolina*, in honour of the gods of Capitoline Rome. The name alone was enough to fill Jewish hearts with horror but Hadrian insulted the Jews further by proposing that the site of the Jewish Temple, Mount Moriah, should be graced with the erection of a temple in honour of Jupiter.

Since the destruction of AD 70 the annual tax due to the Temple had been forcibly diverted to rebuild and maintain a new Temple to Jupiter on the Capitoline Hill in Rome. Hadrian's plans to bring this 'strange' god, whom the Jews were thereby already financing, to Jerusalem signalled the end of any hope of reinstating sacrifice to Yahweh on the site of Solomon's Temple. Even worse, there were rumours that a new law to ban circumcision was going to be imposed which caused the children and grandchildren of the Jews who had survived the events of AD 70 to take up arms again against Rome.

In AD 132, after much preparation involving the stockpiling of weapons and supplies, the Jews of Judaea under the leadership of Simeon Ben Kosevah erupted into rebellion.[10] The Tenth Legion departed from Jerusalem to confront the uprising in the countryside and Ben Kosevah and his followers entered the Holy City in great number. Kosevah appears to have been a practical soldier intent on restoring Jewish independence. The Temple Mount was the focus of his planned insurrection. Backed by his uncle, named Eleazar after the Zealot leader of AD 70,[11] Kosevah instilled a new regime in the city. Gentiles were forced to leave Jerusalem and it is alleged that Kosevah reinstated the sacrificial offering to Yahweh in the ruins of the Temple. Although there is no archaeological evidence to support this, Kosevah's coins, struck over existing Roman and Greek provincial issues, indicate this may be true. One coin has particularly significant links with the Temple.

The obverse of one of the overstruck or reminted silver tetradrachms shows four standing columns flanking the dotted outline of what appears to be a chest or doorway. Suggestions made as to the identity of the dotted outline have been diverse. Rabbi Leibel Reznick in his recent work *The Holy Temple Revisited* makes a claim, popular amongst Orthodox Jews, that the scene depicted on the coin represents the entrance to a 'Third Temple' constructed under the rule of Kosevah out of the ruins of the Second.[12] Ya'akov Meshorer of the Israel Museum, however, in his publication *Ancient Jewish Coinage* states categorically that Kosevah used the design of the Temple on the coin to symbolize a concept rather than an actual Temple.[13] The 'concept', according to a succession of numismatic scholars, is that the four pillars represent the Inner Sanctum, or Holy of Holies, of the tabernacle of Moses, as described by Josephus in *Antiquities*.[14] The design in the centre of the coin appears to stand on a higher level behind the columns and symbolizes the end-on view of the Ark of the Covenant hidden behind the Holy Veil, hence its dotted outline. The two dots or circles on the end panel represent the ends of the carrying poles or staves and the domed top, the covering of the cherubim. This scholarly assessment, although ultimately unprovable, does provide a logical explanation for the representation found on this coin which, if correct, provides proof that even in AD 132 the Jews of Jerusalem, descendants of the priests and Levites of the First Temple, actively believed in the continued presence of the Ark, somewhere within the Temple Mount. Kosevah's silver denominations call for the 'Redemption of Israel' and for the 'Freedom of Jerusalem'. On surviving medium and large bronzes the title 'Shimon Prince of Israel' is legible, demonstrating the high level of revolutionary fervour which existed within the rebellion. Many of Ben Kosevah's followers, including the legendary scholar Rabbi Akiva, viewed Kosevah's emergence as fulfilling a prophecy in the Book of Numbers: 'There shall come forth a star out of Jacob, and a sceptre shall arise out of Israel.'[15]

Kosevah changed his name to Bar Kokhba, or 'Son of the Star', and assumed the role of Davidic Messianic Prince of a New Israel. Kokhba did not have the universal approval of his people. Many rabbis opposed his status and, fearing the consequences of another revolt against Rome, nicknamed him 'Bar Koziba' – 'Son of Lies'.

The fears of the rabbis were unfortunately borne out. As Jews across Palestine joined the rebellion to evict the Romans from Judaea, Rome reacted in a predictable and bloody fashion. The complete eradication of the guerrilla war employed by Kokhba's forces necessitated violent suppression and after three years of warfare, in AD 135, with almost a thousand villages devastated and half a million Jews dead in their wake, the Roman army reached Jerusalem.[16] The city, without walls, was undefendable and Bar Kokhba was compelled to retreat eastwards into the Judaean wilderness. He made a last-ditch stand at the Jewish stronghold of Bethar, ten kilometres to the south-west of Jerusalem, and died during the Roman attack. Kokhba's revolt represented the last serious attempt to restore a permanent Jewish presence on the Temple Mount. The practicality of opposing Rome was futile and this time the Emperor imposed the severest punishment on the Jewish people by permanently removing all traces of monotheism in the city. Jerusalem was transformed into a pagan capital of 'strange gods and goddesses'.

Hadrian's plans, however, were tempered by the casualty list at the end of hostilities. Initially he had wanted to build a temple to Jupiter on the Mount but the Kokhba revolt cost the Roman army an embarrassingly high number of dead, which when announced to the senate dissuaded Hadrian from carrying out this particular part of his plan. But the site was nonetheless treated ruthlessly.

The traditional Roman ritual for the foundation of a 'new' city involved the ploughing up of the chosen area. Although the abundance of stone in Jerusalem would have made this an impossibility, levelling did take place. Hadrian's statue was erected on the Temple Mount platform and a temple to Venus – the Roman equivalent of the goddesses Aphrodite or Ashtoreth – was built in the heart of Jerusalem, west of the Temple Mount. No Jew was permitted to reside in Aelia Capitolina or to enter its precincts. The penalty for disobeying this law was death. 'Ba'alistic' worship had made a triumphant return to the City of David.

A PLACE OF SCORN

Over the course of the next century and a half Aelia Capitolina prospered and grew as a pagan polytheistic city. But at the beginning of the fourth century AD events began to unfold which would result in bringing back to the city monotheistic worship. In AD 312 Flavius Valerius Constantine, son of the Roman Emperor Constantius Chlorus, challenged his rival Maxentius for control of the western Roman Empire. The armies of Constantine and Maxentius met at the Milvian Bridge in Italy. In the moments before battle began, Constantine saw the symbol of the Christian faith, the cross, in the sky above the battlefield.

After his victory he willingly attributed his success to the intervention of the God of the Christians and changed his cult allegiance from Sol Invictus to the God of Jesus. The Christian 'cult' was elevated to the position of the official religion of Rome's western empire replacing the ancient pagan rituals which had ousted the cult of Yahweh from Jerusalem. This was an astute move by Constantine. Although pagan worship still remained at the heart of his empire, Christianity, despite severe periods of persecution, had become successfully integrated throughout the Roman Empire. Many Roman Christians, therefore, saw Constantine's victory as immensely significant: the incident at the Battle of Milvian Bridge was an unquestionable sign of the divine intervention of Christ. In AD 324 Constantine conquered Licinius, his brother-in-law and co-emperor, in the East and transferred his capital from Rome to Byzantium – modern-day Istanbul, which he renamed Constantinopolis. With the Christian Church now close to the spiritual helm of empire a new need arose to channel the religious energies of the faithful in one unified direction. Constantine realized that Christian pilgrims required sites at which to worship. Jerusalem at a stroke became the centre of spiritual attention for the citizens of the empire.

Constantine's logical course of action was to demolish the pagan temples of the city and create Christian shrines in their place. Jerusalem was still a city of pagan monuments, ironically built out of stone taken from the Temple Mount.[17] However, the Christian architects faced the problem that was encountered by every generation of archaeologists in the city in their quest to identify a site predating Roman occupation; the exact location of sites which could be associated with Jesus were somewhere under the foundations of Aelia Capitolina, laid several centuries previously on top of the rubble of New Testament Jerusalem. Undeterred, Byzantine archaeologists made calculations and began digging.

In AD 327 the tomb of Jesus was discovered to the north-west of the Temple Mount. The site on the edge of a Hadrianic quarry was soon announced to include Golgotha as well, and foundations for a new church – the Anastasis, or Resurrection – were laid. The Byzantine Anastasis was lined with marble and gold – in an attempt to imitate Herod's Temple. The Anastasis was a focal point for Christian pilgrimage in Jerusalem disassociated from the Jewish Temple Mount.

But, despite interest in the places of Jesus' passion and crucifixion,

the Temple Mount was not entirely ignored by the Christian architects. A sixth-century mosaic map discovered at Madaba, east of the
Jordan river, suggests that there was a structure on the Mount
during the Byzantine era, mentioned by Christian pilgrims:[18]

> At the southern edge of the Temple Mount, also known as the
> 'Temple Mount Corner,' the Madaba Map indicates the existence of
> a structure that is not further identified. According to Christian tra-
> dition, this is the place where Jesus was tempted by Satan, and it is
> possible that a building was erected there to commemorate that
> event; in any case, some of the pilgrims of this era mention the build-
> ing at the Temple Mount Corner.[19]

This location at the south-east angle was also discussed by
Byzantine pilgrims as the place where Solomon had written the
Book of Wisdom and the spot from where James, brother of Jesus,[20]
was thrown to his death in AD 62. Whether Solomon wrote the Book
of Wisdom on this part of the Mount will never be proven.
However, Byzantine identification of the south-east angle as the
place of James' death does have some archaeological foundation.

The New Testament relates how, as James lay injured on the
slopes of the Kidron below the south-eastern angle, a fuller, so
named from the fuller's earth used in the cleansing and thickening
of cloth, put him out of his misery with a club. Fulling has ancient
associations with the Lower Kidron. A young man called Reverend
Hanauer who assisted Warren as an interpreter was the first person
this century to draw attention to the numerous ancient fullers' vats
which were carved out of the rock, standing to the south of the
south-east angle.[21] Hanauer's discovery gives credence to the story
in the New Testament as well as to the identification of the location
given by Byzantine pilgrims.

Constantine died in AD 337 after successfully creating a pilgrim
city for Christianity. But his actions caused nothing but dismay
amongst the Jews of Palestine who longed for a Messianic return
and the foundation of a new Temple to Yahweh. Constantine's
Byzantine successors, Constantius I and II, imposed increasing
restrictions on Jews for a further generation until in AD 361 Julian
succeeded to the throne. Julian, who was brought up as a Christian,

reacted strongly against the faith of his birth and as his reign progressed he attempted to restore the pagan worship of his Roman ancestors. Surprisingly, he also looked in favour upon the monotheistic Jews and in AD 362 granted them the right to rebuild the Temple on the Mount.[22] They began to clear the ancient site and to lay foundations but in May of the following year an earthquake, not uncommon in the region,[23] struck Jerusalem and caused fire to break out on the Temple Mount. The Christians were jubilant at what they perceived as an act of godly intervention to prevent the Jews from completing their work and, as if to fulfil the divine plan, within a month Julian was killed in battle. Jovian, a Christian to the core, was elected to the throne of the Roman Empire and he reimposed stringent measures on the Jews of Palestine. Banned once again from residing in the city of their faith, they could only visit the Mount as pilgrims and lament the absence of worship on the most holy site of their ancestors.

Throughout the remainder of the Byzantine period, the Temple Mount continued to be a religious no man's land. However, in AD 410 Saint Jerome, a Christian writer prominent for his hatred of heretics, reported the presence of Hadrian's statue next to a monument to Capitoline Jupiter on the Temple Mount.[24] If his account is accurate, despite Hadrian's reservations about building a temple to the king of Roman deities, the figure of Jupiter had at least gained a foothold on the Mount.

With few exceptions, such as with Julian's concessions, the Byzantine era was characterized by a steady decline in Christian attitudes towards the Jews. This gradually degenerated into outright disrespect for the holiest place in the Jewish faith. But, as with the Jews before them, time was running out for the Christians. By the beginning of the sixth century AD they were forced to face new perils which would alter their own claim to monotheistic supremacy for ever. Weakened by internal division, Jerusalem was invaded by the Persians in AD 614. An army led by the general Shahrbaraz surrounded the city. Jerusalem held out for three weeks until at the end of May the Persian army broke through the Byzantine defence. Pouring through the gates and out into the streets, the Persian soldiers showed little mercy and over 60,000 people, including women and children, were killed.[25] The Persians looted the city, then departed, leaving it in the hands of the Jews who found their aspirations of a new covenant on the Mount suddenly rekindled. But resurgent Jewish hopes were finally dashed by the conditions of a truce made between Persia and the Emperor Heraklius of Byzantium in AD 629. Heraklius was permitted to retain Jerusalem and he entered the city via the Golden Gate which today stands at the northern end of the *haram*. His triumph, however, was short lived. In AD 571 a child was born into the Quraysh tribe of northern Arabia, some seven hundred kilometres from Jerusalem. Named al-Amin – the faithful – he became known as Muhammad, 'the highly praised',[26] and his life changed the appearance of Temple Mount beyond recognition.

THE COMING OF ALLAH

Information about Muhammad's early life is scant. His father 'Abdullah died before he was born and when he was six his mother Aminah died. Muhammad's grandfather 'Abd-al-Muttalib looked after him until his death when his paternal uncle abu-Talib took charge of his upbringing. His marriage at the age of twenty-five to Khadijah a wealthy Qurayshite widow changed his life and gave the tribes of Arabia a man who would unite them in monotheistic faith.

Muhammad's marriage offered him the possibility to pursue a desire close to his heart – to commune with his inner self – and he spent an ever increasing amount of time meditating within a small cave on a hillside called Hira. Here, in a series of visions, he received instructions to spread the word of one, all-powerful God who would reward the faithful after death and punish unbelievers with hell. The basic message was hardly different from that of the warning to wayward Jews from the Old Testament prophets and Muhammad's reception from his fellow Arabs was predictably the same: like Jeremiah, prophet of Yahweh, Muhammad, prophet of Allah, was soon perceived as a *nadhir* or Prophet of Doom.[27]

The Quraysh were the custodians of al'Ka'bah, the sanctuary at Mecca which was built to protect a piece of sacred black granite. The

Ka'bah was the main centre of pilgrimage for the polytheistic tribespeople of the Arabian region who erected numerous idols around the Black Stone. Muhammad's words threatened the economic interests of the tribe and, although his wife and her cousin Waraqah ibn-Nawfal followed his calling, the Qurayshite aristocracy opposed all demands to join Muhammad in his monotheistic path.

Muhammad soon gained enough support from the lower classes of his society to be recognized as a threat by his opponents. By AD 615 ninety-four Meccan families, disciples of Muhammad, decided to extricate themselves from danger. They fled Mecca and sought refuge in the domain of the Christian Negus of Abyssinia, leaving Muhammad temporarily isolated.[28] Undaunted, Muhammad continued his work. He began to realize the powerful role that the Bible played in uniting Christians and became determined to create a similar book for his own followers. He began to compile his own mystical experiences which included his famous 'night journey' to the Temple Mount of Jerusalem.

Muhammad described how he was carried off in his dreams on the back of the winged horse Burak, which had the face of a woman and the tail of a peacock. Burak transported him to Mount Moriah in Jerusalem. Here Muhammad began his ascent or *mi' raj* through the celestial spheres to the seventh heaven encountering as he did Jesus Christ, King David, Moses, Abraham, Adam and finally the angel Gabriel who confirmed Muhammad as the Prophet of Allah – the almighty God. Here, above the *sakhra* in Jerusalem, Muhammad was given instructions on how the Moslem faithful should pray.

By AD 622 opposition to his work had grown to such an extent that Muhammad felt obliged to look elsewhere for a place to continue his efforts at converting his fellow Arabs. A deputation of seventy-five men offered him and his people refuge in Medina, the home town of his mother, so he slipped quietly away from Mecca. Muhammad entered Medina on 22 September AD 622 preceded by two hundred of his followers. Muhammad's journey from Mecca to Medina became known as the *hijrah* or 'flight' and from this moment his fortunes changed. He won his first battle in AD 624 when, supported by only three hundred followers, he defeated a Meccan force of one thousand men at Badr, twenty-five kilometres south-west of Medina.[29] This victory spurred him on. His religiously inspired military fervour was soon directed against Jewish inhabitants of Arabia who farmed the date plantations of the Arabian region. In AD 627 Muhammad killed over six hundred of these Jews for daring to support his enemies. The survivors were banished from the region. Similar treatment was meted out to the Jews of Medina and in AD 629 the Jews who inhabited the oasis of Khaybar to the north of Medina were also expelled. These last years of Muhammad's life saw the consolidation of Islam or harmony with God. Wishing to make a complete break from the influences of Judaism and Christianity, Muhammad decreed Friday the Moslem holy day of the week and replaced the use of trumpets and bells as a call to prayer by the *adhan* or call from the minaret. In January AD 630, in the eighth year of the *hijrah*, Muhammad's armies finally conquered Mecca. He entered the sanctuary, the Ka'bah, where the Black Stone was positioned, and smashed the many idols that stood around it. The area around the Stone and the Ka'bah he then declared *haram*, or sacred, and ordered that in future, as Jews had refused to join him in praying towards Jerusalem, all Arabs should pray towards this spot.[30]

Muhammad died in Medina on 8 June AD 632, having united the tribes of Arabia through his revolutionary work. For a year after Muhammad's death his collection of thoughts and sayings, the Qur'an, or Koran, was preserved by men known as the *huffaz* or memorizers. The *huffaz*, however, were a dying breed and to safeguard the Koran Muhammad's words were written down. The original manuscript was kept in Mecca and three perfect copies were forwarded to the Islamic military camps: at Damascus in Syria, at Basra close to the head of the Persian Gulf and at al-Kufah on the river Euphrates, one hundred kilometres south of Baghdad. But despite the unifying effect of the Qur'an, allegiances between the Bedouin tribes of Arabia were, as T.E. Lawrence discovered in 1917, less than easy to maintain. Islam in its purest sense required the surrender of self to the purpose of God and after Muhammad's death the movement he had nurtured nearly foundered through intertribal rivalry. But the timing of the Islamic movement was fortuitous. Persia and Byzantium had fought each other to a standstill and the Arab armies, when united, swept all before them. By AD 636, they entered Palestine and by July of the following year they were encamped in force on the hills surrounding Jerusalem. The city surrendered to the Islamic army in February AD 638 with the Christian Patriarch Sophronius escorting in person the entry of the conquering army. The Islamic leader, Caliph 'Umar, joined his successful Moslem forces for the occasion. It was his responsibility to establish the status of Jerusalem and draw up the necessary regulations for civilian rule of the city. In these aspects he was magnanimous and for once the streets of Jerusalem were not awash with the blood of the innocent. The Patriarch gave 'Umar a tour of the Christian sites of the city and when 'Umar arrived at the Temple Mount he was shocked.

Following the departure of the Persians from Jerusalem, the Temple Mount had suffered terrible indignities. Disposing of waste was as much a problem in ancient cities as in modern, and the citizens of Jerusalem, as Warren found out in the nineteenth century, believed they had an immediate answer. What could not be flushed down drains was dumped, and the Byzantines decided that the Temple Mount platform was the ideal location. The new conqueror of the city was aghast at the desecration of such a holy site. Climbing up over a mound of rubbish spilling out of a gateway, 'Umar picked up a handful of dung and threw it over the wall of the platform, a gesture of his intention to cleanse the site and restore the Mount to its holy status. The officials accompanying 'Umar followed his example.[31]

In 1870 a contemporary of Charles Warren, E.H. Palmer, published a *History of the Haram* which he had compiled from the Arabic historians Jelal ed din es Siyuti and Kemal ed din ibn Abi Sherif.[32] Palmer was, like Warren, meticulous in his research and his account of 'Umar's visit describes how As Sakhra, the exposed area of rock now under the Dome of the Rock, was uncovered by 'Umar's entourage. The Caliph, who discovered a natural surface to the Temple Mount, reportedly forbade anyone to pray at the site until three showers of rain had fallen on the *sakhra*.[33] By imposing this regulation of symbolic purification 'Umar wished it to be known that religious sanctity had been restored to the Mount. By AD 638 political divisions within the Moslem world caused 'Abd al Malik the ruling Caliph to turn his attention towards the architectural development of the Temple Mount. Since the conquest of 'Umar, a simple wooden structure erected at the southern end of the Temple Mount platform on the site of the present-day Aqsa Mosque had been used as a shelter for the pilgrims who wished to visit and pray, but this was about to change. 'Abd al Malik forbade his Syrian followers to make the pilgrimage to Mecca as his political rival, Zobeir, was in control of the region. He therefore decided that the Mount, already revered as the third most holy site of Islam, should be developed to rival Mecca. Plans were drawn up to convert the ruins of Herod's Temple complex into a sacred *haram* or enclosure.

THE DOME OF THE ROCK AND THE AQSA MOSQUE

'Abd al Malik assembled a workforce of skilled artisans and craftsmen and set aside an amount of money equivalent to seven years of revenue from Egypt to finance his scheme. He gave his architect the design of the *qubbet* or dome he wished to build over the *sakhra* and commissioned the preliminary construction of a scale model. The model so pleased him that he ordered for it to remain in place as a permanent fixture of the *haram* architecture. Work began immediately on the main building which was a construction of extraordinary internal harmony and, judging from the dimensions, the architect was well trained in the science of mathematics. The building was constructed as an octagon which if seen in plan would fit inside a circle of just under fifty-five metres in diameter.

There has been much discussion in recent years amongst scholars of the Temple Mount about the possible existence of a Byzantine church on the site of the *sakhra*.[34] But this seems unlikely given the well-documented Christian abuse of the site: the Byzantine Christians would hardly have turned the location of a church into a rubbish-tip. There is, however, substantial evidence to suggest that 'Abd al Malik used the knowledge of Byzantine architects to develop the model and the full-scale plan of the Qubbet as-Sakhra, or the Dome of the Rock. In a book published in 1924 under the auspices of the *British Archaeological Review*, K.A.C. Creswell laid out in great detail the striking similarities between the Dome of the Rock, the Byzantine Cathedral at Bosra and two Christian Byzantine structures of Jerusalem: the Anastasis at 'Golgotha' and the Church of the Ascension on the Mount of Olives. Creswell measured the ground plans of each building and his findings are persuasive:

> To sum up, the steps of evolution of the plan of the Qubbet as-Sakhra would appear to be as follows:
>
> The Anastasis, AD 327–335. Inner Circle 20.90 metres in diameter, with outer circle 36.52 metres in diameter (internal measurement).
>
> The Church of the Ascension, before AD 378 (according to Vincent and Abel). Inner circle, probably of same diameter as last. Outer octagon, measuring 15.80 metres a side, derived from inner circle by same system as in Qubbet as-Sakhra.
>
> The Cathedral at Bosra, AD 513. The first example of a double ambulatory. Central circle probably 14.946 metres in diameter, intermediate octagon, 10.58 metres a side; outer circle 36.10 metres (approximately that of the Anastasis), set in a square exterior.
>
> The Qubbet as-Sakhra [Dome of the Rock] AD 688–691. Inner circle 20.37 metres (approximately that of the Anastasis); intermediate octagon, 15.82 metres a side externally, almost exactly the same as that of the Church of the Ascension. Circumscribing circle, which fixed the outer octagon, derived from intermediate one by same method as at Bosra.[35]

The images obtained from aerial infra-red photography conducted in 1998 show that the *haram* platform contained an outer pavement in line with the outside walls of the Qubbet as-Sakhra, which is otherwise indiscernible to the naked eye.[36] This shows that whether or not there was a previous Christian church over the *sakhra*, the Qubbet as-Sakhra was constructed on an extensive site levelled specifically for that purpose. Inside the *Sakhra* the bedrock of the Temple Mount was left exposed in the centre. The cupola or dome, 24.5 metres in diameter, was built over the sacred stone. Its height, 54.9 metres, was exactly the same measurement as the circumference of the main building.

On completion of the Qubbet as-Sakhra the two men commissioned with executing the works, Rija ibn Haiyah el Kendi and Yezid ibn Sallam, confessed to 'Abd al Malik that they had 100,000 gold dinars left over from their job. As they declined the offer of the Caliph to retain the money as a personal bonus, it was melted down, hammered into gold sheets and added as a plating to the outside of the dome. The Crescent of Islam was placed at its pinnacle and a massive cover of felt and leather was made to protect its gilt finish from the erosion caused by winter rain and snow. The opening of the Dome of the Rock in AD 691 was preceded by a cleansing of the *sakhra* which then became a ritual. Using a distillation of *khaluk*, an aromatic plant, the sacred rock was washed and the air inside the dome filled with incense from the aloe plant, spread by gold and silver censers. Rija and Yezid had also paid for the construction of a latticed ebony screen to surround the *sakhra*, adding further to the mystique of the sacred location.

Visitors to the *sakhra* can enter a cave underneath the rock by going down a flight of fourteen steps. The cave, which is carved out of the solid rock, has a level floor and a domed top. In the centre of the roof, just above head height, is a hole one metre in diameter which pierces the ceiling to the surface level of the *sakhra* above. There have been many suggestions that the *sakhra* was the site of the altar of sacrifice which once stood outside the Temples of Solomon and Herod and that the cave underneath was used for the collection of blood and animal refuse. Wilson, who so capably surveyed it in 1864, believed it was a cistern for the collection of pure water for use in the Temple.[37] The validity of these observations, however, must stand or fall on the question of elevation. The ground level of the Temple, as Warren deduced and Conder chose to ignore, was higher than the surface of the *sakhra*. In reality this cave was probably an ancient tomb or hidden chamber lying underneath the Temple floor, in much the same way as vaults exist under Christian cathedrals and churches, and it had at some stage been converted for use as part of a drainage channel or as a cistern.

Warren was convinced that because of the position of Cistern V to the south-east of the Dome of the Rock, the Temple altar – and thus the Temple – had also stood to the south of the *sakhra*, making

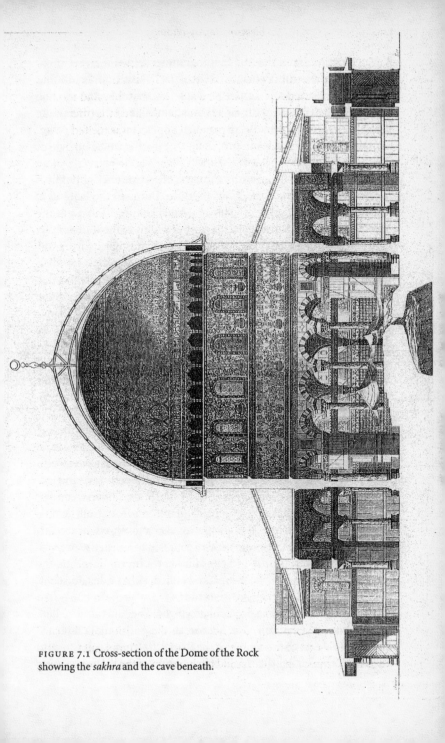

FIGURE 7.1 Cross-section of the Dome of the Rock showing the *sakhra* and the cave beneath.

it even more probable that the chamber under the *sakhra* was some-how connected to the drainage system of the Jewish Temple Mount. Warren recognized the importance of the *sakhra* to the overall archaeological picture of the *haram* and before leaving Jerusalem in 1870 he performed two deeds, one highly secret and the other extremely risky, if not foolhardy in a place long established by the Moslems as holy to the Islamic faith.

By the middle of the seventh century AD, the Moslem Caliphs had successfully established the *sakhra* and the Dome of the Rock as a Moslem shrine. In AD 705 'Abd al Malik restored the El Aqsa Mosque which had stood since the time of 'Umar to the south of the Dome of the Rock. The Aqsa Mosque, which in translation from the Arabic means 'the Remote', was so called either because of its distance from Mecca[38] or because of its proximity to the *sakhra*, the place which the Moslem clerics believed was the exact centre of the earth and the gateway to heaven.[39] Both buildings were lit by lamps suspended from chains: 230 in the Aqsa and 155 in the Qubbet as-Sakhra. Every Friday and festival day one thousand candles were lit to illuminate the buildings for the faithful.

It is known from Moslem sources[40] that Jews also participated in the design and layout of the *haram*. In the prevailing trend of Islamic benevolence, neither Jews nor Christians were totally excluded from the site. Some were given menial tasks within the precincts. In return for an exemption from the annual poll-tax, a fixed number of ten Jewish families were offered the task to sweep out the *haram* area and clean the lavatories which stood around the perimeter. Jews were also employed to make glass lamps, candelabras and wicks, receiving in return exemption from poll-tax for their family members. The Moslems also employed a similar number of Christian servants whose job it was to brush the mats of the *haram* and clean out the conduits and cisterns that honey-combed the area, which were constantly filled with the dirt and dust swept across the *haram* by Jewish brooms.[41]

'Abd al Malik died on 8 September AD 705. The sanctuary he had created was so beautiful that a later successor to the caliphate, Abdullah el Mamun who ruled over Jerusalem from AD 813 to 833, attempted to alter 'Abd al Malik's inscription of dedication on the

Dome of the Rock and credit himself with the glory of its construction.

During the period of Moslem history from the completion of the Qubbet as-Sakhra in AD 691 up to the First Crusade in 1099, many buildings were restored. 'Abd el Malik's son, Caliph el-Walid al-Malik, rebuilt the Aqsa Mosque, replacing the basic timber structure erected at the time of 'Umar with a mosque of stone and marble. However, part of the southern end of the Temple Mount where the Aqsa was situated was extremely unstable. Herod's 'sixty-cubit' extension in the eastern sector of the southern wall was based on sound and probably Solomonic foundations but at the western sector there was a severe problem. Herod, in order to achieve his expansion of the Temple Mount, had been unable to extend the platform eastwards because of the steepness of the sides of the Kidron valley. He had, therefore, been forced to build on the accumulated infill of the Tyropoeon valley which once separated the Temple Mount from the Upper City. This was the perfect course for water and when it rained the natural substructure under Herod's massive blocks of stone could easily move. Warren and his sergeant, Henry Birtles, almost lost their lives when just such a shift caused the partial collapse of one of their underground galleries. Whenever an earthquake occurred in the region, the foundations of the south-western end of the *haram* suffered further damage. So began a fight against nature which has continued until the present day.

In AD 747 an earthquake devastated Jerusalem. The Dome of the Rock was damaged and Walid's Aqsa Mosque collapsed. Two years later an 'Umayyad army was defeated in battle on the Za'b river and the 'Umayyad dynasty which had ruled Jerusalem since AD 661 was replaced by that of the 'Abbasids. The new rulers, now based in Baghdad, stripped gold and silver from the *haram*[42] in order to finance the basic restoration of Jerusalem's infrastructure and no sooner was their task of repair completed than in AD 771 there was another earthquake. The Aqsa was rebuilt from the rubble, this time on a grander scale. The next major earthquake occurred in AD 1033 which caused the collapse of the northern end of the Aqsa. Rebuilt by the middle of the century on a smaller scale, the Aqsa was once again restored to its primary religious function.

From the eighth to the eleventh centuries Jerusalem stood on the political periphery of the Moslem world. Byzantium with its capital Constantinople was still a major power in the region, forming an effective barrier against the westward spread of Islam. Despite this, Christian pilgrimage to Jerusalem had grown and by the eleventh century AD Jerusalem had a well-established Byzantine Christian presence. Pilgrimage was a source of wealth and Armenian and Italian immigrants skilled in trades and crafts settled in the city giving it a vibrant and cosmopolitan atmosphere. But towards the end of the eleventh century the rulers and church leaders of the European Christian world were struggling to preserve order within their own borders. Feudal society, kept in check by the alliance of church and state, was becoming gradually more sophisticated and, in consequence, people were less willing to obey the laws governing their existence. The initial warning of impending discontent amongst the populace had come as early as the anniversary celebrating the first Christian millennium. In AD 1000 the Second Coming had been expected and there was much dismay when this did not happen.

The scenario was repeated in AD 1033 – the official Church millennium of Christ's crucifixion. Church councils, backed by local bishops and barons, organized mass gatherings of the poor to commit them by oath to keep the peace and obey commandments. The Church threatened excommunication for non-compliance, a powerful weapon in a superstitious society governed by the Holy Sacraments. In spite of early successes in maintaining law and order, heresy escalated in the eleventh century. Many poor Christians regarded the removal of a Church which had grown rich on tithes taken from the labourer as the first step towards a new age. Manichaeanism was one such heresy. Based on the teachings of Mani, a third-century monk from Persia, Manichaeanism advocated the Zarathustran principles of good and evil, claiming that the constant fight waged between the two forces was responsible for all things on earth. Such a philosophy, which negated the importance of Christ's resurrection, struck terror into the heart of the Church. Many of the Manichaean leaders were disaffected monks who had left the security of their monasteries to follow an individualistic path to God. They preached the complete abolition of Church sacraments and promoted repudiation of the cross. In an age when life-expectancy hovered around thirty, death was an ever-present reality and such a radical religion drew ardent support from Christians across Europe. The Church looked desperately for a cause to unite the people in the established faith. The situation in Palestine at the end of the eleventh century gave them the perfect opportunity.

Since 1073 the Seljuk Turks had ruled Jerusalem. The Seljuks displaced the Egyptian Fatimid dynasty which had governed the region since AD 983. Although banditry had always existed in Palestine – even Warren went armed in the nineteenth century – under the Seljuks attacks on Christian pilgrims increased. This moved the Pope, Urban II, to intervene. In a society so governed by the Old and New Testaments the idea of liberating Jerusalem was easy to promote: Jerusalem was still considered by medieval Christians to be the centre of the world. This is confirmed by maps of the medieval period.

Since the seventh century AD,[43] Jerusalem had been at the centre of the known world. Based on a format which is now described as the T–O system, the medieval map was simple and by consequence powerful. The 'T' stood within the circular 'O' of the oceans, dividing the continents of Asia, Europe and Africa. Jerusalem was at the centre of the map at the intersection of the upright and cross of the 'T'. From this evidence alone, it is apparent that Jerusalem, which to the vast majority of people must have seemed as remote as the moon, was nevertheless of the greatest symbolic importance.

With the authority of his bishops challenged by heretical forces and Christian pilgrims threatened, Pope Urban II had found the answer to all his problems. A popular 'Crusade', so called from *la croix* – the French word for the cross which every participant wore stitched to their tunics, was organized to march eastwards to wrest the holy places from Moslem control and bring Jerusalem back into the fold of Christendom. To all 'Crusaders' Urban promised remission of sins, wealth and the possibility of acquiring property.

In 1095 he preached a chilling sermon at Clermont in southern France:

Let none of your possessions detain you, no solicitude for your family affairs, since this land which you inhabit, shut in on all sides by the seas and surrounded by mountain peaks, is too narrow for your large population; nor does it abound in wealth; and it furnishes scarcely enough food for its cultivators. Hence it is that you murder one another, that you wage war, and that frequently you perish by mutual wounds. Let therefore hatred depart from among you, let your quarrels end, let wars cease, and let all dissensions and controversies slumber. Enter upon the road the Holy Sepulchre; wrest that land from the wicked race, and subject it to yourselves. The land was given by God into the possession of the children of Israel.

Jerusalem is the Navel of the World; the land is fruitful above others, like another Paradise of Delights.[44]

The promise of fruitful land as well as the remission of sins acted as a powerful incentive on his audience. To allow the harvest to be gathered Urban decreed that all those willing to 'crusade' should be ready to depart their homes by 15 August 1096 and rendezvous at Constantinople, capital of Byzantium, later in the year. But there was little attempt to follow the advice of the Pope, and still less inclination to proceed with any semblance of self-discipline. News of Urban's appeal spread like wildfire and the 'Crusaders' made no distinction between Moslems and the children of Israel. Indeed, as if to emphasize the supremacy of Christian belief, they instigated what can only be described as a human holocaust before they had even reached Palestine, and the Jews were their sacrificial victims.

In Europe many Jews were industrious and capable businessmen who were prominent figures within their communities. Preparations for a long journey such as a Crusade were expensive and Jewish lenders were resented by the less intelligent members of a Crusader society who could not reconcile borrowing money from Jews – the race of people they held responsible for 'killing' Jesus – in order to equip themselves for the job of liberating the city in which he had been put to death. The Pope's call to arms was therefore a perfect excuse for many individuals to express their views. Gathering support as they went, many 'Crusaders' left the land before the August date. Throughout the spring and early summer of 1096 groups rampaged through the valley of the Rhine massacring Jews in the cities of Worms and Mainz, despite attempts by some local bishops to protect them. Similar atrocities took place in the Moselle valley in France.[45] Despite such a bloody demonstration of the Crusader spirit, Christian consciences were remarkably unswayed by this behaviour and preparations continued as planned. In every country of Europe common Crusaders were joined by the nobility with the majority drawn from France and Germany. The Crusaders congregated around three leading figures: Godfrey de Bouillon, Duke of Lower Lorraine, Bohemond I of Taranto and Raymond IV, Count of Toulouse. By 1097 an estimated 60–100,000 people travelled into Byzantine Christian territory to rendezvous outside Constantinople.[46] Alexius, the Byzantine Emperor, had the difficult task of maintaining peace and stability while his kingdom served as a unification point for the Crusade. By spring 1098, all the principal leaders swore on oath to protect the life, honour and possessions of Alexius. At the end of April, the Crusader armies headed south on the ancient trading route towards Palestine in the direction of Jerusalem. An army from northern France which was under the command of Robert of Normandy, the eldest son of William the Conqueror, joined them on 3 June to assist in the siege of Nicaea, seventy kilometres south-east of Constantinople.

It took another fourteen months for the Crusader forces, numbering around 80,000 men, to fight their way through Turkey and Syria into Palestine. But by the evening of Tuesday, 7 June 1099, they set up camp outside the city walls.[47] The Egyptian Fatimid dynasty had retaken control of Jerusalem from the Seljuk Turks and the governor, Iftikhar ad-Dawla, who was well informed by his couriers of the progress of the Crusader army, prepared as best he could for the oncoming battle. Iftikhar ad-Dawla sent a message to Cairo requesting reinforcement and attempted to block or poison the water sources available to the approaching Crusaders. Jerusalem with its copious cisterns, many of which were located on the Temple Mount, had an adequate quantity of fresh water to withstand a long siege and the city was well stocked with food but, as a last measure aimed at preserving supplies, Christians of all denominations were expelled from the city.

The number of Crusaders who reached Jerusalem was insufficient to mount a full-scale assault around the perimeter of the city.
They made an attempt on 13 June to breach the city's defences from
the north but failed as they lacked the scaling ladders and siege
towers necessary for a cohesive attack. With the heat of the summer
upon them and food scarce, they soon realized that they would have
to take the city by applying the maximum amount of force to the
minimum area within the shortest space of time. The Crusaders set
about constructing siege engines and towers. Timber was scarce
around Jerusalem so they had to fetch it from as far away as Samaria,
more than thirty kilometres to the north.[48] With the shipbuilding
expertise of the Genovese several movable siege towers were
completed by the second week of July and an assault was planned
for the night of 13–14 July.

In order to split the enemy forces, the main attack was opened
simultaneously against the walls in the south-west sector of the city
and the eastern part of the northern wall. By the morning of the 14th
the siege tower commanded by Godfrey de Bouillon, Duke of
Lower Lorraine, was rolled against the northern wall and by midday
his men succeeded in bridging the gap between the top of their
tower and the battlements. This foothold was all that was required
to precipitate the fall of the city. Lowering ladders to enable reinforcements to join them, the Crusaders cleared a section of the
wall. A party of men descended into the city streets and opened the
Gate of the Column – the Damascus Gate – to the Crusader army
who were waiting outside. The Christians burst into the northern
part of the city, cutting their way through the narrow streets
towards the Temple Mount. Jews tried in vain to mount a defence of
their own quarter which lay in the path of the Crusaders, but they
stood little chance. The Christians systematically slaughtered
everyone. Many Moslems headed for the Temple Mount, seeking
sanctuary in the Aqsa where they hoped to avoid the butchery whilst
Iftikhar and his bodyguard barricaded themselves into the Tower of
David in the Upper City. In exchange for a substantial ransom
Iftikhar and his men were finally permitted to leave Jerusalem. As
they left, the Crusaders closed in on the surviving Moslems and Jews
of the city. The Moslems in the Aqsa were cut down and the Jews

locked into their synagogue. The Christians then set fire to the building.[49] An estimated thirty thousand men[50] exterminated virtually the entire population of Jerusalem which is believed to have been approximately the same number.[51]

The Crusaders carried out the worst excesses on the Temple Mount that had ever been seen; they believed this was God's justice. Raymond of Aguiles, chaplain to Raymond of Toulouse, who witnessed the events on the Mount, thought it was a 'just and splendid judgment of God that this place [the Temple Mount] should be filled with the blood of unbelievers, since it had so long suffered from their blasphemies'. Aguiles appeared to revel in the gory detail, confessing with some pride that on the site of the Temple 'men rode in blood up to their knees and bridle reins'. [52] If any mounted knights had been constrained to pick their way on horseback through mounds of bodies on the Mount on the afternoon of 15 July 1099, then the sight that met their eyes must have been apocalyptic. Pope Urban II died in Rome on 29 July before news of the Christian victory in Palestine reached him. The Christian world was shocked by reports of the massacre.

Urban's flock had done their work so well that the 'wicked race' had almost been eradicated in Jerusalem. Some of the Jews and Moslems who survived the slaughter of 15 July were saved from execution by Crusaders who anticipated a ransom.[53] Whilst arrangements were being made for their release the Jewish and Moslem prisoners were told to remove the bodies of their fallen kith and kin. Fellow Christians in need of money also helped clear the human remains. The stench of decaying corpses pervaded the air and as late as Christmas, five months after the massacre, the smell was still noticeable.[54]

KINGS OF CHRIST

Such bloodshed was an inauspicious beginning to the rebirth of Christian rule and the conquerors of Jerusalem were divided about the future of the city. In the aftermath of victory few Crusaders wanted to consider the appointment of a king for the city which had once mocked and crucified Jesus as King of the Jews. The factional nature of the Crusader army, all with a different leader vying for power, raised further problems. If someone had to rule, then who should be chosen? After much deliberation and considerable intrigue, the crown was offered to Raymond IV of Toulouse who refused it on the grounds that to wear a crown of gold would show disrespect to Jesus who had worn one only of thorns. Godfrey de Bouillon was the next choice and he accepted the leadership on the condition that he could adopt the title of 'Baron and Defender of the Holy Sepulchre'.[55]

It was an historic moment. A Christian ruled again over the site of Jesus' trial and crucifixion seemingly putting to an end the reign of the Infidel. However, lines of communication with Europe were precariously extended overland through Byzantium, Palestine was far from conquered, and from a strategic point of view the future of the Crusaders was bleak. The most direct route from which to receive reinforcements was via the Mediterranean sea, which left Crusaders as perennial hostages to the weather. Winter storms made travel by ship extremely hazardous between the months of November and March. The problem of resupply, in particular the replacement of horses which was essential in the maintenance of military supremacy in the region, was a constant worry for the Christians.

Godfrey de Bouillon was not burdened by the responsibility of the kingdom for long. After returning from a banquet at Caesarea he fell ill. There were rumours that he had been poisoned, but he may have contracted typhoid fever from fruit he had eaten in Caesarea.[56] He died on Wednesday, 18 July 1100 at the age of forty. He was buried five days later in the Church of the Holy Sepulchre. Once again the need for a leader arose. Godfrey had stipulated in his will that power should pass into the hands of the Patriarch Daimbert. But the Patriarch was with the Crusader army besieging Acre. An urgent message was sent to Godfrey's brother Baldwin who was in Edessa, inviting him to travel to Jerusalem to claim the throne. Baldwin arrived before the Patriarch, and took over control of the city. He was proclaimed King of Jerusalem on Sunday, 11 December 1100, taking the title of Baldwin I King of the Latins.

The Temple Mount, once cleansed of its dead, had already been transformed into the seat of Latin power within Jerusalem. Before his death Godfrey had converted the Aqsa Mosque into his palace and with the coronation of Baldwin, the Christian status of the Mount was reaffirmed. In 1115 work began on converting the Dome of the Rock into a Christian church. The Crescent of Islam on the pinnacle of the dome was replaced by the Christian cross and an altar was installed on the surface of the *sakhra*. One contemporary account by Fulcher of Chartres, a chronicler who followed the Crusader army to Jerusalem, describes how the chippings from the *sakhra* left over from the work of installing the altar were sold to pilgrims for their equivalent weight in gold.[57] In an extraordinary, but not unexpected, snub to the Jews, the converted Dome of the Rock was renamed the Templum Domini – the Temple of the Lord. The Templum Domini was not finally consecrated until 1142, but the Temple Mount had by this early stage in the history of the Latin Kingdom become established as the official centre of power in the Holy Land.

Now that the city was secure the civic and religious authorities looked for further sites of possible interest on the Mount that could be made into shrines for the increasing number of pilgrims. The miniature replica of the Dome of the Rock which 'Umar had left in place a few metres to the east of the main building was converted into a chapel in honour of James, Jesus' brother. James' site of death, the south-east angle, was the highest surviving section of the original Herodian platform. This, and the fact that the angle is visible from the Garden of Gethsemane – the place where Jesus spent his last night before being crucified, gave rise to another legend of the Crusader period. The Reverend Hanauer – Charles Warren's interpreter – mentions in his work *Walks in and Around Jerusalem* that the largest corner stone in the angle was 'the one referred to in Psalm CXVIII, Verse 22 and alluded to by our Lord in Saint Matthew, Chapter XXI Verse 42, as "the stone which the builders rejected" '.[58] Herod's final landscaping of the south-eastern angle was not completed during Jesus' lifetime and the painted marks of Herod's inspectors rediscovered by Warren in 1868 would have been visible to him. When referring to Psalm CXVIII Jesus may have had in mind the 'rejected' stones which lay within the base courses beneath the corner stone identified by the medieval legend. In 1998 photographs of the south-east angle revealed a small but distinct carved triangle twelve courses below Hanauer's 'rejected stone'.[59] Further inspection showed that the oxidized surface of the triangle was similar to the rest of the surface of the stone, suggesting that the carving was many hundreds of years old. It was a perfect 'set square' having one angle of 90 degrees and two of 45, matching the wooden set square that would have been used as the principle tool of measurement by Herod's masons. Precise measurements have always been of great importance to the masons of the Mount where close-fitting blocks of limestone were used to create most of the architecture. The Crusaders were influenced in their thinking on this matter by the huge perfectly joined blocks of stone supporting the *haram* platform and amongst these Crusaders were nine knights who in 1120 founded a military Order. They became known as the Knights Templar and their masons replicated faithfully the mathematical dimensions of the Dome of the Rock in the architecture of every major headquarters of the Order.

THE POOR KNIGHTS OF CHRIST

King Baldwin I died on 2 April 1118 of fever contracted while fighting in Egypt. During his reign he conquered most of Palestine, including the port of Acre which was a vital lifeline for Jerusalem. An upsurge in shipping from Europe followed this victory and pilgrimage increased dramatically. But the routes pilgrims took overland from Europe and the countryside surrounding the Holy City were still dangerous because of marauding Seljuk cavalry. In order to protect the pilgrims' routes the Order of the Knights Templar was created but their role in Christian society developed into far more than this as they became involved in the 'sacred science' of building and the perpetuation of Masonic 'secrets'.

After Baldwin's death his brother Eustace renounced his claim to the throne. Baldwin I's cousin, also named Baldwin, accepted the honour and was the first Latin king to be crowned in Jerusalem at the Church of the Holy Sepulchre. At some date between mid-January and mid-September of 1120,[60] the founding nine members[61] of the Knights Templar were sworn to vows of poverty, chastity and obedience in the presence of Warmund of Picquigny, the Patriarch of the kingdom whose religious seat was the Church of the Holy Sepulchre. Baldwin II gave up his residence at the Aqsa for a palace in the city outside the Temple Mount and handed over the Aqsa to the Knights Templar. The Templars were established at the very heart of ancient Jerusalem, on the site of the Temple of Solomon.

The evolution of the Order's official title indicates that the Templars were keenly aware of the historical importance of the site. They originally called themselves Pauperes Commilitones Christi – Poor Knights of Christ, but by the middle of the eleventh century documents were describing the Order as Milites Christi Templique Salomonici,[62] indicating their sense of allegiance to Solomon who built the First Temple. The Templars played a crucial part in the history of the Latin Kingdom of Jerusalem. They were key figures in the affairs of diplomacy between the Christians and Moslems and as their numbers multiplied both their military contribution to the Christian Kingdom of Jerusalem and their financial wealth increased. By 1128 the Templars were requested by their founding Grand Master Hugh de Payns to adhere to the Latin Rule of Saint Benedict, the requirements of which – chastity, poverty and obedience – he deemed the most suitable for the Order in view of their military role. The Templars wore an unemblazoned plain white surcoat which for twenty-seven years from their foundation in 1120 – until 1147 when a red cross was added – symbolized chastity and poverty. In so doing they followed a prestigious line of people dedicated to monotheism on the Mount. The dress of the Levites was white, with little or no ornament, and the Essenes wore a simple white tunic belted at the waist.

By the early 1170s the Templars had not only consolidated the Mount as a place of pilgrimage but also as a headquarters of considerable sophistication: the *haram* had in the eyes of the German monk and pilgrim Theodoricus been architecturally transformed by the Order. The complex had its own splendid underground cisterns which were full of water and the area above on the Temple Mount platform was 'full of walking places, lawns and council chambers'.[63] The Templars uncovered a number of underground chambers which they used as 'wash-rooms, stores, grain rooms, stores for wood and other domestic stores'.[64] The Aqsa was subjected to considerable renovation. A new façade was built and an extension created on the eastern side of the mosque, in which the Templar administration was housed. Living quarters were situated in the south-western angle, but restricted space there meant that only some of the three hundred knights and one thousand sergeants present in Palestine by the end of the 1170s[65] could be accommodated at this location.

Elsewhere on the Mount, further changes were made by orders of the Patriarch. A convent was constructed north-east of the Dome of the Rock and the Golden Gate in the eastern wall was converted into a church. The doors of the church were opened twice-yearly to the public: on Palm Sunday and on the Feast of the Exaltation of the Relic of the True Cross – a fragment of wood which had been 'discovered' by the mother of the Emperor Constantine seven centuries previously during the building of the Anastasis and which was 'identified' as a piece of Christ's cross.

Despite the considerable efforts of Christians to establish themselves on the Temple Mount Christian presence there soon came to an end. Baldwin II abdicated the throne in 1131 in favour of his son-in-law Fulk of Anjou who ruled Jerusalem for twelve years before dying of head wounds inflicted when falling from his horse chasing a hare. Baldwin II's son succeeded him and was crowned Baldwin III. The reign of Baldwin III was notable for the Christian loss in 1144 of the city of Edessa which since 1031 had been part of Byzantium. This sent shock waves throughout Christendom and calls were made for another Crusade to reinforce the Christian position in the Near East. The Second Crusade was a costly fiasco for the Christians in both manpower and prestige. It was intended principally to restore Crusader dominance of Syria, but internal dissension led to ignominious failure. Under the command of King Louis VII of France and King Conrad III of Germany and reinforced by knights from Palestine, the Crusader army attempted to conquer

Damascus. Arguments between the Germans, the French and the Knights from Jerusalem about the future status of Damascus started the moment the siege began. After only five days and amidst much acrimony, orders were given by King Louis and King Conrad for the army to disperse. The invincibility of the Crusaders was now seriously compromised and following the events outside Damascus the Moslems, fully aware of the internal divide within the forces of the West, looked on Christian-dominated Palestine as a promising area for Islamic reconquest.

Baldwin III died at Antioch in Syria in 1162 and was succeeded by his brother Amalric. Amalric ruled the Kingdom of Jerusalem for a further twelve years. He was a successful and courageous leader and by 1167 had secured the southern approaches to his kingdom through military success in Egypt. There, Amalric had depended heavily on the ambassadorial qualities of the Knights Templar, some of whom possessed the added advantage of speaking Arabic.[66] In return for their services the Templars were granted land and privileges within the kingdom which increased their political influence. By the time of Amalric's death in 1174 the Templars had consolidated sufficient land and titles, both in Palestine and in Europe, to permit the Order to function independently from the crown and to act as bankers in their own right. The outlook for the Kingdom of Jerusalem was much bleaker. The throne of Jerusalem passed to Baldwin III's son, Baldwin IV, and on his death from leprosy in March 1185 Baldwin IV's seven-year-old nephew was crowned as Baldwin V. Baldwin V lasted little more than a year. He was poisoned, it is said, by his mother Sibylla who wished her second husband, Guy de Lusignan, to become king.[67] The Kingdom of Jerusalem, riven by internal feuding and deadly intrigue, was disintegrating from within. In July 1187, less than a year after Guy's accession to the throne, a battle took place which would precipitate the fall of Jerusalem to Moslem forces.

The Seljuk Turks, who had made great gains in Syria against the Christians and who for a decade had fought a series of minor encounters with the Crusaders in Palestine, were marching towards Jerusalem under their charismatic leader, Salah ed-Din. On 4 July 1187 the flower of European chivalry including Guy the King of

Jerusalem and four hundred Knights Templar met Salah ed-Din in a major battle which took place approximately sixty kilometres to the north of the city at a location named the Horns of Hattin. The projecting rock formation which formed the summit, and gave the place its name, was occupied by the Crusaders the night before as their camp. It was an ill-considered choice. Lacking in water and exposed to the heat of the sun, the Crusader army soon found itself trapped by Salah ed-Din in an inferno of their own making. Gerard de Ridefort, the ruling Grand Master of the Templar Order, was primarily responsible for the situation in which the army found itself, having insisted that the army stay there. Cut off from water by the forces of Salah ed-Din, the Crusaders had no choice but to charge downhill in an attempt to break out of their encirclement. Although a small contingent escaped, the bulk of the Crusader army did not. Hundreds of foot soldiers and cavalry fell on the rocky hillside and the plight of the Christians, desperate for water, was worsened by the outbreak of fire which took hold of the scrub creating intense smoke and roasting many of the wounded alive. By mid-afternoon the Christian army was defeated. The King of Jerusalem was taken prisoner by the Moslems and the Relic of the True Cross which had accompanied the army was in the hands of the Infidel. The Bishop of Tyre, who had carried the relic, was dead on the field of battle and the survivors, who hoped to be ransomed, soon found that Salah ed-Din was in an uncompromising mood. Normally of benevolent character, he had been hardened by a decade of Templar brutality meted out to innocent Moslems of the region. He handed his prisoners over to fanatics within his army and 230 Templars were beheaded. Gerard de Ridefort, Grand Master of the Temple, and Guy – his king – were amongst the few captives spared.

The Kingdom of Jerusalem could little afford such losses, and Crusader strongholds fell like dominoes. Salah ed-Din, or Saladin as he was known to the Crusaders, swiftly captured Tiberius, Acre, Ashkelon and Gaza and by mid-September he was marching on the Holy City. By 20 September he was outside Jerusalem's walls. The defending Crusaders were pitifully small in number. Only two knights were left to command a scratch force and Balian de Ibelin, a knight who arrived on the eve of the siege to rescue his wife and children – under oath to Saladin not to remain in the city or bear arms, found himself forced to assist the Crusaders. In a desperate attempt to resist Saladin, Ibelin knighted thirty men of the city and every young boy over the age of sixteen to try to instigate leadership amongst the citizens.[68] Such measures, however, were futile. Saladin had found the weak point of Jerusalem's defences in the northern wall and by 29 September his military engineers succeeded in opening a breach. Ibelin, faced with inevitable defeat, left the walls of the city under truce to parley with Saladin. Ibelin made it clear that the Christians would fight to the bitter end, and if that happened the sacred buildings of the Temple Mount would be damaged or even destroyed. Once a price of 30,000 gold dinars was fixed for the population of Jerusalem, Christian surrender was agreed. On Friday, 2 October 1187, on the anniversary of Muhammad's night journey from Mecca to the *sakhra*, Moslem troops re-entered the Holy City, less than ninety years after the bloody conquest by the leaders of the First Crusade. Mercifully for the inhabitants of the city, the contrast between the comportment of Saladin's forces and the Christian behaviour of 1099 could not have been greater.

8

The Triumph of Islam,
1188–1916

Al-Malik al-Nasir al-Sultan Salah-ed-Din Yusuf was forty-nine years old when he conquered Jerusalem. Of Kurdish parentage, he was by 1187 a veteran military campaigner. He had survived numerous battles and much deadly in-fighting between members of his own faith. His desire to rid Palestine of the Crusaders was matched only by his ambition to spread the word of Islam. Since the death of Muhammad in AD 632 the prophet's followers had been divided by a dispute concerning his correct hereditary line. Saladin was born into the Sunnite tradition which recognized one of Muhammad's earliest converts, Abu Bakr, as the true successor. The Shia Moslems, on the other hand, believed a successor should be found in the family of Ali, Muhammad's cousin and son-in-law.

Once the city was under his control, Saladin immediately focused his attention on the holy site of the Temple Mount. His men set to work on restoring the *haram* to its former Moslem status. The golden cross was taken down from the pinnacle of the dome over the *sakhra* and was beaten with clubs as it was carried in a triumphant procession through the streets of the city. The altar and every vestige of Christian infrastructure was removed from the interior of the building.

The Aqsa was converted back to its function as a mosque and on Friday, 9 October 1187, Saladin attended a ceremony of rededication, helping to sprinkle the holy places with rose-water. Moslem rule on the Mount has endured almost without interruption until the present day. Despite dynastic change between the Arabs who controlled the Mount, this continuity allowed for an architectural and archaeological stability which has enabled the rich heritage which lies both above and below ground to be preserved.

Saladin encouraged the study of theology on the *haram* by conse-crating the *madrasah* style of theological seminary.[1] The scholars of the *madrasah* relied on the verses of the Koran and the early Moslem poets to provide the main structure for their studies, a system of learning not dissimilar to that chosen by Christian uni-versities in the later Middle Ages. Christian presence in the city was tolerated under the new regime. The Church of the Holy Sepulchre was left intact and in Christian hands. Saladin saw little point in destroying a church with such strong religious connections. However, the experience of Christian Crusader domination had had a profound effect on the Moslems, so the Moslem rulers embarked on extensive building, just as the Knights Templar did before them, in order to reinforce their claim over the Temple Mount and to eradicate the nightmare that a Latin kingdom would ever visit Jerusalem again. The Jews, like the Christians, were treated with a certain respect and they had moderate reasons to be hopeful of a new era. Forbidden access to Jerusalem by Rome fol-lowing the destruction of the Temple Mount in AD 70 and again by the Crusaders in 1099, the Jews were by 1190 allowed to take up residence within the walls of the city close to the Temple Mount and build a synagogue. But the consolidation of the Mount into a place of Moslem worship meant that the prospect of a return to Yahwistic sacrifice on Mount Moriah was unlikely.

The Christian disaster at the Horns of Hattin in 1187 encouraged the organization of another Crusade – the Third – which brought together Saladin and Richard Coeur de Lion who landed in Palestine in 1191. Richard's arrival signalled renewed hope for the Crusaders who, under the leadership of the French, had been bogged down for three years outside the city of Acre which they were attempting to recapture. Richard took command and within four weeks Acre capitulated to the Christians. Saladin realized that he was facing a formidable enemy.

Richard and Saladin had dramatically contrasting characters. Although both had been schooled in the harsh atmosphere of medieval political intrigue and had been hardened by battle, Richard was as crude as Saladin was cultured. But they developed a mutual respect for each other. Richard lived for battle and showed few religious inclinations. Saladin on the other hand regarded armed conflict as merely the means through which to pursue his ambitions for the establishment of universal Islam. Richard's ultimate goal was to recapture Jerusalem and Saladin was determined to prevent him from achieving this. Richard marched south from Acre, with the intention of turning east towards the Holy City. Saladin followed him and the two armies clashed on the sands of the coastal village of Arsuf. The outcome was victory for Richard, obtained largely through his personal example of courage and the stalwart behaviour of his Knight Templar bodyguard.

With Saladin expelled from the coast, the road to Jerusalem now lay open to Richard's advance but conquering the city was not yet a practical option. The Crusader forces had inadequate resources to maintain a supply of material and manpower for such an offensive so Richard delayed his march inland. He asked Saladin for a truce and set his initial demands high by suggesting that Saladin hand over the whole of Palestine west of the Jordan river, the city of Jerusalem and the Relic of the Holy Cross captured at Hattin, in return for peace. When Saladin refused, Richard resorted to another tactic. On 20 October he proposed a union of marriage between his sister, Queen Joanna of Sicily, and al-Adil, Saladin's brother. As a wedding gift the couple could be given Jerusalem which would at a stroke bring to an end the conflict between the Moslems and Christians. This rash, if not naive, solution was treated by Saladin with great amusement. Richard's plan was bold in concept but considering the prevailing mentality of the Christian world, totally unworkable. Joanna was the last to be consulted and her horror when she heard of the proposal reflected the general Christian attitude that Moslems were the Infidel and that peace with them was not an option. Negotiations for a truce dragged on and Richard made a final military effort towards Jerusalem. By Christmas he was at Latrun, the strategic western gateway to the hills of Jerusalem, and on 3 January 1192 he reached the castle of Beit Nuba, twenty kilometres to the north-west of the Holy City.[2] In high winds and torrential rain Richard made the difficult decision to abandon the advance. Within sight of Jerusalem's walls, he retreated.

As he walked away Richard the Lionheart refused to look at the view of Jerusalem, apparently saying out loud: 'Blessed Lord God, I pray thee not to let me see thy Holy City that I could not deliver from the hands of thy enemies.'[3] Refusing to be defeated Richard made a further abortive attempt to reach Jerusalem in July. This time Saladin rode out of the city to watch the Crusader army retrace their steps out of the hills down towards the coast and away from his territorial domain.[4] Throughout 1192 battle continued between Richard and Saladin with Richard winning a stunning victory against heavy odds at Jaffa on 5 August. But this was Richard's final effort. Saladin was in constant possession of reinforcements and when Saladin's army had regrouped, threatening the city of Ashkelon, Richard offered peace. A five-year armistice was signed leaving Saladin's forces in control of Jerusalem and its environs in exchange for the right of Christian pilgrims to visit the Church of the Holy Sepulchre. Richard, now known to the Arabs as 'Melec [King] Ric', refused to go to Jerusalem on this pilgrimage. He sailed away from Palestine on 9 October 1192.

The Mediterranean storms of the winter had begun early and he was shipwrecked off the Dalmatian coast. Richard tried to reach France on foot but was captured and imprisoned by Duke Leopold of Austria whom he had insulted during the siege of Acre. On Wednesday, 3 March 1193, whilst Richard languished in captivity, Saladin died in Damascus. Saladin had saved Jerusalem and the Temple Mount for Islam, but the scourge of the Crusades was not yet over and the sacred location was to suffer further indignity at the hands of the Christians. A Fourth Crusade was launched from France and Germany in 1202 which, much to the horror of Pope Innocent III who initially sanctioned it, resulted in the sacking of Byzantine Christian Constantinople in 1204 and the installation of a French nobleman, Baldwin Count of Hainault and Flanders, as the new Emperor of Byzantium. The savagery of the attack on Christians by Christians sealed the fate of the Latin Kingdom of Jerusalem. No Crusaders of the Fourth Crusade had set foot in Palestine and the religious zeal of many Christians – as Pope Innocent III had by this time realized – was now outweighed by motives of personal gain.

Despite the débâcle of the Fourth Crusade the lure of Jerusalem still beckoned. In 1218 the Christian West launched a Fifth Crusade against the Moslems, on this occasion attacking Egypt in the hope of gaining a southern base from which to invade Moslem-held Palestine. The Ayyubid ruler Sultan Al-Mu'azzam 'Isa took the extraordinary decision to pre-empt a Christian attack on the Holy City by ordering the demolition of the walls of Jerusalem. The Christian advance did not materialize and the city lay exposed and undefendable, although still in Moslem hands. However, the Moslems were now threatened from within. Saladin had held power over the Ayyubid dynasty with a firm hand, but the various ambitions of his seventeen sons had produced a complicated and much contested succession to his throne, leading to a fragmentation of Moslem unity.

In 1227 the Holy Roman Emperor Frederick II launched the Sixth Crusade. Frederick was born in Sicily, the grandson of Frederick Barbarossa of Germany. He could speak six languages including Arabic.[5] Despite his linguistic ability, his much vaunted liberal attitude towards sex did not endear him to the Church which longed to excommunicate him. Frederick was under Papal oath to embark on a Crusade and when he fell ill on board ship bound for Palestine he left the Crusader fleet to recuperate at Pozzuoli in Italy. The newly elected Pope Gregory IX used the incident to enforce the will of the Church. He excommunicated Frederick and banned him from pursuing a holy war in the name of Christianity. Undeterred, Frederick, now fully recovered, left Brindisi in southern Italy on 28 June 1228 for the Holy Land. With only a weak force at his disposal it was unlikely that his mission would be successful but the terrifying historical legacy of his bloodthirsty Crusader predecessors came to his aid. Nine months previously, on 11 November 1227, Al-Mu'azzam had died and Al-Kamil his brother, wishing to prevent the rightful inheritance of Al-Mu'azzam's heir, had marched his army into Jerusalem and claimed the city. Al-Kamil wished to gain control of the Ayyubid dynasty by dominating Syria, and news of Frederick's Crusade, together with the dangers posed to his own succession from members of his own family, led him to conclude that any armed resistance to Frederick would precipitate the ruin of his own ambitions. On 18 February 1229 Al-Kamil and Frederick signed a peace treaty. The Moslems agreed to hand Jerusalem back to the Christians but to retain control of the Temple Mount. The Jews, once again, had to leave.

When he arrived in Jerusalem Frederick was shunned by both Christians and Moslems. Only the Order of the Teutonic Knights, a German military Order not dissimilar to the Templars, showed any enthusiasm for the terms of the Christian occupation. In taking Jerusalem without raising a sword in anger Frederick had done what six Crusades before him had failed to do. However, for most Christians his treaty represented a compromise with the enemies of Christ. The Templars in particular were outraged at the thought of Moslems being permitted to stay on the Temple Mount. At his coronation at the Holy Sepulchre Frederick was obliged to place the crown of the Kingdom of Jerusalem on his own head as no priest would do it for him. Without political support his cause was hopeless and on 1 May 1229 Frederick left Palestine in disgrace. He never went back.

Jerusalem continued in this state of truce for another ten years, when a temporary Moslem reoccupation in 1239 signalled the end of Frederick's agreement. But the Moslems had their own, internecine conflict to resolve and Jerusalem was handed back to the Christians. Even though no major battles took place bandits roamed the surrounding countryside preying on pilgrims travelling to the city and on one occasion they even raided Jerusalem itself.[6] But more organized and deadly attackers were about to descend on the city. In 1244 a force of Khwarizm Turks swept through Syria and entered Palestine. On 11 July they attacked Jerusalem. With no walls to defend the city and a virtually ineffective garrison, Jerusalem soon fell and the Khwarizmians went on the rampage massacring Christians who were not lucky enough or fast enough to escape. Jerusalem and the Temple Mount were now back in Moslem hands but the Khwarizmians, who were only interested in plunder, did not stay long and the massacre they carried out forms only a small part of Jerusalem's bloody history. However, in the 1970s an inscription came to light on the wall of the Temple Mount which confirms their presence.

Carved in Hebrew on a Herodian block on the seventh course from the pavement under Robinson's Arch close to the south-western angle are the following words: 'You shall see, and your heart shall rejoice; your bones shall flourish like the grass.'[7] This is a phrase taken directly from the Book of Isaiah. Since discovery of the 'Isaiah Inscription' much controversy surrounds the dating of it and the reason for its obscure location. Dan Bahat in *Carta's Historical Atlas of Jerusalem* states that 'It appears that this verse was engraved at a time of stress for the Jewish inhabitants of the city and perhaps owing to some threat on the inscriber, he abandoned his task before he had finished.'[8] However, the archaeologists of the Israel Antiquities Authority excavation at Robinson's Arch between 1994 and 1997 have proposed a more dramatic answer to the mystery. Directly below the inscription the archaeological team found several human burials.[9] Whilst one body was definitely Christian because of its east–west orientation and the coin found in its mouth, the religious denomination of the others was uncertain. This led to the conclusion that the Isaiah Inscription was directly linked to the unidentified corpses found below it and had been placed there to indicate the presence of Jewish remains. The archaeological dating of the graves matches the period during which the Khwarizmian massacre took place when Jews were still an unwelcome minority in the city. The epitaph on the Temple Mount wall is, therefore, a poignant one. At least one Jew, deprived of access to the Temple Mount, managed to leave the sign of Jewish burial close to the sacred site of Mount Moriah in the hope that one day, at the Coming of the Messiah, the body laid to rest there would resurrect 'and flourish' in accordance with the Jewish scriptures.

The Khwarizmian massacre put an end to any hopes of further Christian rule in Jerusalem. Depopulated and ruined, the city reverted to Ayyubid rule from Egypt. In 1248 King Louis IX of France began to prepare for the Seventh Crusade. After two years the Crusaders disembarked at Damietta on the coast of Egypt. Despite early successes in battle, hunger and disease weakened his army and Louis was defeated. The Ayyubid Sultan Turanshah imprisoned Louis and marched the survivors of his Christian army southwards into captivity. The Sultan was merciless. He ordered that all captives too weak to walk be killed and that for one week three hundred Crusaders should be executed, per day, by their guards. But the days of the Ayyubid dynasty were also numbered. On 2 May 1250 Turanshah was killed at a banquet by soldiers of one of his Mamluk regiments; an Islamic revolution had begun.

MAMLUKS AND OTTOMANS

The Mamluks were by origin a non-Islamic people from the Eurasian steppes. Defeated and enslaved several centuries previously by the soldiers of Islam, they rose in the ranks of the army to a senior position. The Ayyubid dynasty was considered by many Moslems as corrupt and weak and their overthrow brought fresh enthusiasm into the Moslem world. Having murdered Turanshah and consolidated their position in Egypt, the Mamluks looked further afield to pursue their military ambitions. On 3 September 1260 the Mamluk Sultan Saif ad-Din Qutuz defeated the Mongols at the battle of Ayn Jalut, seventy kilometres north of Jerusalem. This battle was pivotal in the history of the Temple Mount as it secured the region from the scourge of the Mongols, allowing the Mamluks to rule over the *haram* for three hundred years, during which time Jerusalem and the Moslems prospered.

This period of tranquillity on the Temple Mount was reaffirmed by Mamluk military success against Crusader strongholds. The Mamluks were responsible for dealing the last blows against the Latin Kingdom in Palestine, which was precipitated by the fall of Acre in the summer of 1291. With the loss of Acre, so crucial to receiving supplies and reinforcements from Europe, the remaining Crusader fortresses fell in quick succession, and in the middle of August 1291 the deserted Templar castle at Athlit, south of Haifa, was destroyed.[10] Trust in the Templar knighthood was badly shaken by the loss of the Latin Kingdom of Palestine. The Templars had many enemies of their own faith envious of their success. By the beginning of the fourteenth century the Templars were in possession of vast amounts of property across Europe and within every kingdom they held key positions of power. From their Temple in Paris they kept the finances of the French king stable by supervising the national accounts. The Order acted as international bankers with bishops, princes and kings as their satisfied customers, but it was the greed of the French monarchy which, in the end, led to their destruction.

In 1312 the French king, Philippe le Bel, in need of money, decided to target the most vulnerable community in his kingdom, the Jews. For this he required the help of the Templars who, in addition to their other services, were bailiffs to the crown. The money raised from the Jews was, however, insufficient to meet Philippe's requirements so he decided to seize the assets of the Knights Templar. Philippe realized that a sustained attack serious enough to destroy their Order could only be successful by making serious allegations against them. The fear of heresy which had persisted throughout the thirteenth century within Christian society was still at the beginning of the fourteenth century strong enough to bring down the Order. Philippe accused the Templars of blasphemy, of practising deviant sexual acts during their 'secret rituals' – which included spitting on the cross – and of worshipping a reliquary human head encased in silver. Templar knights were arrested in raids across France. Many were imprisoned and tortured and some were executed, although the nature of trial and punishment varied greatly depending on the alliances of the court and the place at which it sat. Knights who 'confessed' were not always punished with death but were integrated into other religious orders such as the Cistercians and Augustinians with which their own Rule governing Templar practices had so much in common. The last Grand Master of the Order, Jacques de Molay, was burnt at the stake in Paris in 1314.

Much of the mystery surrounding the Knights Templar involves the identity of the 'secret' from which they derived an enormous amount of power. It has often been stated[11] that they excavated on the Temple Mount in search of 'relics' and, given their standing in society and their physical presence on the *haram*, they would have encountered little difficulty in conducting such work.

THE 'SECRET' OF THE KNIGHTS TEMPLAR

Existing Templar records reveal nothing which throws any light on this matter. Until 1187 and the fall of Jerusalem to Salah ed-Din, the manuscripts of the Temple were kept in the Aqsa which the Templars had taken over as their headquarters in 1120.[12] In 1926 workmen in Jerusalem found a letter written on parchment hidden in the roof space of the Aqsa Mosque. Addressed to Gerard de Ridefort, the Tenth Grand Master and architect of the Crusader defeat at Hattin, it recounts an episode of internal policy regarding one of the Order's members who had disobeyed the Rule:

> Brother Gerard de Ridefort, Seneschal of the soldiers of the Temple of the Ordoni Friars of Vendome, Commander in Jerusalem, greetings.
>
> You know that Robert de Sourdeval has disembarked at Tyre. The commander of our house in this city has received him; on hearing of this we have assembled our Chapter at Feve, and there were one hundred knights or more [present]. We have asked their advice on what we should do in this case and in the end we have decided by a united voice and common consent to send to Tyre five of our brother knights to divest him of his surcoat, to take him to Acre and to guard him there in a private room until the first ship of the season makes the crossing [of the Mediterranean].[13]

It appears from this letter that the Templar authorities were imposing the Rule of their Order with great strictness, but what Robert de Sourdeval had done to lose his Templar status is unknown as most of the Templar records are missing. The archive of the Latin kingdom has almost completely disappeared and, apart from this original letter, only two other documents are known to exist.[14] Despite this lack of information there can be no doubt that the financial success of the Templar Order was based on the accumulation of property and that some kind of recognition of this wealth was reflected in their 'rituals'. As the Templar wealth was based on property, mathematical and architectural knowledge of building technique would have been fundamental to the 'secret'. The mathematical symbol for Pi, an essential number for intricate calculations of proportion within architectural construction, has been found on gravestones and buildings of the Templar period in locations as distant from one another as Syria and Scotland.[15] The fact

that the Templars named their Order after the Temple of Solomon
– the most perfect building of ancient Israel – reinforces the importance of mathematics to the success of the Templar Order.
Templar interest in the site of the *sakhra*, which they renamed
Templum Domini, demonstrates that they probably believed the
sakhra to be the exact site of Solomon's Temple. The 'secret' of
Solomon's perfect building was fully incorporated into the
structure of the Dome of the Rock:

> That the idea is very ancient cannot be denied, since various relation-
> ships of this sort are to be found in the Great Pyramid, where
> amongst other things, the height bears to the circumference of the
> base the same relationship as the diameter of a circle bears to its
> circumference.
>
>   That literature contains no reference to this remarkable system
> goes for nothing, as craft secrets of this sort were no doubt only
> imparted under vows of secrecy... Some of the ratios involved, such
> as the square root of two (as in the Dome of the Rock), and especially
> that which the diameter of a circle bears to its circumference... are
> fundamentals in time and space, they go right down to the very basis
> of our own nature and of the physical universe in which we live and
> move, and may very well appeal to us subconsciously.[16]

Whether or not they were aware of the subconscious appeal that
such craft secrets may have instilled in the imagination of the
members of their Order, the Templar leadership had their minds
fully concentrated on the practical matters of spreading the influence of their brotherhood. They applied their 'secret' knowledge to
their architecture by copying the proportions of the Dome of the
Rock in their churches all across Europe, the most notable examples
being at Temple in London, and Laon and Metz in France.[17] As
architects the Templars were, therefore, actively involved in the
preservation of Solomonic masonic knowledge. They can also be
firmly linked to Solomon's architect and Master Mason, Hiram
Abiff.

  The Knights Templar have long been recognized as custodians of
a Freemasonic legend surrounding Hiram. In England 'Templar'
Freemasonic Lodges have existed since at least the second half of the

nineteenth century and in Scotland for several centuries longer. The Knights Templar had strong links with Scotland and allegedly sought refuge there following the repression of 1312–14. The ruins of the ancient village church of Temple which today lie just to the south of Edinburgh stand on the site of the first Scottish Templar preceptory founded in the twelfth century under King David I.[18] The graveyard contains several Masonic headstones displaying the essential tools of Freemasonry, including the set square, which was the basic instrument of building construction. Thirty kilometres from Temple lies the chapel of Rosslyn Castle, an extraordinary testament to Freemasonic legend and ritual. In 1312 the crown of Scotland was still well disposed towards the Order and Rosslyn was an obvious place of refuge. Rosslyn, owned by the St Clair family, was visited by the founding Master of the Templar Order Hugh de Payns in the summer of 1128 when he returned from Palestine to recruit for the Order. Payns eventually married a Katherine St Clair thus forging a Templar link with the location.[19] In Rosslyn chapel stands a pillar with definite Judaic and Masonic features, which connect it to the Temple of Solomon. The 'Apprentice Pillar', approximately three metres high, is intricately carved from limestone with a scene of Abraham's attempted sacrifice of Isaac, with the ram caught in the thicket carved into the top of the pillar.[20] Its beauty is alleged to have provoked the jealousy of the Master Mason who was in charge of building the chapel and he killed the apprentice who finished it – a clear analogy to the legend of Hiram Abiff, although, in the case of the Rosslyn legend, it was the Master Mason (Hiram Abiff) who committed murder.

The organization of craftsmen into separate skilled 'free' bodies or guilds was part of the Templar heritage.[21] During the Middle Ages monasteries, castles, churches and cathedrals were built by Masons from various guilds. These craftsmen possessed 'secrets' intrinsic to their skills, which were jealously guarded to protect the monopoly they had on their particular trade. Thus, not unlike the builders of the First and Second Temples of Jerusalem, the medieval stonemasons identified their work with carved symbols, some of which are still visible on the Apprentice Pillar.[22] The medieval Church opposed scientific investigation and the Masonic craft system was adopted in some secrecy to perpetuate and investigate the scientific inheritance of the ancient world. If the Templars had employed a 'Freemasonic' ritual within their Order this would explain why Philippe le Bel's attack on them went largely unchallenged by a Church which stood against the unauthorized advancement of science. But what indications are there to connect the Templars to Masonic activities at the Temple Mount where they established themselves?

Two things, the set square and the reliquary head found in the Temple in Paris, hold clues. The examples of set squares found on Templar gravestones in Scotland match one found on a Crusader gravestone at Athlit Castle in Israel.[23] This suggests that the 'secret' of architecture played an important role in the lives of the Templars who were buried there. The identity of the silver reliquary head presents another more complicated conundrum as information is scant. What is certain, however, is that the Templars adopted the idea of such a relic while they were in Palestine. In 1149 Nur ed-Din sent a head to the Caliph of Baghdad. It was the skull encased in silver of Prince Raymond of Tripoli, whom his forces had killed in battle. In the recent past the Templar reliquary has been identified as either Hugh de Payns, John the Baptist or Hiram Abiff. With the Order's obvious respect for the sacred science of building – evidence of which can be seen in their replication of the Qubbet as-Sakhra – Hiram's remains, which may indeed have been concealed somewhere on the Mount, would – if found and identified – have become an object of reverence. The Templars, therefore, could perhaps have preserved a skull they believed was Hiram's and used it in their ceremonies. Although this theory is purely speculative, what we do know is that the Templars had dug on the *haram* and according to a pilgrim eyewitness, Bishop Otto of Freising, the Templars established a cemetery 'not far from the Temple of the Lord' (the Dome of the Rock) the precise location of which has never been discovered. They converted 5000 square metres of the vaults under the south-eastern section of the platform, which they named Solomon's Stables, into storage quarters and accommodation. Still in existence, Solomon's Stables were converted in 1998 into the largest mosque of the *haram*.

THE MOSLEM CONSOLIDATION

As Templar property was redistributed in Europe, the Mamluks began the preservation of their inheritance in the Holy City. During the first century of Mamluk rule there were only modest changes on the *haram*. The dome over the *sakhra* was regilded in 1317 and colonnades added to the northern and western perimeter which, with a view of the Qubbet as-Sakhra, became the much favoured site of Islamic religious schools. But in 1376, control of Jerusalem, which had been ruled from Damascus, reverted to Cairo, the Mamluk capital. This meant that the city received greater attention from the caliphate including an increase in funds which prompted a further upsurge in building on the *haram*. The Temple Mount prospered under a programme of architectural improvement, renovation and beautification. A new fresh-water supply was brought in to service the pilgrims, who required both refreshment and somewhere to clean their feet before entering the Aqsa and the Dome of the Rock. The Sultan Qait Bey erected a fountain to the south-west of the Dome of the Rock in front of the western colonnades, adding to their air of serenity so essential to such a holy site.

The Mamluks have been described as the last medieval dynasty of the Arab world,[24] and their style of architecture incorporates a mixture of Arabic and Gothic building styles. Their constructions reflect a strong hybrid of Middle Eastern and European traditions. Mamluk monuments often display an alternating pattern of geometric red and white stonemasonry as in the existing entrance to the façade of the *madrasah* Ashrafiyya constructed on the *haram* in the fifteenth century, which is one of the architectural glories of the Mount.

The Jews, so long the victims of political change in a city which was once their own, returned in the second half of the fourteenth century to Jerusalem in large numbers. There was a resurgence of Messianic activity when in 1350 an Ashkenazi – or mid-European – Jew, Isaac ha-Levi Asir ha-Tikvah ('the hopeful'), arrived in Jerusalem to set up a yeshiva or Jewish religious school. Despite ha-Tikvah's expectations, however, the Moslem presence on the

Mount was immovable and the vast dispersal of Jews across Europe and the countries bordering the Mediterranean, in comparison to the modest Jewish community of Jerusalem, did little to rekindle hopes of an alternative to Moslem control. The Temple Mount was well established in the diaspora as the lost heart of the Jewish faith which one day, when God so willed it, would be returned to the people of Israel.

Towards the end of the fourteenth century Christian attacks on Spanish Jewry led many hundreds of Sephardic Jews to return to Jerusalem. The Jewish community in the city was thus greatly enriched by these immigrants[25] although old conflicts between Jews and Christians were rekindled. In 1428 the Jews attempted to seize a site known as Mount Zion on the south-west of the Old City, which they were convinced was the site of King David's tomb. The Pope, Martin V, issued an edict prohibiting sea captains from transporting any Jew across the Mediterranean to the Holy Land. Despite such anti-semitism, worsened by periodic clashes between Christians and Jews in Jerusalem, the Mamluk authorities managed to keep the peace. However, Mamluk rule was about to end. In 1453 the Ottoman Turk dynasty extinguished Christian Byzantium by occupying Constantinople. The Ottomans were innovative and by the end of the fifteenth century had introduced vital changes into their army which would procure them an expansion of empire – at Mamluk cost.

In 1516 Ottoman use of gunpowder, which Warren much later employed surreptitiously in his excavations in Jerusalem, brought an end to the Mamluk era and heralded a change of Moslem rule in Jerusalem. On 24 August a Mamluk army under the command of the Sultan Qansawh al-Ghawri was defeated by Salim I, leader of the Ottoman Turk dynasty.[26] Salim's victory was ensured by the Mamluk refusal to countenance the use of firearms and artillery which his own forces had comprehensively adopted. With the fall of Cairo in 1517, the entire region of the Near East came within the sphere of the Ottoman Turks who would steer Jerusalem and the Temple Mount into the twentieth century.

In 1520 Salim's son, Suleiman, succeeded to the sultanate and, in line with new military thinking that fortifications had to be strong enough to withstand the assault of cannon, the walls of Jerusalem were reinforced. Suleiman further improved the water supply and the buildings around the *haram*, following which he decided to architecturally upgrade the exterior of the Qubbet as-Sakhra. The lower section of the outside of the octagonal building was lined with Carrara marble and the intervening section between this belt of marble and the dome above was overlaid with blue ceramic tiles, visually lifting the golden dome towards the sky. Although Suleiman did not allow Jews onto the Mount to pray, the Ottoman conquest of Jerusalem was a fortuitous event for them. In 1492 there was a mass expulsion of Jews from Spain. In 1501 Provence followed suit. These Jews migrated east into Ottoman territory to set up communities in Salonika and Istanbul and when Jerusalem fell to Suleiman in 1516 many moved to Jerusalem. They were given refuge on the condition that they paid a poll-tax and acknowledged the rule of Islam. Suleiman, in his quest for architectural excellence in the Islamic tradition, did not ignore the religious needs of the emigrant Jews. A section of the western wall of the *haram* was turned into a Jewish prayer enclave. This stretch of wall included eight courses of the original Herodian structure. Jews who prayed at the wall could face eastwards towards the position of their ancient Temple. The area soon became known as the Wailing Place of the Jews, a name which Wilson used on his survey of 1864–5, because of their custom of lamenting at the wall the loss of the Temple and the past glories of Israel. The area was later called the Wailing Wall and then, after Israeli conquest of the city in 1967, simply the Western Wall.

Suleiman's heirs continued to enrich the Moslem architecture and ritual on the Temple Mount, emphasizing the permanence of the Islamic faith. Many Jews of the diaspora, however, still yearned for a new era of Judaism which would be heralded by the Coming of the Messiah. This desire manifested itself in a succession of false Messiahs throughout Europe, amongst them Abraham ben Eliezer ha-Levi and Solomon Molkho. In 1626, the most famous, Shabbetai Zevi, was born in Smyrna, modern-day Turkish Izmir. Between 1642 and 1662 Zevi travelled throughout the Ottoman Empire developing his own particular brand of Judaism which ran counter to the Judaic Law. Zevi lived in Jerusalem and then moved to Gaza where he met a Jewish Ashkenazi named Nathan. Nathan became Zevi's 'prophet' and he was proclaimed as the long-awaited Messiah. Zevi's fame spread amongst the diaspora and the Sultan Mehmet IV, fearful of disruption to the civil order of his empire, felt obliged to arrest and try him for sedition. Given the choice of converting to Islam or being put to death, Zevi chose the former. He was deported to Albania where he died on Yom Kippur of 1676.

'Shabbetainism' lived on after Zevi's death giving rise to several prophets and false Messiahs in Poland and Italy, the most notable being Jacob Frank who died in 1791 at the age of sixty-five. Poland in the eighteenth century was a hotbed of Jewish religious activity. Israel Ba'al Shem Tov, a mystic and healer, was born in 1700. His charismatic leadership as a rabbi gained him a dedicated following from fellow rabbis and Jewish scholars. After his death in 1760 his successor, Dov Baer of Mezhirech, welded his disciples into a movement known as the Hasidim or 'Pious Ones'. The Hasidim were at odds with members of their own faith, the Mitnageddim or 'Opponents' who accused them of introducing dangerous innovations into Judaism which upset the status quo the Jews had achieved with the authorities in Poland. In 1777 several hundred Hasidim led by Rabbi Menahem Mendel left Poland to found a Hasidic community in Palestine.

Further west the Christian nations of western Europe were moving towards industrialization, a change which threatened the existence of many traditional communities, not least those who lived under Islam. For most of the eighteenth century Jerusalem was isolated against the changes taking place in Europe and protected from the social and economic revolution happening there. As the period of Ottoman domination lengthened into the seventeenth and eighteenth centuries the city of Jerusalem gradually declined in political and military importance. Although the *haram* was still recognized as a sacred place of pilgrimage and was maintained by successive Pashas or officers of high rank, government from Istanbul resulted in a weakness of local command and a subsequent deterioration in civil order. The Arab families of Jerusalem resented interference from outside and the people of the city felt subjected to an increasingly corrupt system of taxation by Pashas who had little power to collect the dues on a fair basis. Almost inevitably, the countryside of Judaea around Jerusalem once again became the playground of bandits.

In many respects Jerusalem was a strategic backwater. The Ottoman domination of ancient Byzantium and Syria had left Palestine with an infrastructure little changed from medieval times. These conditions were reflected in the state of the Jewish population. Despite the several 'Messianic' revivals in Europe, by the end of the eighteenth century Jewish presence in Jerusalem was noticeably modest. The community struggled in a general state of poverty and under deplorable conditions, in bitter contrast to the days when Jerusalem was the proud capital of Judah. However, by the end of the eighteenth century French ambition to dominate the Middle East once more brought the region back into the political and military focus of the European powers of England and France. In 1799 French forces invaded Palestine and Egypt, with Napoleon Bonaparte at their head.

IN SEARCH OF THE BIBLE

As the historian Barbara Tuchman revealed in her history of Palestine *Bible and Sword*, Napoleon was the first head of state 'to propose the restoration of a Jewish state in Palestine'[27] and he did so in the most emotive terms. Napoleon's proclamation to the Jews of the diaspora was flamboyant, but it was designed to leave the Jewish people of his own empire in no doubt as to the nature of his own convictions.[28]

> Israelites, arise! Ye exiled, arise! Hasten! Now is the moment, which may not return for thousands of years, to claim your political existence as a nation among nations, and the unlimited natural right to worship Jehovah in accordance with your faith, publicly and most probably forever.[29]

Bonaparte dreamt of defeating the Ottoman Empire and securing the Middle East and thus the overland gateway to India for France.

On 1 August 1798 his Mediterranean fleet was virtually annihilated by
Lord Nelson at Aboukir Bay – the Battle of the Nile – forty kilometres east of Alexandria. Despite this setback Napoleon Bonaparte's
army continued their campaign, marching into Palestine in the
spring of 1799. By 18 March Napoleon was outside the walls of Acre,
and the future for a Jewish-controlled Jerusalem stood on defeat or
victory. The Ottomans tried to defend the walls of Acre and a British
fleet under Admiral Sir Sidney Smith stood offshore ready to attack
Napoleon's troops with cannon fire. After attempting for a month to
capture Acre, Napoleon's army, weakened by casualties and disease,
were routed when men of Sir Sydney Smith's squadron stormed
ashore to attack the French lines and on 20 May 1799 Napoleon
turned his back on the dream of re-establishing 'the ancient
Jerusalem'.[30] The siege of Acre shattered Napoleon's plan of
conquering the Middle East, bringing to an end his vision of a
restored Israel. Two changes arose as a result of Napoleon's attempt
to win the Holy Land, both of which affected the Temple Mount.

Napoleon had taken a corps of scientists, archaeologists and historians with him to Egypt, and their study of the Great Pyramid at
Giza, the Rosetta Stone and other ancient Egyptian monuments
when published in Europe sparked off a wave of public curiosity into
past civilizations. This interest grew during the nineteenth century
into a thirst for information concerning the lost history of the
Middle East. This developed, particularly in England, into a retracing of the 'biblical past' which eventually found its investigative
apogee with the expeditions of Wilson and Warren. The second
change was purely political. Following Napoleon's retreat from
Egypt, Muhammad Ali, an Albanian Moslem and a veteran of the
Battle of the Nile, became ruler of Egypt. In 1831 his army crossed into
Palestine and successfully reduced the fort of Acre which had so
resolutely defeated the army of Napoleon in 1799. Muhammad Ali
ruled Jerusalem for only nine years but during this period he
brought the city into the western world. Secular courts were set up,
breaking the stranglehold of the religious authorities, and equal
rights were extended to members of all religious denominations in
the city. In 1839 a British Consulate was established in Jerusalem and
many of the major European powers copied the British example.

In 1799 Napoleon Bonaparte had thought of building a canal between the Mediterranean and the Red Sea. The proposal, which had first been considered in the seventeenth century by Louis XIV, was resurrected under Napoleon III in 1862 and in 1866 the Ottoman Sultan Mehemet Ali gave his consent to the project. The arrival of Charles Wilson in Jerusalem in 1864 was no mere coincidence. For centuries Russia, who wanted to expand into the Balkans, had coveted Ottoman territory. England and France were gravely concerned about these Russian ambitions to expand southwards. If Russians captured Constantinople they would control the eastern Mediterranean and threaten French and British communications with the Middle East and India. The Turkish Ottoman Empire was viewed by the Russian Czar as moribund and, wishing to precipitate its end, Nicholas I demanded that the Ottoman Sultan cede to him the rights of the holy places of Jerusalem and jurisdiction over all Christian Orthodox Russians living within the Ottoman Empire. When the Sultan refused, the Crimean War began. Russia defeated a Turkish fleet off the coast of the Black Sea at Sinope, and Britain and France sent an expeditionary force to Sebastopol to fight the Russians. The Anglo-French alliance prevented Czar Nicholas from achieving his objective. The war came to an end in 1856 with the signing of the Treaty of Paris which compelled Russia to respect the territorial integrity of the Turkish Ottoman Empire. The experience of the Crimea sharpened British awareness of the strategic importance of the eastern Mediterranean. By 1860 most of India was under British domination and news that the French were building a canal from the Mediterranean to the Red Sea – thus shortening the sea voyage to India by weeks if not months – brought a mixed response from the British who viewed French ownership of the Canal with disquiet. The work went ahead as scheduled and on 17 November 1869 the Suez Canal was opened.

The control of the Suez Canal stayed in French hands until 1875 when the Ottoman Sultan's grandson and major shareholder in the Canal, Khedive Ismail, went bankrupt. Within two days the British Prime Minister Benjamin Disraeli secured a loan from the Rothschild bank giving the British government the £4,000,000 necessary to purchase Ismail's shares. Britain bought Khedive Ismail's controlling interest and the Canal was in British hands. With such a vital lifeline for her empire secured, Britain became even more closely involved with the future of the Ottoman Empire, an involvement which had begun with the arrival of Charles Wilson in 1864 and which reached its peak in 1917 with the recapture of Jerusalem by a Christian army after an interval of over nine hundred years.

ENGLISHMEN ON THE MOUNT

Charles Wilson's Royal Engineer successor, Charles Warren, would have been aware of the tremendous results that Wilson had achieved through his survey. There is no record of why Warren was chosen to follow in Wilson's footsteps, but documentation which hitherto has remained private may provide us with an indication as to his suitability for the task. Before being posted to Jerusalem, Warren had served for over six years in Gibraltar between 1858 and 1865. It was there that he met Henry Birtles, the non-commissioned officer who was to become his faithful and resolute companion, sharing his adventures and misfortunes throughout the excavations at Jerusalem. The Gibraltar posting was hardly exotic but for a young engineer officer the experience was invaluable. During his six years on the Rock, Warren was involved with the design and construction of new gun batteries and with opening up new caves for storage of matériel. The guns of the Rock were the guarantee of British naval access to the Mediterranean, and the system of tunnels and galleries necessary to supply and serve the batteries which Warren learnt about in Gibraltar provided him with a professional training of how to excavate the Temple Mount of Jerusalem. Charles Warren's appointment to Jerusalem was also personally fortuitous. He had a keen interest in the history of past civilizations and Jerusalem with its legendary Temple of Solomon presented an excellent opportunity to engage in matters close to his heart, in particular the pursuit of Freemasonry.

Since the seventeenth century Freemasonry had played an increasing role in the hierarchy of English society. What had begun in the Middle Ages as an organization for craftsmen mutated into a powerful cultural organization with strong aristocratic affiliations and, since the time of George IV who became involved in English Freemasonry, with royal patronage as well. By the nineteenth century Freemasonry was soundly integrated into military circles, and it was in Gibraltar that Warren began his illustrious career as a Master Freemason. Despite recent attempts by the United Grand Lodge of England to publicize positive aspects of Freemasonry such as its contributions to charity, since the early eighteenth century Freemasonry has become increasingly mysterious and deliberately closeted from society. No man can ask to become a Freemason. A candidate is chosen, discussed and then approached by two 'brothers' of the Masonic Lodge who wish to recruit him. In Warren's case this duty fell to [Brother] Sergeant (later Major) Irwin and [Brother] P.M. Gould.[31] Warren's father, a distinguished general who had served in the Crimea, was also a Freemason. The Masonic tradition of loyalty and service to the crown and the brotherhood of Masons could not have found a more willing apprentice than in Charles.

On 30 December 1859 at the age of nineteen Lieutenant Charles Warren, RE, was initiated into the Royal Lodge of Friendship, then Number 345, now Number 278.[32] He made rapid progress within Masonic circles. In 1860 Warren joined the Inhabitants Lodge, Gibraltar, Number 153 (formerly Number 178) and the Royal Arch in October 1861. He became a Master of the Gibraltar Lodge, Number 43, in the same month. In November he joined the Royal Europa Chapter of Gibraltar, Number 14. The Rock of Gibraltar, it seemed was a hive, not just of military but Masonic activity as well. In 1863, four years before he left for Jerusalem, Warren became a Freemasonic Knight Templar, joining the Calpe Preceptory of Knights Templar, Number 50. In July 1865 Warren returned to England and was appointed Assistant Instructor at the School of Engineering at Chatham. In 1866 he was elected a Fellow of the Geological Society of London and one month later he became an Associate of the Institute of Civil Engineering.

At the end of 1866 the newly established Palestine Exploration Fund requested the assistance of an officer and three NCOs to continue the pioneering survey work undertaken by Charles Wilson. It is unclear whether the PEF had imagined the use of tunnels and galleries to achieve this end, but Warren, who was recommended for the post, was clear from the beginning about the spirit in which he would undertake his duty. His grandson, biographer and fellow Mason Watkin Williams wrote of Warren: 'It was somewhat in the role of Crusader that Warren accepted the charge, as he was stirred by the longing to reveal to the Christian world those Sacred places hidden by the debris of many a siege, and jealously guarded by the Turkish Musselmans.'[33]

Twenty-six years after his induction into Freemasonry, Warren stated to an assembly of fellow Masons that 'Masonry had a great effect for good in assisting to keep up discipline in our army.'[34] His next overseas posting gave him ample opportunity to test this effect.

Charles Warren arrived in Palestine on 15 February 1867, disembarking from a storm-swept Mediterranean at the port of Jaffa. He went straight to Jerusalem where he met the Turkish authorities, and in March, having not yet received the necessary instruments of survey for his team of Royal Engineers to continue work, he departed for the valley of the Jordan in order to study the life and customs of the Ta'amireh Bedouin. The Ta'amireh were native to the area and Muhammad adh-Dhib, a descendant of this tribe, discovered the Dead Sea Scrolls at Qumran in 1947. Warren was kindly received and, although he was able to converse only in sign language, his hosts offered him their best hospitality. At night, devoured by fleas under the goat-hair quilt of his bedding, and unable to leave his tent because of the ferocious attentions of the watch dogs of the camp, Warren found himself caught in a nomadic existence reminiscent of the ancient tribes of Israel who under Moses wandered across the desert with their herds, carrying with them the Ark of the Covenant. At the end of April 1867 Warren reached the southern end of the Jordan plain. Alone in the thorn bushes which cover that region, he became hopelessly entangled in the undergrowth. He saw a Bedouin approaching and, realizing he was not from the local tribe, Warren was afraid he would have his throat cut. Just able to reach and draw his revolver he persuaded the man, at gunpoint, to free him. This experience was a stern initiation into the reality of the tribal life of the Jordan valley. Back in Jerusalem the rule of tribal law was as strict as in the countryside of Judaea. Nine months later, on New Year's Day 1868, Warren revealed that he had been witness only a few days beforehand to an horrific scene.

A Ta'amireh Bedouin, a member of the same tribe with whom he had lived nine months previously in the Jordan valley, had murdered a fellow Moslem from Jerusalem. The Bedouin had been apprehended and Warren's experience, recorded in a letter written from the comfort of the Mediterranean Hotel in Jerusalem, to the Palestine Exploration Fund in London, was brutally shocking.

> The widow and brother-in-law of the murdered one, finding justice lagging, telegraphed to Constantinople, and obtained a *firman* for the Ta'amirah's execution: his family offered £200 for his release, but the widow of the Jerusalemite was too public spirited or too vindictive to allow such an offer to have any effect upon her, and it was settled that the man should be decapitated.
>
> He was brought out for that purpose to the Jaffa Gate; but his family still seemed to think there was hope for him, and when the time was up made a last appeal to the widow of his victim. During the short conversation which took place with her, the convict opened his mouth, eyes, and nostrils in his endeavours to hear her replies, and when he was put out of his dreadful suspense by finding her inflexible, he appeared to be already suffering the pangs of death.
>
> The execution was truly barbarous; the unfortunate man first got a cut across his shoulders, and turned round to say, 'You are hurting me;' then the amateur executioner, finding that sixteen blows did not sever the head from the body, turned the man on his back, and sawed away at his throat as if he were killing a sheep. Eventually he managed to get the head and part of the shoulder off the trunk, and together they were left during the day for the diversion of the multitude.[35]

This experience would have brought to life the bloody reality of the history through which Warren was digging. He had just completed a tunnel through the stones which had fallen from the Mount during the destruction of AD 70, when thousands of Jews had been slaughtered in the confined space of the Temple Courtyards in only one day.

If Ottoman justice was barbaric, the sanitary conditions in which

Warren had to work were no better. Jerusalem in the 1860s was a demanding site. Despite previous experience of hardship under military conditions, the non-commissioned officers who accompanied the survey could never have been fully prepared for the rigours of working in the Holy City. Centuries of accumulated rubbish lay within the immediate area surrounding the Temple Mount, and the cisterns, secret passages and chambers which riddled the Mount area were more often than not choked with raw effluent from the population of the city. The slightest cut in such contaminated soil could lead to infection, and this before even drinking any water. Everyone in Warren's party at one time or another became seriously ill.[36] It was perhaps a miracle or a testament to individual physical fitness that only one member of the survey died while there. Corporal Duncan succumbed to fever on 10 August 1868 and was buried in the Protestant graveyard to the west of the Old City under a tombstone formed from a broken column which Warren had discovered underground in the area of Robinson's Arch.

Warren faced a running battle of wits with the Turkish authorities. He had a *firman* or official permit to conduct excavations but there were constant interferences from the local land and property owners, most notably Abu Saud who owned a large building adjoining the *haram* wall north of Robinson's Arch. To overcome this problem Warren opened up new shafts which enabled him to stay one step ahead of any interruptions.

In late January 1870 Warren and Birtles entered an underground vaulted area on the outside of the western wall. Birtles was injured when one of the walls he was attempting to climb gave way, collapsing on top of him. This did not, however, dissuade Warren and Birtles from continuing. During the course of their inspection Warren discovered an ancient chamber which 'acquired the name "The Masonic Hall" from some circumstances connected with its discovery'.[37] Gaining entrance via a steep sloping passage, Warren was lowered by rope. He found himself in a 'large rectangular vaulted chamber of ancient construction, with a column or pedestal sticking up from the centre'.[38] The walls were built of well-jointed square stone and at each corner stood a pilaster with distinctive capitals. Warren described the chamber as 'having the appearance of being the oldest piece of masonry visible in Jerusalem, with the exception of the Sanctuary walls [which he believed in places to be Solomonic] and perhaps as old as they'.[39] One particular section of the southern wall also excited his interest. At the beginning of his work Warren attempted to drive a shaft below the Single Gate, a blocked entrance to Solomon's Stables, approximately thirty metres from the south-eastern angle of the *haram*. Owing to sickness,[40] he and Birtles stopped work, but in a letter to the PEF dated 22 October 1867, Warren wrote:

> In a former letter I stated that I believed that there was another system of vaults under the present vaults [of Solomon's Stables] … and in a sketch I showed a point where I expected the entrance would be … on Wednesday, to our great delight the hoped-for entrance was found. I send you a plan which I made yesterday immediately it was open; you will see that the stones are of great size, one of them 15 feet long … The passage is 3 feet wide, and is perpendicular to the south wall of the Sanctuary … after 60 feet [inside the *haram*] the roof stones disappear. On the east there is a passage blocked up … At present I have no clue as to the use of this passage.[41]

Warren later concluded that this passage was the Kidron outlet for the drainage of the altar of Solomon's Temple, via Cistern V.

Despite his endeavours, the immensity of the site and the complexities of investigating it meant that Warren reached only a fraction of the archaeological area buried under the *haram*. He realized he would not be able to penetrate as much of the Temple Mount area as he wished but his curiosity got the better of him. Warren noticed, inside the Qubbet as-Sakhra, 'something peculiar about the northern portion of the [*sakhra*] rock'.[42] Alone in the building, he vaulted over the protective railing onto the *sakhra* to investigate two pieces of stone flagging which lay side by side set into its surface. He managed to get his fingers into the joint between the flagstones and realized that there was a hollow underneath. The cave under the *sakhra* had a circular stone lid set into the floor which covered the entrance to a narrow shaft known to the Moslems as the Well of Souls. It was forbidden for Warren to investigate this entrance, but he believed he now had a chance to do so via the flagstones above.

Accordingly, he made arrangements to carry out a clandestine investigation starting from the surface of the *sakhra*.

A few days later Warren, escorted as usual by two *zaptis* or Turkish soldiers to watch over his movements, entered the *haram* with an iron lever the length of his arm hidden up the sleeve of his jacket, in the company of two ladies and Captain E. Warry of the Royal Artillery. Warren had planned his mission with military precision. Corporal Ellis was ordered to wait at the entrance to the Gate of Muhammad with a ladder and a rope, and Sergeant Birtles was scheduled to arrive shortly afterwards at another gateway. Warren sent one *zapti* to let in Ellis and the other to find Birtles who was under instructions to wander around the *haram* pretending to look for him. As Ellis stood with the rope and ladder and Birtles walked the *haram* in search of their officer, Warren and his friends slipped inside. The ladies insisted that the mosque officials inside show them the cave under the *sakhra* and once the party had trooped down the flight of stairs and out of sight, Warren scrambled onto the sacred rock. A Moslem official of the shrine – and Warren's accomplice – watched Warren's progress in an increasing state of terror. It took Warren three minutes to lever the northernmost piece of flagging from its bed of mortar. As he dislodged each piece of cement, Warren hid the evidence of his sacrilege by pushing it between the gap in the two stones, into the hole below. Then using both hands he lifted the flagstone. As he did so the muscles of his left arm, which had been permanently damaged in a fall in Gibraltar, gave way. The stone was too heavy to hold with just one arm and it fell with a crash into the hole below causing 'an echo which shook the building and reverberated all over the place'.[43] Warren would have been exposed had it not been for the quick thinking of his female companions in the cave below: 'When at last they heard the crash above them, and the echo around, they showed no signs of emotion though it was impossible for them to imagine what had happened; one, with woman's wit, silenced the arising suspicion of their guide by asking if the wind had not risen, as the door [to the Dome] had slammed with a noise.'[44]

His Moslem friend was now frantic, terrified that 'they should all get murdered'.[45] He begged Warren to get off the *sakhra*. Warren responded by disappearing down the hole. At the bottom, he found a channel filled with soft earth or dust. About three feet deep and two wide, it ran northwards for about eleven feet where it was blocked by rough masonry. After measuring the channel Warren extracted himself and rejoined his Moslem companion on the other side of the railing. Warren's survey of this channel tallied with his assessment of the position of the altar outside Solomon's Temple which he situated to the south of the *sakhra* over Cistern V. He concluded: 'The solution I propose is that above this rock was the chamber of the washers of the Temple: here were the innards etcetera, cleaned, and this gutter carried the blood and refuse to co-mingle with that from the Altar, and then run into the Kidron by the passage we discovered under the Single Gate.'[46]

The First Book of Kings describes how Solomon set five of the ten lavers for the washing of entrails on the northern side of the Temple entrance, so presumably Warren was referring to this. If he was correct, his findings on the *sakhra* substantially reinforce his own view of the position of Solomon's Temple.[47] Several days after his investigation Warren returned to the site and noticed that the flagstone had been replaced. No mention was made of the episode by the Turkish authorities although Warren's attentive escort became even more anxious about keeping him in his sight.

Judging by his actions on the *sakhra*, the position of Solomon's Temple held a particular fascination for Warren and before he left Jerusalem, he indulged in a further secret spectacle under the Temple Mount in the guise of a Freemasonic Knight Templar.

FREEMASONRY UNDER THE MOUNT

Warren did not publicize his Masonic activities and after his death in 1927 Freemason's Hall in Great Queen's Street, London, continued to protect his Freemasonic record from public scrutiny. On 4 February 1936 the Deputy Grand Secretary of the United Grand Lodge of England wrote a letter to Watkin Williams, Warren's grandson and biographer:

Dear Sir and Brother,

I regret not having replied earlier to your letter of the 12th January. I have taken advice on the matter to which you refer. It is felt that it would be inappropriate for a reference to be made in the biography of your grandfather, the late General Sir Charles Warren, beyond the brief statement of his Masonic services which are outlined in the first paragraph on page No. 17a, and perhaps some abbreviation of the two following paragraphs.

The account of the speech which follows in your notes, it is thought should certainly be omitted.

Yours faithfully and fraternally.
Dep. G.S.[48]

The 'speech' that was the cause of so much concern had been made by Warren in response to the toast of 'Brethren who have done Good Service across the Seas', at the Installation banquet of the Moira Lodge, Number 92, on 7 December 1885,[49] in which he referred to the Temple Mount:

Brethren ... I am deeply impressed with the good done by Masonry in foreign lands, and the important feature it is in bringing together so many who would not otherwise have an opportunity of knowing each other ... In Palestine, Masonry brought together persons of different races and creeds, who were otherwise not likely to have met, and I may mention among others whose acquaintance I made, the name of Herr Petermann, of Berlin, the distinguished occidental linguist. While grubbing among the ruins of the Temple of King Solomon, I had ample opportunity of observing the good work of Masons in Palestine, and my thanks are due to many for the valuable assistance they gave me in my work. On one occasion I had the pleasure in assisting in opening a Lodge in a cavern which runs nearly under the old Temple, the members of which, though few in number, represented the East and West. There was an Englishman, an American, a German, a Frenchman, an Armenian, and a Greek, and also a Hebrew.

If Warren believed the Temple to have been situated to the south of the Qubbet as-Sakhra there were only two caverns 'nearly under the old Temple' accessible, without arousing suspicion, to eight men. The first was the erroneously entitled 'Solomon's Quarries', a vast underground quarry which stretched southwards from the northern wall of the Old City. This place is, in fact, a quarry of the Herodian period and during the second half of the nineteenth century when Warren was in Jerusalem it was a regular meeting place for Freemasons. The second was the cave under the *sakhra* itself. Warren is not precise about which of the two locations the meeting was held in, but the fact that it was conducted at all at the centre of Ottoman-controlled Jerusalem was extraordinary. Six hundred and eighty years after the last Crusader Knight Templar had been expelled from the Holy City, Warren held a Templar Masonic meeting underneath the Templum Domini.

Warren's interest in things Templar extended to the study of architecture and the mathematics that were necessary for building. Contrary to the scholastic thinking of his time – perhaps because of his Masonic experience – he was convinced about the important role mathematics played in the construction of ancient buildings:

> the difficulty is that all the mathematicians I have yet met have an instinctive repugnance to believing that the ancients knew anything about Pi, and they will not help to put the matter in a clear light. I hold that the ancients <u>knew</u> much more than they could <u>express</u>. Archimedes said that Pi lay between 22/7 and 223/71. That shows that he did know a good deal about Pi. I must get this paper put in such a form that mathematicians will consider it, and they have a very fixed machinery for everything. I think of sending it to Dr Glaisher of Cambridge who is one of the first in pure mathematics.[50]

Charles Warren's archaeological work represents an invaluable contribution to our understanding of the history of the Temple Mount. It is evident from his letters that his strongest desire was to go deep into the Mount although, despite his conviction that 'in places there may be objects of the greatest interest hidden', there is no indication to suppose that in the places he did enter he ever found any trace of the Ark of the Covenant. But his insistence that

Cistern V, because of the drainage channels leading from it, gave the position of the Temple altar, suggests that the legendary relic of the Solomonic Temple was probably never far from his mind. Warren even went to the extent of superimposing the ground plan of the Temple, including the Holy of Holies, on a copy of Wilson's 1:500 survey of the *haram*.[51] Perhaps it was this interest that caused him to behave in such a rash manner on the *sakhra*, an act which if observed by the Turkish authorities would have meant the end of his excavations if not his army career.

When he returned from Palestine in 1870 Warren established the Quatuor Coronati Lodge, described in Freemasonic circles as 'the first Masonic lodge of [historical] research in the world'.[52] All nine founding members were leading authorities in the field of Masonic history, archaeology and anthropology. Warren had great pride in belonging to a Freemasonic Knight Templar Order. Amongst his possessions when he died was a sword concealed inside a walking stick. It was the sword traditionally carried by the 'Tyler' or guard of a Lodge to protect against intrusion from outsiders. Warren had removed the hilt to fit it into the stick. On the blade was etched the Christian Cross, the Masonic Compasses and a Cross of the Knights Templar.

The next British officer to arrive in Jerusalem, Captain Montagu Parker, was not sent by the PEF but came in a private capacity. He arrived in 1909 at the head of an expedition to find the treasures of King David and King Solomon and to search for the Ark of the Covenant.

MONTAGU BROWNLOW PARKER AND THE ARK OF THE COVENANT

Born on 13 October 1878, Montagu Brownlow Parker was the second son of the 3rd Earl of Morley, a family which owned a vast amount of property in south Devon. Parker was commissioned into the Gloucester Regiment in 1898, joining the Third Battalion. The following year he transferred to the Grenadier Guards and fought in the South African war against the Boers where he was wounded, although not seriously. He returned to England and from 1901 until 1906 he was aide-de-camp to successive commanding generals. In 1907 he was made a captain but two years later he resigned in order to pursue an adventure which would gain him international notoriety.

In 1908 Parker met the self-styled 'biblical scholar', Valter H. Juvelius. Juvelius had apparently deciphered a coded message within the text of the Book of Ezekiel which described the precise location of the 'treasure' of Solomon's Temple hidden deep inside the Mount. Parker was convinced that Juvelius' research was genuine and he and Juvelius formed a working partnership. There are confusing reports about the 'treasure' which Parker and Juvelius believed lay concealed under the *haram*. Newspaper articles of the time record a search for the jewels of King Solomon, the tombs of David and Solomon and the Ark of the Covenant. But if Juvelius was half the biblical scholar he professed himself to be, both he and Parker would have been aware from the start of their research that the Babylonians – according to the Old Testament Second Book of Kings – had looted the Temple of its 'treasures' in 586 BC. Given this factor it is likely that they imagined they would find, not gold and silver from the Temple, but the tombs of the Jewish kings and, quite possibly, the Ark containing the Ten Commandments.

There is no information concerning the exact nature of the 'coded message'. So perhaps Juvelius had picked up on the passage in the Second Book of Chronicles describing the request by King Josiah for the Levites to 'put the holy Ark in the house which Solomon the son of David king of Israel did build'.[53] Once he realized that the Ark was probably still somewhere under the Mount, in an undisclosed location, he may have deliberately concocted the story about the Book of Ezekiel in order to convince Parker that he knew exactly where the treasure lay. This would explain why, whilst Parker was busy raising money for the expedition, Juvelius hired a Danish clairvoyant to guide the team in their search.[54] But whatever the truth behind Juvelius' 'evidence', Parker was sufficiently enthused by the prospect of unearthing the greatest archaeological treasure of all time. He spent the winter of 1908–9 visiting family friends of his father, the 3rd Earl, in England, Europe and America, and succeeded in raising over $125,000 for an excavation.[55]

In the summer of 1909 Parker left for Palestine aboard the private yacht of his friend Clarence Wilson, who together with Captain R.G. Duff and a Major Foley had joined the expedition. The intrepid explorers were inspired by the work undertaken by Warren in the City of David where, with the help of Birtles, he had investigated the Gihon Spring connected to Hezekiah's Tunnel. Juvelius was certain that in this complex of underground channels they would discover a secret route leading northwards to the southern end of the Temple platform, which would allow them access to a concealed chamber deep within the bowels of the Mount itself, where the 'treasure' would then be found. But Juvelius and Parker, together with their team of companions – and the investors – were bitterly disappointed.

In 1950 Bertha Spafford Vester, a life-long resident of Jerusalem and mother-in-law of the present owner of the American Colony Hotel in the Arab quarter north of the Damascus Gate, wrote the following account of the first stages of the 'Parker Expedition':

> an agent, acting mysteriously on behalf of a group of 'notable Englishmen,' came to Jerusalem for the acquisition of property to 'build schools and hospitals for the people on behalf of the Turkish Government.' According to his accounts, he enjoyed the patronage of the Grand Vizier, the Minister of the Interior, *et al.* Soon it evolved that the property sought was the hill situated to the south of the city… The local authorities ordered the municipal architect to make plans of the entire hill for the purchasers… and handed the property over to the Englishmen…
>
> The Englishmen came to Jaffa by yacht and, in due time, to Jerusalem.
>
> They brought with them many cases of implements for excavation. Nothing more was said about a hospital or a school… We heard of gay dinner parties given by the Englishmen… and of their using oranges for target practice, with the little Jewish children from the nearby 'box colony' scrambling about to gather the smashed fruit… They were certainly the oddest archaeologists ever to visit Jerusalem. Frederick and I met some of them at a reception and found them charming, but we were puzzled by their complete lack of archaeological knowledge.'[56]

It was not long, as Bertha Spafford Vester recounts, before 'all kinds of stories were afloat – that they were trying to find the royal Tomb of David and the Kings of Judah; that they sought the buried temple treasures; that they were after the Ark of the Covenant that was hidden there, etcetera, etcetera.'[57] Parker and his companions spent the rest of the summer and early autumn clearing one of the many shafts sunk by Warren on the slopes of the Davidic city hoping that they would find an entrance to a tunnel leading to the Mount. But if Parker had been fortunate in war and rich in connections, both luck and money now deserted him.

The winter rains came early, preventing the continuation of work, and in November Parker returned to London to raise further funds and organize a new team for the next season of digging. In August 1910 Parker arrived back in Jerusalem with 'expensive and perfect [digging] machinery' and engineers who had experience in digging the London Underground to assist him.[58] But he found a changed atmosphere in the Holy City. The Turks were suspicious of the motives of the expedition and the Jews had found in Baron Edmond de Rothschild an advocate for their objections to Parker's work. The Baron purchased his own small parcel of land in the City of David several hundred metres to the south of Parker and set up in competition with Parker by excavating there. The Turks consequently gave Parker an ultimatum: he must finish his investigations by the end of the summer of 1911 or leave. This placed him in an impossible position as there was no hope of excavating a gallery to the Mount within this time. His excavation of Warren's old shaft had come to nought. So he turned his attention to Hezekiah's Tunnel which had been explored by Warren and Birtles forty years earlier. He dug throughout the winter, but the tunnel led him away from rather than towards the Mount and there was no indication of subsidiary galleries in that direction. By April simple mathematics demonstrated that if a tunnel were to be found his team would not have time to clear the necessary distance to the *haram*.[59] So Parker resorted to a last desperate gamble. By offering the Turkish governor, Ahmed Bey, $25,000, Parker and a handful of companions were smuggled into the *haram* at night dressed in Arab disguise. A week of clandestine excavation at the south-eastern corner in the hope of finding a connecting shaft to a secret chamber produced no result, and on the night of 17 April they entered the Dome of the Rock to investigate the exposed bedrock of Mount Moriah. In the cave under the *sakhra* they broke up the flagstone floor which, as Wilson had shown in his survey of 1864–5 contained the entrance to the Well of Souls.

According to a letter in *The Times*, published on 4 May 1911, Parker's party had procured a copy of Professor Conrad Schick's report on the well. Schick, a German architect and model-builder, had investigated the location in 1887. However, Wilson had already confirmed in 1866 that the shaft led to a drain, which in turn ran out into the valley of the Kidron, in a similar way to the drain explored by Warren but at a deeper level. Spafford Vester had perhaps been right to question the archaeological capabilities of the Parker team. The noise of breaking flagstones attracted the attention of an attendant who, unaware of Parker's complicity with the governor, and finding the cave full of disguised excavators, raised the alarm. Leaving the governor to handle the rioting which now exploded across the city, Parker and his companions fled Jerusalem in a wild bid to seek refuge in Clarence Wilson's yacht which was moored at Jaffa.

According to Spafford Vester, 'the "Parker Fiasco" came nearer to causing anti-Christian riots and even massacre than anything that had happened during our long residence in Jerusalem.'[60] The party of the Young Turks, who challenged the established Ottoman hierarchy across the empire, were blamed for condoning the Christian sacrilege of the *sakhra* and Moslems faithful to the Ottoman regime latched onto the incident in order to stir up anti-Western sentiment at a time when Moslems were pouring into the streets for the Feast of Nebi Musa. The celebrations comprised a march in the honour of the prophet Moses – instituted by the Mamluks – which had been held annually in order to counterpoise Christian pilgrim presence at Easter. Jerusalem was on the brink of anarchy and, as the anonymous letter writer from Jerusalem reported to *The Times*, 'Christian throats were jeopardised for several hours.'[61] Parker escaped arrest by persuading the Turkish soldiers to allow him and his friends to row out to Clarence

Wilson's yacht to have a meeting in more comfortable surroundings than would be possible on shore. Once they reached the safety of the yacht the Englishmen immediately weighed anchor and sailed away from the Holy Land leaving behind at the site of their excavation in David's City, two tin buckets, a ladder and a broken pipe, which were uncovered by archaeologists in 1998.

The baggage of Parker and his friends had been searched by the Turkish soldiers who confirmed that it contained no treasure. But despite Parker's lack of success, the 'Parker Affair' – the Christian desecration of the Dome of the Rock – entered the legend of The Temple Mount. All manner of new rumours and statements concerning the expedition began to circulate including a Reuter's Agency report which claimed that 'members of the expedition declared that they expected to find a manuscript which would set at rest all doubts as to the Resurrection of Christ.'[62] But what Parker needed was some good luck. He arrived back in England with his mission and his reputation in tatters. The Turkish government demanded that Parker and his accomplices be sent back to Jerusalem and hanged. This did not dissuade Parker from preparing another excavation, telling a correspondent of *The Times* on 16 September that he and his friends were still determined to look 'for the tombs of David and Solomon'. At the end of October 1911 he arrived in Jaffa on board Clarence Wilson's yacht only to be warned by his friends that it would be unwise for him to disembark. He sailed away from the shores of Palestine empty-handed.

Six months previously, whilst Parker's party was sailing back to London after their undignified escape, the *New York Times* published a full-page article complete with photographs of the *haram* and a reconstruction of the Ark of the Covenant. Under a banner headline HAVE ENGLISHMEN FOUND THE ARK OF THE COVENANT?, the story of the 'Parker Fiasco' was explained, as was the biblical history concerning the relic. The article claimed that in New York it was believed that 'the excavating expedition which has been digging around the sacred precincts in Jerusalem went there with the object of finding the Ark.'[63] The person who wrote the article had contacted Dr Solomon Schechter, head of the Jewish Theological Seminary of New York, who explained the existence of a Jewish religious tradition: 'Some of the Talmudic writers set forth a belief that the sacred Ark had been hidden just about where it was reported to be found, under [the ancient site of] the Temple of Solomon.' Dr Schechter added further, stunning information: 'A place had been made there, says the tradition, so that in case of fire or destruction by enemies the Ark and the other treasures of the Temple could be quickly hidden. The legend went that the Ark would not be brought forth until the day when the Messiah should bring the scattered people of Israel back to their land and Temple.' The article in the *New York Times* summed up Schechter's information with a conclusion about the Mount which, in the late 1990s, is still pertinent: 'There are of course many chambers under the Mosque [Dome of the Rock] and foundations and hidden places that have not been explored.'

This was the last major article to be published internationally on the Parker Affair. But even though Parker disappeared from the headlines, the first step towards the mass-return of the scattered people of Israel to Jerusalem – the precondition, according to the Talmudic tradition, for the re-emergence of the Ark – was about to happen. In 1914 Great Britain went to war and Moslem Turkey was on the side of the enemy.

One God and the Millennium,
1917–2000

The outbreak of the First World War initiated the terminal decline of the Turkish Ottoman Empire. In October 1914 Turkey joined an alliance with Germany and Austria bringing her into conflict with Great Britain, France and Russia. In February 1915 Turkish forces marched south-east from Palestine and traversing the northern Sinai launched an attack against the Suez Canal. They were thrown back by the British and retreated across the Sinai into Palestine.

The British retaliated in 1915 by attacking the Turks in Mesopotamia and Gallipoli. Although the Mesopotamian campaign was partially successful in 1917, the Gallipoli plan – to force a quick end to the Turkish Empire by steaming through the Dardanelles with battleships and shelling Constantinople from the sea – was disastrous. The Turks were assisted by German liaison officers who advised them on how to use mines and artillery and they were well equipped with small-arms: since 1904 the German Mauser factory at Obendorf had been producing the latest design of their bolt-action rifle, based on the proven German model 1898 Mauser, specifically for use by the Turkish infantry. The Turks fought British and Commonwealth troops to a standstill on the rocky peninsular of Gallipoli. Offshore, losses amongst the British and French warships lying in wait for a dash through Dardanelle Straits to Constantinople necessitated a naval withdrawal from the area. With mounting casualties and no prospect of a breakthrough the British decided to evacuate their army. On 8 January 1916 the Royal Navy took the last British soldiers off the beach at Cape Helles leaving behind over 48,000 British, Commonwealth and French dead.

In Cairo, the British High Command reverted to another strategy to defeat the Turks. They decided to invade Turkish territory across the Sinai advancing up the Mediterranean coast to Gaza and on to Jerusalem and Damascus, thereby cutting the Ottoman Empire, which stretched from Constantinople to Mesopotamia, in two. In March 1917 the British reached Gaza but were beaten off in their attempt to capture the city. A second unsuccessful attack was made in April. By May the Egyptian Expeditionary Force had a new commander, Edmund Allenby, who was under orders from the British Prime Minister Lloyd George to conquer Jerusalem by Christmas and thus provide a war-weary British public with a moral-boosting victory. Allenby attacked and captured Gaza. It took his British Expeditionary Force two months to reach the outskirts of Jerusalem. His army fought a campaign which stands out as probably the most successful and least recognized of the First World War. Allenby's conquest was dependent on the role played in his campaign by T. E. Lawrence who since 1916 had been working to protect the eastern flank of the British army as it advanced from Egypt and into Palestine. This Lawrence achieved by single-handedly masterminding an uprising of the Arabian tribes.

Lawrence grew up in Oxford and went to university there. In 1909 aged twenty-one, he left Jesus College to walk around Syria on foot. Lawrence wished to obtain first-hand knowledge of the Crusader castles and when he arrived home a year later he was fluent in several Arab dialects. The essay he wrote of his findings earned him a four-year scholarship from Jesus College and he decided to return to the Middle East and pursue his archaeological interests. From 1910 to 1913 he excavated at Carchemish in south-eastern Turkey under Sir Leonard Woolley where he gained valuable experience in dealing with Moslem Arabs of various tribal origins. This experience was put to good use when in the winter of 1913–14 the War Office in London were anxious to have an accurate map of the Sinai desert. They commissioned Lawrence, Woolley and Colonel Newcombe from the British army to carry out a survey of the Sinai peninsula for the Egyptian government. At the outbreak of war in 1914, Lawrence enrolled in the British army and was posted to Cairo to join the Military Map Department of the Intelligence Service. Lawrence's qualities as a linguist and as someone capable of understanding the Arab mentality were slowly recognized and in October 1916 he was sent to Saudi Arabia to investigate the potential for an Arab uprising against Ottoman Turk occupation. Lawrence's 'Arab Revolt' was principally directed against the Ottoman railway system, which ran from Syria through Palestine into the Arabian peninsula. By wrecking the railway link between the northern and southern parts of Ottoman territory he completely disrupted the Turkish lines of communication and supply. To the British public Lawrence's exploits of ambushing Turkish soldiers, blowing up railway bridges and derailing troop trains became legendary, obscuring the less glamorous achievements of Allenby, his commander-in-chief. However, the success of the campaign depended on the capture of Jerusalem and fourteen months later, by the beginning of December 1917 Allenby's forces were prepared for an assault. The religious status of Jerusalem was of great concern to Allenby. Before he launched his attack he issued the following communiqué to Chetwode, his general in command: 'I place no restriction upon you in respect of any operation which you may consider necessary . . . except that on no account is any risk to be run of bringing the city of Jerusalem or its immediate environs within the area of operations.'[1]

After ten days of hard fighting the Turks withdrew from the city and headed north, leaving Jerusalem at the mercy of the British forces. At half past eight on the morning of 9 December, the Mayor of the city, Hussein el Husseini, in the company of his Chief of Police and two gendarmes, walked towards the British positions with a white flag. The Mayor's surrender was accepted by two British soldiers, and the Ottoman rule of the Holy City came to an end. At 12.30 p.m. the keys of the city were handed over to Major General Sir John Shea, commander of the 60th Infantry Division who was acting on behalf of Allenby. Jerusalem had been 'liberated' by a Christian-led army, and a victory procession was hurriedly organized for the next day. On 10 December Allenby passed through Suleiman's walls at the head of the procession which walked from the Jaffa Gate into the Old City. T. E. Lawrence had not worn regular army uniform since the beginning of the Arab Revolt and when he was invited to participate in the victory parade he

hurriedly borrowed articles of uniform from several of his col-
leagues in order to comply with the minimum requirements of
dress laid down in British army regulations. The processional entry
into the Old City had a profound effect on him and he later
described it as 'the supreme moment of the war'.[2]

However, his experiences in the desert also revealed the spiritual
side of his character, dramatically changing the way he viewed
Christian belief. In 1916 he had visited a spring at Wadi Rumm
which was big enough to bathe in. An old man with a grey beard and
'a hewn face of great power' sat down on Lawrence's clothes which
he had spread out in the sun and, having scrutinized Lawrence,
leant towards him and uttered the words, 'The love is from God;
and of God; and towards God.'[3] Before this encounter Lawrence
had believed that only the Christian faith possessed the capacity to
transmit God's love to the people of the world. Semites, he believed,
'were unable to use love as a link between themselves and God'.[4] In
one short sentence, the old man at Wadi Rumm altered Lawrence's
perception of the supremacy of his own Christian brand of
monotheism, a fact Lawrence later admitted when describing the
meeting in his book on the Arab Revolt, *Seven Pillars of Wisdom*.[5]

On the *haram* Allenby's conquest made little difference to daily
life. The British military encouraged Moslems to continue to worship in the Aqsa. Allenby even went to the lengths of placing an
armed guard of Indian Moslem troops outside the Dome of the
Rock. But, whilst the religious status of the *haram* was ensured, the
political situation in Jerusalem was heading for an abrupt change.
One month before Allenby's occupation the British government
had issued a declaration which had profound repercussions for the
future of Jerusalem, eventually leading to the creation of a new
Israel and a revival of the Jewish 'Messianic' dream.

THE RETURN TO ZION

Zion: Holy Hill of Jerusalem.

Zionism: Colonising of Palestine as modern Jewish scheme.

The Pocket Oxford Dictionary, 1924

Since the eighteenth century the idea of Jews returning to their ancestral land, fuelled by Messianic movements such as Shabbetainism, had gradually been gaining a wider international acceptance. By the end of the nineteenth century this momentum received another stimulus. Bloody pogroms against Jews in Russia in the 1880s reinforced the conviction of many Jews that a return to Palestine represented the only future for the Jewish people. In the last decade of the nineteenth century, the Jewish diaspora found a champion for a mass Jewish return to the Holy Land.

Theodor Herzl was a Viennese journalist and the author of *Der Judenstaat* (the Jewish State) which was published in 1896 and shook his people out of a political apathy. Herzl declared that the only way to prevent the continuation of anti-semitism was for the Jews to have their own state run on modern, democratic and secular lines. A year later the First Zionist Congress, a meeting organized by Jews who wished to return to Palestine, was held in Basle to discuss how to create 'a home in Palestine secured by public law' for the Jewish people.[6] Herzl in his opening address to the Congress drew attention to the ancient Temple and the *sakhra,* reminding his fellow Jews of the significance of the sacred site on Mount Moriah.[7] Herzl's address was enthusiastically received and 'Zionism' became a recognized political movement whose goal was to return the Jews to the Land of Israel. Herzl did not live to see the realization of his dream but his efforts were tireless. He negotiated ceaselessly with heads of government in London and Constantinople, where in October 1898 he met Kaiser Wilhelm II. Herzl followed the Kaiser, when on his tour of the Middle East, to continue discussions about the future of Palestine. They met again in Jerusalem on 2 November 1898 when the Kaiser was visiting the Temple Mount. Their meeting was brief and inconclusive; no one, it seemed, was willing to consider seriously the establishment of a Jewish homeland. Eventually, however, the British in 1902 suggested a solution to the Jewish proposal. The British government put forward a plan that Uganda, which was sparsely populated and had farming potential, be handed over to the Zionists. The suggestion of transporting Israel to Africa was not met with unanimous glee, and the proposal was quickly shelved.

Two years later, at the age of forty-four, Herzl died. The Zionist movement had lost its founding father and factionalism broke out within the organization. Its lack of serious international recognition hampered the achievement of its aim and, despite the popular appeal to many Jews of the Zionist cause, when war broke out in 1914 the number of Jews supporting it was only one per cent of the total Jewish population throughout the world. A start, however, had been made. In Palestine fifty-nine Jewish colonies had been set up. Most were farming communities in the style of kibbutzim which contained an estimated twelve thousand settlers.[8] The pioneering example set by the settlers greatly encouraged the Zionist cause. Active lobbying for Zionism continued in the political arena of Europe and by the time of the British victory in Palestine in 1917 negotiations between Zionists and members of the British government had resulted in support for the main point in the Basle Declaration of 1897: 'the acquisition of an internationally recognised legal right to colonise Palestine'.[9] This agreement was primarily the result of the efforts of one man who also succeeded in re-establishing unity within the ranks of the Zionist organization.

Since his arrival in England from Russia in 1904, Chaim Weizmann, a chemist, had cultivated friends in high places, some of whom were Jewish or sympathetic to the Zionist cause, including Lloyd George, Sir Herbert Samuel and Arthur Balfour. Weizmann's contribution to the British war effort was also significant. By 1915 Britain was desperately short of munitions for the Western Front and Weizmann used his knowledge of chemistry to produce large quantities of acetone, a chemical mixture necessary for the production of high explosives. In 1917 Weizmann's friendship with influential political contacts and the help he had given Britain during the war brought political dividends. Lloyd George became Prime Minister and he appointed Arthur Balfour to lead the Foreign Office. In July the Balfour Declaration giving Jews the right to settle in Palestine had been hammered out between the Zionists and the British government and on 2 November 1917 Balfour sent Lord Rothschild, who was acting representative of the Zionist Federation, a letter in which he declared the government's position:

I have much pleasure in conveying to you, on behalf of His Majesty's Government, the following declaration of sympathy with Jewish Zionist aspirations which has been submitted to, and approved by, the Cabinet.

'His Majesty's Government view with favour the establishment in Palestine of a national home for the Jewish people, and will use their best endeavours to facilitate the achievement of this object, it being clearly understood that nothing shall be done which may prejudice the civil and religious rights of existing non-Jewish communities in Palestine, or the rights and political status enjoyed by Jews in any other country.'

I should be grateful if you would bring this declaration to the knowledge of the Zionist Federation.

Yours sincerely,
Arthur James Balfour

Sir Winston Churchill said that the Balfour Declaration had 'often been supposed as an ill-considered, sentimental act',[10] and it is clear that the creation of a 'national home for the Jewish people' within Palestine was from the very outset wide open to interpretation.

Very few people opposed the British government. In January 1918 T. E. Lawrence was sent as an envoy to deliver to the Arab leader King Hussein the British government's 'proposals for the future of Palestine'. The document began with an apology: the lack of any previous communication was because British officials were 'unable to get in touch with the Palestinian Arabs, as they were fighting against us',[11] an acceptable if somewhat naive explanation. The proposal went on to guarantee that the *haram* would 'not be subjected directly or indirectly to any non-Moslem authority'. The British government were aware that they were unlikely to encounter any serious resistance to the Declaration. Arab leaders, although uneasy about the scope to which the Balfour Declaration could be exploited, welcomed the prospect of Jewish immigration with caution. Later in the year King Hussein called upon the Arab population in Palestine 'to bear in mind that their sacred books and their traditions enjoined upon them the duties of hospitality and tolerance' and he exhorted them to 'welcome the Jews as brethren and co-operate with them for the common welfare'.[12] In 1918 Hussein's son, the Emir Feisal, issued a statement to a representative of Reuter's Agency, published in *The Times* on 12 December: 'The two main branches of the Semitic family, Arabs and Jews, understand one another...Arabs are not jealous of Zionist Jews, and intend to give them fair play.' This was reinforced by an agreement of mutual co-operation between Weizmann and Feisal which was drawn up in the spring of 1919. But 'fair play' soon degenerated into conflict. In 1920 and 1921 rioting broke out in Jerusalem and towards the end of the decade a more serious outbreak occurred, sparked off – almost inevitably – by an incident at the Temple Mount.

On Yom Kippur of 1928 members of the Jewish Orthodox community erected a wooden screen at the Wailing Wall in order to separate male and female worshippers. The Supreme Moslem Council on the *haram* immediately declared the screen to be a 'permanent structure' and as such an infringement of their right of jurisdiction over the holy location. Powerless to remove it, the Moslems began general maintenance and building work close to the Wall with the intention of disrupting the Jewish prayers. The stalemate continued into the heat of the summer and in August, on the anniversary of the destruction of the First and Second Temples, a group of young Jews marched to the Wall and, unfurling the Zionist flag, sang the Zionist national anthem. Riots broke out across Palestine and 133 Jews were killed, most of them members of the Orthodox from Jerusalem, Hebron and Safad.[13] There were also a number of Arab casualties.

T.E. Lawrence, who took an active role in post-war negotiations about the future of the Middle East, had foreseen the signs of such potential conflict.

The Jewish experiment is...a conscious effort on the part of the least European people in Europe, to head against the drift of ages, and return once more to the Orient from which they came...The success of their scheme will involve inevitably the raising of the present Arab population to their own material level...and the consequence might be of the highest importance for the future of the Arab world. It might well prove a source of technical supply rendering them independent of industrial Europe, and in that case the new confederation might become a formidable element of world power. However, such

a contingency will not be for the first or even for the second generation, but it must be borne in mind in any laying out of foundations of
Empire in Western Asia. These to a large extent must stand or fall by
the course of the Zionist effort.[14]

Lawrence's words can be read as either anti-Jewish or tragically
prophetic. Arab society in Palestine was based on the ancient tribal
principles of family obedience and respect of religious law. In this
regard Ottoman rule had done the Palestinians a great disservice, by
leaving them politically unprepared as a society for the techno-
logical and political revolution of the twentieth century. Zionism
was a new and vibrant movement, and the Balfour Declaration
made any criticism of the Zionists' aims difficult to uphold. The
Arabs in Palestine were left at a severe political disadvantage.

In 1922 the League of Nations invested Great Britain with a
Mandate for the government of Palestine. Military rule was super-
seded by civilian and in Jerusalem Sir Herbert Samuel took up
residence as the first High Commissioner. During the course of the
next fifteen years Jewish immigration continued at a trickle, while
many Zionist pioneers, disillusioned at the reality of life under
the Mandate, returned to their country of origin. The Mandate
required Britain to recognize the Zionist organization as the agency
with co-authority for the creation of a Jewish homeland, whilst at
the same time refraining from 'prejudicing the civil and military
rights of existing non-Jewish communities in Palestine'.[15] On 7 July
1937 the British government produced the Peel Report on the future
of the Mandate which recommended the partitioning of Palestine
and the creation of a Jewish state which would consist of a corridor
of territory stretching from Jaffa on the Mediterranean coast up to
and including Jerusalem. An Arab rebellion broke out and Britain
had to send reinforcements to control the situation. In October 1937
the District Commissioner of Galilee and his escort were ambushed
by terrorists and killed while travelling by car.

This period of violence coincided with a rapid rise in Jewish
immigration. From 1937, the rise of the Nazis and the threat of war
in Europe provoked an escalation of Jewish refugees and by 1939 the
number of Jews in Palestine stood at just over a quarter of the Arabic

population. This increase created serious tension between the Jewish and Arab communities and the British were fighting on a daily basis to keep the peace. Grave damage was inflicted to the prestige and morale of the British forces, and the Christian army, which had come to Jerusalem in 1917 with hopes of ruling peacefully, became the object of hatred for many Jews and Arabs who, because they wished for their own sovereignty, were determined to force the British out of Palestine.

Throughout the history of the Temple Mount events far from it have affected its destiny. Up until 1939 change in Jerusalem was normally initiated by a single battle, but the National Socialist Party of Germany broke this historical pattern and in so doing altered for ever the history of the Jewish people. The word given to the 6,000,000 Jews murdered by the Nazis between 1933 and 1945 – the 'Holocaust' – could not be more appropriate. The name which, for three millennia before the Nazi era, had described a whole sacrifice to Yahweh, is now a permanent memorial of the Nazi regime's attempt to extinguish all trace of the Jews by burning their bodies. It is one of the terrible ironies of history that had it not been for this human holocaust the modern state of Israel may never have come into existence as early as 1948 when the British relinquished their Mandate. By 1945 it was undeniable, even to people who found it hard to believe that the Nazis had committed mass-murder in such a cold-blooded way, that Hitler's dream of ridding Europe of all Jews had very nearly succeeded. Herzl's idea of a Jewish state had become a matter of necessity which no one could now deny.

On 29 November 1947 the General Assembly of the United Nations adopted a resolution in favour of dividing Palestine between Jews and Arabs, and for Britain to be released from their obligations. The Jews were given control of the Negev, the coastal plain and part of eastern Galilee, and the Arabs were to keep western Galilee, Samaria and the rest of central Palestine from the Mediterranean coast at Ashkelon up to the Jordan river. Jerusalem was to be left as an 'international' city accessed by a corridor from Jewish territory to the west. Fighting between Arabs and Jews broke out almost immediately, with the British, preoccupied by their preparations for departure, unwilling to intervene. Six months later on 14 May, the day before the British Mandate expired, David Ben-Gurion, the newly elected Prime Minister, proclaimed the creation of a new Israel. After nearly 1900 years, Israel was reborn as a nation.

The odds were heavily stacked against the survival of the new country. Five Arab armies from Egypt, Transjordan, Iraq, Syria and Lebanon, comprising an estimated total of 40,500 soldiers well equipped with tanks and artillery and air support, crossed into Palestine determined to help defend the rights of the Palestinian Arabs and destroy the Jewish state. Opposing them was a scratch force of 13,000 trained Israelis out of a population of 600,000. The Israelis had no more than 10,000 rifles, 600 machine guns of various kinds, two pieces of obsolete artillery and a handful of aircraft of Second World War vintage – several of them ex-German Luftwaffe Messerschmitt 109s flown over from Czechoslovakia.[16] Despite the overwhelming odds against them, the Israelis resisted the Arab onslaught. The fighting was particularly fierce in and around Jerusalem, where the Israelis were drawn into combat against the Arab Legion of Jordan which was properly trained and officered by the British. After three weeks of desperate conflict a truce was ordered by the United Nations. This lull in the fighting saved Israel. The country was able to airlift supplies of arms from the United States and Czechoslovakia and reinforce her fledgling air force. British arms supplies to the Arabs had been suspended under the terms of the United Nations truce and when fighting resumed after one month, the tide of advantage had turned in Israel's favour. By the time a second truce was called on 18 July Israel had captured most of Galilee and had either contained or pushed back the Arab armies in all other sectors.

Jerusalem, however, was still divided. From West Jerusalem an Israeli-occupied salient stretched eastwards into Jordanian-occupied territory, with its front abutting the west wall of the Old City. The Temple Mount and the Wailing Wall still lay firmly in Arab hands. But despite this, the Israeli army managed to withstand the worst the Arabs could throw at them and a new spirit of defiance took hold of the Jewish people. Many Jews who had served in the British army during the Second World War, together with survivors of the concentration camps and Nazi persecution, formed the nucleus of an army which in 1967, would recapture East Jerusalem and unite the city and the Temple Mount under the flag of Israel.

THE RETURN TO THE MOUNT

On 23 January 1950 the Israeli government established Jerusalem as the capital of Israel and on 5 July the Law of Return – or right of all Jews to settle in Israel – was constituted. The first clause laid the foundation for modern Israel and effectively put an end to the state of forced diaspora which had existed since Roman times. Every Jew, it confirmed, 'has the right to come to this country as an *oleh* or immigrant'. This law, prompted by the Holocaust, gave birth to the grounds for future conflict between Arabs and Jews as it cleared the way for a large influx of religious Orthodox Jews to Jerusalem, which put great pressure on an already delicate religious balance which existed within the Old City. In 1950, however, the Jerusalem Jewish Orthodox community exerted little influence on Israeli or Arab affairs. Since the Declaration of the State of Israel in 1948 the government had conducted its business on secular lines without interference from religious elements within its society and for the next two decades of Israel's existence the Orthodox movement found neither the opportunity nor the reason to intervene.

To survive, Israel was obliged to create, train and maintain a modern army. It successfully achieved this and, as the economy grew, so the standard of living of the ordinary Israeli citizen rose – faster than that of the Palestinian Arabs. This increase in Jewish prosperity – as T.E. Lawrence predicted – by the early 1960s created resentment amongst the Palestinians. The Arab countries surrounding Israel still dreamt of conquering the whole of Palestine and by the mid-1960s relations between Israel and her Arab neighbours were extremely fragile. On 22 May 1967 Egypt closed the Straits of Tiran cutting off Israel's southern shipping route into the Red Sea and with Egypt's refusal to remove the air and naval blockade, war was inevitable.

In the early hours of 5 June the Israelis made a pre-emptive strike against the Egyptian air force, beginning the Six-Day War. By 10 June the Sinai peninsula, extensive parts of the Golan and the entire West Bank up to the Jordan river and the Dead Sea had been conquered by Israel and a ceasefire was called. The Israeli army, air force and navy had achieved a stunning victory. Yitzak Rabin, Chief of Staff and future Prime Minister of Israel, declared: 'All this has been done by the Israel defence forces alone, with what we have, without anything or anybody else.'[17] Jerusalem fell to Israeli troops on 7 June, including the Wailing Wall and the Temple Mount. The fighting in East Jerusalem was ferocious. The narrow streets and tall buildings of the Old City made any attack difficult and the Arab troops defended the site of their *haram* with determination. Israeli troops advanced house by house. By the late morning of 7 June the area by the Wailing Wall was filled with victorious Israeli paratroopers, many of them in tears, praying in thanks for the deliverance of their Holy City. The Chief Rabbi of the Israeli Armed Forces, General Shlomo Goren, stood clutching the Torah – the Books of Moses – which he had carried into battle. He made an emotional speech:

> We have taken the city of God, we are entering the Messianic era for the Jewish people. And I promise to the Christian world that we are responsible for, we will take care of, the holy places of all religions here…We took an oath today, while capturing the city, on our blood we took an oath that we will never give it up, we will never leave this place. The Wailing Wall belongs to us. The Holy place was our place first, our place and our God's place. From here we do not move. Never. Never.[18]

The words of Rabbi Goren reflected the feelings of many Jews. Both in Israel and abroad Zionism was seen as the realization of a divine plan, and the recapture of Jerusalem, after almost two thousand years, reinforced this conviction. Some Jews, however, did not believe that Jerusalem had been conquered through the will of God. This ideological difference became immediately apparent through the actions of Moshe Dayan who was sworn in as Defence Minister only eight hours after the outbreak of the war.

Dayan went to the Wailing Wall to visit the scene of Israel's most symbolic victory. Like Rabin, Dayan represented the military leadership of post-war secular Zionism. He was not particularly religious, although on this occasion he gladly paid homage in public to the God of his people. On a scrap of paper he wrote the words, 'May peace be upon all Israel,'[19] and inserted it into a gap between the Herodian stones of the Wall now under his jurisdiction. In the days that followed he endeavoured to effect this wish by holding negotiations with the Arabs. On 17 June 1967 Dayan attended a meeting with Moslem officials inside the Aqsa Mosque. Sitting barefoot on a carpet, in accordance with the tradition of his hosts, he assured the Palestinian Arabs that the status of the *haram* would remain unchanged; the entire area inside the walls of the Mount would continue as an Islamic sanctuary. Many Jews saw this as appeasement provoking a rift which, as the millennium approaches and religious issues on the Temple Mount come under increasing scrutiny, haunts Israeli society. As a direct result of Dayan's decision the Temple Mount Faithful, a group dedicated to the expulsion of the Arabs from the *haram* and the re-establishment of Jewish prayer on the Temple Mount, was founded, with the hope that within the lifetime of its members all the aims of the movement would be realized.[20] Ideological differences between the religious and secular elements of Israeli society were already beginning to threaten the national unity which had only just won back Jerusalem for Israel.

ANCIENT STONES AND SACRED BONES

Non-violent opposition to Dayan's policy on the *haram* continued throughout the 1970s and into the early 1980s. Then, in 1984, an attempt was made by a zealous ultra-Orthodox group to blow up the Qubbet as-Sakhra in the hope of precipitating a removal of Moslems from the Mount. The leader of this extremist faction, Yehuda Etzion, was arrested on 29 May 1984 and jailed.

Etzion's attempt was widely reported as an act of extreme desperation conducted by a fringe minority. But the number of ultra-Orthodox Jews in Jerusalem is in fact rising and they are no longer a minority. Many have come as immigrants and it is the youthful members of this Orthodox community who are responsible for the drastic changes taking place in the city, including a stricter observance of the sabbath and more direct confrontation with the Moslem authorities who control the *haram*. New religious institutions, or yeshivas – the Jewish equivalent of the Moslem *madrasah* – have sprung up in the city and money has poured in from wealthy Jews in the United States to assist the needs of the city's growing population. Many Orthodox Jews believe the future of the city belongs only to them. The Jewish quarter, which overlooks the Temple Mount, has been rebuilt and restored to a standard which makes the adjoining Arab sections of the city look poor and decrepit.

In October 1990 a rumour began to spread that the Temple Mount Faithful under the leadership of Gershon Solomon were preparing to infiltrate the *haram* and conduct a Jewish prayer meeting on the Mount. The group broke into the *haram* on the anniversary of Yom Kippur carrying with them a stone which they intended to lay on the ground as the foundation stone of the Third Jewish Temple. The Israel Defence Force and the police attempted, unsuccessfully, to quell the ensuing riot and in a running battle which raged around the Dome of the Rock and the entrance of the Aqsa eighteen Palestinians were shot dead. Gershon Solomon's extreme actions stemmed from his personal experience of the 1973 Arab–Israeli conflict when he had been severely wounded.

In the immediate aftermath of 1967 Dayan, predicting the outbreak of a conflict, had tried to find peace with the Arabs: 'The war [he declared] has strengthened us abroad and given us a potential for a new, unified Israel. But I am not sure a new Israel will emerge ... our main goal is peace with the Arabs. Until we achieve that, all else is marginal.'[21] In 1973 war broke out yet again. On the Day of Atonement – Yom Kippur – Egypt and Syria crossed into Israeli-held territory in the Sinai and the Golan Heights, attempting to stretch Israel's defences to breaking point and defeat her. Although other Arab nations such as Libya provided troops and matériel in a desire to share a glorious victory over the forces of Zionism, Jordan's King Hussein abstained from involving his country in the conflict. After ten days of fighting Israel had repulsed the Arab attack and inflicted great damage on the Egyptian and the

Syrian armies. In the Sinai Israeli troops crossed the Suez Canal into Egypt and surrounded the Third Egyptian Army in the Great Bitter Lakes south of Ismalia. In the Golan Heights Israeli tanks advanced into Syria but the United Nations intervened to broker a ceasefire. Had King Hussein of Jordan attacked, opening a third front just forty kilometres from Jerusalem, the outcome of the war may well have been different.

The experience of the Yom Kippur War pushed Israel to pursue a more aggressive policy of retaliation towards her neighbours. After 1973 Arab terrorist attacks organized from Lebanon continued to target Israeli civilians and Israel responded in the early 1980s with a series of military operations in the southern half of the country which created a buffer zone of protection between Jewish settlements in northern Israel and Arab terrorist bases. The conflict, which still continues, claimed the lives of scores of Israelis which convinced Yitzak Rabin that the only possible way to find a lasting peace in Israel was to make concessions to her Arab neighbours. On 4 November 1995 in Tel Aviv, Dayan's prayer for peace received a setback which in 1967 would have been unimaginable. Prime Minister Rabin, the architect of Israeli victory in the 1967 war and the man whose military brilliance had effectively given Jerusalem back to the Jews, was shot dead by Yigael Amir, a young member of a religious Jewish Orthodox yeshiva.

Tragically, a new threat to Israel's stability had emerged, not from Arab neighbours but from ultra-Orthodox Israelis. The conflict between the interests of the secular state and the religious Orthodox who wish to impose restrictions on non-religious Jews has in the late 1990s begun to overshadow the entire nation. The intransigent policies of Benjamin Netanyahu, elected after Rabin's assassination, have only compounded the issue. Netanyahu was able to form a government only through the support of a handful of the minority Orthodox political parties in the Knesset, the Israeli parliament. Netanyahu has been dependent on Orthodox support to maintain his majority and religious Orthodox influence in government decisions is now out of all proportion to their national representation. Many secular Israelis feel uncomfortable, if not threatened, by a religious minority which is making its presence felt in everyday life. Some refuse to live in Jerusalem or even visit the city which they believe has become tainted by religious extremism. Nowhere is this problem so deeply felt than in the archaeological excavations being carried out around the area of the Temple Mount.

The excavations which began in 1967 outside the south-western corner of the Temple Mount were completed in 1997 and evidence has been exposed that the Second Temple was destroyed. The Herodian blocks which once formed part of the western perimeter of the Temple platform lie in a massive heap on the pavement below Robinson's Arch that was once the main entrance to the Temple area. To many archaeologists and historians the fallen stones are symbolic of the folly of the Zealots in AD 70 – the peril of mixing religion with politics. But to the religious Orthodox this archaeological exposure represents an unwelcome intrusion into the past, an attitude which has brought them increasingly into conflict with the scientific and artistic community within their state. As any archaeologist will agree, the ground of Jerusalem is in effect a mass graveyard and every excavation, however minor, stands a good chance of disturbing ancient bones. To the Orthodox community, this disturbance constitutes a violation of the sanctity of the human body which they contend extends beyond life into the realm of death. The remains of the Jewish dead, they argue, should be allowed to rest in peace.[22]

Archaeological excavations are closely monitored by the Orthodox communities. As the 'watch' for human bones has intensified, the relationship between Israeli archaeologists and Orthodox Jews has deteriorated with threats and acts of violence and vandalism against the archaeological community frequently made.[23] This situation, combined with all the other tensions in the city, such as the desire of the Orthodox to reinstate Jewish prayer ritual on the Islamic Mount, has produced an explosive atmosphere. Jerusalem has become a cauldron of ultra-Orthodox religious extremists dedicated to the 'reclaiming' of land close to the Temple Mount. Since 1996 this fanatical religious momentum has received the backing of Evangelical Christians who see the ultra-Orthodox attempt to recolonize the City of David and the Temple Mount as a legitimate target for their support. The Netanyahu government has done little to prevent such action, even when the law is broken. In 1997 a

Palestinian house on the ancient site of the Davidic city was taken over and heavily fortified by Jewish religious extremists. The house stands on the hillside immediately above the entrance to Hezekiah's Tunnel, the main site of Parker's two-year excavation in search of the Ark. In June 1998 the ultra-Orthodox acquired three more houses apparently legally, much to the consternation of both Moslems and Jews. A demonstration ensued, conducted by members of the Jewish 'Israel, Peace Now' movement who viewed this action by the ultra-Orthodox extremists as a deliberate attempt to provoke the Palestinian inhabitants of the area.

The problems of the City of David in the late 1990s were foreseen by the early leaders of Zionism. In 1917, immediately following the Balfour Declaration, Achad Ha'am, the 'leader' of the cultural faction of Zionism, made the following statement: 'If you build your house...in a place where there are other inhabited houses, you are sole master only so far as your front gate...beyond the gate all inhabitants are partners.'[24] The gates of the Jewish-controlled houses above the entrance to Hezekiah's Tunnel are firmly locked, alarmed and protected by armed guard. In the City of David there is no prospect nor suggestion nor any likely hope of the partnership which Achad Ha'am recognized as crucial to the success of peaceful co-existence between Jew and Moslem. Furthermore, Israeli governmental policy has tacitly approved the acquisition of Arab land and property, a policy which can only result in widening the gap between rich and poor, Jew and Moslem. But if the words of Achad Ha'am were heeded, the claim of repossessing biblical lands would rest on a matter of equality, and Jewish rights to recolonize the land of their forefathers could be examined with greater fairness. One 'Peace Now' demonstrator on the site of David's city asked the simple but thorny question: 'Does an immigrant Jew from Brooklyn have more right over a Palestinian Arab to live on the ancient site of King David's City?' The archaeologist may go one step further and remind the ultra-Orthodox that a non-Jewish population existed at David's city before David built his capital and as this was so, who were the people he displaced and who are their genetic descendants?

In July 1998 a new section of excavation on the site of David's city was revealed to the public by the Israel Antiquities Authority. The team, led by Professor Ronnie Reich and Eli Shukrun, have discovered that the Gihon Spring was incorporated into a Canaanite city eight hundred years before the arrival of David in Jerusalem making it 'one of the most complex, unique and well protected systems in the Middle East'.[25] The ultra-Orthodox, however, despite the evidence that non-Jewish settlers once inhabited the City of David, prefer to ignore the questions thrown up by archaeology and to concentrate on their religious faith. They fervently believe that the true Messiah will be revealed in Jerusalem and that God's promise to redeem the people of Israel and raise the dead to new life will soon come true.

For the ultra-Orthodox the City of David is an important site to recolonize. It was from the Davidic city that Solomon transported the Ark of the Covenant – which his father David had brought to Jerusalem – up to the Mount. The ultra-Orthodox also believe that the Ark will play a crucial role in the religious ritual which is necessary to prepare the way for the coming of the Messiah. When a 'pure' red heifer without any blemish of other colour is successfully reared, the Orthodox must sacrifice it and from its ashes make a paste. This will be used to purify ceremonially the foundations of a new, or Third, Jewish Temple which has to be constructed on the site of the Dome of the Rock and the Aqsa. The Ark of the Covenant then has to be brought forth from its hiding place and placed inside the Temple. The 'true' Messiah will then make his entrance into Jerusalem.

The Orthodox are apparently on the verge of rearing an unblemished red heifer and plans for the Third Temple exist on computer. The whereabouts of the Ark, however, is still a mystery.

THE ARK AND THE MOUNT

Since the Ark's disappearance in 620 BC, there have been many different theories about where it is. From the early 1980s interest in the Ark of the Covenant has intensified. The story of the Ark has been popularized by such films as *Raiders of the Lost Ark* which emphasized its mystical properties and involved the Nazis in the search for its secret location. Many books have been written on the subject, including Graham Hancock's *The Sign and the Seal* which claims that the Ark was transported to Ethiopia in the tenth century BC and is still preserved at Axum.[26] Dr Vendyl Jones, an archaeologist who has been digging at Qumran in search of the Ark for more than thirty years, is convinced that the relic was moved out of Jerusalem before the Babylonian destruction, through a natural tunnel thirty kilometres long, and was deposited in a cave close to the site of the Qumran settlement.[27] In September 1998 the *Sunday Times* reported that a British biblical scholar, Michael Sanders, was preparing to mount an expedition to excavate the ruins of an Egyptian temple of the tenth century BC at Dhahiriya, forty kilometres south of Jerusalem. Sanders is convinced that the Ark was pillaged from the Temple of Solomon in 925 BC in a raid by the Egyptian Pharaoh Shishak, and from there transported to Dhahiriya where the tablets of stone – the Ten Commandments – were buried under the floor of the Egyptian temple. The Knights Templar have also been connected with the search for the Ark but there is no record in existence which credits them with finding it. Similarly, the treasure vaults of the Vatican have been promoted as another popular, unconfirmed location for the Ark. Some Jews believe that Jeremiah took the Ark to Mount Nebo in Jordan, forty kilometres west of Jerusalem, in 586 BC. But Orthodox Israelis such as Gershon Solomon of the Temple Mount Faithful firmly dismiss the Axum theory and all the others which place the Ark outside Jerusalem. Gershon Solomon claims that the Ethiopian Jews of Axum are known to have built replicas, and that the Ark, far from being in Africa, is still hidden under the Temple Mount. Solomon's theory is backed up by archaeologists such as Ja'acov Bilich and Meir ben Dov of the Israel Antiquities Authority who see the Mount as a perfect place for concealment.[28]

With these facts in mind, plus the evidence in the Bible that the Levites had hidden the Ark from King Josiah in 620 BC, I decided to see at first hand just how easily the Ark could have been hidden in the substrata of the Mount. In August 1998 I entered a shaft close to the Temple Mount in the company of a television crew. Armed with ropes and portable lamps we made our way under the Temple Mount. At a depth of seven metres we found ourselves totally cut off from the noise of the city. By lamplight we filmed sights last seen by Charles Warren and Sergeant Birtles over one hundred and thirty years ago. This was the closest I could come to the substrata interior of the *haram* and I could easily imagine the Ark of the Covenant hidden only metres away but still protected as it had been for over twenty-five centuries from the 'monotheistic' world above. For a few moments I experienced the euphoria that Warren must have felt when by the light of a candle he had examined the base stones set into the natural rock of Mount Moriah at the south-east angle. With the thought that the Ark might still be under the Mount I tried to visualize what it looked like.

The Ark was a practical box, in which to transport – and protect – two tablets of stone, which has been given extraordinary significance. Even the exact location of Mount Sinai, where the Ark was constructed, has for centuries been debated. Whilst Warren was busy digging in Jerusalem Charles Wilson was in the Sinai desert carrying out an ordnance survey to establish the precise location of Moses' encounter with God. Wilson, after exhaustive research, identified Jebel Musa as the ancient Mount Sinai, although this location, and indeed the whole of the Exodus route from Egypt to Canaan, is still challenged by biblical scholars. If we were to embark on the reconstruction of the Ark, however, the directions given in the Bible are precise.

A wood that matched the fine grain of the gum arabic, or *Shittim*, wood found in the Sinai desert would be used to build the carcass. The frame would be erected with a mortise and tenon method of joinery and the side panels fitted into grooves in the frame before gilding. Following the Egyptian method of gilding, the finished woodwork would be covered in gesso, which once hard and sanded down would receive a coat of size or glue to take the gold leaf. Once the carcass was complete, the top would be hinged to the body according to the description given by Josephus in *Antiquities*.[29] Two cherubim based on winged animal figures of similar cherubim of the period would then be added to the top. To complete the replica four brass rings, cast from bronze and gilded, would be fitted to the sides of the Ark in order to take the carrying poles used by the Levites whose task it was to carry the sacred container.

In autumn 1998 I completed a replica based on this description. Although heavy, the replica sat easily on the shoulders, suggesting that it would have been possible to carry it over rough terrain. The alleged magical power of the Ark was measured by finding out if the Ark could function as a primitive receptacle for static electricity – the only logical explanation for the biblical tradition that it had the power to strike dead those, such as Uzza, who touched it. Static is a complex scientific field as it relies on the conditions of humidity, insulation and the electrical conductivity of other materials to manifest itself and, although the Ark contained one of the best conducting materials – gold – it is not clear whether this may have been sufficient to produce enough of a shock either to frighten Uzza to death or to stop his heart. Calculations proved that a significant voltage could have been produced by the Ark by reason of the alternating section of its construction, with gold insulated from wood turning it into a primitive accumulator. The Bible tells us that soon after Uzza's death David instructed the Levites that only they should carry the holy relic.[30] Perhaps they were aware of how to protect themselves from static shock through the basic principle of insulation and thus found themselves with a job for life.

If the Ark has remained hidden inside the Mount since the time leading up to the Babylonian destruction, then locating the chamber by traditional methods would not be easy. It would require a massive excavation of the *haram*. In 1998 I took infra-red photographs of the surface of the Mount from a helicopter. The octagonal shape of the external pavement of the Dome of the Rock was immediately apparent, shown by a 'light area' on the surface. However, the use of film sensitive to the infra-red wavelength of light would result in any area, such as an underground chamber or cistern, showing up as a darker area because of the air inside the cavity being cooler than the solid mass of rock or stone surrounding it.

One place on the *haram* surface shows an anomaly when compared to images of the same area photographed with 'normal' film. Cistern V lies just to the south-east of the Dome of the Rock and three black lines, one thick and two thin, can be seen on the infra-red photograph to run out from under the wall of the Dome of the Rock directly to the north-western corner of Cistern V. This suggested that Warren was perhaps correct in his view that the channel he had investigated on the *sakhra* – which he identified as the drainage channel for the 'northern' lavers – did in fact continue south-eastwards to the altar position over the north-western end of Cistern V. This lends considerable weight to Warren's theory about the location of King Solomon's Temple. It proves that Cistern V was a central drainage point for the area and therefore the most likely place for the altar of the Temple to be situated.

Other means of investigating the substrata of the Mount do exist, although every method has its limitations. The use of 'geophysics', the electronic mapping of surfaces, would be hampered by the thickness of the paved surface of the *haram* area. Side imaging radar, the reading of ground density by satellite, a technique used by the United States to investigate the bunkers and palaces belonging to Saddam Hussein, would enable a deep penetration of the Mount, although access to such a satellite-based system is not available to the public. We therefore have only the infra-red evidence to fall back on, but it does seem to support Warren's theory. If he was right, and the Solomonic Temple lay to the south of the Dome of the Rock, then the most probable location of an underground chamber would be between the Dome of the Rock and the Aqsa Mosque. Archaeological excavation of this area would give us a strong chance of finding the Ark of the Covenant.

The chances of obtaining permission to excavate on the *haram* are at present, extremely slim. But what would happen if by some means, in the future, the Ark was located and unearthed intact? Some investigators such as Dr Vendyl Jones believe it would herald a golden age of peace.[31] When I asked the Chief Rabbi of Israel, Rabbi Israel Meir Lau, the same question he told me it would confirm to the world the truth of the Bible.[32] The Grand Mufti of Jerusalem and Preacher of the Aqsa Mosque, Sheikh Muhammad Hussein, stated that the word of the Koran was 'above everything' and therefore any such discovery would, naturally, have no relevance to Moslems.[33] The Orthodox Jews not only expect the Ark to

FIGURE 9.1 (a) Standard exposure of the Haram compared to (b) an infra-red photograph showing the channels leading to the eastern end of Cistern V. (Author's photographs.)

be found, but they believe it will happen soon, confirming the imminence of the Messianic Coming. However, as the Orthodox wish to build the Third Temple on the *haram*, discovery of the Ark would probably only serve to precipitate conflict between the Jewish Orthodox and the Moslems of Jerusalem.

BLOOD ON THE MOUNTAIN

In September 1998 the security forces in Jerusalem planned a number of exercises to combat right-wing[34] attacks on the Temple Mount. The Israeli Defence Minister, Yitzhak Mordechai, when asked about this threat made a statement on Army Radio: 'We are approaching the year 2000. In 2000 all kinds of extremists – Christian, Moslem, and Jewish – could suddenly get "divinely inspired" and do serious things...any such action could spark a huge fire.' The Israelis fear that Jewish or Christian extremists may attempt to blow up the Dome of the Rock or the Aqsa Mosque and that Moslem fanatics may carry out a bombing against Jews at the Western Wall. Israel's General Security Service has tightened security around the Prime Minister and the President of Israel, believing on the basis of their intelligence reports that Jewish religious extremists wish to begin a campaign of political assassination in order to force the Israeli government to bend to religious Orthodox demands for the expulsion of the Moslems from the *haram*.

The *haram* faces an uncertain future, a doom-laden scenario brought on by ancient jealousies and religious differences made worse by the actions of politicians such as Hanan Porat, the Knesset member of the National Religious Party who, in September 1998, announced the formation of a convention to discuss the building of the Third Temple. With such wilful disregard of the Moslem heritage of Jerusalem within the Israeli parliament it is not an exaggeration to say that the Holy City represents the hardest problem facing the international community for the new millennium.

But the year AD 2000 offers a new and exciting challenge for Israelis and Palestinians. The place where almost four thousand years ago Abraham's hand was stayed by God from committing violence to a child does possess the chance of a permanent peace. A full and lasting agreement over inter-faith co-operation on Mount Moriah would succeed in breaking a cycle of violence which has repeatedly undermined the hopes and dreams of hundreds of generations of religious faithful from the time of David and Solomon up to the present day. If Jerusalem could find peace, the city would become a beacon of hope for the third Christian millennium. In the late 1990s there has been constant use in the media and amongst politicians of the word 'vision'. Perhaps the only real vision is the attainment of a lasting peace in the city of King David, Jesus of Nazareth and the prophet Muhammad. The choice, after three thousand years – to be nearer to God or to a recurrence of bloodshed on Mount Moriah, rests in the hands of every member of every faith.

Afterword

Since the publication of *Blood on the Mountain* in May 1999 further developments have cast new light on two aspects of the history of the Temple Mount. The first concerns Axum in Ethiopia, the second, my infra-red photographs taken in Jerusalem in 1998. Both are relevant to the fate of the Ark.

In 1992 Graham Hancock, author of *The Sign and the Seal*, claimed he had traced the Ark of the Covenant to a small chapel in Axum. But he was unable to produce any solid proof: the Ethiopian authorities had steadfastly refused to grant him access to the interior of the chapel or release any pictures of the famous relic which, according to him, lay inside.

Subsequent newspaper articles bolstered Hancock's theory and reporters still endeavour to gain entry to the chapel. They certainly have good reason to do so as throughout the twentieth century not a single foreigner has been allowed to see the Axum 'Ark'. In fact, only one person has ever recorded a precise description: Dimotheos Vartabet Sapritchian, an Armenian priest from Jerusalem, who travelled to Axum in the nineteenth century.

In *The Sign and the Seal* Hancock stated that 'the Armenian legate [Dimotheos] had been duped and shown one of the many replicas [of the Ten Commandments] kept at Axum ... They [the Ethiopian priests] had not shown him the Ark.' Hancock goes on to dismiss Dimotheos's eye-witness report, but is careful not to diminish his own theory that the original Commandments and the Ark of the Covenant were *somewhere* inside the chapel.

Contrary to Hancock's interpretation, Dimotheos's account suggests that there is a different basis to the Ethiopian claim. The contents of Dimotheos's book, a rare copy of which is held by the Bodleian Library of Oxford, are surprising.

During the winter of 1866–7 the British Foreign Office had found themselves faced with an embarrassing crisis, entirely of their own making. In 1866 the Christian Emperor of Abyssinia, Tewodros II, or 'Mad King Theodore' as he was known to the British press, had attempted to open diplomatic relations with Great Britain. His missive had languished in the 'In' tray at the Foreign Office for months. Incensed at the lack of British response to his friendly overtures, Tewodros arrested the British Consul in Massawa and imprisoned him on the mountainous Abyssinian Plateau at Magdala. The Consul was soon joined in prison by his relief – fresh from London – followed by a group of German missionaries. Noel Temple-Moor, the British Consul in Jerusalem, was instructed by London to ask the Armenian authorities in the Holy City to intervene and persuade Mad Theodore to release his captives immediately.

Isaac de Kharpert, the Patriarch to the Armenian Library of the Convent of Saint James in Jerusalem, was chosen by his superiors to deal with the British request. Isaac and a fellow priest of Saint James' – Dimotheos Sapritchian – set off on 13 April 1867, bound southwards for Abyssinia. However, their progress proved too slow for the Foreign Office – it took the two priests several weeks just to reach Egypt – and the British government, increasingly concerned about the welfare of their consuls, dispatched an expedition under Sir Robert Napier, a hero of the Indian Mutiny, to secure the release of the hostages by use of military force. Consequently, when the two Armenians finally arrived in Abyssinia in June they found Napier's force already there and fully engaged in war against Theodore. Under the prevailing circumstances Isaac and Dimotheos decided that rather than make an undignified return to Jerusalem they would stay and explore the country.

Dimotheos's account of their journey, published in 1871, relates the difficulties they encountered: poor communications, recurring sickness and a dire scarcity of food constantly hindered their progress. However, in spite of such problems, by 1869 the Armenians had reached their main goal: the town of Axum, the spiritual centre of Ethiopia, where they had heard that the most important relic of the Ethiopian Church was to be found. This was a *tabot* or tablet of stone reputed to be the original tablet of the Ten Commandments given by God to Moses on Mount Sinai. Before viewing the *tabot* Isaac and Dimotheos needed the permission of the Axum clergy which presented them with a dilemma. The Ethiopian priests in charge of the chapel said that the *tabot* could only be shown to Isaac and Dimotheos if they would first admit to its authenticity. Dimotheos, perhaps undiplomatically, pointed out that according to the Bible the Ten Commandments had been written on *two* tablets of stone and not one, which cast immediate doubt on their whole story. With theological battle-lines thus drawn, the Axum priesthood recounted a long and bizarre 'historical' explanation in support of their belief.

They told Isaac and Dimotheos how their ancestral King Menelik – the legendary son of Solomon and the Queen of Sheba – had stolen the *tabot* from the Temple of Jerusalem in the tenth century BC. Nine hundred years later, an Ethiopian named Ezekiel had carried it back to the Holy City of Jerusalem where Ezekiel showed Jesus the *tabot* and asked: 'Do you accept the Commandments or not?' Jesus did not reply, but turning the tablet over in His hands he wrote with His finger dipped in gold 'accept all that you find here'. Ezekiel returned to Axum with the tablet, and as the centuries passed this *tabot* became the supreme reliquary symbol of the Ethiopian Christian Church.

Having ended their fantastical account the priests of Axum found Isaac and Dimotheos still unmoved and continued to refuse them access to the relic. Instead, they launched into a lengthy debate on the origins of their Christian faith, declaring that only when all discussion was exhausted would they finally take the two Armenians inside the chapel.

While Isaac and Dimotheos were held up from entering the chapel, Napier's force managed to secure the release of the two British Consuls – and the German missionaries – by killing nineteen hundred Ethiopians for the loss of just two British soldiers. Dismayed by the rout of his men, which he witnessed from a fortress on the summit of Mount Magdala, Mad King Theo committed suicide by putting the barrel of a loaded pistol into his mouth and pulling the trigger. His death left Abyssinia temporarily in the hands of the British; it also precipitated a rapid end to Isaac and Dimotheos's debate with the priests at Axum.

On receiving the news of Theodore's death the surviving Crown Prince of Ethiopia, Dedjadjmatch-Kassa, decided to cultivate a friendship with the Armenians by intervening personally in Church affairs. He went quickly to Axum and broke the doctrinal stalemate by dismissing his own priests, declaring them rude, uncultured and incompetent. He then took Isaac and Dimotheos into the chapel and showed them the 'Ark of the Covenant'.

The relic bore little resemblance to the gilded Ark of the Covenant which is described in the Bible as being almost two metres long. The Axum 'Ark' was a small wooden box less than half that size which, in Dimotheos's opinion, had been fabricated on the Indian sub-continent – a not unlikely scenario given Ethiopia's ancient trading position on the Red Sea route between the Middle East and India. The *tabot* inside was reddish in colour, 24 centimetres high by 22 centimetres wide and 3 centimetres thick. It had a floral motif carved around its edge, a further chain motif inside this and in the centre, set in two columns of five, the 'Ten Commandments'. The Commandments were composed not in ancient Hebrew but, according to Dimotheos, in Ethiopian, albeit of 'Turkish style'. Towards the bottom of the tablet there were two symbols which neither Dimotheos nor the Ethiopian priests could decipher, although the engraving printed in Dimotheos's book suggests they were probably the letters I and S, or *Iesu Signore* – Jesus the Lord – a Latin legend found on many Christian objects of the medieval period. Isaac and Dimotheos were clearly embarrassed by the fake and when pressed by their host to give a final verdict they politely agreed its Mosaic provenance. On leaving the chapel they found, much to their relief, a British honour guard awaiting to escort them back to the coast and the road for home. Once safely back in Jerusalem, Dimotheos admitted that the tablet showed no sign of belonging to the time of the Jewish Exodus from Egypt: he reckoned it to be a crude and mistaken relic of the original stone tablets given by God to Moses. He dated the Axum *tabot* as thirteenth or fourteenth century AD. Disappointed not to have stumbled on the most famous relic of Biblical history, Dimotheos none the less felt indebted to the British and dedicated his account of *Two Years in Abyssinia* to Queen Victoria.

It is hardly surprising that upholders of the Axum 'Ark' theory today prefer to ignore the existence of Dimotheos's book, which shows that in 1869 Isaac and Dimotheos had seen what was according to them a fake Ten Commandments or *tabot* and an imitation 'Ark' as well. The myth of the existence of the 'true' Ark of the Covenant at Axum, successfully established by Hancock, has subsequently been bolstered by further reports and books such as *The Ark of the Covenant* published in 1999 by Weidenfeld and Nicolson and written by Stuart Munro-Hay and Roderick Grierson. In terms of historical accuracy Dimotheos's explanation is by far the most plausible. With this in mind I redoubled my efforts both in the archives in London and on the ground in Israel for evidence that the original Ark of the Covenant may still be under the Temple Mount of Jerusalem.

I discovered that Roman engineers included revetments of gum acacia – the wood used to construct the Ark – in a massive limestone ramp which was constructed to launch the final assault on the zealot garrison at Masada in AD 73. Large pieces, exposed by a new tourist path cut into the side of the ramp, are now visible. The wood has survived in near perfect condition for nearly two millennia; many pieces still show the burnished cut-marks of Roman axes. The fact that these pieces of wood have survived so well suggests that the wooden carcass of the Ark of the Covenant, if buried under the limestone of Mount Moriah, would still be intact. So, given the ban by the Moslem authorities on digging on the Mount, I wondered whether infra-red photographs might reveal any evidence which would narrow down the Ark's hiding place.

During the summer of 1999 I traced the path of the channels shown on my aerial infra-red photographs of the area around the Dome of the Rock taken the year before. There was no visible mark on the ground nor, apart from a crack in the corner of a paving slab which emitted a current of cold air from below ground, was there any indication of the vast chamber, Cistern V, which had once served as the central drainage point to the ancient Temple complex.

Cistern V extends southwards for 54.5 metres and is 15 metres deep. Although Warren in his research into the underground of the Temple complex had not recorded the presence of the channels which showed up in my photograph leading into Cistern V from the *sakhra*, he had predicted their existence. Whilst studying the intricate architecture of the Noble Enclosure it became increasingly obvious to me that the Arab engineers who had constructed the Dome over the *sakhra* in AD 691 would have worked with detailed engineering designs of the entire *haram*. Since that time, with the brief exception of a period of eighty-nine years in the twelfth century, the Moslems have exercised control over the Mount. It is unlikely that the information from such ancient maps would not have been available to the Ottoman engineers of the nineteenth century.

Both Wilson and Warren, however, had apparently conducted a fresh survey, for which there is a logical explanation: Moslem distrust of foreign investigators of the *haram* probably prohibited them access to Ottoman records and archives. But my research had thrown up another reason, which had at its basis, British national pride. An Italian, Ermette Pierotti, had pre-empted Wilson and Warren's mission by nearly a decade and, although he was, like the two British officers, a trained military engineer, the Biblical scholars of Victorian England had labelled him *anathema:* he was a gentleman fallen from grace.

Charged with desertion from his unit and complicity in the embezzlement of regimental funds, Pierotti had been cashiered by a military tribunal sitting at Genoa in 1849. By 1856, at the age of thirty-five, he was trying to make a living as a civil engineer in Ottoman Jerusalem, a lone outcast with, it seems, one ambition: to unravel the historical and archaeological mystery of the Temple Mount. Pierotti assisted the Turkish engineer Assad Effendi in the restoration of the main aqueduct to the *haram* during the summer of 1856, which enabled him to observe many of the underground cisterns of the Mount. He spent the following year writing up his observations and acquainting himself with the subterranean workings of the *haram* and the surrounding city. By 1858 Pierotti realised that the key to understanding the history of the Jewish

Temples lay within the mapping of the cisterns and conduits which had served the Mount since the first millennium BC. His access to the underground was restricted to the area under repair by Assad Effendi, but the course of nature then intervened to Pierotti's advantage. During the winters of 1858 and 1859 little rain fell in Jerusalem. The Moslem authorities, anxious to improve a rapidly dwindling supply of water to the sacred precincts of the *haram*, took Pierotti on as an assistant engineer. This gave him the opportunity he needed to complete a book based on the water systems of the *haram*. On the eve of Wilson's departure for Palestine in 1864 Pierotti's *Jerusalem Explored* was published in England. The general response from British enthusiasts of the Holy Land was damning. In a series of letters to *The Times*, Pierotti was accused of plagiarism and dubious scholarship. The events of Pierotti's trial in Genoa were then discovered by his adversaries and the facts revealed which dealt a fatal blow to his already damaged prestige. He did, however, have his advocates including his English translator Thomas G. Bonney who wrote back to *The Times* in Pierotti's defence. His critics, according to Bonney, were mistaken: Pierotti's work was original and his character, far from being flawed displayed 'all the signs of a true Christian gentleman'.

At the end of his own survey in 1874 Warren concluded that many of the cisterns and passages shown on Pierotti's maps were inaccurately drawn. Warren was undoubtedly partially correct in this criticism. But, although Pierotti's British adversaries could not admit it at the time publicly, many of them regarded Pierotti's discoveries as groundbreaking: all his original maps of the *haram* are carefully preserved at the headquarters of the Palestine Exploration Fund in London, whose members were amongst his harshest critics.

In the autumn of 1999 I studied Pierotti's maps and found that they indicated mysterious channels and secret passages which are missing from the later surveys conducted by Warren and Wilson. Several of these passages are relevant to the position of the Holy of Holies – the last known resting place of the Ark. Pierotti pinpoints an ancient passageway connecting the Gihon Spring – which we know to be the main water source of the ancient City of David – to the *haram* and although Pierotti did not explore the length of the tunnel, an elderly Bedouin, who secretly entered the *haram* by this route in the 1840s, described it to him in detail. Pierotti attempted to confirm the Bedouin's story by exposing a section of the tunnel: perhaps the maverick archaeologist Montagu Brownlow Parker, who was convinced of the existence of such a passage was not so crazy after all. I became convinced that Pierotti's claims were genuine when I first noticed his survey of underground channels leading outwards from the Dome of the Rock: the course of one of the channels shown on my infra-red photograph taken in 1998 is clearly visible on Pierotti's map.

The evidence of Pierotti's maps and Dimotheos's book have convinced me that the present day Moslem *haram* stands guard over a secret chamber – a purpose-built room deep within the bowels of Mount Moriah – which has protected the Ark of the Covenant since the time of King Josiah in the seventh century BC. Given the present ban on excavating the Mount, the only possible way of continuing the search for the Ark is to seek out and study all the engineering maps of the *haram* still in existence. If the missing sections of the arterial water system under the *haram* could be filled in the entire historical development of the Temple Mount could be accurately revealed. This would give us a three-dimensional map and accurate coordinates for the Temple of Solomon. For the first time the exact position of the Holy of Holies could be determined. Any tunnel leading from the Holy of Holies to an underground chamber containing the Ark – a secret known only to the Levites on the eve of the Babylonian invasion – could then after being concealed for over two and a half millennia be easily located.

Richard Andrews
April 2000

Acknowledgements

There are many people who have assisted me in the writing of this book. Ursula Bender has encouraged me from the initial stages of research as have Vivienne Schuster and Diana Mackay. In Jerusalem Silvia Krapiwko of the Israel Antiquities Authority has worked ceaselessly to provide me with the latest archaeological information concerning the Temple Mount and the City of David. Ja'acov Bilich and Professor Ronnie Reich have also been generous with their time and expertise, providing me with information about, and access to, the Robinson's Arch site. Siegfried Aust's excellent news report of 1997 led to the commissioning of a television ZDF Terra 'X' documentary based on my work. The process of filming has meant working in dangerous tunnels, sometimes up to the waist in cold water and enduring long hours in the summer heat of Jerusalem and Qumran: my thanks to producer George Graffe, cameraman Manes Avni, soundman Misha and Gideon Gadi, our superb location manager in Israel, and to Ralf Gemmeke and Alex Seip of UNIT TV, Mainz who filmed the UK sequences. Thanks also to Nir Toib of G.M. Communications, Tel Aviv and his crew, who produced unique interview material with Gershon Solomon and with the Jewish religious Orthodox community of Jerusalem. Mrs Valentine Vester, Najati Tahhan, Mahadi Tahhan, Yousef Rasas, Hani Shebeita and George at the American Colony Hotel, Jerusalem have all given freely of their time. Adnan Husseini and his staff at the offices of the Waqf have kindly allowed me access to the most revered places on the *haram*. Hava Zimuky has given me the facts when I most needed them.

In England, Dr Rupert Chapman at the PEF has given me

enthusiastic help whenever I have asked. Brian Tremain has spent time helping me with photography. Dr Yolande Hodson has advised me on the history and methods of the Victorian cartographers. Christopher Warren has provided me with superb material concerning the life and work of his great-grandfather, Sir Charles Warren. David Ruskin has given me specific information on ancient coinage. Richard Boulton has provided newspaper archive material with a magician's touch.

Most authors, at some stage, rely on the skill of their editor to point them in the right direction; I have Rebecca Wilson to thank for her long hours of dedicated work. My thanks also to Elmar Klupsch of Gustav Lubbe. Gillian and David Holl, John and Deborah Andrews and the other members of my family have all given me invaluable support. Finally my thanks to Gina and to my daughter Sophie for their care and patience throughout the project.

Notes

NB Unless otherwise indicated references to Josephus are taken from *Whiston's Josephus*, published by W.P. Nimmo, Hay & Mitchell, Edinburgh. (Reprint of Josephus' *Antiquities of the Jews, The Wars of the Jews* and other writings, translated by William Whiston, first edition, 1806.)

Foreword, pp. xv–xviii

1. This name, once universally used to describe an exposed section of the Herodian, Second Temple wall, used as the 'praying place' of the Jews, has now been changed by the Israelis to 'Western Wall'.
2. The Internet Web Site for the Temple Mount gives periodic confirmation of this situation.

Introduction, pp. 1–5

CHAPTER 1 *Mount Moriah*, pp. 7–21

1. This hidden agenda was later confirmed by Wilson himself. See *Wilson's Memo: On a proposed Survey of Palestine*, PEF Archives: PEF WS/3 (1869).
2. W.A. Seymour (ed.), *A History of the Ordnance Survey* (1980) pp. 154–156.
3. Gibson, S., and Jacobson, D., *Below the Temple Mount of Jerusalem* (1996) p. 14.
4. Wilson quoted in the *History of the Corps of Royal Engineers*, The Institution of Royal Engineers (1954) Chapter 3, Part 3, pp. 268–9.
5. *History of the Corps of Royal Engineers* (1954) Chapter 3, Part 3, p. 270.

6. Between 14 and 16 June 1997, the author searched for Wilson's benchmarks around the *haram* and within the Old City. Of a total of nine shown on the Ordnance Survey, he found the remains of three, the clearest of which is on the southern side of the Lion's (Saint Stephen's) Gate, reproduced in this book. For an appraisal of these and others left by Wilson around the city walls, see the report by M. Shurman, 'Wilson Bench Marks in the Old City of Jerusalem', *Palestine Exploration Quarterly*, No. 126, 1994, which includes an excellent explanatory note on the origin and meaning of bench-marks by Yolande Hodson.

7. The exact number of victims of Jack the Ripper remains undetermined.

8. 'Uru' in Babylonian script meaning city as recorded in the Tell el-Amarna letters of circa 1400 BC: see Smith, G.A., *Jerusalem From the Earliest Times to 70 AD*, vol. I, p. 252 for an extensive discourse on the use of the name 'Ur' or 'Uru' in the composition and evolution of the name of Jerusalem.

9. *Historical Atlas of the Jewish People*, general editor E. Barnavi, English editor M. Eliav-Feldon, (1992) p. 2.

10. Genesis XVII: 17.

11. Genesis XXII: 2.

12. There remains much argument about his and other datings of Old Testament events. Archaeological discoveries this century, and the ongoing excavations in Israel, Syria and Egypt, in particular those concentrating on the influence of the ancient Egyptian dynasties, are gradually narrowing the possible time frame of biblical events.

CHAPTER 2 *The Holy of Holies, 1290–963 BC, pp. 22–35*

1. This dating of the Exodus, impossible to verify with precise accuracy, has been given variously at between 1295 and 1275 BC.

2. David Rohl has spent much time and effort in proposing a new chronology, explained in his book *A Test of Time* (1996). His theories, however, remain strongly opposed by Egyptologists. His treatment of Solomonic Jerusalem remains unsupported by archaeological stratigraphic evidence.

3. The scholarly uncertainty which surrounds the historical veracity of the Old Testament has spread to the story of the Israelite defeat of the Canaanites. For a recent and alternative view to the accepted history,

see details of the seminar attended by Professor Whitelam and Israel Finkelstein at Tel-Aviv University, as reported by Karen Glaser in *Jewish Chronicle*, 30 May 1997. Finkelstein supports Whitelam, suggesting that the rise of early Israel was not 'a unique event' but 'rather just one of many, cyclical events'.

4. 1 Samuel XXXI: 10.

5. 1 Chronicles X: 10.

6. 1 Samuel V, complete text.

7. See Armstrong, K., *A History of Jerusalem* (1996) pp. 38–40 for an in-depth explanation of Jebusite/Davidic relationships.

8. For a full explanation of the scholarly linkage, see Israel Exploration Society (ed.), *The New Encyclopaedia of Archaeological Excavations in the Holy Land*, p. 700.

9. Mollett, J.W., *Dictionary of Art and Archaeology* (1883) p. 21.

10. This parallel is drawn by Graham Hancock in *The Sign and the Seal* (1992), see plates 56 and 57.

11. Exodus XXXI.

12. Kenyon, K., *Digging up Jerusalem* (1974).

13. Information given to the author in confidence, and verified.

14. Miller, J.M., 'Solomon: International Potentate or Local King?' *Palestine Exploration Quarterly*, 1990–1, versus Millard, A.R., 'Texts and Archaeology: Weighing the Evidence: The Case for King Solomon', *Palestine Exploration Quarterly*, 1990–1.

15. 2 Chronicles III: 2.

16. 1 Kings V: 1.

17. 2 Chronicles II: 3.

18. 2 Chronicles II: 9.

19. 2 Chronicles II: 17.

20. Conder, C.R., *The City of Jerusalem* (1909) p. 119.

21. Conder, C.R., *The City of Jerusalem* (1909) pp. 118–19.

22. Warren, C., *The Recovery of Jerusalem* (1871), Conclusions.

23. Warren, C., *The Recovery of Jerusalem* (1871) p. 67.

24. There exists a current school of thought which downgrades the importance of the Solomonic era, and the biblical account of the Temple, claiming that Solomon simply restored an earlier, Canaanite Temple on the site of Mount Moriah. See Lipinski, E., *Phoenicia and the Bible: Proceedings of the Conference held at Leuven, 15–16 March 1990*

(1991). This thesis, however, is hamstrung by the one problem common to all researchers of the Solomonic Temple period: little or no archaeological evidence.

CHAPTER 3　*The Navel of the World, 962–954 BC, pp. 36–56*

1. 1 Kings VI: 18.
2. 1 Kings VI: 21.
3. 1 Kings VI: 32.
4. Kathleen Kenyon, Director of the British School of Archaeology in Jerusalem 1951–66, whose fascination and enthusiasm for the beauty of Jerusalem's archaeological past remains undeniable, found the constant use of gold by Solomon as going beyond the pale, describing, with some understatement, the abundant use of the metal by Solomon, as set forth in the First Book of Kings, as 'somewhat ostentatious'. Kenyon, K., *Digging up Jerusalem* (1974) p. 120.
5. 1 Kings IX: 24.
6. 1 Kings XI: 1.
7. 1 Kings VII: 13–14. 2 Chronicles II, verses 13–14, gives his name as Huram and although it is probable that this discrepancy is historically insignificant, the similarity with the name of the king suggests that the name was titular, signifying master, or lord; see Baigent, M. and Leigh, R., *The Temple and the Lodge* (1989) pp. 176–7.
8. The word *Abba* in Hebrew means father, Abiff being a probable derivation in the sense of leader or master.
9. The names given to these massive pillars have entered into the rites of Freemasonry as passwords between Masons, the knowledge of each word being a recognition of differing grade, or degree, within Masonic rank.
10. Based on the Egyptian royal cubit of 21 inches or 53.35 centimetres.
11. See *Bible et Terre Sainte*, Numéro 25, janvier 1960.
12. The site of Succoth lies midway between Jericho and Bet She'an, on the eastern bank of the river Jordan. Zarthan (Zeredathah in Chronicles) is probably Zarathan, or Zeradah, ten kilometres closer to Jerusalem, on the western bank of the Jordan.
13. Josephus, *Antiquities*, VIII: III: 4.
14. 1 Kings VII: 23.

15. 1 Kings VII: 64.
16. Josephus, *Antiquities*, VIII: III: 6, and 2 Chronicles IV: 6 and 10–11.
17. 1 Kings VII: 50.
18. 1 Kings VII: 47.
19. Josephus, *Antiquities*, VIII: III: 7–8.
20. 1 Kings VI: 36.
21. Josephus, *Antiquities*, VII: III: 9.
22. Whiston, W., *The Complete Works of Josephus*, Dissertation V: 3.
23. 1 Chronicles XIII: 10.
24. 2 Chronicles V: 12.
25. Josephus, *Antiquities*, VIII: III: 8.
26. Electrum was prized by the ancient Egyptians as the most precious of alloys and was used by Tuthmosis III to plate two columns which stood at the gates of his Theban temple. These were sacked by the Syrian King Ashurbanipal. Their combined weight was given as 2500 talents, or 166,650 pounds. Queen Hatshepsut plated two obelisks at Karnak and the columns of the Temple. The columns and the grooves into which the plates of electrum were once set can still be seen today; see Desroches-Noblecourt, C., *Tutankhamen* (1963) pp. 33–4.
27. The Bible is not specific concerning the day or the month.
28. Josephus, *Wars*, I: XXI: 1.
29. Josephus, *Antiquities*, VIII: IV: 1.
30. Josephus, *Antiquities*, VIII: VI: 1.
31. Williams, W., *The Life of General Sir Charles Warren* (1941) p. 49.
32. Warren, C., *Underground Jerusalem* (1876) p. 345.
33. Warren, C., *The Recovery of Jerusalem* (1871) p. 60.
34. Exodus XXX: 4.
35. 1 Kings VIII: 8. (Author's underlining.)
36. 2 Chronicles V: 9. (Author's underlining.)
37. Pfeiffer, R., *Introduction to the Old Testament* (1952) p. 812.
38. Preservation of secret knowledge was not uncommon in ancient times. Contemporary works such as Michael Drosnin's *The Bible Code* (1998) have successfully enlarged on the written codification of secret knowledge – a method which is suspected by many scholars to be inherent in similar bodies of work such as the New Testament and the Dead Sea Scrolls: see Mack, Burton L., *The Lost Gospel* (1993) and Vermes, Geza, *The Dead Sea Scrolls: Qumran in Perspective* (1994).

39. Contrast 1 Kings VIII: 4.

40. Pfeiffer, R., *Introduction to the Old Testament* (1952) pp. 796–8.

41. When one remaining fact is taken into consideration, this probability increases, for as the Chronicler himself informs us, the Levites were set one further duty by Solomon beyond that of music making, porterage and door keeping. They were to be guardians: 'over the treasures of the house of God, and over the treasures of the dedicated things'. (1 Chronicles XXVI: 20).

42. See Fernández-Armesto, F., *Truth* (1997).

43. Josephus, *Antiquities*, VIII: IV: 2.

CHAPTER 4   *God's Covenant, 953–597 BC, pp. 57–101*

1. Josephus, *Antiquities*, VIII: IV: 2.

2. 2 Chronicles VI: 12.

3. Josephus, *Antiquities*, VIII: IV: 3.

4. 2 Chronicles VII: 7.

5. Josephus, Antiquities, VIII: IV: 5.

6. 2 Chronicles VII: 15.

7. 1 Kings IX: 4–6.

8. Warren, C., *The Recovery of Jerusalem* (1871) pp. 312–14.

9. Warren, C., *The Recovery of Jerusalem* (1871) p. 316, and Warren, C., *Underground Jerusalem* (1876) pp. 78–9.

10. The British Academy, *Text of the Old Testament* – The Sweich Lectures, 1916, Oxford University Press.

11. Warren, C., *The Recovery of Jerusalem* (1871) p. 111.

12. Warren, C., *The Recovery of Jerusalem* (1871) Introduction, p. xv.

13. Kenyon, K., *Digging up Jerusalem* (1974) pp. 115–16.

14. Kenyon, K., *Digging up Jerusalem* (1974) pp. 111–12.

15. Ezra III: 12–13.

16. Comments made to author.

17. This method explained by Dan Bahat is also visible in the south-eastern corner of Solomon's Stables to which the author was granted access in July 1998 by the authorities of the Waqf.

18. This block can be seen in the southern portion of the jumbled stones from the Temple destruction below Robinson's Arch, facing west. Confirmation of the authenticity of the marks was made by Professor

Ronnie Reich of the Israel Antiques Authority who conducted the dig exposing this stone, to the author in 1998.

19. For a detailed synopsis see John F. Healey, *The Early Alphabet* (1990).

20. Psalm XLVIII: 1.

21. 1 Kings IX: 27–8.

22. Kenyon makes the point in *Digging up Jerusalem*, p. 107: 'It is generally (though not universally) accepted that the Queen of Sheba ruled an area in South Arabia.'

23. 1 Kings X: 1.

24. 1 Kings X: 2.

25. 1 Kings X: 10. Based on the talent being equivalent to approximately twenty-seven pounds.

26. 1 Kings X: 2.

27. 1 Kings X: 13.

28. 1 Kings X: 14–15.

29. 1 Kings X: 16–18.

30. 1 Kings X: 21.

31. Baigent, M. and Leigh, R., *The Temple and the Lodge* (1989) p. 182.

32. Horne, A., *King Solomon's Temple in the Masonic Tradition* (1972) p. 277.

33. Frazer, Sir James, *The Golden Bough* (1922) pp. 191–2.

34. As related to the author by senior Freemasons. See also Horne, A., *King Solomon's Temple in the Masonic Tradition* (1972) for comprehensive written reference.

35. 1 Kings XI: 28.

36. 1 Kings XI: 40.

37. David Rohl in his study of Egyptian chronology *A Test of Time* (1996) presents compelling evidence that the Biblical Shishak can be identified not, as has been traditionally upheld, with Shoshenk I, founder of the 22nd Dynasty, but instead with Rameses II.

38. 2 Chronicles XII: 3.

39. 1 Kings XIV: 22–4.

40. 2 Chronicles XII: 9.

41. 2 Chronicles XII: 7.

42. See Meek, T.J., *Hebrew Origins* (1960) p. 136: 'As Moses was the founder of the Levitical priesthood so Aaron was . . . the traditional founder of the bull cult.'

43. Meek, T.J., *Hebrew Origins* (1960) pp. 134–47.

44. Exodus XXXII: 26–8.

45. 1 Kings XI: 7.

46. Meek, T.J., *Hebrew Origins* (1960) p. 140.

47. 2 Chronicles XXII: 11.

48. 2 Chronicles XXIII: 2–6.

49. 2 Chronicles XXIII: 7.

50. 2 Chronicles XXIII: 9.

51. 2 Chronicles XXIII: 15.

52. Smith, G.A., *Jerusalem from the Earliest Times to 70 AD* (1908) vol. II, p. 107.

53. Meek, T.J., *Hebrew Origins* (1960) pp. 150–1.

54. 2 Kings IX: 11, and Jeremiah XXIX: 26.

55. Meek, T.J., *Hebrew Origins* (1960) p. 171.

56. Isaiah I: 11, 15, 17.

57. 2 Kings XVI: 8.

58. 2 Kings XVI: 3.

59. 2 Chronicles XXVIII: 2–3.

60. 2 Kings XVI: 13.

61. 2 Chronicles XXVIII: 24.

62. 2 Chronicles XXVIII: 23.

63. 2 Kings XVI: 17.

64. Smith, G.A., *Jerusalem from the Earliest Times to 70 AD* (1908) vol. II, p. 266.

65. Smith, G.A., *Jerusalem from the Earliest Times to 70 AD* (1908) vol. II, p. 267.

66. 2 Kings XVIII: 15–16.

67. Evidence exists that Sennacherib made a further attempt to exact tribute from Jerusalem between 690 and 689 BC. For an in-depth explanation see Smith, G.A., *Jerusalem from the Earliest Times to 70 AD* (1908) vol II, pp. 148–74.

68. 2 Kings XIX: 35.

69. 2 Kings XX: 14–17.

70. Smith, G.A., *Jerusalem from the Earliest Times to 70 AD* (1908) vol II, p. 190.

71. 2 Chronicles XXXIII: 6.

72. Smith, G.A., *Jerusalem from the Earliest Times to 70 AD* (1908) vol II, p. 267.

73. 2 Kings XXI: 16.
74. Smith, G.A., *Jerusalem from the Earliest Times to 70 AD* (1908) vol II, p. 263.
75. Ezekiel XLIII: 9.
76. 2 Chronicles XXXIII: 22–4.
77. Jeremiah II: 8.
78. 2 Kings XXIII: 2.
79. 2 Kings XXIII: 10.
80. 2 Kings XXIII: 20.
81. Josephus, *Antiquities*, X: V: 1.
82. 2 Chronicles XXXVI: 5.

CHAPTER 5 *From Destruction to Jesus, 596–4 BC, pp. 102–164*

1. 2 Kings XXIV: 9.
2. 2 Kings XXIV: 12.
3. 2 Kings XXIV: 13.
4. 2 Chronicles XXXVI: 9.
5. 2 Kings XXIV: 16.
6. Josephus, *Antiquities*, X: VII: 1.
7. 2 Kings XXIV: 14, 16.
8. Jeremiah XXIV: 2.
9. Jeremiah XXIV: 6–7.
10. Jeremiah XXIV: 9–10.
11. Jeremiah XXVI: 23.
12. Jeremiah XXVIII: 3–4.
13. Jeremiah XXVIII: 9.
14. *The Oxford Dictionary* gives a definition: *object like* yoke, *in form or function.*
15. Jeremiah XXVIII: 11.
16. Robinson, T.H., *A History of Israel* (1932) vol. 1, p. 438.
17. Robinson, T.H., *A History of Israel* (1932) vol. 1, pp. 439–40.
18. Jeremiah XXXVII: 21.
19. Jeremiah XXXVIII: 6.
20. Josephus, *Antiquities*, X: VIII: 1.
21. Jeremiah XIV: 16.
22. This date fluctuates from year to year and there are several

interpretations of past calendar dating: 2 August is held as the most probable.

23. Josephus, *Antiquities*, X: VIII: 2.
24. 2 Kings XXV: 4.
25. Josephus, *Antiquities*, X: VIII: 2.
26. 2 Kings XXV: 4.
27. 2 Kings XXV: 8.
28. 2 Kings XXV: 9.
29. 2 Kings XXV: 14–15.
30. 2 Kings XXV: 12.
31. 2 Kings XXV: 24.
32. Osterley, W., and Robinson, T., *A History of Israel* (1932) vol. 1, p. 442.
33. Josephus, *Antiquities*, X: VIII: 5.
34. Jeremiah XXXVIII: 7–11.
35. Jeremiah XXXVIII: 28.
36. Jeremiah XXXIX: 14.
37. Jeremiah XL: 4.
38. Keller, W., *The Bible as History* (1980) pp. 302–4.
39. 2 Chronicles XXXV: 3.
40. Jeremiah LII: 25–7.
41. Extracts from the Lamentations of Jeremiah, I: 1; I:8; V: 18.
42. There is strong scholarly argument to support the theory that, although compiled by eyewitnesses of the destruction, Jeremiah himself was not the author of the Book of Lamentations; for further clarification see Pfeiffer, R.H., *Introduction to the Old Testament* (1953) pp. 720–4.
43. Jeremiah LII: 28–30.
44. Josephus, *Antiquities*, X: IX: 7.
45. For illumination on this matter see Smith, G.A., *A History of Jerusalem from Ancient Times to 70 AD* (1908) vol. II, pp. 296–7.
46. Jeremiah XLI: 5.
47. 2 Chronicles XXXVI: 21.
48. Ezekiel I: 27.
49. Ezekiel II.
50. For a discussion of this see Oesterley W., and Robinson, T., *A History of Israel* (1932) vol. II, pp. 42–50.
51. Oesterley W., and Robinson T., *A History of Israel* (1932) vol. I, p. 453.

52. Isaiah XLV: 1, 2, 3, 7.

53. Ling, T., *A History of Religion East and West* (1968) pp. 75–82.

54. As given by Jeremiah LII: 30.

55. Josephus, *Antiquities*, XI: I: 3.

56. Josephus, *Antiquities*, XI: I: 3.

57. Josephus, *Antiquities*, XI: I: 3.

58. Josephus, *Antiquities*, XI: I: 3.

59. Ezra IV: 24.

60. Ezra VI: 1–5.

61. Haggai I: 4.

62. See Pfeiffer, R.H., *Introduction to the Old Testament* (1953) and Haggai I: 15.

63. Ezra III: 12. These tears are commonly interpreted as being tears of disappointment; however, an emotional response to the realization of the exilic prophecies is a far more plausible explanation.

64. Ezra III: 7.

65. Haggai II: 1–5.

66. Ezra VI: 11.

67. Josephus quotes these dimensions from Hecataeus, in *Flavius Josephus against Apion*, I: 22. Calculation of size is based on the Egyptian royal cubit of 21 inches, 53.35 centimetres.

68. *Mishnah, Yoma*, 5, 2.

69. Pfeiffer, R.H., *Introduction to the Old Testament* (1953) p. 266.

70. Named in the *Yoma* as Bet Hiddudo.

71. The word *Yoma* is derived from the Aramaic meaning 'the day'. It is uncertain whether the *Yoma* description was specific only to the period of the Second Temple under Herod; however, the detailed involvement of the priesthood indicates that it might in fact refer to the time of Zerubbabel. The *Yoma* describes how following a ruling by the High Priest, only a fellow priest could lead the goat away; see *Mishnah, Seder Moed* (1994) vol. II, p. 79.

72. *Mishnah, Yoma*, 6, 6.

73. Isaiah 1: 18.

74. Frazer, Sir J., *The Golden Bough* (1922) p. 578–9.

75. Frazer, Sir J., *The Golden Bough* (1922) pp. 577–82.

76. Isaiah LXV: 1–12.

77. There is much controversy surrounding this dating due to haphazard

compilation of the Books of Nehemiah and Ezra, but the majority of modern scholarly opinion supports this dating. R.H. Pfeiffer in *Introduction to the Old Testament*, p. 829, comments: 'Written by Nehemiah himself after 432 [BC] these Memoirs report frankly and vividly, as one would do in a personal diary not for publication, the actual events and the emotions they aroused in the writer.'

78. Whether on horseback or by mule remains unclear, Nehemiah simply says 'the beast that I rode upon', Nehemiah II: 12.

79. More accurately Jackal's Well; see Kenyon, K., *Digging up Jerusalem* (1974) p. 181.

80. Nehemiah II: 13.

81. Kenyon, K., *Digging up Jerusalem* (1974) p. 181.

82. Nehemiah II: 15.

83. G.A. Smith on pp. 81 and 82 of volume I of *Jerusalem from the Earliest Times to 70 AD*, says the following: 'Josephus, who several times mentions the Kidron, describes it generally as a valley or gorge, and once by the Greek word for "winter" or "storm torrent," by which it is also called in the New Testament [John XVIII: 1.] It is in this sense that we must take the Hebrew term nahal as applied to the Kidron in the Old Testament. [2 Samuel XV: 23, I Kings XV: 13, II Kings XXIII: 6, 12, Jeremiah XXXI: 40.] Translated *brook* in our versions, *nahal* means no more than a valley down which a transitory stream may flow after heavy rain ... the fact that the Kidron is called in two passages *the* Nahal, and that no other Jerusalem valley gets the name, implies that neither in the Tyropoeon nor elsewhere about the City was there a flow of water worthy even of the name *storm* or *winter brook*.'

84. Nehemiah VI: 15; Josephus in *Antiquities*, XI: V: 8 gives the length of building at two years and four months.

85. Nehemiah III: 1–32.

86. Nehemiah IV: 18.

87. Nehemiah IV: 21–3.

88. See Nehemiah X–XII.

89. Nehemiah XIII: 1–2.

90. For a detailed description of Temple tithes and taxes, see Smith, G.A., *Jerusalem from the Earliest Times to 70 AD* (1908) vol. I.

91. Nehemiah XIII: 10–14.

92. Nehemiah XIII: 15–16.

93. Nehemiah XIII: 25–6.

94. Nehemiah XIII: 30.

95. For dating see Oesterley, W., and Robinson, T., *A History of Israel* (1932) vol. II, pp. 128–39.

96. This title is given to Ezra by Artaxerxes, King of Persia: Ezra VII: 11–12.

97. Ezra VII: 15.

98. There is much scholarly dispute surrounding the authenticity, or otherwise, of Ezra. For analysis see Oesterley, W., and Robinson, T., *A History of Israel* (1932) vol. II, Chapter X.

99. Ezra VII: 25–6.

100. Ezra X: 11.

101. Ezra X: 13.

102. Ezra gives the date of the assembly as the twentieth day of the ninth month (X: 9) and the date of examination as being the first day of the tenth month (X: 16).

103. Ezra X: 10.

104. The site of the battle of Issus is situated near the Mediterranean coast, with the river Pyramus to the north and west and the Orontes to the south; Oesterley and Robinson, *A History of Israel* (1932) vol. II, p. 189.

105. Oesterley, W., and Robinson, T., *A History of Israel* (1932) vol. II, p. 198.

106. Kathleen Kenyon on p. 189 of her work *Digging up Jerusalem*, stating archaeological evidence, dates the schism to 'probably early in the third century BC'.

107. Oesterley, W., and Robinson, T., *A History of Israel* (1932) vol. II, p. 201, and Pfeiffer, R.H., *Introduction to the Old Testament* (1953) p. 811.

108. There remains considerable confusion surrounding the events leading up to the Seleucid conquest of Jerusalem. For a sound historical assessment see Oesterly, W., and Robinson, T., *A History of Israel* (1932) vol. II, p. 207.

109. Josephus, *Antiquities*, XII: III.

110. Smith, G.A., *Jerusalem from the Earliest Times to 70 AD* (1908) vol. I, p. 401.

111. A substitution was made by using the words 'Adonai' meaning 'Lord' or 'El Elyon' meaning 'Most High'.

112. Josephus, *Antiquities*, XII: III: 3–4.

113. Smith, G.A., *Jerusalem from the Earliest Times to 70 AD* (1908) vol. II, p. 429.

114. 2 Maccabees III.

115. Smith, G.A., *Jerusalem from the Earliest Times to 70 AD* (1908) vol. II, p. 432.

116. Daniel VIII: 5–11.

117. R.H. Pfeiffer in his *Introduction to the Old Testament* also gives the alternative dating of the first century AD.

118. Smith, G.A., *Jerusalem from the Earliest Times to 70 AD* (1908) vol. II, p. 434, and 2 Maccabees V: 21.

119. Josephus, *Wars* I: I: 1.

120. Josephus, *Antiquities,* XII: V: 4.

121. W.O.E. Oesterley, Late Professor of Hebrew and Old Testament Exegesis at King's College London, draws a definite conclusion to support this possibility; see p. 224 of vol II of his *History of Israel.* However, the words of the accepted translations of Josephus still retain an ambiguity surrounding the matter.

122. Josephus, *Antiquities*, XII: V: 4.

123. As suggested by contemporary apocalyptical additions to the words of the Old Testament Book of Zechariah. The dating of Chapters IX–XII is given by W. Oesterley and T. Robinson in their *History of Israel* vol. II, p. 245 gives these a second century BC origin. For an alternative view see Pfeiffer, R.H., *Introduction to the Old Testament* (1953) pp. 607–12.

124. Zechariah IX: 9.

125. Josephus, *Antiquities*, XIII: 5.

126. In all probability built by the son and heir of Onias III, this sanctuary only survived until AD 73, that is, three years after the final destruction of the Jerusalem Temple in AD 70. See Box, G.H., (ed.) *Judaism in the Greek Period* (1932) vol. V, p. 34, and Josephus, *Antiquities* XIII: III: 1.

127. See Baigent, M., and Leigh, R., *The Dead Sea Scrolls Deception* (1991) pp. 252–57.

128. Archaeological analysis of the Qumran site indicates an initial communal presence from 150–140 BC.

129. Josephus, *Wars*, I: VII: 6.

130. Josephus, *Antiquities*, XIV: VII: 1.

131. Josephus, *Wars*, I: XIII: 9.

132. See Josephus, *Antiquities*, XIV: XV for a full explanation of the composition of Herod's own forces.

133. Josephus, *Antiquities*, XIV: XV: 14.
134. Josephus, *Antiquities*, XIV: XVI: 2.
135. Josephus, *Wars*, I: XVIII: 3.
136. Josephus, *Antiquities*, XVII: VI: 5.
137. As uniquely reported in the New Testament Gospel of Matthew.
138. Josephus, *Antiquities*, XV: XI: 1.
139. Josephus, *Antiquities*, XV: XI: 1.
140. Kathleen Kenyon, drawing from a lifetime of experience, expressed little doubt in the extent of Zerubbabel's intervention: 'One can nevertheless take it as certain that Zerubbabel's work was based on Solomon's foundation. Ruined as it was, the Temple had remained in existence.' Kenyon, K., *Digging up Jerusalem* (1974) p. 177.
141. Warren, C., *Underground Jerusalem* (1876) p. 81.
142. The distance from the south-eastern corner to the Straight Joint when measured undergound by Warren at bedrock level was 108 feet, or 32.91 metres, the nineteen-centimetre discrepancy between the underground base level and the present-day ground level encountered being due to the setting-back of each successive course towards the inside of the platform in order to offset the external perspective.
143. Josephus, *Antiquities*, XV: XI: 1.
144. Josephus, *Wars*, I: XXI: 1. Measurements of the Solomonic Temple area, excluding the Royal Palace, are also given in the *Mishnah*, Tractate *Middot*: 2.
145. Rabbi Leibel Reznick, on pages 56–7 of his book *The Holy Temple Revisited*, claims that according to Talmudic Law Jewish priests would be allowed to enter a non-Jewish cemetery, thus invalidating the purpose of the cemetery.
146. Rabbi Leibel Reznick, *The Holy Temple Revisited* (1996) pp. 55–9.
147. Measurements taken as the mean width and length across the area: Herodian, 300 metres by 475 metres; Solomonic, 220 metres by 335 metres.
148. Josephus, *Antiquities*, XVI: XI: 6.
149. Josephus, *Antiquities*, XV: XI: 3.
150. Josephus, *Antiquities*, XV: XI: 3.
151. Josephus, *Wars*, V: V: 2. The archaeological discovery of such a plaque in Greek, the replica of which can be seen in the Rockefeller Museum, Jerusalem, confirms this.

152. Josephus, *Antiquities*, XV: XI: 5.
153. Smith, G.A., *Jerusalem from the Earliest Times to 70 AD* (1908) vol II, p. 502.
154. Josephus, *Wars*, V: V: 4.
155. The geometric development of the hexagram is too intricate to investigate in this volume but information can be readily found in any relevant mathematical treatise.
156. Josephus, *Antiquities*, XV: XI: 3.
157. Bahat, D., *Ancient Jerusalem Revealed* (1994) p. 181.
158. Official weight of an empty 747 is 176,847 kilograms; fully laden, 377,850 kilograms.
159. Josephus, *Antiquities*, XV: XI: 5.
160. Josephus, *Wars*, V: V: 6.
161. Josephus, *Wars*, V: V: 6.
162. For a matching comparison of style see Israel Exploration Society (ed.), *The New Encyclopaedia of Archaeological Excavations in the Holy Land* (1993) p. 739.
163. Josephus, *Antiquities*, XV: XI: 5.
164. Josephus, *Wars*, I: XXXIII: 1.
165. Rabbi Leibel Reznick, on page 5 of his book *The Holy Temple Revisited* (1991), shows a photograph of a statue 'believed to be of King Herod'.
166. Josephus, *Wars*, I: XXXIII: 3.
167. Josephus, *Wars*, I: XXXIII: 3.
168. Josephus, *Wars*, I: XXXIII: 5.
169. Josephus, *Antiquities*, XVII: VI: 5.

CHAPTER 6 *From Jesus to Destruction, 3 BC–AD 70, pp. 165–193*

1. Josephus, *Antiquities*, XVII: VIII: 3, and *Wars*, I: XXXIII: 9.
2. Matthew II: 9.
3. For a balanced assessment of the complexities of this argument see Keller, W., *The Bible as History* (1980) pp. 359–69.
4. Josephus, *Antiquities*, XVII: IX: 3.
5. Josephus, *Antiquities*, XVII: IX: 3.
6. Josephus, *Wars*, II: III: 2.
7. Josephus, *Antiquities*, XVII: X: 3.
8. Josephus, *Antiquities*, XVII: X: 10.
9. Brownrigg, R., *Who's Who in The New Testament* (1971) p. 208.

10. Matthew II: 23.

11. Numbers VI: 13.

12. Luke II: 27.

13. Luke II: 46.

14. Crossan, J.D., *The Historical Jesus* (1991) Appendix 2, p. 452, and Josephus, *The Jewish War*, translation G.A. Williamson, II: 56.

15. Thiering, B., *Jesus the Man* (1992) complete text.

16. The detail of this account, given to an archaeologist by Muhammad adh-Dhib in the 1990s, contradicts that of several other versions.

17. As certified by the author during his own search in 1998.

18. Interview with General Sharon, Baigent, M., and Leigh, R., *The Dead Sea Scrolls Deception* (1991) p. 54.

19. See Vermes, G., *The Dead Sea Scrolls* (1994) p. 53, for this dating.

20. Translation of fragments from Qumran document 4 Q 521, from the translation given by Eisenman, R., and Wise, M., *The Dead Sea Scrolls Uncovered* (1992) p. 23.

21. The only indication that Jesus may have ever identified himself with a Messianic role came through the word of the Gospels written after his death, which declared that he had made reference to his 'father' in heaven. Matthew XX: 23.

22. Smith, G.A., *Jerusalem from the Earliest Times to 70 AD* (1908) vol. I, pp. 361–4.

23. Matthew XXII: 21.

24. Extracts from the Gospel according to Matthew, XXIII: 5, 6, 7, 13, 17.

25. As with the birth date of Jesus, there remains much controversy surrounding the date of his crucifixion, which observers place between AD 30 and 33.

26. Matthew XXI: 13.

27. At the time of Jesus' betrayal, the standard silver coin used in payment at the Temple was the Tetradrachm or Shekel of Tyre. For a concise explanation of the use of Shekalim, see Pinhas Kehati, *Mishnah, Seder Moed* (1994) vol. II, Tractate, *Shekalim*. A hoard of 561 coins, which included many examples of the Tyrian *Shekalim*, was found during excavations at Qumran in 1955. For photographs of this hoard and other Qumran material, see *Scrolls from the Dead Sea,* Israel Antiques Authority Exhibition Catalogue, Vatican Apostolic Library, 30 June–2 October 1994.

28. In the Gospel according to Mark, Jesus answers in the affirmative.

29. Bahat, D., *Carta's Historical Atlas of Jerusalem* (1986) p. 29.

30. Matthew XXIV: 2.

31. Josephus, *The Life of Flavius Josephus*, 75.

32. John XIX: 33.

33. Mark XV: 43–5.

34. For a thorough explanation of this theory see Thiering, B., *Jesus the Man* (1992) pp. 108–28.

35. Hippolytus drew further comparisons of the life of Jesus with the dimensions of the Ark of the Covenant; for further clarification see Robin Lane Fox, *Pagans and Christians* (1986) p. 267.

36. Josephus, *Wars*, II: IX: 3.

37. Josephus, *Wars*, II: IX: 4.

38. At Vienne where he had been banished by Nero.

39. Josephus, *Wars*, II: X: 1.

40. Josephus, *Wars*, II: X: 4.

41. Josephus, *Wars*, II: X: 4.

42. A cohort represented a tenth of a Roman legion which was anything from 3000 to 6000 men strong.

43. Josephus, *Wars*, II: XII: 1.

44. The excavated pavement below Robinson's Arch at the southern end of the western wall of the *haram* is now believed to date from the time of Agrippa II and includes the only known example from the ancient world of a drain cover, cut from solid stone.

45. Josephus, *Wars*, II: XIII: 2.

46. Josephus, *Wars*, II: XIII: 4.

47. According to Josephus from the Latin, *Sicae*, or sickles, *Antiquities*, XX: VIII: 10. The word is still used in contemporary Italian to describe an assassin.

48. Josephus, *Wars*, II: XIII: 3.

49. Josephus, *Wars*, II: XIV: 9.

50. Josephus, *Wars*, II: XVI: 4.

51. Josephus, *Wars*, II: XIX: 9.

52. Josephus, *Wars*, V: II: 2.

53. Josephus, *Wars*, V: I: 4.

54. Josephus, *Wars*, V: I: 3.

55. Josephus, *Wars*, V: X: 1.

56. Josephus, *Wars*, V: XI: 1.
57. Josephus, *Wars*, V: XII: 1.
58. Josephus, *Wars*, V: XII: 3.
59. Josephus, *Wars*, V: XIII: 3.
60. Josephus lays the blame for this practice on the Arabian and Syrian auxiliaries, and not on the regular Roman army, although it is unlikely that they were the sole perpetrators.
61. Josephus, *Wars*, VI: I: 7.
62. Josephus, *The Jewish War*, transl. Williamson, G.A., revised by Mary Smallwood (1981) p. 358.
63. Josephus, *The Jewish War*, transl. Williamson, G.A., revised by Mary Smallwood (1981) p. 359.

CHAPTER 7   *From Rome to Saladin, 71–1187 AD, pp. 194–227*

1. Josephus, *Wars*, VI: VIII: 3.
2. Josephus, *Wars*, VI: VIII: 3.
3. There is a popular view that the Ark was taken by Titus and is now in the vaults of the Vatican, despite no historical reference of this. In 1998 the author interviewed individual members of the ultra-Orthodox community in Jerusalem who firmly believe this to be the case.
4. Josephus, *The Life of Flavius Josephus*, 75.
5. Josephus, *The Life of Flavius Josephus*, 75.
6. Josephus, *Wars*, VI: IX: 4.
7. The stamps of the Tenth Legion, known as the 'Fretensis', comprised lettering with either a dolphin or a boar and, less commonly, a ship.
8. This ash deposit is clearly visible between the excavated blocks under Robinson's Arch.
9. Kenyon, K., *Digging up Jerusalem* (1974) p. 257.
10. Variously spelt as Kosiba, Koseba, Cozeba, etc.
11. There is controversy surrounding the identity of his uncle whom most commentators describe as being a priest. For clarification of the issue based on the evidence of coinage, see Ya'akov Meshorer, *Ancient Jewish Coinage* (1982) vol. II, pp. 136–8.
12. Reznick, Rabbi Leibel, *The Holy Temple Revisited* (1996) pp. 155–6.
13. Meshorer, Y., *Ancient Jewish Coinage* (1982) p. 140.
14. Josephus, *Antiquities*, III: VI: IV.

15. Numbers XXIV: 17.

16. Based on figures given in Dio Cassius.

17. Eusebius, *Proof of the Gospel*, VIII: III: 11–12.

18. The Bordeaux Pilgrim, *Itinerary from Bordeaux to Jerusalem*, translation by Aubrey Stewart (1887).

19. Bahat, D., *Carta's Historical Atlas of Jerusalem* (1986) p. 39.

20. Brownrigg, R.B., *Who's Who in the New Testament* (1971) p. 99.

21. Hanauer, Reverend J.E., *Walks in and around Jerusalem* (1926) pp. 356–7.

22. Chadwick, H., *The Early Church* (1967) vol. I, Penguin Books, London, p. 156.

23. Jerusalem lies on the geological edge of the rift valley which runs north–south through the valley of the Jordan and Dead Sea. Qumran was severely damaged by earthquake during its time of occupation.

24. Hanauer, Reverend J.E., *Walks in and around Jerusalem* (1926) p. 178.

25. Antiochus Strategos, *Conquest of Jerusalem*, XIV: 14–17.

26. Hitti, P.K., *History of the Arabs* (1940) p. 111.

27. *Al-Qur'an, A Contemporary Translation* by Ahmed Ali (1990) 67, *The Kingdom*.

28. Hitti, P.K., *History of the Arabs* (1940) pp. 113–14.

29. Hitti, P.K., *History of the Arabs* (1940) p. 116.

30. *Qu'ran*, sura 2: 125.

31. This story, with at times some embellishment, is still told by official guides of the *haram* in Jerusalem.

32. Jelal ed din es Siyuti, *The History of the Temple of Jerusalem* (1836), translation by the Reverend J. Reynolds, and *The Work of Kemal ed din ibn Abi Sherif* (1817), translation by Paul Lemming.

33. Palmer, E.H., 'History of the Haram Es Sherif', published in the *Palestine Exploration Quarterly* 1870–1, in three sections.

34. Internet Web Site, *Temple Mount*, 1997–8.

35. Creswell, K.A.C., *The Origin of the Plan of the Dome of the Rock* (1924) pp. 29–30.

36. Photographs taken by the author.

37. For an excellent description and assessment of all the historical theories, see Gibson, S., and Jacobson, D., *Below the Temple Mount in Jerusalem* (1996) pp. 283–9.

38. As alluded to in the Koran i.e. 'the Remote Place of Adoration'. See Palmer, E.H., 'History of the Haram Es Sherif (1870–1) p. 132.

39. Palmer, E.H., 'History of the Haram Es Sherif' (1870–1) p. 132.

40. Tradition quoted in Le Strange, G., *Palestine Under the Moslems: A Description of Syria and the Holy Land from AD 650 to 1500*, translated by Alexander P. Watt for the Committee of the PEF (1890) p. 142.

41. Palmer, E.H., 'History of the Haram Es Sherif' (1870–1) p. 130.

42. There is uncertainty surrounding the fate of the gold covering to the Dome of the Rock. Some writers state that it was removed at this time, but Palmer specifically mentions the removal of gold and silver from the doors alone. See Palmer, E.H., 'History of the Haram Es Sherif' (1870–1) p. 166.

43. Nebenzahl, K., *Maps of the Holy Land* (1986) p. 33.

44. Translation from Gies, F., *The Knight in History* (1984) p. 21, taken from: *Historia Hierosolymitana* by Robert the Monk.

45. Runciman, S., *A History of the Crusades* (1990) vol. I, pp. 136–9.

46. Runciman, S., *A History of the Crusades* (1990) vol. I, p. 165.

47. Runciman, S., *A History of the Crusades* (1990) vol. I, p. 278.

48. Runciman, S., *A History of the Crusades* (1990) vol. I, p. 282.

49. Runciman, S., *A History of the Crusades* (1990) vol. I, p. 287.

50. Runciman, S., *A History of the Crusades* (1990) vol. I, p. 285.

51. Armstrong, K., *A History of Jerusalem* (1996) p. 274.

52. Krey, A.C., *The First Crusade: The Accounts of Eye Witnesses and Participants* (1921) p. 266.

53. Prawer, J., *The History of the Jews in the Latin Kingdom of Jerusalem* (1988) pp. 23–4.

54. Chartres, Fulcher of, *A History of the Expedition to Jerusalem, 1095–1127* (1969) I: p. 33.

55. Hitti, P.K., *History of the Arabs* (1953) p. 639.

56. Runciman, S., *A History of the Crusades* (1990) vol. I, p. 312.

57. Chartres, Fulcher of, *A History of the Expedition to Jerusalem, 1095–1127* (1969) I: XXXI: pp. 5–10.

58. Hanauer provided further support to the legend, saying that Dr Frankel, author of *Nach Jerusalem*, had been told the same account in 1856. See Hanauer, Reverend J.C., *Walks in and around Jerusalem* (1926) pp. 180–1.

59. Discovered and photographed by the author.

60. There has always existed much discrepancy concerning the dating of formation of the Order; for this dating, see M. Barber, *The New Knighthood* (1994) p. 9.

61. This number, although established in legend, is contradicted by the evidence of Michael the Syrian who mentions thirty knights, with Hugh de Payns at their head, responding to the call of the king. See Barber, M., *The New Knighthood* (1994) p. 7.

62. As evident in documents of land transaction recorded in Albon, M, d'., (ed.) *Cartulaire général de l'Ordre de Temple* (1913) Bodleian Library reference 127324195.

63. Theodoricus, XVII, pp. 26–7, *Jerusalem Pilgrimage 1099–1185*, editor Wilkinson, J., with Hill, J., and Ryan, W.F., The Hakluyt Society 167 (1988).

64. Theodoricus, XVII, pp. 26–7. *Jerusalem Pilgrimage 1099–1185*, editor Wilkinson, J., with Hill, J., and Ryan, W.F., The Hakluyt Society vol. no. 167 (1988).

65. Barber, M., *The New Knighthood* (1994) p. 94.

66. Runciman, S., *A History of the Crusades* (1990) vol II, p. 373.

67. *Beeton's Dictionary of Universal Biography 1862–3*, p. 119.

68. Runciman, S., *A History of the Crusades* (1990) vol. II, p. 464.

CHAPTER 8   *The Triumph of Islam, 1188–1916, pp. 228–264*

1. Hitti, P.H., *History of the Arabs* (1940) p. 661.

2. Runciman, S., *A History of the Crusades* (1990) vol. III, p. 61.

3. Tuchman, B., *Bible and Sword* (1957) p. 72.

4. Runciman, S., *A History of the Crusades* (1990) vol. III, p. 69.

5. Runciman, S., *A History of the Crusades* (1990) vol. III, p. 175.

6. Runciman, S., *A History of the Crusades* (1990) vol. III, p. 193.

7. Isaiah LXVI: 14.

8. Bahat, D., *Carta's Historical Atlas of Jerusalem* (1986) p. 43.

9. Led by Ronnie Reich and Ya'akov Bilich.

10. Hitti, P.K., *History of the Arabs* (1940) p. 658.

11. See Baigent, Leigh and Lincoln, *The Holy Blood and the Holy Grail* and K. Laidler, *The Head of God*.

12. M. Barber in *The New Knighthood* (1994) p. 311 claims they were kept in the Temple of Solomon, by which he means presumably the headquarters of the Order, or the Aqsa.

13. Author's translation from the original held in the Aqsa Museum, Jerusalem.

14. One from the County of Tripoli in 1152 and one from the Kingdom of Jerusalem in 1166. It is probable that the documentation was destroyed in the last days of the Latin kingdom.

15. Kilmartin Church, Argyll, and by Warren in Syria. See *Journal of the PEF* (1871) AGM, p. 332.

16. Creswell, K.A.C., *The Origin of the Plan of the Dome of the Rock* (1924) pp. 11–12.

17. Le Strange, G., *Palestine under the Moslems* (1890) p. 130.

18. As described by the official notification on site.

19. Barber, M., *The New Knighthood* (1994) p. 14.

20. Part of this scene is now missing.

21. Brydon, R., *The Guilds of Masons and the Rosy Cross* (1994) complete text.

22. A good place to view these is amongst the ruins of Jervaulx Abbey in Yorkshire, where many fallen blocks of stone have been made into boundary walls.

23. For example, at Temple Church near Edinburgh.

24. Hitti, P.K., *History of the Arabs* (1940) p. 671.

25. Documents of the Moslem tribunal between the years 1391 and 1394 discovered in the Aqsa Mosque in 1975 bear testament to Jewish involvement in the affairs of the city.

26. Hitti, P.K., *History of the Arabs* (1940) pp. 703–4.

27. Tuchman, B., *Bible and Sword* (1957) p. 162.

28. Barbara Tuchman in *Bible and Sword* describes his proclamation as play-acting, designed as 'a military stratagem' but this is curious as the Jews of the diaspora had no army, and very little political influence worldwide.

29. Tuchman, B., *Bible and Sword* (1957) p. 163.

30. Tuchman, B., *Bible and Sword* (1957) p. 166, and *Le Moniteur*, 22 May 1799.

31. Private papers courtesy of Christopher Warren.

32. Hitherto unpublished extract from *The Life of Major General Sir Charles Warren* by Watkin W. Williams, Charles Warren's grandson and fellow Mason, by courtesy of Christopher Warren. Each lodge is allocated a number for reasons of clarification.

33. Extract taken from internal Freemasonic publication written by Brother A.C.F. Jackson, 11 September 1986, by courtesy of Christopher Warren.

34. Hitherto unpublished extract from *The Life of Major General Sir Charles Warren* by Watkin W. Williams, Charles Warren's grandson and fellow Mason, courtesy of a descendant of Sir Charles Warren, P. 17c., by courtesy of Christopher Warren.

35. Warren, C., 'Letters to the PEF', *Palestine Exploration Quarterly* (1867–70) London p. 56.

36. For confirmation of this see Warren, C., *The Recovery of Jerusalem* (1871) pp. 51–5.

37. Warren, C., *The Recovery of Jerusalem* (1871) p. 87.

38. Warren, C., *The Recovery of Jerusalem* (1871) p. 87.

39. Warren, C., *The Recovery of Jerusalem* (1871) p. 89.

40. On his return to Chatham in 1870 Birtles was prescribed quinine for malarial fever. *Service Record, Sergeant Major H. Birtles*, PRO.

41. Warren, C., *The Recovery of Jerusalem* (1871) pp. 132–3.

42. Warren, C., *Underground Jerusalem* (1876) p. 402.

43. Warren, C., *Underground Jerusalem* (1876) p. 404.

44. Warren, C., *Underground Jerusalem* (1876) p. 405.

45. Warren, C., *Underground Jerusalem* (1876) p. 405.

46. Warren, C., *Underground Jerusalem* (1876) p. 406.

47. Perhaps Warren was also aware of the description in the *Mishnah* which describes the blood channel into the Kidron. See *Yoma* IV: 6.

48. Correspondence courtesy of Christopher Warren.

49. Extract from the unpublished text of Watkin W. William's *Life of General Sir Charles Warren*, courtesy of a descendant of Sir Charles Warren, 17b.

50. Extract from a letter to Watkin Williams, 24 August 1924. By courtesy of Christopher Warren.

51. Warren Archive, PEF, London.

52. Extract taken from internal Freemasonic publication written by Brother A.C.F. Jackson, 11 September 1986.

53. 2 *Chronicles*, XXXV: 3.

54. Silberman, N.A., *In Search of Solomon's Treasures* (1980) p. 33.

55. Silberman, N.A., *In Search of Solomon's Treasures* (1980) p.33.

56. Vester, B. Spafford, *Our Jerusalem* (1950) pp. 227–8.

57. Vester, B. Spafford, *Our Jerusalem* (1950) p. 228.

58. *The Times*, 16 September 1910.

59. Silberman, N.A., *In Search of Solomon's Treasures* (1980) p. 37.

60. Vester, B. Spafford, *Our Jerusalem* (1950) p. 227.
61. *The Times*, 4 May 1911.
62. *The Times*, 4 May 1911.
63. The *New York Times*, 7 May 1911.

CHAPTER 9 *One God and the Millennium, 1917–2000, pp. 265–290*

1. Massey, W.T., *How Jerusalem was Won* (1919) p. 158.
2. Garnett, D., *The Essential T.E. Lawrence* (1951) p. 167.
3. Garnett, D., *The Essential T.E. Lawrence* (1951) p. 143 (extract from *Seven Pillars of Wisdom*).
4. Garnett, D., *The Essential T.E. Lawrence* (1951) p. 143.
5. Garnett, D., *The Essential T.E. Lawrence* (1951) p. 143.
6. Tuchman, B., *Bible and Sword* (1957) p. 289.
7. Taylor, A.R., *Prelude to Israel* (1959) p. 4.
8. Taylor, A.R., *Prelude to Israel* (1959) p. 8.
9. Point Two of the Basle Declaration, 1897.
10. Churchill, W., *House of Commons Report*, 23 May 1939.
11. Jewish Agency for Palestine (ed.), *Documents Relating to the Palestine Problem* (1945) p. 16.
12. *Al Qibla* (Mecca) No. 183, 23 March 1918.
13. Marlowe, J., *The Seat of Pilate* (1959) pp. 114–15.
14. Jewish Agency for Palestine (ed.), *Documents Relating to the Palestine Problem* (1945) p. 37; extract from T.E. Lawrence, *Oriental Assembly*, p. 92.
15. Jewish Agency for Palestine (ed.), *Documents Relating to the Palestine Problem* (1945), excerpts from the Mandate, 24 July 1922.
16. Marlowe, J., *The Seat of Pilate* (1945) p. 255.
17. *Newsweek Magazine*, 19 June 1967, p. 15.
18. *Newsweek Magazine*, 19 June 1967, p. 16.
19. *Newsweek Magazine*, 19 June 1967, p. 20.
20. In August 1998 the author interviewed Gershon Solomon, founder of the Temple Mount Faithful, who told him that the Dome of the Rock and the Aqsa Mosque should be dismantled and sent to Mecca.
21. *Newsweek Magazine*, 19 June 1967, p. 21.
22. *New Scientist Magazine*, June 1996, p. 49.
23. Author's interview with archaeologists of the Israel Antiques Authority

and his own experience while witnessing religious demonstrations in 1998.

24. Taylor, A.R., *Prelude to Israel* (1959) p. 32.

25. Press release, Israel Antiques Authority, Jerusalem, July 1998.

26. Hancock's deduction in *The Sign and the Seal* is largely based on his interpretation of the eye-witness account of an Armenian priest, Dimotheos Vartabet Sapritchian, who together with his Patriarch visited Axum in 1869. Hancock concluded that Sapritchian was only shown a replica tablet of the Ten Commandments and that the Ark was hidden elsewhere. Sapritchian, however, was shown the *tabot* which the Ethiopians claimed to be the unique tablet containing the Ten Commandments (in direct contradiction to the two stones described in the Bible). This relic was clearly a fake: the Commandments were written in 14th century Abyssian script. Furthermore, the Ethiopians laid no claim to the original Ark of the Covenant: they kept their *tabot* in a small wooden chest, or 'ark' made in India, which they also showed to Sapritchian. For further information see: Sapritchian, Dimotheos, *Deux Ans de Sejour en Abyssinie*, Jerusalem 1871, pp. 135–147.

27. Interview with the author, Qumran, August 1998.

28. Ja'acov Bilich, *Sunday Times*, 26 July 1998 and Meir ben Dov, as discussed with the author.

29. Josephus, *Antiquities*, III: VI: 5.

30. 1 Chronicles XV: 2.

31. Interview with the author, Qumran, July 1998.

32. Interview conducted August 1998, Jerusalem.

33. Interview with the author, July 1998.

34. Amy Klein and news agencies, Jerusalem.

Bibliography

Biblical, Mishnaic and Qu'uranic extracts taken from:

The English Version of the Polyglot Bible (Samuel Bagster & Sons, London, 1854).

Al-Qu'ran, A Contemporary Translation, by Ahmed Ali (Princeton University, Princeton, 1990).

Mishnah, Seder Moed, a new translation with a commentary by Rabbi Pinhas Kehati (Moar Wallach Press, Jerusalem, 1994).

Abel, Le P.F.-M., *Les Livres des Maccabées* (J. Gabalda et Cie, Éditeurs, Paris, 1949).

Aharoni, Y., *Excavations at Ramat Rahel* (Jerusalem, 1962).

Albon, M. d' (ed.), *Cartulaire général de l'Ordre de Temple* (Paris, 1913). (Bodleian Library reference 127324195).

Armstrong, Karen, *A History of Jerusalem* (HarperCollins, London, 1996).

Bahat, Dan, *Ancient Jerusalem Revealed* (Israel Exploration Society, Jerusalem, 1994).

Bahat, Dan, *Carta's Historical Atlas of Jerusalem* (Carta, Jerusalem, 1986).

Baigent, Michael and Leigh, Richard, *The Dead Sea Scrolls Deception* (Jonathan Cape, London, 1991).

Baigent, Michael, Leigh, Richard and Lincoln Henry, *The Holy Blood and the Holy Grail* (Jonathan Cape, London, 1982).

Baigent, Michael and Leigh, Richard, *The Temple and the Lodge* (Jonathan Cape, London, 1989).

Baker, G.P., *Twelve Centuries of Rome* (G. Bell & Sons, London, 1934).

Barber, Malcolm, *The New Knighthood: A History of the Order of the Temple* (Cambridge University Press, 1994).

Barber, Malcolm, *The Trial of the Templars* (Cambridge University Press, 1978).

Barnavi, Eli (general editor), Eliav-Feldon, Miriam (English editor), *Historical Atlas of the Jewish People* (Schocken Books, New York, 1992). Originally published by Alfred A. Knopf, Inc., New York, 1992).

Beeton's Dictionary of Universal Biography (London 1862–3).

Betz, Otto and Riesner, Rainer, *Jesus, Qumran and the Vatican* (SCM Press, London, 1994). (Original German edition published by Brunnen-Verlag, 1993).

Bevan, Edwyn, *Jerusalem under the High Priests* (Edward Arnold, London, 1924).

Boardman, J., Griffin, J. and Murray, O. (eds), *The Oxford History of the Classical World* (Oxford University Press, 1986).

Bordeaux Pilgrim, *Itinerary from Bordeaux to Jerusalem,* translated by Aubrey Stewart (Palestine Pilgrims' Text Society, vol. I., London, 1887; New York, 1971).

Box, G.H. (ed.), *Judaism in the Greek Period* (Clarendon Press, Oxford, 1932).

Brandon, S.G.F., *The Trial of Jesus of Nazareth* (Batsford, London, 1968).

Brauer, George C. Jr., *Judea Weeping* (Thomas Y. Crowell, New York, 1970).

Bray, Warwick and Trump, David, *Dictionary of Archaeology* (Penguin, Harmondsworth, 1982).

The British Academy, *Text of the Old Testament* (Oxford University Press, 1916).

Brownrigg, R., *Who's Who in the New Testament* (Weidenfeld & Nicolson, London, 1971).

Brox, Norbert, *A History of the Early Church* (SCM Press, London, 1994). (Translated from Kirchengeschichte des Altertums, 4th edn, Patmos-Verlag, Düsseldorf).

Brumbaugh, R.S., *Plato's Mathematical Imagination* (Indiana University Press, Bloomington, 1954).

Brydon, Robert, *The Guilds of Masons and the Rosy Cross* (Rosslyn Chapel Trust, Midlothian, 1994).

Busch, Fritz Otto, *The Five Herods* (Hale, London, 1958).

Cary, M., *A History of the Greek World from 323 to 146 BC* (Methuen, London, 1932).

Chadwick, Henry, *The Early Church* (Penguin, London, 1967).

Chartres, Fulcher of, *A History of the Expedition to Jerusalem, 1095–1127* (University of Tennessee Press, Tennessee, 1969).

Churchill, Winston, *House of Commons Report*, 23 May, 1939.

Conder, C.R., *The City of Jerusalem* (John Murray, London, 1909).

Conybeare, F., 'Antiochus Strategos', Account of the Sack of Jerusalem' (*English Historical Review*, No. 25, 1910).

Creswell, K.A.C., *The Origin of the Plan of the Dome of the Rock* (Chiswick Press, London, 1924).

Crossan, John Dominic, *The Historical Jesus: The Life of a Mediterranean Jewish Peasant* (Harper, San Francisco, 1991).

Crossan, John Dominic, *Who Killed Jesus? Exposing the Roots of Antisemitism in the Gospel Story of the Death of Jesus* (Harper, San Francisco, 1995).

Daillez, Laurent, *Les Templiers, ces inconnus* (Librairie Académique Perrin, Paris, 1972).

Desroches-Noblecourt, Christiane, *Tutankhamen* (*The Connoisseur* and Michael Joseph, London, 1963).

Dimont, Max I., *Jews, God and History* (Mentor, New York, 1994).

Dix, G. and Chadwick, H., (eds), *The Treatise on the Apostolic Tradition of St. Hippolytus of Rome, Bishop and Martyr* (The Alban Press, London, 1992).

Drosnin, M. *The Bible Code* (Weidenfeld and Nicolson, London, 1998).

Eisenman, Robert and Wise, Michael, *The Dead Sea Scrolls Uncovered* (Element Books, Shaftesbury, 1992).

Eusebius, *Ecclesiastical History* (Abraham Miller, London, 1650).

Evergates, Theodore (ed. and transl.), *Feudal Society in Medieval France* (University of Pennsylvania Press, Philadelphia, 1993).

Ferguson, *The Temples of the Jews* (John Murray, London, 1878).

Ferguson, Everett, *Backgrounds of Early Christianity* (William Eerdmans, Grand Rapids, Mich., 1987).

Ferguson, G., *Signs and Symbols in Christian Art* (Oxford University Press, 1954).

Fernández-Armesto, Felipe, *Truth* (Bantam, London, 1997).

Filoramo, Giovanni, *A History of Gnosticism* (Blackwell, Cambridge USA and Oxford UK, 1990).

Foote, Shelby, *The Civil War: A Narrative*, 3 vols (Pimlico, London, 1992).

Fox, Robin Lane, *Pagans and Christians* (Viking, London, 1986).

Frazer, Sir James George, *The Golden Bough* (Macmillan, London, 1922).

Freising, Otto of, *Gesta Friderici.*

Garnett, David, *The Essential T.E. Lawrence* (Jonathan Cape, London, 1951).

Gibson, S. and Jacobson, D., *Below the Temple Mount in Jerusalem* (BAR International, Series 637, Tempus Reparatum, Oxford, 1996).

Gies, Frances, *The Knight in History* (Harper & Row, New York, 1984).

Gilbert, Martin, *First World War* (HarperCollins, London, 1995).

Ginsberg, H.L., BASOR 109, (1948).

Glaser, Karen, report in: *Jewish Chronicle,* (London, 30 May 1997).

Glubb, John Bagot, *A Soldier with the Arabs* (Hodder & Stoughton, London, 1957).

Hanauer, Reverend J.E., *Walks in and around Jerusalem* (London Society for Promoting Christianity amongst the Jews, London, 1926).

Hancock, Graham, *The Sign and the Seal* (Heinemann, London, 1992).

Harley, J.B., *Ordnance Survey Maps: A Descriptive Manual* (Ordnance Survey, Southampton, 1975).

Healey, John F., *The Early Alphabet* (British Museum Press, London, 1990).

Hengel, Martin, *Earliest Christianity,* translated by John Bowden from the German (SCM Press, London, 1986).

Herodotus, *The Histories,* translated by Henry Cary (Henry G. Bohn, London, 1848).

Hitti, P.K., *History of the Arabs* (Macmillan, London, 1940).

Hoehner, H.W., *Herod Antipas* (Cambridge University Press, 1972).

Horne, A., *King Solomon's Temple in the Masonic Tradition* (The Aquarian Press, Wellingborough, Northamptonshire, 1972).

Institution of Royal Engineers, *History of the Corps of Royal Engineers* (Chatham, 1954).

Israel Antiques Authority Exhibition Catalogue, *Scrolls from the Dead Sea* (Vatican Apostolic Library, 30 June–2 October 1994).

Israel Exploration Society and Carta (ed.), *The New Encyclopaedia of Archaeological Excavations in the Holy Land,* vol. II (Simon and Schuster, New York/London, 1993).

Jacquot, F., *Défense des Templiers II* (Féchot et Letouzey, Paris, 1882; Reprint: C. Lacour, Nîmes, 1992).

Jennings, H., *The Rose Cross and the Age of Reason* (Chatto & Windus, London, 1870).

Jennings, H., *The Rosicrucians* (Chatto & Windus, London, 1879).

Jewish Agency for Palestine (ed.), *Documents Relating to the Palestine Problem* (London, 1945).

Joseph, Morris, *Judaism as Creed and Life* (George Routledge & Sons, London, 1920).

Josephus, Flavius, *The Complete Works of Josephus*, translated by William Whiston (Kregel Publications, Grand Rapids, Mich., 1960).

Josephus, Flavius, *The Jewish War*, translated by G.A. Williamson, revised by Mary Smallwood (Penguin, London, 1981).

Josephus, Flavius, *Whiston's Josephus* (W.P. Nimmo, Hay & Mitchell, Edinburgh, 1890). (Reprint of Josephus' *Antiquities of the Jews, The Wars of the Jews* and other writings, translated by William Whiston, 1st edn, 1806).

Keller, Werner, *The Bible as History*, new revised edition (Hodder & Stoughton, London, 1980).

Kenyon, Kathleen, *Digging up Jerusalem* (Ernest Benn, London, 1974).

Kersten, Holger and Gruber, Elmar, *The Jesus Conspiracy* (Element Books, Shaftesbury, 1994). (Translated by the authors from the German original published by Albert Langen/Georg Müller Verlag, Munich, 1992).

Knight, Steven, *The Brotherhood: The Secret World of Freemasons* (Granada, London, 1984).

Krey, August C., *The First Crusade: The Accounts of Eye Witnesses and Participants* (Princeton and London, 1921).

Laidler, K., *The Head of God* (Weidenfeld and Nicolson, London, 1998).

Lambert, Malcolm, *Medieval Heresy, Popular Movements from the Gregorian Reform to the Reformation* (Blackwell, Oxford UK and Cambridge USA, 1992).

Lange, Nicholas de, *Atlas of the Jewish World* (Facts on File, New York 1992).

Lawrence, T.E., *Oriental Assembly* (Williams & Norgate, London, 1947).

Lawrence, T.E., *Seven Pillars of Wisdom* (Jonathan Cape, London, 1922).

Lemming, P., *The Work of Kemal Ed din ibn Abi Sherif* (London, 1817).

Léonard, E.G., *Introduction au Cartulaire Manuscrit du Temple 1150–1317* (Édouard Champion, Paris, 1930).

Le Strange, G., *Palestine under the Moslems: A Description of Syria and the Holy Land from AD 650 to 1500* (translated by Alexander P. Watt for the Committee of the PEF, London, 1890).

Ling, T., *A History of Religion East and West* (Macmillan, London, 1968).

Lipinski, E., *Phoenicia and the Bible: Proceedings of the Conference held at Leuven, 15–16 March 1990* (Peeters Press, Leuven, 1991).

Livingstone, Elizabeth A. (ed.), *The Concise Oxford Dictionary of the Christian Church* (Oxford University Press, 1977).

Lizerand, Georges, *Le Dossier de l'affaire des Templiers* (Librairie Ancienne Honoré Champion, Paris, 1923).

Ludemann, Gerd, *The Resurrection of Jesus*, translated by John Bowden (SCM Press, London, 1974). (Original German edition published by Vandenhoeck and Ruprecht, Gottingen, 1994.)

Mack, Burton L., *The Lost Gospel: The Book of Q and Christian Origins* (HarperCollins, New York, 1993).

Marlowe, John, *The Seat of Pilate* (The Cresset Press, London, 1959).

Massey, W.T., *How Jerusalem was Won* (Constable, London, 1919).

Mazar, Amihai, *Archaeology of the Land of the Bible 10,000–586 B.C.E.* (Doubleday, New York, 1990).

Mazar, Benjamin, *The Mountain of the Lord* (Doubleday, New York, 1975).

McManners, John (ed.), *The Oxford History of Christianity* (Oxford University Press, 1990).

Meek, T.J., *Hebrew Origins* (Harper & Brothers, New York, 1960).

Meshorer, Ya'akov, *Ancient Jewish Coinage* (Amphora Books, Israel, 1982).

Millard, A.R., 'Texts and Archaeology: Weighing the Evidence: The Case for King Solomon' (*Palestine Exploration Quarterly*, London, 1990–1).

Miller, J. Maxwell, 'Solomon: International Potentate or Local King?' (*Palestine Exploration Quarterly*, London, 1990–1).

Mollett, J.W., *Dictionary of Art and Archaeology* (Sampson Low, Marston, Searle & Rivington, London, 1883).

Nebenzahl, Kenneth, *Maps of the Holy Land* (Abbeville Press, New York, 1986).

Nock, A.D., *Early Christianity and its Hellenistic Background* (Harper, New York, 1964).

Oesterley, W.O. and Robinson, T.H., *A History of Israel* (Clarendon Press, Oxford, 1932).

Pace, Edward, *Ideas of God in Israel* (George Allen & Unwin, London, 1924).

Palmer, E.H., 'History of the Haram Es Sherif' (*Palestine Exploration Quarterly*, London, 1870–1).

Pfeiffer, Robert H., *Introduction to the Old Testament* (Adam & Charles Black, London, 1952).

Phillips, Jonathan (ed.), *The First Crusade, Origins and Impact* (University Press, Manchester, 1997).

Prawer, J., *The History of the Jews in the Latin Kingdom of Jerusalem* (Clarendon Press, Oxford, 1988).

Reznick, Rabbi Leibel, *The Holy Temple Revisited* (Jason Aronson, New Jersey, 1996).

Ritmeyer, Leen, *The Temple and the Rock* (Ritmeyer Archaeological Design, Harrogate, 1996).

Robinson, James M. (general editor), *The Nag Hammadi Library in English* (E.J. Brill, Leiden, 1988).

Rodinson, Maxime, *Mohammed* (Penguin, London, 1971).

Rogerson, John, *The New Atlas of the Bible* (Guild Publishing, London, 1985).

Rohl, David, *A Test of Time* (Century, London, 1996).

Rosslyn, The Earl of, *Rosslyn Chapel* (Rosslyn Chapel Trust, 1997).

Runciman, Steven, *A History of the Crusades*, 3 vols (Penguin, London, 1990). (First edition published by Cambridge University Press, 1952).

Schonfield, Hugh, *The Essene Odyssey* (Element Books, Shaftesbury, 1984).

Sear, David R., *Greek Coins and their Values*, vol I (Seaby Publications, London, 1979).

Seymour, W.A. (ed.), *A History of the Ordnance Survey* (Dawson, Folkestone, 1980).

Shurman, Michael M., 'Wilson Bench Marks in the Old City of Jerusalem' (*Palestine Exploration Quarterly*, No. 126, London, 1994).

Silberman, N.A., *In Search of Solomon's Treasures* (BAR, London, July/August 1980).

Simons, J., *Jerusalem in the Old Testament, Researches and Theories* (E.J. Brill, Leiden, 1952).

Sinclair, Andrew, *The Sword and the Grail* (Century, London, 1993).

Smith, A.L., *Church and State in the Middle Ages* (Clarendon Press, Oxford, 1913).

Smith, George Adam, *Jerusalem from the Earliest Times to 70 AD* (Hodder & Stoughton, London, Volume I, 1907; Volume II, 1908).

Soggin, J. Alberto, *I manoscritti del mar morto* (Newton Compton, Rome, 1978).

Spong, John Shelby, *Born of a Woman* (HarperCollins, New York, 1992).

Spong, John Shelby, *Resurrection: Myth or Reality?* (HarperCollins, New York, 1994).

Stade, Bernhard, *Geschichte des Volkes Israel* (G. Grote'sche Verlagsbuchhandlung, Berlin, 1887).

Sturzo, Luigi, *Church and State* (The Centenary Press, London, 1939).

Suetonius, Gaius, *The Twelve Caesars*, translated by Robert Graves (Penguin, London, 1979).

Sussmann, Ayala and Peled, Ruth, *Scrolls from the Dead Sea* (Library of Congress, Washington DC, in association with The Israel Antiques Authority, 1993).

Siyati, Jelal ed din es., *The History of the Temple of Jerusalem*, translated by Reverend J. Reynolds (A.J. Valpy, London 1936).

Tacitus, Cornelius, *The Histories*, translated by W.J. Brodribb and A. Church, edited and abridged by Hugh Lloyd-Jones (Sadler & Brown, Chalfont St Giles, 1966).

Taylor, Alan R., *Prelude to Israel: An Analysis of Zionist Diplomacy 1897–1947* (Philosophical Library, New York, 1959).

Theodoricus, *Jerusalem Pilgrimage 1099–1185*, (ed. Wilkinson, J. The Hakuyt Society London, 1988).

Thiering, Barbara, *Jesus of the Apocalypse* (Doubleday, New York and London, 1996).

Thiering, Barbara, *Jesus the Man* (Doubleday, New York and London, 1992).

Thomson, William M., *The Land and the Book* (T. Nelson & Sons, London, 1881).

Tibble, Steven, *Monarchy and Lordships in the Latin Kingdom of Jerusalem 1099–1291* (Clarendon Press, Oxford, 1989).

Tuchman, Barbara, *Bible and Sword* (Redman, London, 1957).

United Grand Lodge (ed.), *Constitutions of the Ancient Fraternity of Free and Accepted Masons* (London, 1984).

Vermes, Geza, *The Dead Sea Scrolls: Qumran in Perspective* (William Collins, London, 1977). (Revised edition published by SCM Press, London, 1994).

Vermes, Geza (ed.), *Journal of Jewish Studies*, vol. XXXI, No. 2 (Oxford Centre for Postgraduate Hebrew Studies, 1980).

Vester, B. Spafford, *Our Jerusalem* (Evans Brothers, London, 1950).

Warren, Sir Charles, *The Ancient Cubit and our Weights and Measures* (Richard Bentley & Sons, London, 1903).

Warren, Sir Charles, *Plans, Elevations, Sections Shewing the Results of the Excavations at Jerusalem 1867–1870* (PEF, London, 1884).

Warren, Sir Charles, *The Recovery of Jerusalem* (Richard Bentley & Sons, London, 1871).

Warren, Sir Charles, *Underground Jerusalem* (Richard Bentley & Sons, London, 1876).

Watson, Sir Charles M., *The Life of Major-General Sir Charles Wilson* (John Murray, London, 1909).

Welch, Adam C., *The Work of the Chronicler, Its Purpose and its Date*, The Schweich Lectures of the British Academy 1938 (Humphrey Milford, London, Oxford University Press, 1939).

Whitelam, Keith, *The Emergence of Israel: A Historical Perspective* (Stirling University 1996).

Wilkinson, J. (ed.) with Hill, J. and Ryan, W.F., *Jerusalem Pilgrimage 1099–1185* (The Hakluyt Society, London, 1988).

Williams, Watkin W., *The Life of General Sir Charles Warren* (Basil Blackwell, Oxford, 1941).

Wilson, Edmund, *Israel and the Dead Sea Scrolls* (Farrar Straus Giroux, New York, 1978). (1st edn 1954.)

Wilson, Sir Charles, *Ordnance Survey of Jerusalem* (Southampton, 1865).

Wilson, Sir Charles, *Memo: On a proposed Survey of Palestine* (1869) Palestine Exploration Fund Archives: PEF WS/3, London.

Wilson, Sir Charles (ed.), *Picturesque Palestine, Sinai and Egypt* (London, n.d.).

Woolley, C. Leonard, *Dead Towns and Living Men* (Humphrey Milford, London, Oxford University Press, 1920).

Index